ENCYCLOPAEDIA OF INDIA, PAKISTAN AND BANGLADESH

ENCYCLOPAEDIA OF INDIA, PAKISTAN AND BANGLADESH

(In 9 Volumes)

(Volume 8)

OM GUPTA

ISHA

ISHA BOOKS

Delhi-110033

Encyclopaedia of India, Pakistan and Bangladesh
(In 9 Volumes)

ISBN : 81-8205-389-7 (Set)
ISBN : 81-8205-397-8 (Vol. 8)

Rs. 6300 (Set)

Published in 2006 in India by
Isha Books
D-43, Prithviraj Road,
Adarsh Nagar, Delhi - 110033
e-mail : ishabooks@hotmail.com

Laser Typesetting : Vinayak Printers, Delhi
Printed at : Salasar Imaging Systam, Delhi

Preface

According to Oxford dictionary Encyclopaedia is a book or aset of books that gives information on many subjects or many aspect of one subject. This encyclopaedia does that on India, Pakistan and Bangladesh. It is the first work of its kind. There have been anthologies on India but there is no compendium of information in an alphabetical order. Even Britannica could go as far as four-volume encyclopaedia on Indian history.

Encyclopaedia is an extension of a dictionary. The latter gives you meanings of words while the former gives facts about people, places and events. No one can claim to compile all the facts and that of a sub-continent called India. But then it is the prerogative of the editor to pick up his entries that he considers would be useful to his reader. Generally we soon find our comfort levels in a language. And rarely consults a dictionary and lesser an encyclopaedia. But those who dare, find the experience worth it. It can be easily compared to a human body. In our daily life we tend to be our own quacks and medicate on the basis of common sense. If we refer to a doctor we come to know the actual cause of the symptom and get relieved on knowing the gravity of the situation or the absence of it. One would realize that encyclopaedia reveals the fundamentals of any situation, person or the event and we feel at home with that information.

A dictionary and an encyclopaedia can easily enlarge the process of learning even to an uninitiated person. It is truer in case of humanities. Popular myth about encyclopaedia is that it is meant to be referred to in a library only. The librarians, the world over keep encyclopaedia in such zealously guarded protection that the generally refrain from asking for it. Since the advent of internet in our life, the bulkiness of encyclopaedias has disappeared. That is why we have divided this enterprise in nine volumes. Encyclopaedias are generally global in its expanse. Even subject-related encyclopaedias give the global perspective.That is why country-specific encylopaedias have never been seriousy attempted. We hope that this effort will fill that volume. Traditionally encyclopaedias don't deal with factual data e.g. Indian exports, population figures, GDP. That is the job of annual reference books. They are also different from alamans in as much as that they don't give dated entries. That will become texts on history. Encyclopaedias need to be updated. A country is alive and kicking. People and events continue to play role in various aspects of life. Hence they need to be added. That is why either annual supplements or updation needs to be done in encyclopaedias. We would strive for that.

Regarding its contents only those entries have been included that continue to influence the life of a nation. There are historical figures who might have played a significant role in their times but if those deeds have no relevance to the present they have been excluded. Another example is literary awards. They always create controversies because their selection at times is subjective. Hence only universally accepted meritorious work has found place in these volumes. In this context a debatable point need to be stated. Who is more important book or the author. Conventionally work is an end product and only that is a measure of the author's importance but then a prolic writer might have produced a large body of creations. Hence to save space the author is entered with all his important work.That is also an international practice.

Lastly, why India, Pakistan and Bangladesh have been clubbed together. Before India's independence they were one nation. They share a common heritage and composite culture. Their post-independence history is different but 22their foundation is undivided. In order to appreciate the historical context better it is necessary to cross-refer and that was possible when they are juxtaposed.

Om Gupta

Q

Qaem Amrohvi : Qaem Amrohvi, real name Syed Zarif-ul-Hassan Naqvi, was a very famous Urdu poet, philosopher and thinker. His verses are basically in the praise of Ahl al-Bayt (A.S.). He belonged to Naqvi Syed family, and a close relative of Raees Amrohvi. In 1974, he moved to Kuwait and settled there. During the days of Gulf War, he came back to Pakistan. He died in 1990 in Karachi. His book "Gul-hae Rang Rang" is a collection of beautiful poetries.

Qasim Razvi : Qasim Razvi was an Islamic fundamentalist activist and political leader in the Hyderabad State, now a part of India. Razvi headed the militant Islamic group, the Razakars, and advocated independence for Hyderabad under the rule of the Nizam Usman Ali Khan. Razvi is also believed to have held views that Hyderabad would eventually join Pakistan in a major war against India, evidenced by some of his speeches and publications in Hyderabadi newspapers. Razvi was politically powerful and a close advisor of the Nizam, whom he encouraged to defy the Indian government and block the accession of Hyderabad into India. At the height of the crisis, Razvi had placed his allies in influential posts, and was virtually dictating the Nizam's policy on the issue. Razvi even traveled to Delhi, India's capital and had a stormy meeting with Indian leader Sardar Vallabhbhai Patel.

After Operation Polo, Razvi was placed under house arrest and tried under Indian laws on seditious activities and inciting communal violence. Released in the 1950s, he migrated to Pakistan.

Qawwali : Qawwali is the devotional music of the Sufis. Originally performed mainly at Sufi shrines throughout what is now India and Pakistan, it has also gained popularity in the mainstream, especially through the work of artists like Nusrat Fateh Ali Khan. Qawwali is a vibrant musical tradition that stretches back more than 700 years.

The roots of Qawwali can be traced back to 8th century Persia. However, Qawwali in the form we know it today was essentially created by Amir Khusrau in the late 13th century in India.

During the first major migration from Persia, in the 11th century, the musical tradition of Sama migrated to the Indian Sub-continent, Turkey and Uzbekistan. Rumi and his Mevlana order of Sufism have been the propagators of Sama in Central Asia. Amir Khusrau of the Chisti order of Sufis is credited with fusing the Persian and South Asian musical traditions, to create Qawwali as well as the Hindustani classical music tradition. The word "Sama" is used (or is the preferred name) in Central Asia and Turkey, for forms very similar to Qawwali. And even in India and Pakistan, the formal name used for a session of Qawwali is "Mehfil-e-Sama".

Qawwali : Qawwali is the devotional music of the Sufis. Originally performed mainly at Sufi shrines throughout what is now India and Pakistan, it has also gained popularity in the mainstream, especially through the work of artists like Nusrat Fateh Ali Khan. Qawwali is a vibrant musical tradition that stretches back more than 700 years.

The roots of Qawwali can be traced back to 8th century Persia. However, Qawwali in the form we know it today was essentially created by Amir Khusrau in the late 13th century in India.

During the first major migration from Persia, in the 11th century, the musical tradition of Sama migrated to the Indian Sub-continent, Turkey and Uzbekistan. Rumi and his Mevlana order of Sufism have been the propagators of Sama in Central Asia. Amir Khusrau of the Chisti order of Sufis is credited with fusing the Persian and South Asian musical traditions, to create Qawwali as well as the Hindustani classical music tradition. The word "Sama" is used (or is the preferred name) in Central Asia and Turkey, for forms very similar to Qawwali. And even in India and Pakistan, the formal name used for a session of Qawwali is "Mehfil-e-Sama".

Qazi Hussain Ahmad : Qazi Hussain Ahmad is the president of the Pakistani Islamist party Jamaat-e-Islami. He also leads the Muttahida Majlis-e-Amal or MMA. Qazi Hussain Ahmed was born at Ziarat Kaka Sahib in Nowshera, NWFP, Pakistan in 1938. His father Qazi Muhammad Abdul Rab was a great religious luminary and a farmer by profession. Qazi Hussain Ahmed was first elected as member of the Senate of Pakistan in 1986 for a term of six years. He was re-elected as such in March 1992, but he resigned in 1996 as a protest against the corrupt political system. Mr. Ahmed has widely traveled abroad to represent the Jamaat at the international forums, leading goodwill missions as well as in his personal capacity to mediate on issues concerning the Muslim Ummah. His services during the Iran-Iraq and Gulf wars, the Balkan (Bosnia) crisis and the post-Soviet power struggle in

Afghanistan, have been widely commended and appreciated by those of a similar ideological disposition.

Qilla Abdullah : Qilla Abdullah or Killa Abdullah or Abdullah Qilla (fort) is a district in the north west of Balochistan province of Pakistan. Prior to 1975 Qilla Abdulla was part of Pishin district. Due to administrative reasons Qilla Abdullah was separated from Pishin and was made a new District on 14th June, 1993. The District also consist of one tehsil Chaman and two sub-tehsils : Dobandi and Gulistan. The district consists of two sub-divisions : Chaman and Gulistan. The district Qilla Abdullah is named after Sardar Abdullah Khan Achakzai, who was a man of great influence. He was one of the two great leaders of the rebellion at Kabul, Afghanistan, in 1841, during which the British envoy was also killed. He bought Dehsora Karez from Kakars and Chashma Inzergai from the Ashezai Achakzai, in the early part of the 19th century. He then built a fort (Qilla) and gave the place his own name.

Qilla Saifullah : Qilla Saifullah or Killa Saifullah or Saifullah Qilla (fort) is a district in the north west of Balochistan province of Pakistan. Qilla Saifullah was notified as a district on 14th December 1988. Previously it was part of Zhob District and known as Upper Zhob sub-division. About two years ago Kashatoo sub-tehsil of Zhob District was transferred to Qilla Saifullah district with a new name, Badinai. After the inclusion of Badinai sub-tehsil, (whose area is not known) in Qilla Saifullah district, the district was re-organised as far as administrative division is concerned. At present the district is divided into two sub-divisions : Qilla Saifullah and Muslim Bagh.

Qisas and Diyat Ordinance 1990 : With the passing of the Qisas and Diyat Ordinance in 1990, the victim (or heirs of the victim) of a crime now have the right to inflict injuries on the offender identical to the ones sustained by the victim. The law also allows offenders to absolve themselves of the crime by paying compensation to the victim or their heirs. In the already existing system of bribery and corruption, it gives free hand to the people with money. The Human Rights activists say that in effect this means, that rich people can get away with willful murder.

Qissa Khwani Bazaar Massacre : The massacre of the Qissa Khwani bazaar (the story tellers market) in Peshawar, modern day Pakistan on April 23, 1930 is considered a defining moment in the non violent struggle to drive the British out of India. It was the first major confrontation between British troops and non violent demonstrators in the then peaceful Peshawar city and some estimates at the time put the death toll from the shooting at nearly 400 dead. The shooting down of hundreds of unarmed people triggered protests across the subcontinent and catapulted the then newly formed KK (Khudai Khidmatgar) movement onto the National scene.

Quaid-e-Azam Mausoleum : Quaid-e-Azam Mausoleum is the mausoluem of Quaid-e-Azam Mohammad Ali Jinnah, foundar of Pakistan. It is located in Karachi, Sindh, Pakistan. Quaid-e-Azam Mausoleum is the beautiful Mughal style building that is the most famous landmark of Karachi.

Quaid-i-Azam University : Quaid-i-Azam University (sometimes romanized as Quaid-e-Azam) lies in Islamabad, Pakistan. The largest public sector University of the Capital, Islamabad. It was founded in 1965 and made a university in 1967 as the University of Islamabad. It was renamed in 1976. The name means "Great Leader" and refers to title of Mohammad Ali Jinnah.

Quamrul Hassan : Quamrul Hassan (1921-1988) was a Bangladeshi artist. Hassan was born in Kolkata, India. In Bangladesh, Hassan's fame as an artist is perhaps only second to that of Zainul Abedin. Hassan is often referred to in Bangladesh as Potua, a word usually associated with folk artists, due to his down to earth style. In addition of his artistic legacy, two of Hassan's work have come to be part of Bangladesh's political history. The first of this is a monstrous rendiiton of Yahya Khan, the Pakistani president who ordered genocide in Bangladesh. The second was just before his death, mocking the then dictator of Bangladesh, Hossain Mohammad Ershad. This skecth was titled Desh aaj bisshobeheyar khoppre (Our land is now in the hand of the champion of shamelessness).

Queen Victoria : The title Empress of India was given to Queen Victoria in 1877. The title was created some years after the formal incorporation into the British Empire of Britain's possessions and protectorates on the Indian subcontinent, comprising modern-day India, Pakistan, Bangladesh, and Burma (though the latter would be made a separate colony in 1937). It is said Victoria's desire for such a title was motivated partially out of jealousy of the Imperial titles of her royal cousins Wilhelm I of Germany and Alexander II of Russia. Prime Minister Benjamin Disraeli is usually credited with creating the title for her. Also, the title was created when it became evident that Queen Victoria's daughter, Victoria the princess royal, would out-rank her mother when she ascended the imperial throne of Germany.

When Victoria died, and her son Edward VII ascended the throne, his title became Emperor of India. The title continued until India and Pakistan became independent from the United Kingdom at midnight on 14/15 August 1947. The title was given up in 1948 by George VI, then King of the United Kingdom, with retrospective effect to August 15, 1947.

When signing their name for Indian business, a King-Emperor or reigning Queen-Empress used the initials R I

(Rex/Regina Imperator/Imperatrix) or the abbreviation Ind. Imp. (Indiae Imperator/Imperatrix) after their name (while reigning Queen-Empresses used the initials R I, consorts of King-Emperors simply used R). This was also used on many British coins, including some 1948 coins of George VI. When a male monarch held the title, his Queen Consort assumed the title Queen-Empress, but unlike Queen Victoria, they themselves were not reigning monarchs but the consorts of reigning monarchs.

Quetta : Quetta is the capital of the province Balochistan in Pakistan. The spelling of 'Quetta' is an erroneous English derivation from kwatta meaning 'fort' in the Pushtu language. Quetta is also known as the "fruit garden" of Pakistan. It is located in the densely populated Quetta District, which lies in the northeast of the province, and is situated in a river valley near the Afghani border, with a road to Kandahar in the northwest.

Quetta District : Quetta district is a district in the north west of Balochistan province of Pakistan. In March 1883, the Khan of Kalat leased Quetta to the British authorities. In April 1883 it was combined with Pishin into a single administrative unit. In 1975, Quetta and Pishin were made separate districts. Now the district consists of two sub-divisions: Quetta city and Quetta Sadar. The district also comprises one Tehsil (Quetta) and one Sub-Tehsil (Punjpai). Over 99% of the people of the area are Muslims. The population of Quetta district is estimated to be over 850,000 in 2005.

Quila Rai Pithora : Quila Rai Pithora was a seven gated strong fort in Delhi built by Prithviraj. Quila means Fort; Rai Pithora was more well-known as Prithviraj. Quila Rai Pithora is supposed to be the First City of Delhi, built by Prithviraj, a Chauhan King and also the last Hindu King of Delhi.

Quit India Movement : The Quit India Movement (Bharat Chhodo Andolan) was the final call, the definitive organized movement of civil disobedience for immediate independence of India from British rule issued by Mahatma Gandhi on August 9, 1942 and made famous by his slogan Do or Die (Karenge Ya Marenge in Hindi). Unlike the previous two Gandhi-led revolts, Quit India was more controversial, and specifically designed to obtain the exit of the British from Indian shores

On July 14, 1942, the Indian National Congress passed a resolution demanding complete independence from Britain. The draft proposed that if the British did not accede to the demands, massive civil disobedience would be launched. However, it was an extremely controversial decision. A prominent Congress national leader Chakravarti Rajgopalachari quit the Congress over this decision, and so did some local and regional level organizers. Jawaharlal Nehru and Maulana Azad were apprehensive and critical of the call, but backed it and stuck with Gandhi's leadership till the end. Sardar Vallabhbhai Patel and Dr. Rajendra Prasad were openly and enthusiastically in favor of this revolt, as were many veteran Gandhians and experienced freedom-fighters, socialists like Asoka Mehta and Jaya Prakash Narayan, and young, more radical Congressmen. Thousands of college students were also enthusiastic about this revolt.

The Congress had lesser success in rallying other political forces under a single flag and mast. Smaller parties like the Communist Party of India and the Hindu Mahasabha opposed the call. Mohammed Ali Jinnah's opposition to the call led to large numbers of Muslims cooperating with the British, and the Muslim League obtaining power in the Imperial provincial governments.

On August 8, 1942 the Quit India resolution was passed at the Bombay session of the All India Congress

Committee (AICC). At Gowalia Tank, Bombay, Gandhi urged Indians to follow non-violent civil disobedience. He told the masses to act as an independent nation and not to follow the orders of the British. Hundreds of thousands of people all over the country responded to the call. Many thousands of revolutionaries who employed violent means and were outside the Congress rallied to the call of their non-violent resister brothers and sisters.

The British swiftly responded by mass detentions. A total over 100,000 arrests were made nationwide, mass fines were levied, bombs were air-dropped and demonstrators were subjected to public flogging. Hundreds of resisters and innocent people were killed in police and army firings. Many national leaders went underground and continued their struggle by broadcasting messages over clandestine radio stations, distributing pamphlets, and establishing parallel governments. The British sense of crisis was strong enough that a battleship was specifically set aside to take Gandhi and the Congress leaders out of India, possibly to South Africa or Yemen, but such a step was ultimately not taken out of fear of intensifying the revolt.

The entire Congress leadership was cut-off from the rest of the world for over three years. Gandhi's wife Kasturba Gandhi died and personal secretary Chandhara Sakhidev died in a short space of months, and Gandhi's own health was failing. Despite this, Gandhi went on protest 21-day fasts and maintained a superhuman resolve to continuous resistance. Although the British released Gandhi on account of his failing health in 1944, Gandhi kept up the resistance, demanding the complete release of the Congress leadership.

Though the revolt shook the foundations of British rule, its forceful and quick suppression did reduce the force of the revolt. By early 1944, India was mostly peaceful again, while the entire Congress leadership was incarcerated. A sense that the movement had failed depressed many nationalists, while Jinnah and the Muslim League, as well as Congress opponents like the Communists and Hindu extremists, sought to gain political mileage, criticizing Gandhi and the Congress Party.

The movement in fact, had succeeded. The war had sapped a lot of the economic, political and military life-blood of the Empire, but the powerful Indian resistance had shattered the spirit and will of the British Raj to continue ruling India, and had made it clear that after the war, even a greater, larger movement would be launched and would succeed, as no excuse or distraction from the issue would remain.

In addition, the British people and the British Army seemed unwilling to back a policy of repression in India and other parts of the Empire even as their own country lay shattered by the war's ravages. The writing was on the wall, and freedom only a matter of time.

By early 1946, all political prisoners had been released, and the British openly adopted a political dialogue with the Indian National Congress for the eventual independence of India. On August 15, 1947, India won its freedom.

Qur'an : The Qur'an, also transliterated as Quran, Koran, and less commonly as Alcoran, is the holy book of Islam. Muslims believe that the Qur'an is the literal word of God in Arabic and the culmination of God's revelation to mankind, revealed to Muhammad, the final prophet of humanity, over a period of twenty-three years through the angel Gabriel.

Quraishi Magan Thakur : Quraishi Magan Thakur (17th century) is one of the noted poets of medieval Bangla

Literature. Quraishi Magan Thakur, who wrote the poetical work called Chandravati and Magan Thakur of the Siddiq family, who was the chief minister of Arakan, are believed to be the same person. Magan Thakur's father Badai Thakur (Shribada Thakur) was also a minister of Arakan. The Rosang King Narapatigi (1638-45), in his old age, entrusted Magan Thakur with guardianship of his only daughter. Magan Thakur was made the chief minister when the princess became the queen after the death of the king.

Qutb Complex : The Qutb complex is an array of monuments and buildings at Nehru Place in Delhi, India, the most famous of which is the Qutub Minar. This complex was first constructed by Qutb-ud-din Aybak, the first ruler of the Slave Dynasty, and the son of Akbar in his new city called the Qila-Rai-Pithora near Prithivraj Chauhan's older city. The complex was added to by many subsequent rulers, including Iltutmish and Ala ud din Khilji as well as the British.

The most famous monument situated in the complex is the Qutub Minar; other important constructions in the complex are the Quwwat-ul-Islam mosque, the Ala-I-Darwaza, the Alai Minar and the iron pillar.

Qutb Complex : The Qutb complex is an array of monuments and buildings at Mehrauli in Delhi, India, the most famous of which is the Qutub Minar. This complex was first constructed by Qutb-ud-din Aybak, the first ruler of the Slave Dynasty, and his successor Iltutmish (aka Altmash) in his new city called the Qila-Rai-Pithora near Prithivraj Chauhan's older city. The complex was added to by many subsequent rulers, including Iltutmish and Ala ud din Khilji as well as the British.

The most famous monument situated in the complex is the Qutub Minar; other important constructions in the complex are the Quwwat-ul-Islam mosque, the Ala-I-Darwaza, the Alai Minar and the iron pillar.

Qutb Shahi Dynasty : The Qutb Shahi dynasty (whose members were also called the Qutub Shahis) was the ruling family of the kingdom of Golconda in southern India. They were Shia Muslims and belonged to a Turkmen tribe from the Turkmenistan-Armenia region. The dynasty's founder, Sultan Quli Qutbl Mulk, migrated to Delhi with some of his relatives and friends in the beginning of the 16th century. Later he migrated south to Deccan and served Bahmani sultan Mohammad Shah. He conquered Golconda and became the Governor of Telangana region in 1518, after the disintegration of the Bahmani Kingdom into the five Deccan sultanates. Soon after, he declared independence from the Bahmani Sultanate, took title "Qutub Shah," and established Qutb Shahi dynasty of Golconda.

Qutb Shahi Dynasty : The Qutb Shahi dynasty (whose members were also called the Qutub Shahis) was the ruling family of the kingdom of Golconda in southern India. They were Shia Muslims and belonged to a Turkmen tribe from the Turkmenistan-Armenia region.

The dynasty's founder, Sultan Quli Qutbl Mulk, migrated to Delhi with some of his relatives and friends in the beginning of the 16th century. Later he migrated south to Deccan and served Bahmani sultan Mohammad Shah. He conquered Golconda and became the Governor of Telangana region in 1518, after the disintegration of the Bahmani Kingdom into the five Deccan sultanates. Soon after, he declared independence from the Bahmani Sultanate, took title "Qutub Shah," and established Qutb Shahi dynasty of Golconda.

This dynasty was the first Muslim dynasty to rule Telugus. This effectively divided the Telugu nation into two countries, one Muslim ruled country (Telanagana State) and the other a Hindu ruled country. The dynasty ruled Golconda for 171 years, until the Mughal emperor Aurangzeb's armies conquered the Deccan in 1687. Even then, Telangana State continued to be ruled by Muslims until the Hyderabad State joined the Indian Union in 1948 with the military intervention of New Delhi.

Qutb-ud-din Aybak : Qutb-ud-din Aybak was a ruler of Medieval India, the first Sultan of Delhi and founder of the Slave dynasty (also known as the Mamluk dynasty). He served as sultan for only four years, 1206-1210.

Qutb-ud-din was a Turk of the Aybak tribe and was born somewhere in Central Asia. When yet a child, he was captured and sold as a slave (mamluk). He was purchased by the chief Qazi of Nishapur, a town in the province of Khorasan in northeastern Iran. The Qazi treated him like one of his own sons, and Aibak received a good education, including training in archery and horsemanship. When his master died, his master's sons, who were jealous of Aibak, sold him to a slave merchant. Qutb-ud-din was purchased by Sultan Muhammad Ghori, ruler of Ghowr in central Afghanistan.

Qutb-ud-din rose through the ranks to become Muhammad's most trusted general; his greatest military successes occurred while he was still a subordinate of Muhammad. Qutb-ud-din was responsible for most of Muhammad's conquests in northern India. He was left in increasingly independent charge of the Indian campaigns and the exaction of levies from the areas in India that were under Muhammad's hegemony, as Muhammad concentrated on Central Asia after 1192.

Muhammad Ghori established no real state, plunder being his aim; he made no nomination or provision for his succession. Upon his death in 1206, Qutb-ud-din Aybak, after a brief power struggle, succeeded in establishing himself as ruler of Muhammad's empire in Afghanistan, Pakistan, and northern India; Muhammad's Central Asian possessions had been captured by none other than the notorious Mongol warlord, Ghengis Khan.

The areas over which Qutb-ud-din established his rule were those over which he already exercised coercive power as Muhammad's local receiver-general of periodic exactions and levies. Therefore, although his formal tenure as ruler was only four years, Qutb-ud-din managed to establish a defined administrative system, something never contemplated by Muhammad. This was achieved despite his having to quell rebellions by nobles like Taj-ud-din Ildiz and Nasir-ud-din Qubachah. Qutb-ud-din ruled initially from Lahore and later moved the capital to Delhi; he is hence considered the first Muslim ruler of South Asia.

Qutb-ud-din Aybak initiated the construction of Delhi's earliest Muslim monuments, the Quwwat-ul-Islam mosque and the Qutub Minar. These was completed by his successor, Iltutmish. Aibak, so barbaric in dealings with the non-Muslims, was otherwise known as "Lakh Baksh" or "giver of hundred thousands" because of his generosity. He was thus a pious Muslim, praised by contemporary Muslim clerics. He also patronized Nizami and Fakh-i-Mudabbir, both of whom dedicated their works to Aibak.

Qutb-ud-din died accidentally in 1210. While he was playing a game on horseback, his horse fell and Qutb-ud-din was impaled on the pommel of his saddle. He was buried near the Anarkali Bazaar in Lahore. Shams-ud-din Iltutmish, another ex-slave of Turkic ancestry who was married to Qutb-ud-din's daughter, succeeded him as sultan of Delhi.

Qutb-ud-din Aibak's tomb was destroyed during the Mongol attack on Lahore in 1241. In the early 1970's, during a particularly jingoistic phase in the history of the Islamic Republic of Pakistan, a new cenotaph was constructed over that site.

Qutb-ud-din Aybak : Qutb-ud-din Aybak was a ruler of medieval India, the first Sultan of Delhi and founder of the Slave dynasty (also known as the Mamluk dynasty). He served as sultan for only four years, 1206-1210.

QQutb-ud-din Aybak initiated the construction of Delhi's earliest Muslim monuments, the Quwwat-ul-Islam mosque and the Qutub Minar. These was completed by his successor, Iltutmish. Aibak, so barbaric in dealings with the non-Muslims, was otherwise known as "Lakh Baksh" or "giver of hundred thousands" because of his generosity. He was thus a pious Muslim, praised by contemporary Muslim clerics. He also patronized Nizami and Fakh-i-Mudabbir, both of whom dedicated their works to Aibak.

Qutub Minar : Qutub Minar is the tallest brick minaret in the world, and an important example of Indo-Islamic Architecture. The tower is in the Qutb complex at Delhi, India. The Qutub Minar is 72.5 metres high and visitors must climb 379 steps to get to the top. The diameter of the base is 14.3 metres wide while the top floor measures 2.7 metres in diameter.

Inspired by the Minaret of Jam in Afghanistan and wishing to surpass it, Qutb-ud-din Aybak, the first Muslim ruler of Delhi, commenced construction of the Qutub Minar in 1193; but could only complete its basement. His successor, Iltutmish, added three more stories and, in 1368, Firuz Shah Tughluq constructed the fifth and the last story. The development of architectural styles from Aybak to Tughluq are quite evident in the minaret. Like earlier towers erected by the Ghaznavids and Ghurids in today's Afghanistan, the Qutub Minar comprises several superposed flanged and cylindrical shafts, separated by balconies carried on Muqarnas corbels. The minaret is made of fluted red sandstone covered with intricate carvings and verses from the Qur'an, and is built on the ruins of Lal Kot, the Red Citadel in the city of Dhillika. According to John Keay's "History of India," 27 previous Hindu and Jain temples were destroyed and their materials reused to construct the minar.

The Qutb Minar's size makes it visible from far around. The purpose for building this beautiful monument has been speculated upon, apart from the usual role of a minaret—that of calling people for prayer in a mosque- in this case the Quwwat-ul-Islam mosque to the northeast of minar in AD 1198. It is the earliest extant -mosque built by the Delhi Sultans.Other reasons ascribed to its construction are as a tower of victory, a monument signifying the might of Islam, or a watch tower for defence. Controversy also surrounds the origins for the name of the tower.

Many historians believe that the Qutb Minar was named after the first Turkish sultan, Qutb-ud-din Aibak but others contend that it was named in honour of Khwaja Qutb-ud-din Bakhtiar Kaki, a saint from Baghdad who came to live in India who was greatly venerated by Iltutmish. According to the inscriptions on its surface it was repaired by Firuz Shah Tughlaq (AD 1351-88) and Sikandar Lodi (AD 1489-1517). Major R.Smith also repaired and restored the minar in 1829

Quwwat-ul-Islam Mosque : Quwwat-ul-Islam mosque (Might of Islam) (also known as the Qutb Mosque or the Great Mosque of Delhi) was built by Qutb-ud-din Aybak, founder of the Mamluk or Slave dynasty. The mosque construction started in the 1190s when Aibak was the commander of Muhammad Ghori's garrison occupied Delhi. The mosque is said to be built by the parts taken by destruction of twenty-seven Hindu and Jain temples. It was the first mosque built in Delhi after the Islamic conquest of India and the best surviving example of Ghurid's architecture.

Expansion of the mosque continued after the death of Qutub. His successor Iltutmish extended the original prayer hall screen by three more arches. By the time of Iltutmish, the Mamluk empire had stablized enough that the Sultan could replace most of his conscripted Hindu masons with Muslims. This explains why the arches added under Iltutmish are stylistically more Islamic than the ones erected under Qutb's rule. The mosque is in ruins today but indigenous corbelled arches, floral motifs, and geometric patterns can be seen among the Islamic architectural structures.

R

Rabab : Rabab is a very ancient instrument found primarily in Afghanistan but in India it is restricted mainly to northwest India. The mystic poets Kabir and Krishnadasa have mentioned it.

The rabab is made of a walnut or cedar soundbox that looks like an elongated half pear joined together along its length. It is a bowed stringed instrument of 53cm length. The top has an upper part covered with a thin sheet of hammered cooper, decorated with three small rosettes. The lower part is covered with goat skin. The instrument also has a peg box, two sheep gut strings that are attached at the bottom of the instrument and pass over a 4 to 5 cm reed bridge. The bow is very curved and made of horse hair.

Rabab is either played as a solo instrument or accompanies singing, especially of long epic poems. The rabab player sits cross-legged, and places the rabab on his right knee obliquely across his body, with the peg box resting against his left shoulder. He places his thumb underneath the strands and uses pressure to control the tension of the bow. The sound produced by the rabab is said to resemble that of the human voice.

Rabindra Jayanti : Rabindra Jayanti (Celebration of the birthday of Rabindrnath Tagore) falling on May,7/8 is the most widely observed cultural festival in West Bengal. All cultural associations and groups in town and village celebrate this day with programmes of song, dance and drama composed by Tagore which run for days together. Meeting and seminars are held for discussion on the different aspects of his encyclopedic personality.

Rabindra Sangeet : Rabindra Sangeet refers to the 2000 odd songs (about 2230) and poetry written and composed by Bengali Nobel-laureatepoet Rabindranath Tagore. These songs are regarded as cultural treasures of Bengal in both West Bengal (India) and Bangladesh, formerly East Bengal. The Rabindra Sangeets, which deal with varied themes are immensely popular with speakers of the language and form a foundation for the Bengali ethos that is comparable to, perhaps even greater than, that which Shakespeare had on the English-speaking world.

In his book Caste and Outcaste, Dhan Gopal Mukerji has said that these songs transcend the mundane to the aesthetic and express all ranges and categories of human emotion. The poet had given a voice to all — big or small, rich or poor. The poorest boatman on the Ganges as well as the rich landlord find expression to their emotional trials and tribulation in the songs of Tagore.

Rabindranath Tagore : Rabindranath Tagore was a Bengali poet, Brahmo (reformed Hindu) philosopher, artist, dramatist, musician, novelist, and songwriter who was awarded the Nobel Prize in Literature in 1913, becoming the first Asian Nobel laureate.

Tagore, also known as Gurudev, revolutionized Bengali literature with such works as Ghore Baire ("The Home and the World") and Gitanjali. Tagore extended wider Bengali art with his many poems, short stories, letters, essays, and paintings. Tagore was also a cultural reformer and a polymath (an adept in many subjects) who modernized Bangla art by challenging the strictures binding it to classical forms. Two of his songs are now the national anthems of Bangladesh and India: the Amar Shonar Bangla and the Jana Gana Mana.

Rabri Devi : Rabri Devi (born 1959) has served three terms as the Chef Minister, of Bihar, India, as a member of the Rashtriya Janata Dal political party. She's married to Indian politician and former Chief Minister of Bihar Lalu Prasad Yadav.

She became the first woman chief minister of Bihar on July 25, 1997; her first term ended on February 12, 1999. Her second term ran from March 9, 1999 to March 3, 2000. Her third (and longest) term began in on March 11, 2000, and ended in 2005, when her party suffered great losses in state elections. Rabri Devi was born in 1959 in the family of Sri Sib Prasad Chaudhary of Salarkalan, Line Bazar, Gopalganj. She married Laloo Prasad Yadav in 1973 at the age of 14. She has two sons and seven daughters. The appointment of Rabri Devi as the Chief Minister of Bihar came under severe criticism, because she was nearly illiterate and had little experience or interest in politics.

Rabwah : Rabwah is a city in the Punjab, Pakistan, which has recently been renamed Chenab Naghar against the will of its residents, as part of the systematic persecution of its Ahmadi population by the Pakistan Government under pressure from Sunni religious fanatics. Its population still refers to it as Rabwah

Radcliffe Line : The Radcliffe Line became the border between India and Pakistan in 1947. The partition of the British Indian Empire required that the territories to be assigned to the two new countries, generally had to have a population matching the majority. Pakistan was set up as a Muslim state while India was predominantly Hindu. The border had already been roughly drawn up by Lord

Wavell, the Viceroy of India, but the final version was set out by Sir Cyril Radcliffe. Radcliffe had never visited India and didn't know anybody in India before his arrival. Thus, he was considered to be unbiased. However, he was ignorant of realities on the ground and this caused avoidable gaffes in the division.

Radio Mirchi : Radio Mirchi is a nationwide network of Private FM radio stations in India."Mirchi" is a Hindi word for Chilli. The station claims to be as "hot" as Chilli. It is one of the subsidiaries of The Times Group. It has a presence in 7 cities in India namely Ahmedabad, Chennai, Delhi, Indore, Kolkata, Mumbai and Pune.

Rafiq Uddin Ahmed : Rafiq Uddin Ahmed (1926-1952) was a language martyr. Rafiq Uddin Ahmed was born at village Paril of Manikganj district in Bagladesh. He matriculated from Baira School in 1949. While a student of Intermediate class at Devendra College in Manikganj he discontinued his studies and moved to Dhaka. There he worked in his father's commercial printing business.

On 21 February 1952, a general strike was called and a mass demonstration staged in Dhaka demanding recognition of Bangla as one of the state languages of Pakistan. The government ban on public gatherings of people in Dhaka under Section 144 of the Criminal Procedure Code. But students and people from all walks of life defied Section 144 and participated in a demonstration. The police opened fire on the demonstration in the premises of Dhaka Medical College Hostel. Rafiq Uddin had joined the demonstration and was shot dead. The police took his body to the morgue of Medical College Hospital. He was buried in Azimpur graveyard at 3 a.m under an army guard. In recognition of his sacrifice during the Language Movement, Rafiq Uddin was awarded Ekushey Padak posthumously in February 2000.

Raga : Raga are the melodic modes used in Indian classical music. "Raag" is the modern Hindi pronunciation used by Hindustani musicians; "Ragam" the Tamil form used by Karnatak Carnatic music musicians.

A raga functions both as description and prescription. It describes a generalized form of melodic practice; it prescribes a set of rules for how to build a melody. It specifies rules for movements up (aarohanam) and down (avarohanam) the scale, which notes should figure more and which notes should be used more sparingly, which notes may be sung with gamaka, phrases to be used, phrases to be avoided, and so on. The result is a framework that can be used to compose or improvise melodies, allowing for endless variation within the set of notes.

Ragda Pattice : Ragda pattice is a popular Indian fast food or snack commonly found in Mumbai. It is usually found at places or stalls that offer chaat-based items like bhelpuri or panipuri. This dish has two main ingredients: the ragda and the pattice. Ragda is prepared by boiling chick-peas in water along with flavouring agents like haldi (turmeric powder) until they are almost dissolved. The patties are pan-fried, mashed potato cutlets. While serving, 2-3 patties are covered with the stew-like ragda and garnished with finely chopped onions, coriander leaves, spicy chutney and sweet sauce.

Raghavendra Swami : Raghavendra Swami (1601-1671), one of the influential saints in Hinduism, lived in the 17th century. He advocated Vaishnavism (worship of Vishnu as the supreme God) and the Dvaita philosophy. He is considered by his devotees to be a reincarnation of Prahlada, the devotee who was saved by Vishnu, in his avatar as Narasimha. Shri Raghavendra Swami is said to have performed many miracles during his lifetime and is believed to continue to bless his devotees to this day.

Raghunath Temple : Raghunath Temple, with seven shrines each with its own Sikhara, is one of the largest temple complex of north India, and is located in the Indian state of Jammu and Kashmir. The temple was built during the period 1835-1860 by Maharaja Gulab Singh and his son Maharaja Ranbir Singh. The temple has many gods, but the presiding deity is Rama, an avatar of Vishnu. While the Hindus were performing puja in the temple complex on 24th November 2002, fidayeen attack by terrorists took place, which resulted into at least 10 deaths, and injuries to several devotees.

Raghuvamsha : Kalidasa's Raghuvamsha tells of the family of Rama and his descendants, including the conqueror Raghu. The warrior Raghu leads a military expedition to Transoxiana. He defeats and subjugates local peoples along the way (presumably on his march through Central Asia) until he reaches the Vankshu, as the ancient Indians called the Oxus River. There, Raghu's army battles the Hepthalites, or White Huns, whom the Indians called Hunas and Mlecchas (barbarians). The Hepthalites are defeated, and the Raghuvamsha boasts of "The exploits of Raghu, whose valor expressed itself amongst the husbands of the Huna women, became manifest in the scarlet color of their cheeks."

Rahimdas : Abdul Rahim Khan-e-Khana, also known as Rahimdas was a poet and the son of Akbar's trusted caretaker, Bairam Khan. After Bairam Khan was murdered, his wife became the second wife of Akbar, which made Abdul Rahim Khan-e-Khan his stepson. He had a high place among Akbar's Navratnas.

Rahimuddin Khan : General Rahimuddin Khan (born 21 July 1926) held the dual posts of Corps Commander and Governor of Balochistan, the largest province of Pakistan, during the regime of General Muhammad Zia-ul-Haq. He was made full General when he was appointed

Charirman Joint Chiefs of Staff in March 1984. His tenure in Balochistan lasted from 1978-1984, and has not been surpassed in length or stability by any Governor since.

He holds the unique distinction that after retirement from his post as Governor, he also served as the caretaker Governor of Sindh following the dismissal of the civilian government by the President General Muhammad Zia-ul-Haq in May 1988. He was also the first and only man to hold dual posts of Corps Commander and Governor of Balochistan, which went through unprecedented stability and economic expansion during his reign.

Rahimyar Khan : Rahimyar Khan is a city in the south of Punjab province in Pakistan. Formerly Rahimyar Khan was also one of the names of the three districts of the former princely State of Bahawalpur until 1955. Today, Rahimyar Khan lies on an important train route which runs south to Sukkur and north to Bahawalpur. As of 2005, it has a population of around 150,000.

Rahul Dev Burman : Rahul Dev Burman, also known as Pancham or Pancham da (June 27, 1939 - January 4, 1994) was a music composer for Bollywood films. He was the son of singer and music composer Sachin Dev Burman and the second husband of playback singer Asha Bhosle.

Pancham was comfortable with all types of music. Be it the romantic Raat kali from Buddha mil gaya (1971), the sexy cabaret Piya tu ab to aaja from Caravan (1971), the ultimate hippie anthem Dum maro dum from Hare Krishna Hare Rama (1972) or the classical Raina beeti jaaye, Pancham proved himself to be a genius. It is said that Dev Anand did not include the complete version of 'Dum maro dum' in Hare Rama Hare Krishna, as he was worried the song would overshadow the film. At times, R D doubled up as a singer too. His most famous song as a singer was Mehbooba from Sholay.

Pancham has also directed music for some regional films, including Bangla, Oriya, Tamil, Telegu and Marathi. He also acted in one of the Bengali film named Nayak. Pancham's non-filmi music comprises of few albums, including 'Pantera' - the international album for which he shares credit with Latin American composer, Jose Flores.

Rahul Dravid : Rahul Sharad Dravid has established himself as an integral part of the Indian National Cricket team with his technical proficiency, stylish strokes and sheer stability.

Rahul was born on January 11, 1973 in Indore, Madhya Pradesh, to parents Sharad Dravid and Pushpa. He started to play cricket at the age of 12. Dravid did well in the junior tournaments to merit selection in the State under-15, under-17 and under-19 tournaments. Meanwhile he finished his bachelors from St. Joseph's College of Commerce.

He made his debut in the Ranji Trophy match against Maharashtra at Pune in 1990-91. He was the youngest Karnataka player to score a maiden century in Ranji. In 1995-96 he broke into the international team. He made his debut in One Day Internationals against Sri Lanka at Singapore in 1996. He is one player who has always shown stability and concentration and delivered solid performances in all the games that he played. Dravid was the highest scorer in the 1999 World Cup, when he along with Sourav Ganguly created a new World record for the highest partnership of 318 runs for any wicket. Rahul's abilities are not confined to batting alone. He bowls right-arm off breaks and now is a good reserve wicket keeper also.

Rahul keeps his cool even in a crisis and thus is a reliable anchor for the Indian team. Since he started playing he has maintained a Test career average of over 50.

Technically his batting is flawless and he has improved with experience especially in Test Cricket.

Dravid has been honoured with the Arjuna Award by the President of India. Rahul Dravid was the 12th Indian to be named one of Wisden's five Cricketers of the Year for the year 2000 after his splendid performance in the 1999 World Cup in England. This talented player with his scores remains a pride to the Indian team

Rahul Sharad Dravid, is married to Vijetha Pendharkar, a Nagpur-based doctor.

Rahul Gandhi : Rahul Gandhi (born June 19, 1970) is a rising Indian politician and member of the Parliament of India from the Indian National Congress. Rahul Gandhi is the scion of India's most powerful political family. Gandhi is the son of Sonia Gandhi, the powerful President of the Indian National Congress, and Rajiv Gandhi, the former Prime Minister who was assassinated in 1991 by Sri Lankan Tamil militants. He was only 14 when his grand-mother, Prime Minister Indira Gandhi, was assassinated by Sikh militants in 1984. His great-grandfather was Jawaharlal Nehru, the distinguished leader of the national freedom struggle and the first Prime Minister of India.

Although, his mother had been the Congress President and Leader of the Opposition since 1998, Gandhi had showed little interest in politics. In 2003, there was widespread media speculation about his imminent entry into national politics; this was not discouraged. Appearing with his mother at public events and Congress meetings, Rahul also went to Pakistan on a goodwill visit to watch a historic Cricket Test match between the two nations. In May 2004, he ran for the Lok Sabha, the lower house of Parliament, from his father's constituency of Amethi in Uttar Pradesh and won by a wide margin. His campaign was directed by his younger sister Priyanka Gandhi Vadra, and his victory generated considerable media excitement and enthusiasm amongst the younger citizens of the country. He leads a new coterie of young MPs, all sons of distinguished Congressmen. Since then, Gandhi has sought to cultivate support from young Indians by carefully working up his profile through the media and staying away from the scandals of coalition politics.

Rahula : Rahula is generally accepted to be the name of the son of the Buddha Siddhartha Gautama. The name in English, roughly translated, is "chain" or "chained one," an interesting philosophical contrast to Buddha, "the awakened one." It can also be translated as obstacle. Siddhartha Gautama named his son Rahula at birth, recognizing the child as a tie that bound him to his wife Yashodhara and the comforts of the life of a householder. In the Dhammapada, the pleasure and joy that a man takes in his wife and children is called a 'soft fetter' that ties individuals to the life of suffering- possibly a reference to Siddhartha's own son.

Although Rahula was part of the family that Gautama essentially abandoned when he began his life as a monk, Rahula, according to several Buddhist sutras, eventually came to be a part of his father's new-founded religious order. He is seen in several anecdotes about Gautama, and he is exclusively portrayed as a student. According to the scriptures, Rahula was first ordained as a novice as a young boy, without his mother's knowledge. The distress that this caused Rahula's mother prompted the Buddha to rule that no young man or woman would be ordained without the knowledge and consent of their parents. Rahula became one among the many Arhats after following the Buddha's teachings.

Rai Dynasty : The Rai Dynasty rulers of Sindh were Buddhists of the Mauryan clan Balhara Jats. Rai was their title. Their capital was at Alore.Their state exdended from Kashmir and Kannauj in the east, Makran and Kewal port in the west, Surat port in south, Kandahar, Sistan, Suleyman, Ferdan and Kekanan hills in the north.

Raichur : Raichur is a district in the Indian state of Karnataka. The population of the district, by the 2001 Census of India, is 1,648,212. Raichur district has five taluks: Raichur, Devdurg, Sindhanur, Manvi and Lingasagur. The capital of the district is the city of Raichur, which is 409 km from the state capital, Bangalore. The thermal power production plant at Shaktinagar in this district provides a large portion of the electricity consumption in Karnataka. Among the historial attractions in the district, notable are the Raichur fort, built in 1294, and the nearby town of Anegundi, which has a number of monuments from the Vijayanagara empire, including the Ranganatha temple, Pampa lake and Kamal Mahal.

Raichur district is one of those few places in India where Gold resources is present. Hutti gold mines is situated in Raichur district and is around 90kms away from Raichur city. All the five talukas mentioned above are very well irrigated and water source is from Tungabhadra dam and Narayanpura dam (Krishna river). Raichur is known for its paddy fields and rice is of extremely superior quality.

Raidas : Raidas or Ravidas (c.1398-c.1448), is considered one of the early northern India poet-Sants. He was initiated by Ramananda and is considered the guru of Mirabai. He was a was a cobbler by caste (and thus an untouchable) and in the tradition of the Sant poets, wrote devotional (Bhakti) poems in secular Hindi. He lived in Varanasi (Benares). His writings have been included in the Sikh's Holy Book "Guru Garanth Saheb".

Raigad District : Raigad District is a district in the Indian state of Maharashtra. It is located in the Konkan region. The district was renamed after Raigad, the fort and former capital of the Maratha leader Shivaji, which is located in the interior forests of the district, on a west-facing spur of the Western Ghats or Sahyadri range.

The district is bounded by Mumbai Harbour to the northwest, Thane District to the north, Pune District to the east, Ratnagiri District to the south, and the Arabian Sea to the west. It includes the large natural harbor of Pen-Mandwa, which is immediately south of Mumbai Harbour, and forming a single landform with it. Part of the district is included in the planned metropolis of New Bombay, and its port, the Jawaharlal Nehru Port.

The district includes Kashid and Kihim beaches, besides the towns of Mahad and Panvel. The district also includes the isle of Gharapuri or Elephanta, located in Mumbai Harbor which has ancient Hindu and Buddhist caves.

Raigarh District : Raigarh District is district of the state of Chhattisgarh, in India. Raigarh is the district headquarters. The district was formed by merging the states of princely states of Raigarh, Sarangarh, Udaipur (Dharamjaigarh) and Jashpur. Jashpur is now a separate district.

Raikal : Raikal is the mandal (sub-district) headquarters and a small town in Karimnagar District, Andhra Pradesh, India. It is about 65 km from the district headquarters Karimnagar. This small town has historical significance for two things. The first is the ancient temple of Kesavanatha Swamy which was built in the 13th century A.D. by the Kakatiyas. This temple's idol is Panchamukhalingeswara Swamy (Lord Siva with five faces) which is believed to be one of the only two existing, the other being at Varanasi. The second attraction is the annual Bhimanna Jatara (Hindu festival) held for 3 days during January - March.

Raipur : Raipur is the capital city of the state of Chhattisgarh, India. The population is 605,131 (agglomeration 922,559) in 2001 census. The city is also the administrative headquarters of Raipur District. It was formerly a part of Madhya Pradesh, before the state of Chattisgarh was formed on November 1, 2000.

Raisen District : Raisen District is a district of Madhya Pradesh state of India. The town of Raisen is the district headquarters. The district is part of Bhopal Division. It is situated between the latitude 22 47' and 23 33' north and the longitude 77 21' and 78 49' east and is bounded in the west by Sehore District, in the north by Vidisha District, in the east and south-east by Sagar District, in the south-east by Narsimhapur District, and in the south by Hoshangabad and Sehore districts. Raisen District takes its name from massive fort. This fort is built on a sandstone hill, at the foot of which settles the town. The name is probably a corruption of Rajavasini or Rajasayan, the royal residence.

Raisina Hill : The Raisina Hill is the most prized estate in Edwin Lutyens' Delhi. The Rashtrapati Bhavan, India's Presidential palace, stands tall at Raisina Hill, flanked by the Secretariat building housing the Indian Prime Minister's Office and several other important ministeries. Other important buildings and structures situated near the Raisina Hill includes the Parliament of India, the Rajpath, the Vijay Chowk and the India Gate.

Raita : Raita is an Indian condiment based on yogurt. The yogurt is seasoned with cilantro, cumin, mint, cayenne pepper, and other herbs and spices. Vegetables such as cucumber and onions are mixed in. A key ingredient in raita is powdered mustard. In fact, the Hindi word for mustard is rai. The mixture is served chilled. Raita has a cooling effect on the palate which makes it a good foil for spicy Indian dishes. Southern Indian cuisine, such as that found in the Bangalore region, often uses finely chopped or diced carrots mixed with dahi yogurt.

Raj Ghat : Raj Ghat, a memorial to Mahatma Gandhi is a simple black marble platform that marks the spot of his cremation on 31 January 1948. It is left open to the sky while a flame burns perpetually at one end. It is located on the banks of the river Yamuna in Delhi, India. A stone footpath flanked by lawns leads to the walled enclosure that houses the memorial. Two museums dedicated to Gandhi are located near by. The memorial has the epitaph Hey Ram, the last words uttered by Gandhi, meaning, Oh Lord!

It has become customary for foreign dignitaries visiting India to pay their respects to Gandhi at the Raj Ghat by laying flowers or wreaths on the platform. Visitors are required to remove footwear before approaching the memorial as a sign of respect. A commemorative ceremony is held every Friday, to mark the day Gandhi died. Prayer sessions are held at the Raj Ghat on Gandhi's birth and death anniversaries.

Jawaharlal Nehru's samadhi is to the north of the Raj Ghat and is known as the Shantivan or Shanti Vana meaning the forest of peace. The area has a beautiful park adorned with trees planted by visiting dignitaries and heads of state. His grandson Sanjay Gandhi's samadhi is adjacent to it.

Raj Kapoor : Raj kapoor was a famous actor, director, producer of Hindi films. Ranbir Raj (Raj kapoor) was born on December 14, 1924. He was the son of Prithviraj Kapoor, who was also a famous actor.

For more than fifteen years, he remained an evergreen hero of the Hindi films along with his contemporaries Dilip Kumar and Dev Anand. He launched his own R.K films banner. Nargis and Raj duo made a popular team and they drew huge crowds. His films are considered as valuable contributions to cinematic art. His famous films are 'Awaara' (1951),' Shri 420 (1955), 'Sangam' (1964), and 'Mera Naam Joker' (1970). Raj Kapoor was the only Indian actor-producer who carved a niche for himself across the continents.

Raj Kapoor won many awards during his life time. Apart from many film fare awards, He won grand prix award (1957), Padma Bhushan(1971), and Dada Saheb Phalke Award (1987). Some of the well known films directed by him are Bobby(1973), Satyam Shivam Sundaram(1978). He died in 1988.

Raja Ram Mohan Roy : Raja Ram Mohan Roy was a zealous Social reformer holding modern and progressive views. He was born in 1772, in a prosperous and orthodox Brahmin family at Hoogly in West Bengal.

He stood firmly against all sort of social bigotry, conservatism and superstitions and advocated English and western education for his countrymen. Raja Ram Mohan Roy was a great scholar too. He made a wide study of different religions of the world including Christianity and Islam. He also knew many languages like English, Persian, Arabic, Latin, French and Hebrew. He was also a great scholar of Bangla and translated Vedas and Upnishads into Bengali.

He was honoured the title 'Raja' by the Moghul Emperor. Raja Ram Mohan Roy believed in the fundamental unity of all religions. In 1814, he founded, 'Atmiya Samaj' and in 1828, the 'Brahma Samaj'. Through these organisations he wanted to expose the religious hypocrisies and to check the growing influence of Christianity on the Hindu society.

By far, the greatest achievement of Raja Ram Mohan Roy as a social reformer was the abolition of 'Sati' in 1829, child marriage and 'Pardha'. He was been rightly called the 'Father of Indian Nationalism'. He died on 27th September 1833, in England.

Raja Ramanna : Raja Ramanna (1925 - September 23, 2004), was an Indian nuclear scientist and was associated with the country's first nuclear test in 1974. Beginning his studies at Bishop Cotton Boys School, Bangalore, Raja Ramanna obtained Ph.D. and L.R.S.M. from London. He specialised in nuclear physics, reactor physics and design, European music and philosophy.

Dr. Ramanna was the director of Bhabha Atomic Research Centre (BARC) for over a decade. It was during this time that India carried out its first nuclear test in Pokhran in 1974, codenamed Operation Smiling Buddha. He has served as director-general of the Defence Research and Development Organisation (DRDO) and as scientific adviser to the defence minister. He was the President of the 30th General Conference of the International Atomic Energy Agency.

He was the Union minister of state for defence in 1990 in the V.P. Singh government. In 1997, he became a Member of Parliament through the upper house, the Rajya Sabha. Dr. Ramanna was also a noted pianist. Raja Ramanna died in Mumbai in 2004.

Raja Ravi Varma : Raja Ravi Varma (1848-1906) was an Indian painter who achieved recognition for his depiction of scenes from the epics of the Mahabharata and Ramayana. Ravi Varma was born in the royal palace of Kilimanoor, which is situated 25 miles from Thiruvananthapuram (Trivandrum), in Kerala, India. Ravi Varma showed talent at a young age. The power and forceful expression of European painting fascinated Ravi

Varma, which came across to him as strikingly contrasting to stylized Indian artwork.

Raja Ravi Varma came to widespread acclaim after he won an award for an exhibition of his paintings at Vienna in 1873. He travelled throughout India in search of subjects. He often modeled Hindu Goddesses on South Indian women, whom he considered beautiful. Ravi Varma is particularly noted for his paintings depicting episodes from the story of Dushyanta and Shakuntala, and Nala and Damayanti, from the Mahabharata. Ravi Varma's representation of mythological characters has become a part of the Indian imagination of the epics. He was—and still is—criticized for being too showy and sentimental in his style. However his work remains very popular in India.

Raja Ravi Varma is most remembered for his paintings of beautiful sari clad women, who were portrayed as very shapely and graceful. He stayed in the city of Bombay in Maharashtra for some years and drew many a beautiful Maharashtrian woman. After a successful career as a painter, Raja Ravi Varma died in (1906) at the age of 58. His paintings are considered to be among the best examples of the fusion of Indian traditions with the techniques of European academic art.

Raja Todar Mal : Raja Todar Mal was the Indian Mughal emperor Akbar's finance minister, who overhauled the revenue system in the kingdom. He succeeded the eunuch Khwaja Malik I'timad Khan in 1560. He introduced standard weights and measurements, revenue districts and officers. His systematic approach to revenue collection became a model for the future Mughals as well as the British. He was also responsible for replacing Hindi with Persian in government accounts. Raja Todar Mal was also a warrior who assisted Akbar in controlling the Afghan rebels in Bengal.

Raja Todar Mal had developed his expertise while working under another able administrator Sher Shah. In 1582, Akbar bestowed on the raja the title Diwan-I-Ashraf. Todar Mal died in 1586, the same year as Akbar's other nau-rathan Raja Birbal. He was famous for his Land reforms, popularly known as 'BANDOBAST SYSTEM'

Rajaconda : Rajaconda's is a fort in India. Its history dates back to the 14th century A.D., when it was constructed by Singama Nayak, the founder of a new clan of kings (previously serving the Kakatiya rulers as military commanders since the 2nd century A.D) and governing the territory of Rajaconda.

The kings of Rajaconda were Recherla Velama cheiftains of the Padma Nayak lineage, who rose to rule over the entire Telangana during the post-Kakatiya and pre-Bahamani period in the Deccan. Rajaconda acted as a buffer State between the muslim Bahamani kingdom and the Hindu Vijayanagara empire and was subsequently taken over by the Bahamanis in 1433 A.D. during the Velama rule.

In 1498, the last governor of Telangana, Qutubul Mulk Dakhani, controlled the territory of Golconda, Warangal, Devaraconda, Rajaconda and Koilconda and went on to build the edifice of the Qutub Shahi dynasty. Rajaconda the fort, offers a good exampe of medieval Hindu fort architecture. The construction is of cyclopean masonary, and the whole fort is devoid of the use of mortar.

Rajaconda forms an ideal case to understand medieval Hindu town planning and architecture. The fort even adheres to Viswakarma's Vasthu Sastra on Hindu fort architecture. One can observe that the fort was structured as upper and lower tiers with the city lying on the south eastern side of the fort, partly sprawling outside the boundary wall.

Rajahmundry : Rajahmundry or Rajamundry is a major city in East Godavari District of Andhra Pradesh state of southern India. Its original name is Raja Mahendri or Raja Mahendravaram. It was the first capital of any known Telugu Kingdom.

The Chalukya ruler Rajaraja Narendra ruled this city around 1022. The city has traces of 11th century fine palaces, and fort walls. However, new archeological evidence suggests that the city may have existed far before the Chalukyas. In the Middle Ages, it was called Raja Mahendra Varam. Later the name underwent various changes to Rajahmahendravaram, Rajahmahendramu, Rajamandramu and Rajahmundhri. It later became Rajahmundry during British rule.

Nannayya, the poet laureate, who was called 'Adi Kavi' (The first Poet) of telugu belonged to this place. He, along with Tikkana and Yerrana, is responsible for the translation of Jaya, Sanskrit version of Mahabharata, into telugu. It is the birthplace of telugu literature. Kandukuri Veeresalingam, who is a social reformer and also the author of Rajashekhara Charithra, the first Telugu novel, is also from Rajahmundry. He himself married a widow and is against bad practices in society.

Rajaji National Park : Rajaji National Park is a national park that encompasses the Shivaliks, near the feet of the Himalayas. Three districts of Uttaranchal: Hardiwar, Dehradun and Pauri Garwhal make up this sprawling park land which been three different protected areas before being merged into one. Those three areas had been the Chilla, Motichur and Rajaji sanctuaries.

Inhabiting the dense green jungles that form the park are an impressive array of creatures - 23 species of mammals - including tigers, leopards, elephants, deer, jungle cat, wild boar and sloth bear - and 315 species of birds are found in Rajaji. The most prominent avian species include pea fowl, woodpeckers, pheasants, kingfishers and barbets, supplemented by a number of migratory species during the winter months. Besides that, the rivers which flow through the park harbour fish such as trout and mahseer.

Rajaparab : Raja is one of the most popular festivals of Orissa, though it is not observed in western Orissa. The first day of the Raja festival is always celebrated in the last day of the solar month of Jaishtha. The festival continues for three days. It is believed that the Earth goddess had started to menstruate on the first day of the Raja and after the third day she is taken to a ritual bath and returned to normalcy. So this is called as the menstruation period of the earth, so the earth is to be avoided like a woman.

Rajarajeswara Temple : The Rajarajeswara temple is a beautiful Shiva temple (Rajarajeswara is one of the names of Shiva) and is located at Taliparamba in Kannur district of Kerala, south India. The temple is regarded as one of the 108 ancient Shiva temples of Kerala. It has a prominent place amongst the numerous Shiva temples in south India. If any problem is encountered in temples of South India, the final solution is sought in this Temple through a prasna, a traditional method of astrological decision making. The prasna is conducted on a peedha (a raised platform) situated outside the temple. The quadrangular sanctum has a two tiered pyramidal roof. In front of the sanctum is the namaskara mandapam. The temple has no kodi maram (flagstaff) as opposed to other temples in Kerala.

Rajarani Temple : Rajarani is a 'love temple', covered with coyly erotic carvings of women and couples. This 11th century Raja Rani temple is aesthetically endearing, sculpted with graceful feminine figures. It is surrounded by well-maintained gardens. It's one of the best of the

Bhubaneswar temples and is famous fro its ornate deul (sanctuary), decorated with some of the most impressive Orissan temples sculptures. This temple is no longer used for worship.

Rajasthan : Rajasthan is geographically the largest state in India. It borders Pakistan to the west, Gujarat to the southwest, Madhya Pradesh to the southeast, Uttar Pradesh and Haryana to the northeast and Punjab to the north. Rajasthan covers an area of 342,239 km^2 (132,139 mi^2;). The state capital is Jaipur. Geographical features include the Thar Desert in western Rajasthan and the termination of the Ghaggar River. One of the world's oldest mountain ranges, the Aravalli Range, cradles the only hill station of Rajasthan, Mount Abu, and its world famous Dilwara Temples. Eastern Rajasthan has two national tiger reserves, Ranthambore and Sariska, as well as Keoladeo National Park near Bharatpur, famous for its bird life.

Rajasthani : The Rajasthani languages are a group of related languages spoken in India and Pakistan. They are chiefly spoken in the state of Rajasthan and adjacent parts of Gujarat, in the Malwa and Nimar regions of western Madhya Pradesh, and the Pakistani states of Punjab and Sind. The Rajasthani languages are classified in the Central Zone of the Indo-Aryan languages, which also includes Hindi and Urdu. Some of the Rajasthani languages are considered by some to be dialects of Hindi; however, many linguists agree that they are sufficiently distinct from Hindi to be considered languages.

Rajendra Prasad : Dr. Rajendra Prasad (December 3, 1884 – February 28, 1963) was the first President of India.

Rajendra Prasad was a great freedom-fighter, and the architect of the Indian Constitution, having served as President of the Constituent Assembly that drafted the

Constitution of the Republic from 1948 to 1950. He had also served as a Cabinet Minister briefly in the first Government of Independent India. He was a crucial leader of the Indian Independence Movement. He was awarded the Bharat Ratna, the nation's highest civilian award.

Rajgarh : Rajgarh is a city in Madhya Pradesh state of central India. Rajgarh is the administrative headquarters of Rajgarh District, and was formerly a princely state under the British Raj. The old town is surrounded by a battlemented wall. Rajgarh princely state was part of Central India's Bhopal Agency. It had an area of 940 sq. mi., and a population of 88,376 in 1901. Estimated revenue, 33,000 (1911); tribute (to Sindhia of Gwalior), 3640. The rulers, whose title was Rawat, were Rajputs of the Ponwar (Umat) clan. Grain and opium were the principal articles of trade.

After India's independence in 1947, the Rawat acceded to the Indian government, and Rajgarh became part of Madhya Bharat state, which was formed out of the western half of the Raj's Central India Agency of princely states. In 1956 Madhya Bharat was merged into Madhya Pradesh state.

Rajgir : Rajgir is an ancient town, and has reference in Mahabharata, Buddhist and Jain texts. Vestiges of its time-honored and magnificent past still remain, eclipsing even the modern state of Bihar, India, in which it is located. Once a great city, Rajgir is but a village today. Rajgir is about 10 km south of Nalanda and 46 km from Bodhgaya.

This place has been associated with Lord Buddha and Mahavira and not only as a place for worship; Rajgir has developed as health and winter resort with its warm water ponds. These baths are said to contain some medicinal properties that help in the cure of many skin diseases. The added attraction of Rajgir is the Ropeway that takes you uphill to the Shanti Stupa and Monasteries built by the Japanese Devotees on top of the Ratnagiri hills.

One may visit Rajgir from Patna. Another way is to come via Begusarai junction or Mokameh, after arriving by train in an overnight journey from Kolkata. Rajgir is a diversion from somewhere midway on the Barauni–Patna highway. It is located in a verdant valley surrounded by rocky hills.

Rajgir Hills : Rajgir hills, lying in central regions of Bihar state, India, are two parallel [[ridge]s extending around 65 km. The highest point in the hills rise to an altitude of 388 meters, but mostly the hills are around 300 meters high. Between these two ridges lie a number of places of historical importance, dating from the period of the Mahabharatha, Gautam Buddha, Mahavira, Mauryas and the Guptas. Currently, Rajgir is the most famous place of the area.

Rajiv Gandhi : Rajiv Gandhi was born on August 20, 1944 in Mumbai. Born to parents, Firoz Gandhi and Priyadarshini Gandhi, he was heir to the political heritage of his mother and grandfather Jawaharlal Nehru, the architect of modern India. He married Sonia Maino, an Italian girl, whom he met during his student days in Cambridge.

Rajiv was a pilot by profession. He was never interested in politics but the sudden death of his younger brother Sanjay in a glider accident in Delhi steered Rajiv Gandhi into it. He won the election from Amethi and became a Member of Parliament in 1981. He was appointed general secretary of the Congress party in 1983. On the October 31, 1984 he took the oath as the Prime Minister of the country.

Rajiv Gandhi was the youngest Prime Minister of the World's largest Democracy. He strengthened India's political, economic and cultural bonds with other countries. He was the first politician at the helm to criticize the power brokers who ruled the roost in the ruling party. Rajiv Gandhi found himself in many controversies during the last two years of his Prime Minister ship. He met a tragic end on 21st may 1991 at Sriperumbudur, by an LTTE (Liberal tigers of Tamil Eelam) Suicide Bomber named Tanu, when he was attending an election meeting. The Government of India conferred the highest honour of the land "Bharat Ratna" on him posthumously. Many foundations have been established to cherish his memory for the welfare of society in the fields of Science and Technology, Arts and Culture, and Health and Medicine

Rajiv Gandhi Khel Ratna Award : Rajiv Gandhi Khel Ratna award is India's highest sporting honour. It was instituted from the year 1991-92 in the memory of Late Rajiv Gandhi, the former Prime Minister of India. The award carries a medal and a scroll of honour apart from a cash component. The award honours either an individual sportsperson or a sports team for outstanding performance in the sports disciplines included in any of Olympics, Asian Games and Commonwealth Games, as well as Billiards & Snooker, Cricket and Chess in a year.

Typically, performances from 1 April of a year to 31 March of the next year are taken into consideration for the award. A selection committee of people affiliated to sports is constituted by the Ministry of Youth Affairs & Sports for selecting the awardee every year. The award may not be given in a year if the committee feels that performances that year have not been up to the mark. No award was given in the year 1993-94 while the award was shared between sportspersons of different disciplines on two occasions. So far, a team event has been awarded only once. The cash component was Rs. 1 lakh in 1991-92. It reached Rs. 3 lakh by 2000-01 and is Rs. 5 lakh (~11,500 USD) in 2004-05.

Rajiv Gandhi Park : Developed by the Vijayawada Municipal Corporation with great care and interest, this park welcomes the tourists at the entrance of the city with its impressive horticultural network.

Rajkumari Amrit Kaur : Rajkumari Amrit Kaur (2nd February 1889, Lucknow – 2nd October 1964), born into the princely family of Kapurthala of Undivided India, was an eminent Gandhian and freedom fighter. Her father was raja Sir Harman Singh, and he has accepted Christianity as his religion, Which Rajkumari inherited as her religion. After India's independence, Rajkumari Amri Kaur was inducted in the cabinet, and became first female Cabinet Minister of India. She was assigned the Ministry of Health. She was also elected the president of World Health Assembly in 1950, a position held by only two women in the first 25 years of WHO's history. She was also instrumental in setting up the All India Institute of Medical Sciences, New Delhi.

Rajmahal : Rajmahal a historic town, is situated on the west bank of the Ganges and located in the hills known as daman-i-khoh during the Muslim rule. The hill runs north south for 193 km from Sahibganj of Santal Pargana to Rampurhat Railway Station of Dumka. The earlier name of the place was Agmahl. Mansingh, on his return from the conquest of Orissa in 1592, named it Rajmahal and on 7 November 1595 laid the foundations of a new capital of Bengal subah there and named it Akbarnagar, after Akbar, the emperor.

Rajnandgaon : Rajnandgaon is a district, as well as the name of the primary town in the district, in the state of Chhattisgarh, in India. The population of the city is

143,727 (2001 census). Asia's only Performing Art and Music University is located in the town of Khairagarh.

Rajnikanth : Shivaji Rao Gaekwad, more popularly known as Rajnikanth, is an Indian film actor working mainly in the Tamil film industry. He is one of Kollywood's highest-paid actors and is considered to be one of the most popular Tamil film stars that his fans call him the Super Star of Tamil Cinema since 1987. Rajinikanth was born on December 12 1949 in Karnataka, India. He was the fourth child to his parents Ramabai and Ramoji Rao Gaekwad. Before starting his career in the film industry, he had to take up all sorts of odd jobs. He served as a bus conductor for Karnataka State Transport Corporation in Bangalore. It was during this time that he nurtured his acting interests by performing in various stage plays.

Powered by a strong desire to become an actor, Rajinikanth went to Madras, the tinsel town of Tamil Cinema. He was helped by a friend to join the Madras Film institute and completed his basic acting course in 1974 at the age of 25. Rajinikanth got his first break in movies when he played a small role in the Kannada movie Katha Sangama by the late director Puttanna Kanagal. Later, he made his entry in the Tamil film world when he played a cancer patient in the movie Apoorva Raagangal (1975). This film was directed by K. Balachandar, whom Rajinikanth considers his mentor, and who named him Rajinikanth.

Rajinikanth is popular for his flamboyant dialogue delivery and characteristic mannerisms. While his contemporary super star Kamal Hassan selects performance oriented roles, Rajinikanth's movies have been safe-bet mass entertainers. His movies invariably have a 'good wins over evil' theme with entertaining action sequences, catchy songs and good-natured humour, which makes his films liked by people of all age groups and all walks of life. Rajinikanth has acted in over 160 films including movies in Telugu, Kannada, Malayalam, Hindi and Bengali. He has also acted in one Hollywood movie (Bloodstone in 1988). Rajinikanth was awarded the prestigious Padma Bhushan award in the year 2000.

Rajpath : Rajpath also known as King's Way (which is what the word means) is the ceremonial avenue of the Republic of India. It runs from Rashtrapati Bhavan through Vijay Chowk and India Gate to National Stadium, Delhi. The New Delhi boulevard is lined on both sides by lawns with rows of trees and ponds. Unarguably the most important stretch of road in India, Rajpath goes straight towards Raisina Hill, India's administrative center. After climbing Raisina Hill, Rajpath is flanked by North Block and South Block. Finally it ends at the gates of Rashtrapati Bhavan. At Vijay Chowk it crosses Sansad Marg and the Parliament House of India can be seen to the right if coming from India Gate.

Rajpramukh : Rajpramukh was an administrative title in India which existed from India's independence in 1947 until 1956. Rajpramukhs were the appointed governors of certain of India's provinces and states. British India, which included modern-day India, Pakistan, Bangladesh and Bhutan, was made up of two types of political units. Fifteen provinces were ruled directly by British officials, either a governor or a chief commissioner, who were appointed by the Viceroy. Princely states were ruled by local, hereditary rulers, who acknowledged British sovereignty in return for local autonomy. At the time of the proclamation of Queen Victoria as Empress of India in 1877, more than 700 Indian princely states and territories enjoyed treaty relations with the British Crown. The exact relationship between the Government of India (under the British rule) and these states varied enormously, ranging from treaties of alliance, defence, protection, or supervision to almost outright control. The British Crown assumed these rights from the British East India Company in 1857 and exercised paramountcy in respect of the internal governance which was exercised by the British Viceroy

Rajput : A Rajput is a kshatriya. Rajputs claim descent from royal dynasties of India. Rajputs reside mainly in northern, western, eastern and central states and territories of India. It is estimated that there are 40 million rajputs.

Rajput Painting : Rajput painting, a style of Indian painting, evolved and flourished, during the 18th century, in the royal courts of Rajputana, India. Each Rajput kingdom evolved a distinct style, but with certain common features. Rajput paintings depict a number of themes, events of epics like the Ramayana and the Mahabharata, Krishna's life, beautiful landscapes, and humans. Miniatures were the preferred medium of Rajput painting, but several manuscripts also contain Rajput paintings, and paintings were even done on the walls of palaces, inner chambers of the forts, havelies, particularly, the havelis of Shekhawait.

The colours extracted from certain minerals, plant sources, conch shells, and were even derived by processing precious stones, gold and silver were used. The preparation of desired colours was a lengthy process, sometimes taking weeks. Brushes used were very fine.

Over a period of around 300 years, beginning from the 16th century, different schools of Rajput painting emerged, and notable among them are Mewar School, Bundi-Kota kalam, Jaipur school, Bikaner school, Kishengarh school, Marwar school, and Raagamala style of painting.

Rajputana : Rajputana (or Rajpootana), which means "Land of the Rajputs" is a region of western India, which now makes up the greater part of Rajasthan state. Under the British Raj, Rajputana was an agency, made up of a number of princely states, whose rulers enjoyed local autonomy. Upon Indian independence in 1947, the local rulers acceded to India, and in 1950 Rajputana was combined with the former British province of Ajmer-Merwara to became the Indian state of Rajasthan.

Rajputana Agency : It was a collection of native states in India, under the political charge of an agent to the Governor-General of India who resided at Mount Abu in the Aravalli Range. The total area of Rajputana was about 127,541 square miles (330,000 km^2). It included 18 states and 2 estates or chiefships.

Rajputana Rifles : The Rajputana Rifles are a regiment of the Indian Army, formerly the 6th Rajputana Rifles when part of the British Indian Army. They were initially created as a regiment of the Bombay Army of the British East India Company, circa 1775. The name Rajputana Rifles comes from the Hindi word Rajput which is derived from the Sanskrit word Rajputra meaning son of a king. The Rajputs are the dominant people of Rajputana, a historic region which is now part of Rajasthan. Other important fighters in this regiment are Jats from Rajasthan, UP and Haryana.

Rajrambha : Rajrambha is the name of Himalayan mountain peak, situated in the Pithoragarh district of Uttaranchal state of India. It means 'celestial nymph (Apsara) in Hindi. This peak is situated south of the Kalabaland Glacier in eastern Kumaun in the Ralam valley. The summit of the peak is 6,537 M.The nearby peaks which forms north-south massif are Suitilla 6,373 M, Chaudhara 6,510 M, Ngalaphu 6,410 M. Rajrambha forms wall between Lasser Yankti and Ralam Valley.It can be approached through Uttari Balati glacier passing Balati plateau.Dhakar or Tidang is the Base camp from where one can climb the Rajrambha peak (6537m).Dakar is near Tawaghat in Pithoragarh district as the last motorable station on the way.

Rajshahi : Rajshahi is a city in Rajshahi District in northwestern Bangladesh. It is situated on the river Padma and has a population of 700,000. Rajshahi is the headquarter of Rajshahi Division, one of the six administrative divisions in Bangladesh. Rajshahi Municipality was established in 1876, one of the first in Bangladesh. Rajshahi is located near many ancient capitals of Bengal, notably Lakhnoiti or Lokhonaboti and Pundra. Rajshahi is home to many educational institutes, and is often is referred to in Bangladesh as education city.

Rajshahi district was a part of Pundru region of ancient Bengal. The capital of Vijay Sen, the king who led military operations in Sri Lanka and Southeast Asia was located 9 miles to the west of Rajshahi town. In medieval ages, the region came to be known as "Rampur Boalia". The administrative district was established in 1772 and the municipal corporation in 1876. It was made a city corporation in 1991.

During the British Raj, it was also known as "Beuleah" and was the administrative headquarters of Rajshahi district in Eastern Bengal and Assam. It was originally chosen as a commercial factory for the silk trade, which was being officially encouraged by the agricultural department of that time. The town contained a government college, and an industrial school for sericulture. Most of the public buildings were severely damaged by the earthquake of the 12th of June 1897. There was a daily steamer service on the Ganges.

Along with all of Bangladesh, Rajshahi witnessed both great atrocities by the Pakistan army and heroic struggles by the freedom fighters during the liberation war in 1971.

The largest mass grave in Bangladesh is located in Rajshahi University, which was used as an army camp during the war. On the other hand, one of the great battles of the war took place near Rajshahi. Captain Mohiuddin Jahangir, who died in battle, was awarded the highest honor (Bir Srhestha) by the Bangladesh government after the war.

Rajshahi College : Rajshahi College is one of the first institutions of higher education in Bangladesh. Established in 1873 in Rajshahicity, it is said to be the third oldest college in Bangladesh after Dhaka College and Chittagong College. Rajshahi College was the first institution in Bangladesh to award a Masters degree. Situated in the city center, Rajshahi College is adjacent to other important educational institutions such as Rajshahi Collegiate School and Barendra Museum.

The origins of the college were in a private English School that had been founded in Rajshahi in 1828 by the concerted efforts of many of the region's most prominent citizens (this school is now known as Rajshahi Collegiate School). In 1836 the school was taken over by the provincial government of Bengal and was converted into a Government Zillah (or District) School. In 1873, again through the concerted efforts and appeals of local citizens, the Zillah School was given the status of an Intermediate College, and F.A. courses were introduced into its curriculum. With further development this college was accorded "first-grade rank" in 1878, which meant that it could teach B.A. courses and be affiliated to Calcutta University. The name "Rajshahi College" came with the first-grade rank in 1878. The year 1881 saw the inauguration of the M. A. classes; B.L. classes were added in 1883. The postgraduate Departments in Arts and in Law continued till 1909 when they were withdrawn because the college could not meet the requirements of the New Regulations of Calcutta University which came into force in that year.

Starting with only 6 students on the roll in 1873, the college counted 100 in 1878, 200 in 1900, 400 in 1910, 800 in 1920 and no less than 1000 in 1924 ; there was only 1 Muslim student at the college in 1873,5 years later it was still 1, but the figure rose to 156 in 1916 and climaxed at 215 in 1924. Subsequently, of course, Muslim numbers rose in the college and after 1947 eventually exceeded the Hindu numbers. Today, in independent Bangladesh, the college has been accorded "University College" status and no longer teaches Higher Secondary or Intermediate courses. Currently, it is part of the National University system of Bangladesh and its curriculum includes only undergraduate and post-graduate courses in a variety of disciplines.

Rajshahi Collegiate School : Established in 1828, Rajshahi Collegiate School is the first modern school to be established in Bangladesh. It is located in the center of Rajshahi, a prominent city in northern Bangladesh. After the British colonial rule started in Bengal in 1757, the British started founding educational centres to create the body of (usually low ranked) officers from the native people. This let to establishment of a number of educational institutions all over India and Bengal in particular. Though a lot of institutions were established in Kolkata and the western part of Bengal, the first school in East Bengal was Rajshahi Collegiate School. Its establishment was followed by those of Jessore Zilla School, Dhaka Collegiate School, Chittagong Collegiate School and Rangpur Zilla School.

Rajshahi Division : Rajshahi Division is in Northwestern part of Bangladesh. The major cities of Rajshahi division are Rajshahi, Rangpur, Bogra and Dinajpur. Rajshahi and the city of Saidpur have airports, with daily flights to the capital city of Dhaka. A major landmark in Rajshahi is the Kantaji Mondir, a Hindu temple north of Dinajpur. The temple is covered entirely with thousands of terra cotta tiles, each with a unique design. Other sites of interest are Sompur Bihara, a large buddhist monastery, a Mohasthangar, home to archeological sites of Hindu, Buddhist and Muslim periods. Barendra Museum in Rajshahi is one of the foremost museums specializing in history of ancient Bengal. Rajshahi is well-known for its fruit, particularly mangoes.

Rajshahi Medical College : Rajshahi Medical College, located in Rajshahi, Bangladesh, is a state sponsored medical school. It is afflilliated with the Rajshahi University. It was established in 1956, the second such instituion in erstwhile East Pakistan after Dhaka Medical College. It has a large hospital that is the central provider for advanced health care in the northern part of Bangladesh. Rajshahi Medical College admits 150 students every year for its M.B.B.S. program. It's dental unit admits a further 50 students. Students are admitted in these prgrams after high school and get a degree after 5 years of study.

Rajshahi University : Rajshahi University is the second largest university in Bangladesh. For a long time, it used to be the only center of higher studies in the northern part of the nation. Rajshahi University was established in 1953. It was the second university in what was then East Pakistan, after University of Dhaka. The campus was designed by architect John Zomanec. Rajshahi University is located in Rajshahi, a city in Bangladesh. The area of the campus in 753 acres (3 km^2), making it one of the largest universities in the region. In addition to degrees in arts, sciences and business, the university has a medical program through Rajshahi Medical College and also houses a number of institutes of higher studies.

Rajula Festival : It is celebrated for one day in honour of Polam Raju or Nagoba deity, a God holding sway over the hills and forests. He is supposed to protect the cattle and the herdsmen. On the full moon day in the month of Ashadha, all the male members, including children with their cattle go to the nearby forest and sacrifice a goat to Rajula deity.

Kheer (rice cooked with milk and sugar) is prepared and a little is given to all the cattle, the rest eaten by the family members. Afterwards a straight line, twenty or thirty metres long is drawn with turmeric powder and cattle are made to cross over it and driven away untended into the forest and brought back on the following day and the men perform the Puja. Women look after the preparation of the feast; a non- vegetarian feast, including Kheer is prepared and eaten with much relish. A goat is sacrificed and its meat is distributed among all. They do not touch the leaf of a teak tree till the function is over. This festival is based on the belief that on the day, if any of the cattle driven away to the forest is killed by a tiger, the village would face a tiger menace throughout the year.

Rajwada : The Rajawada with its 7-storeyed gateway, faces the main square in MP. A mixture of French, Mughal and Maratha styles, the palace has been up in flames three times in its 200 year history. Its lofty entrance archway above a huge wooden door encrusted with iron studs, leads into a vast courtyard enclosed by galleried rooms. The lower three floors are made of stone and the upper floors are made of wood. After the serious conflagration in 1984, it's now not much more than a facade. The New Palace still remain on the north side.

Rajya Sabha : The Rajya Sabha is also known as Council of States or the upper house. Its members are indirectly elected by members of legislative bodies of the states.

The Rajya Sabha has 250 members in all. Elections to it are scheduled and the chamber cannot be dissolved legally. Each member has a term of 6 years and elections are held for one-third of the seats after every 2 years. The composition is specified in Article 80 of the Constitution of India.

Rajyavardhan Singh Rathore : Rajyavardhan Singh Rathore (born January 29, 1970, Jaisalmer, Rajasthan, India) is an Indian shooter who won the first individual silver medal for the country in 2004 Summer Olympics. His event was the Men's Double Trap. In 2005 Commonwealth Shooting Championships in Melbourne, he was the member of the winning team in the double trap event. He won the gold in the individual and team events in Men's double trap at the 2005 Asian Clay Shooting championships at Bangkok. The gold in the individual event was the third consecutive one for Rathore at the annual events after the ones in 2003 and 2004, thus constituting a hat trick.

He is a Lt. Colonel in the Indian Army. He won the Arjuna award in 2003-2004 for shooting and the Rajiv Gandhi Khel Ratna, the highest sporting honour of India, in 2004-2005. He is a recipient of the Padma Shri, a civilian award from the Government of India, and the Ati Vishisht Seva Medal (AVSM), a gallantry award for service presented by the government. He is the first officer (from the Indian Army) below the rank of brigadier to be awarded the AVSM.

Rakaposhi : Rakaposhi is a mountain in the Karakoram region of the Pakistani Himalaya. Rakaposh means "shining wall" in the local language. Rakaposhi is also known as Rakaposhi Peak, Rakapushi and Dumani ("Mother of Mist"). There are magnificent views of Rakaposhi from the Karakoram Highway on the route through Hunza. Rakaposhi was first climbed in 1958 by Mike Banks and Tom Patey of a Britain-Pakistan expedition. Both of them suffered severe frostbite during the ascent. Another climber slipped and fell on the descent and died during the night.

Rakesh Sharma : Rakesh Sharma (born January 13, 1949 in Patiala, Punjab, India) was the first Indian in space. He was a squadron leader in the Indian Air Force and embarked on the mission in 1984. The manned space program of the Indian Space Research Organisation has depended entirely upon Russia, and the first Indian cosmonaut became the 138th man into space.

He spent eight days in space aboard Salyut 7. Launched along with two other Soviet cosmonauts aboard Soyuz T-11 on 02 April 1984, was then-Squadron Leader Rakesh Sharma, a 35 year old Indian Air Force pilot. During the flight, Squadron Leader Sharma conducted multi-spectral photography of northern India in anticipation of the construction of hydroelectric power stations in the Himalayas. In a famous incident, he was asked by the then Prime Minister Indira Gandhi how India looked from the space and he replied, Saare Jahan Se Achcha, (translates to better than all the world) which happens to be the first line of a famous poem by Muhammad Iqbal.

Squadron Leader Sharma and his backup, Wing Commander Ravish Malhotra, also prepared an elaborate series of zero-gravity Yoga exercises which the former had practised aboard the Salyut 7. Retired with the rank of Wing Commander, Rakesh Sharma joined Hindustan Aeronautics Limited (HAL) as a test pilot. He was based at the Aircraft & Systems Testing Establishment (ASTE) in Bangalore and worked on the indigenous Light Combat Aircraft program.

Rakhi Festival : In Bhadon, on the day of the full moon, the *Rakhi festival* is celebrated. On this day sisters tie the multi-coloured thread on the right wrist of their brothers. So long as a sister has not tied the Rakhi to her brother, she is not supposed to eat anything. After she has done so she offers some sweets to her brother and he in return gives her some gift or money. Rakhi is meant to remained the brother of his promise to protect his sister whenever she needs this protection.

Rakhi or Raksha Bandhan : Rakhi or Raksha Bandhan in northern India is the day for brothers and sisters to renew the affectionate ties that bind them. On this day, the Kashmiri Hindus in Srinagar climb the temple of Shankaracharya on a hill top. This is believed to be an abode of Lord Shiva. But the more revered abode is situated in the far off, glacier-bound cave-shrine of Amarnath where pilgrims from all parts of India behold sacred pigeons—believed to be incarnations of Shiva and Parvathi. Those who cannot trek to Amarnath make it to Thanjivara cave—3 km from the town of Bijibrara—to worship the Shiva lingam. The belief is that three pilgrimages to this shrine equal the merit gained by the Amarnath yatra.

Rakhigarhi : Rakhigarhi, or Rakhi Garhi, is a village in Hissar district in the northwest Indian state of Haryana, around 150 kilometers from Delhi. In 1963 archeologists discovered the village was the site of an extensive city, part of the Indus Valley Civilization. Since 1997 the Archaeological Survey of India has undertaken a detailed excavation of the site, revealing the size of the lost city (at least 2.2 km^2) and recovering numerous artifacts, some over 5,000 years old. Evidence of paved roads, a drainage system, a large rainwater collection and storage system, terracotta brick and statue production, and skilled metal working (in both bronze and precious metals) has been uncovered. Jewellery, including bangles made from terracotta, conch shells, gold, and semi-precious stones, have also been found.

Raksha Bandhan : Raksha bandhan or Rakhi is a Hindu festival which celebrates the relationship between brothers and sisters. The literal meaning of the phrase Raksha Bandhan is 'the bond of protection'. Sisters tie a rakhi (a holy thread) around their brothers' wrists. The brother in return offers a gift to his sister and vows to look after her. This festival is typically an occasion for celebration by the whole family. It is not necessary that the rakhi can be given only to a blood brother—any male can be "adopted" as a brother by tying a rakhi on the person. Indian history is replete with women asking for protection, through rakhi, from men who were neither their brothers, nor Hindus themselves. Rani Karnavati of Chittor sent a rakhi to the Mughal Emperor Humayun when she was threatened by Bahadur Shah of Mewar. Humayun abandoned an ongoing military campaign to ride to her rescue. Raksha Bandhan is celebrated on the full moon of the month of Shravana. For example, in the year 2005 it fell on the 19th of August. The rakhi may be bound on other special occasions (not necessarily only among brothers and sisters), as was done during the Indian independence movement.

Raksi Bahini : Raksi Bahini is a para-military force raised in Bangladesh soon after liberation to serve as a law enforcing agency. Jatiya Raksi Bahini Order of 8 March 1972 was intended to restore deteriorating law and order in the country. Immediately after the liberation, the law and order ran fast into a desperate situation. In view of the situation the government resolved to raise a new para-military force, Raksi Bahini, under the total control of the government.

Ralam Glacier : Ralam Glacier is one of the main Himalayan glaciers situated on the hills of Pithoragarh district of Uttaranchal, India. Munsiyari is the base for the trek.This glacier is situated near Ralam Dhura at Ralam

Khal.It lies at the base of the great Himalayan wall. It is situated at an altitude of 2,290 m above sea level.The glacier is glaciologically divided into two parts namely Upper Ralam and Lower Ralam. From Munsiyari to Ralam Glacier it is on 15 km from Ralam village near Sophiya Udiyar.

Ram Bagh : This beautiful garden is named as a tribute to Guru Ram Das, the founder of the city of Amritsar. It is situated in the new part of town and has a museum in the summer palace built by the Sikh Maharaja Ranjit Singh (1780-1839) the Lion of Punjab. The museum contains weapons dating back to Mughal times and some portraits of the ruling houses of the Punjab and a replica of the diamond 'Kohinoor'. To commemorate the memory of his valour Ram Bagh has a lively statue of Maharaja Ranjit Singh saddled on a horse. It's closed on Wednesdays.

Ram Janmabhoomi : Ram Janmabhoomi refers to a tract of land in the North Indian city of Ayodhya which is believed by many to be the birthplace of the King Ram. The name Ram Janmabhoomi simply means "birthplace of Ram."

It is located in Ayodhya in the state of Uttar Pradesh and has found itself at the epicentre of communal politics in modern India. It was commonly believed, by certain sections in India, until about 1990 that an ancient Ram Janmabhoomi temple was demolished and replaced with the Babri Mosque which stood on the site until 1992. Historical opinion on the matter is divided. The site is intensely contested because the mosque—which was unused but had consequentially acquired symbolic value—was forcibly demolished by a group of Hindu rioters on December 6, 1992. Efforts to replace the mosque with a temple had been on since 1947, but had been continually stymied by both the central government and various Indian courts. Its demolition triggered large-scale rioting across India and led to intense communal tensions between the majority Hindu community and the Indian Muslim community. It continues to be a major issue in Indian politics.

Ram Karmabhoomi : Ram Karmabhoomi is the area composing of Rameshwaram, Dhanushkodi, Rama's Bridge, also known as Adam's Bridge where the Hindu deity Rama is believed to have conducted his fight against Ravana to rescue Sita. It is called so because in terms of importance to Hindus it matches Ram Janmabhoomi which is the location of Rama's birth.

Rama's heritage, including the holy city of Rameshwaram is under jeopardy from the launch of the Sethusamudram Canal Project. Though the historical significance of Rama's bridge, has not been proved by NASA, the photos clearly depict the presence of a bridge connecting India and SriLanka. The construction of a canal will destroy this bridge. It is also argued that design of the canal is likely to invite a tsunami that could wash out Rameshwaram, similar to the manner in which Poompuhar was washed away.

Ram Raja Temple : Its soaring spires and palatial architecture, the temple is one of the most unusual in India. It is also the only one in the country where Rama is worshipped as a king. It opens from 0800 to 1230 and from 1900 to 2130. Its fresh pink and cream colour painting is a peculiarity, if compared with other temples. It is interesting to visit during arati.

Ram Thirth : The place of Pujab gets special mention in the great Hindu epic 'Ramayana'. It is the place where Maharshi Valmiki gave shelter to Sita, wife of Rama when she was abandoned after the Lanka Victory. It was here that she gave birth to the twins Lav- Kush. There is a temple here.

Rama Leela : This all -India festival is celebrated in a few important villages and towns in Orissa in the month of Chaitra (March-April). The masks of Rama, Ravana and others of the Ramayana myth are worn by characters in a dramatic re-enactment of the epic happenings. This is accompanied by music and singing and is presented in the form of folk opera. The burning of the huge effigies as practiced elsewhere in India is not prevalent in Orissa. The fair is held in honour of Lord Rama to celebrate the victory of virtue over vice Ravana.

Rama's Bridge : Rama's Bridge, Nala's Bridge or Adam's Bridge is a chain of limestone shoals, between the islands of Mannar, near northwestern Sri Lanka, and Rameswaram, off the southeastern coast of India. The bridge is 30 miles (48 km) long and separates the Gulf of Mannar (southwest) from the Palk Strait (northeast). Some of the sandbanks are dry and the sea in the area is very shallow, being only 3 ft to 30 ft (1 m to 10 m) deep. This seriously hinders navigation. It was reportedly passable on foot as late as the 15th century until storms deepened the channel. A ferry links the island and port of Rameswaram in India with Talaimannar in Sri Lanka; the Pamban Bridge links Rameswaram island with mainland India.

The names Rama's Bridge and Nala's Bridge originate in Hindu mythology. According to the Hindu epic Ramayana, the bridge was constructed at Rama's request by his subjects, including the Vanara Sena (army of monkeys), led by Nala, son of the architect-god Visvakarman. The bridge was supported on floating rocks but the gods were said to have later anchored the rocks to the sea bed, thus creating the present chain of rocky shoals. It was said to have helped Rama to reach Sri

Lanka to rescue Sita from a monster called Ravana, who was then the ruler of Lanka.

The alternate name Adam's Bridge derives from the Christian mythological notion that the biblical Garden of Eden was located on Sri Lanka.

Archeological studies of the bridge are ongoing, and some archeologists claim to have found evidence suggesting that the bridge is man-made. For instance, some researchers from Bharathidasan University, Tiruchirappalli, announced that the "bridge" is only 3,500 years old.

Sea levels rose about 10 or 20 metres in the 6th millennium BCE to reach levels similar to today, so in 6000 BCE the bridge would have been an isthmus situated above sea level. As such, it almost certainly would have been a viable route for humans to have reached Sri Lanka by dry land.

Ramagundam : Ramagundam (including Godavarikhani Town} is a municipality in the Karimnagar district of northern Andhra Pradesh, India. It has a population of 235,540 (agglomeration 236,623 (2001 census}. Ramagundam is situated in the Godavari Valley coalfields and has one of India's largest thermal power stations, run by NTPC. Ramagundam Airport code is RMD. The town Ramagundam gets its name from combination of two words (Rama + Gundam). A famous temple of Hindu god lord Rama is situated in old part of the town and Gundam means water springs.

Ramakrishna Hegde : Ramakrishna Hegde (born August 29, 1926 at Siddapur in north Karnataka) was the chief minister of Karnataka. His parents were Mahabaleshwar Hegde and Saraswati Hegde.

He participated in Quit India Movement of 1942 - Indian freedom struggle and was an active member of

Congress Party. Then he became a prominent member of Janata Party. After the split in Janata party, he became a prominent leader of Janata Dal. He became the first non-Congress chief minister of Karnataka with the support of BJP. First from January 10, 1983 - December 29, 1984 followed by term from March 8, 1985 - February 13, 1986 and finally from February 16, 1986 - August 10, 1988. He has the rare distinction of presenting thirteen finance budgets in the State Assembly.

He was also the deputy chairman of the Planning Commission of India, during the time of V P Singh. He was expelled from Janata Dal by its president Lalu Prasad Yadav, as per the instructions of then Prime minister H. D. Deve Gowda. Ramakrishna Hegde formed 'Rashtreeya Nava nirmana vedike' a social organisation and then 'Lokashakti'. He became the commerce minister in the BJP lead NDA government. He passed away in January 2004 in Bangalore.

Ramakrishna Math : Ramakrishna Math is a religious monastic order set up by Swami Vivekananda to follow the teachings of Sri Ramakrishna. The Ramakrishna Math is headquartered at Belur Math (in West Bengal, India), and shares the location with the related organisation, the Ramakrishna Mission. Ramakrishna Math consists of monks (Sannyasins and Brahmacharins) belonging to a monastic order for men. After the passing away of their Master Sri Ramakrishna in 1886 the young disciples organized themselves into a new monastic order. The original monastery at Baranagar was shifted in January 1899 to a newly acquired plot of land at Belur in the district of Howrah. This monastery, known as Belur Math, serves as the Mother House for all the monks of Ramakrishna Order who live in the various branch centres of Ramakrishna Math and/or the related Ramakrishna Mission in different parts of India and the world.

Ramakrishna Mission : The Ramakrishna Mission is an association founded by Sri Ramakrishna's chief disciple and religious leader, Swami Vivekananda on May 1, 1897. The Mission carries on missionary and philanthropic work in conjunction with householders (Grihastha) disciples.

Ramakrishna Paramahansa : Ramakrishna Paramahansa was a great religious leader of India. He was born in a Brahmin family in the Hooghly district, West Bengal. He taught that God-realisation is the only goal of life. Visions, trances, ecstasies crowded upon him and most of his time was spent in intense spiritual activities. Paramahansa proceeded under various spiritual guides to experience the whole gamut of mystical relationship described in Hindu scriptures. Ramakrishna reaffirmed on the basis of his own spiritual experiments that all creeds and religions led ultimately to the same goal. He exhorted people not to waste time squabbling over this or that religion but to seek God with pure and dedicated heart.

His sayings and story of his life remain to this day a major source of religious guide-lines. Under his great influence he attracted to him a group of young disciples. Outstanding among them was was Swami Vivekananda.

Ramakuppam : Ramakuppam is a small town situated in the Palmaner Taluk of Chittoor District of Andhra Pradesh in India and about fifteen miles from Kuppam. It is probably the last town on the deccan plateau, further south the landscape descends down through a forest range to meet the plains of Tamil Nadu. It has a mixture of all the major religions of india. The two nearest villages are bandarlapalle and manindram. It has got good transport facilities and connected well by road to other towns in the region. A huge population of people reside in the nearby city of Kolar Gold Fields in the state of Karnataka. The Kalki ashram is situated near Ramakuppam called Satya Loka. From KGF you should go towards a bus junction called Rajupeta Road, which is 2,5 km from Satyaloka. Then go towards Ramakuppam, and half the way to Ramakuppam is Satyaloka.

Ramalinga Raju : Ramalinga Raju (born September 16, 1954) who's surname is Byrraju, is an Indian businessman, and a pioneer of the Information Technology industry in India. He is the Chairman of Satyam Computer Services Ltd. It was founded in the late 1980's after venturing earlier into other businesses such as construction and textiles. Raju had acquired a B. Com from Andhra Loyola College at Vijayawada prior to recieving an MBA degree from Ohio University. He has attended the Owner/ President course at Harvard.

Ramanathan Krishnan : Ramanathan Krishnan (born April 11, 1937, in Madras, India) was an Indian tennis player of the 1950's and 60's and one of the greatest Indian players of all time. He was born on 11 April 1937, did M.A. in Economics from Madras University. Tennis soon took a grip on him with his father T.K. Ramanathan, a champion in his own right, being the guiding factor.

Krishnan was a good pupil and soon became a known figure, winning both the junior and senior national championships, the latter for eight years at a stretch. Krishnan became the mainstay of Indian tennis for over a decade and a half and with a world rating which no other player from the country, not even Vijay Amritraj, has been able to match. He was rated among the top ten in the world on five different occasions and was seeded 4 in the Wimbeldon of 1962. He however withdrew of an ankle injury.

Ramanathan Krishnan could rightly be called the architect of Indian tennis after independence. A subtle stroke player with a backhand that stood out, Krishnan ushered in a new era as a 16-year old with a memorable performance against Belgium in the Davis Cup Tournament in 1953. He was already the National Champion at that time and though India lost 0-5, Krishnan left his stamp with a five-set thriller against Jacques Brichant in the first Singles and then another five setter with Sumant Misra as his partner in the Doubles.Being among the youngest to have played in Davis Cup, Krishnan was full of confidence for his Wimbledon debut the next year where he won the junior Singles beating Ashley Cooper in the Finals. He was the first Asian to do so.

From then onwards Krishnan's tennis career was on the upswing and even though never did win the Wimbledon he was forever a favourite with the crowds, twice reaching the Semi-Finals, the only Indian to do so. On both occasions he lost to the eventual champion. Neale Fraser, in 1960 and Rod (Rocket) Laver in 1961. For all his high-profile showing in the Wimbledon, Krishnan will always be known for his performance in the Davis Cup Tournament. He has in fact one of the best records in this team event, winning 50 of the 69 Singles and 19 of the 29 Doubles encounters, the latter in partnership with Jaideep Mukherjea. He was also instrumental in taking India into the Challenge Round in 1966 where the team lost to Australia, the holders. Ramanathan Krishnan has many big victories to his credit but the two he will cherish most are the triumph over Rod Laver in the Davis Cup Zonal Finals against Australia played in Brooklyn (USA) in 1959 and against Thomas Koch of Brazil in the crucial 5th rubber at Calcutta in 1966, It was an incredible Krishnan, trailing two sets to one, 2-5 games and 15-30 down in the fourth set, reserverd the trend to win over five sets.

Ramanuja Acharya : Sri Ramanuja Acharya (traditionally dated 1017–1137 CE) was an Indian philosopher and is recognized as the most important saint of Sri Vaishnavism. He held the Vishishtadvaita or qualified Nondualist belief that the world and Brahman were united, like a soul and a body are. His version of Indian Nondualism differed from Adi Shankara's because he acknowledged the existence of differences, and believed that the identity of an object as a part was as important as the unity of the whole. The Vaishnava Theology espoused by Ramanuja posits that Brahman is not devoid of attributes but is expressed as a personal God, full of infinite good qualities, as Narayana. The Adishesha on whom Lord Ranganatha of Srirangam rests is believed to be Ramanuja.

Ramappa Temple : Ramappa Temple of Andhra Pradesh is located at Palampet near Mulug in Warangal district. This is of tourist importance owing to the existence of the renowned and exquisitely carved sculptures of the Ramappa Temple, and the Ramappa Lake constructed at the time of Kakatiya Ganapati. The temple, built of black basalt with splendid carvings, is 12.19 metres high. The Ramappa lake is a magnificient irrigation work of the 13th century AD, and the place, where the lake stands, is surrounded by thick forests and presents a beautiful natural scenery making it a popular holiday resort.

Ramayana : The Ramayana is part of the Hindu smriti, written by Valmiki. This epic of 24,000 verses in seven kands (chapters or books) tells of a Raghuvamsa (Sanskrit—"Of the Sun Dynasty") prince, Rama of Ayodhya, whose wife Sita is abducted by the Rakshasa, or demon, Ravana. The Ramayana had an important influence on later Sanskrit poetry, primarily through its establishment of the Sloka meter. But, like its epic cousin Mahabharata, the Ramayana is not just a good story. It contains the teachings of the ancient Hindu sages and presents them through allegory in narrative and the interspersion of philosophic and devotional. The characters of Rama, Sita, Lakshmana, Bharat, Hanumana and Ravana (the archvillain of the story) are all fundamental to the grander cultural consciousness of India. Just like Christians historically believe in the birth of Jesus, people of the Hindu religion believe in the birth of Rama.

The Ramayana is set in the Treta Yuga. Many interpret this as 3000 BCE (based on astronomical data in the Ramayana). The Ramayan is ascribed to a single author, Valmiki. Its exact date of creation is unknown, and is estimated to lie between the 4th and 2nd century B.C.E. "The Cultural Heritage of India", Vol. IV, "The Religions", The Ramakrishna Mission, Institute of Culture, says: "The first and the last Books of the Ramayana are later additions. The bulk, consisting of Books II—VI, represents Rama as an ideal hero. In Books I and VII, however Rama is made an avatara or incarnation of Vishnu, and the epic poem is transformed into a Vaishnav text.

As per the traditional astronomical back-projection by Vedic system, the event of the war between Rama and Ravana is supposed to have happened 880,147 years ago, as of April 09, 2005. This is an important observation made in invariably all astronomical almanacs published in India. These almanacs, called Pancang are intended to be used as calendars, ready-reckoner for muhurt, and astrological predictions, and thus subtlely organize and control the life and events in Indian society—especially the Hindu community. Modern scholars even in India are usually sceptic about this claim. Yet several modern researchers as well as traditional practitioners of the Hindu system of time-charts and cosmology subscribe to this. This view has never been accepted by mainstream modern historians in India.

According to Hindu tradition, Rama is an Avatara, an incarnation of Vishnu or God. The main purpose of his incarnation is to demonstrate the ideal human life on earth. Ultimately, Rama slays the rakshasa king Ravana and reestablishes the rule of religious and moral law on earth known in Hinduism as dharma. It has been said that

Brahma promised Valmiki, so long as the mountains and seas endure, so long shall the Ramayana be read by men.

Ramcharitmanas : Sri Ramcharitmanas is an epic poem composed by the great 16th-century Indian poet, Goswami Tulsidas (c.1532–1623) (also transliterated as Tulasidasa). As he mentions in Baal Kaand of the composition, he started writing it in Vikram Samvat 1631 (1574 AD) in Avadhpuri, Ayodhya. It was completed in two years and seven months. A large portion of the poem was composed at Varanasi, where the poet spent most of his later life. It is considered one of the greatest works of Hindi literature.

Raamcharitmaanas is a retelling of the events of the Sanskrit epic Ramayana, concerning the amazing exploits of Rama. The great poem is popularly called Tulsi-krita Ramayana, but entitled by its author Raamcharitmaanas, or the Lake of Rama's Deeds. It is as well known among Hindus in northern India as is the Bible among the rural population of England. The composition is in Avadhi, a local dialect of Hindi, spoken in the Gangetic plain of North India. The language is flowery with free use of metaphors and similes. Many of its verses are popular proverbs in that region; an apt quotation from them by a stranger has the immediate effect of instilling confidence in the listener. As with the King James Bible and Shakespeare, Tulsidas's phrases have passed into common speech, and are used by millions of Hindi speakers (and even speakers of Urdu) without the speakers being conscious of their origin. Not only are his sayings proverbial: his doctrine actually forms the most powerful religious influence in present-day Hinduism; and, though he founded no school and was never known as a guru or master, he is everywhere accepted as both poet and saint, an inspired and authoritative guide in religion and the conduct of life.

Ramcharitmanas : Sri Ramcharitmanas is an epic poem composed by the great 16th-century Indian poet, Goswami Tulsidas (c.1532–1623) (also transliterated as Tulasidasa). As he mentions in Baal Kaand of the composition, he started writing it in Vikram Samvat 1631 (1574 AD) in Avadhpuri, Ayodhya. It was completed in two years and seven months. A large portion of the poem was composed at Varanasi, where the poet spent most of his later life. It is considered one of the greatest works of Hindi literature.

Raamcharitmaanas is a retelling of the events of the Sanskrit epic Ramayana, concerning the amazing exploits of Rama. The great poem is popularly called Tulsi-krita Ramayana, but entitled by its author Raamcharitmaanas, or the Lake of Rama's Deeds. It is as well known among Hindus in northern India as is the Bible among the rural population of England. The composition is in Avadhi, a local dialect of Hindi, spoken in the Gangetic plain of North India. The language is flowery with free use of metaphors and similes. Many of its verses are popular proverbs in that region; an apt quotation from them by a stranger has the immediate effect of instilling confidence in the listener. As with the King James Bible and Shakespeare, Tulsidas's phrases have passed into common speech, and are used by millions of Hindi speakers (and even speakers of Urdu) without the speakers being conscious of their origin. Not only are his sayings proverbial : his doctrine actually forms the most powerful religious influence in present-day Hinduism; and, though he founded no school and was never known as a guru or master, he is everywhere accepted as both poet and saint, an inspired and authoritative guide in religion and the conduct of life.

Ramdhari Singh 'Dinkar' : Ramdhari Singh 'Dinkar' (1908—pril 24, 1974) was one of the most famous modern Hindi poets. He emerged as a rebellious poet with his nationalist poetry in pre-Independence days. Dinkar was awarded the Jnanpith Award in 1972 for Urvashi, a work of poetry, published in 1961. The theme of Urvashi revolves round love, passion, and relationship of man and woman on a spiritual plain, distinct from their earthly relationship. The name Urvashi is derived from the name of an Apsara of the same name (Urvashi), a celestial damsel of the court of Hindu mythological god, Indra.

Ramesh Krishnan : Ramesh Krishnan (born June 5, 1961, in Madras, India) was one of India's foremost tennis players. He epitomised the notion of the gentleman on the field, is the hero of many a Davis Cup wins for the country. He came into the field with the Amritraj brothers, Sashi Menon and Gaurav Mishra in 1981 when India maintained its winning form in the Davis Cup ties.

He helped establish India as an important tennis-playing nation. In 1998 he was awarded the Padma Shree. With his father, Ramanathan Krishnan, the tennis maestro runs the Krishnan Tennis Academy in Chennai, which has been producing some top class junior talent.

Rameswaram : Rameswaram is a town in the southern part of India in the state of Tamil Nadu, on an island separated from the mainland by the Pamban channel. Rameswaram is famous for the Hindu temple dedicated to Lord Rama who, it is believed, had descended on its shores and built a bridge across the Palk Strait to reach Lanka in his quest to rescue Sita from Ravana. Additionally, the temple is famous for being one of the 12 Jyotirlingas of Siva and it is called Ramalingam. Lord Rama had constructed a Siva linga in order to offer thanks to the Lord after killing Ravana. The Jothilingam in the Rameswaram Temple set up by the side of Sri Visalakshi Ambigai Sannithi was established by Vibeeshna.Hence, the temple is a sacred site for both Shaivites and Vaishnavites.

The grandest part of the temple is the 1219 m pillared corridor consisting of 3.6 m high granite pillars, richly carved and well proportioned. The perspective presented by these pillars run uninterruptedly to a length of nearly 230 m. Together, with Kashi it is considered one of the holiest places in India for the Hindus. Hence, it is a bustling pilgrim centre.

According to Purnas, as advised by Rishis, Rama along with Sita and Lakshamana, installed and worshipped the Sivalinga here to expiate the sin of Brahmahatya (Ravana was a Brahmin being and great grandson of Brahma himself). Lord Rama fixed an auspicious time for installation and sent Anjaneya to Mount Kailas to bring a lingam but as Anjaneya could not return in time Sita herself made a lingam of sand and the worship was over when Anjaneya returned with a Lingam from Mount Kailas. Anjaneya was enraged and tried to in vain to remove the Lingam of sand. To pacify Anjaneya Rama had Anjaneya's Lingam (Visvalingam) also installed by the side of Ramalinga and ordered all pujas should first be performed for Visvalingam.

Ramna Park : Ramna Park is a large park and recreation area situtated at the heart of Dhaka, capital of Bangladesh. The park, established originally by the Mughal emperors in 1610, was later developed by the British colonial rulers and local Nawabs in the 19th Century.

Ramna Racecourse : Ramna Racecourse now known as Suhrawardy Uddyan, is located at the heart of Dhaka city. The area is surrounded by the old high court building and the mausoleums of the three National leaders Sher-e-Bangla Ak Fazlul Huq, Khwaza Nazimuddin and Huseyn Shaheed Suhrawardy to the South, Bangla Academy, Atomic Energy Commission, Bangladesh National Museum, Public Library, and the Teachers Students Centre, Institute of Fine Arts and the main mosque of the University of Dhaka to the west, Birdem hospital, Dhaka Club and Dhaka Tennis Complex to the north, and the Supreme Court, the institute of engineers, and the Ramna park to the east.

Ramoji Film City (RFC) : RFC is the world's largest integrated film studio complex, at nearly 2,000 acres. It is also one of Asia's most popular tourism and recreation centres. Opened in 1996, it is located about 25 km from Hyderabad, India. Established by the Ramoji Group, RFC offers comprehensive and international-standard pre-production, production, and post-production resources for film makers.

RFC offers over 500 set locations. Twenty international films, and nearly forty Indian films can be produced simultaneously in the complex. It has attracted not only filmmakers from southern India and Bollywood, but also producers from Hollywood. The RFC infrastructure includes: custom-designed locations & mock-ups, set construction, properties & costumes, shooting stages, cameras and equipment, audio post-production, digital post-production / SFX as well as film processing.

Ramprasad Sen : Ramprasad Sen (1720-1781) was a Bengali song-writer and singer of Hindu devotional songs, specially Shyamasangit (Songs devoted to the goddess Kali). He is almost always referred to as Ramprasad, and his songs are known as Ramprasadi. Ramprasad's life has been the subject of many mytical stories depicting his devotion to and relation with Kali.

Ramsagar : Ramsagar is a man-made water tank located at the village of Tejpur about 8 km south of Dinajpur town. It is considered to be the biggest man-made tank of Bangladesh. It can be approached from the town by a metalled road, which was once known as the 'Murshidabad Sarak'.

Ramzan : Ramzan is the most important month in the religious year of the Muslims. During the Ramzan month, they take their food only before dawn and again after dusk after offering their prayers in the evening. Severe austerity is the key note of this festival. At the end of the month the Muslims congregate in the central place, offer prayers, and exchange greetings.

Ranchi : Ranchi is the capital city of Jharkhand state, India. Ranchi was the center of the Jharkhand movement for a separate state for the tribal regions of South Bihar. Jharkhand was formed on 15th November 2000 by carving out the districts of Chota Nagpur and Santhal Parganas divisions of Bihar. As a part of Bihar, it used to be the summer capital from the time of the British Raj because of its cool climate.

Rangamati : Rangamati is a district in South-eastern Bangladesh. It is a part of the Chittagong Hill Tracts. It is located in the Chittagong Division. The total area of the district is 6116.13 sq km. It is bounded by the Tripura state of India on the north, Bandarban District on the south, Mizoram State of India and Chin State of Myanmar on the east, and Khagrachhari and Chittagong Districts on the west. The district of Rangamati consists of 10 upazilas, 1 municipality, 9 wards, 35 mahallas, 50 union parishads, 162 mouzas and 1347 villages. The upazilas are Baghaichhari, Barkal, Kawkhali, Belaichhari, Kaptai, Juraichhari, Langadu, Nannerchar, Rajasthali and Rangamati sadar.

Ranganthaswami Temple : The Sri Ranganthaswami Temple in Nellore, Andhra Pradesh, India is a Hindu temple dedicated to Lord Ranganatha a resting form of Lord Vishnu. This temple, also called Talpagiri Ranganathaswami temple or Ranganayakulu is one of the oldest temples in Nellore. It is located on the banks of the river Penna and is believed to have been constructed in the 12th century. Just before the main entrance of the temple is a huge tower, called Gaaligopuram, which literally means "wind tower". This tower is approximately 70 feet high and has 10 feet of gold plated vessels on top of it, called kalisams. Every year during the month of march-april(varies according to indian calendar) grand festival is celebrated. these are called Brahmotsavam.

Rangeet River : The Rangeet River is a tributary of the Teesta River, the largest river in the Indian state of Sikkim. The river originates in the Himalayan mountains in West Sikkim district. A perennial river, it is fed by the melting snow of the Himalayas in early summer, and the monsoon rains in July-August. It is popular among rafting enthusiasts owing to its turbulent waters. The tortuous river joins the Teesta at Teesta Bazaar on the border of West Bengal and Sikkim. During its final few kilometres, it forms the boundary between these two states. The river flows past the towns of Jorethang, Pelling and Legship.

Rangpur : Rangpur is a district in Northern Bangladesh. It is a part of the Rajshahi Division. The District is bordered on the north by Nilphamari District, on the south by Gaibandha District, on the east by Kurigram, and on the west by Dinajpur district. Rangpur town is the district headquarters. The soil composition is mainly alluvial soil (80%) of the Teesta River basin, and the remaining is barind soil. The temperature ranges from 32 degrees Celsius to 11 degrees Celsius, and the annual rainfall averages 2931 mm.

The district has 3 municipalities (namely, Rangpur Sadar, Badarganj, and Kaunia), and eight Upzillas, namely, Badarganj, Gangachara, Kaunia, Rangpur Sadar, Mithapukur, Pirgachha, Pirganj, and Taraganj. Rangpur town, covering an area of around 43 square kilometers, lies on the bank of Ghagat river, and was turned into a municipality long back in 1869. The current population of the Rangpur municipality is 251,699, with 52 % male and 48 % female, and the literacy rate is 54.6 %.

Mansingh, a commander of the Mughal emperor, Akbar, conquered Rangpur in 1575, but it be completely integrated with the Mughal Empire only by 1686. Names of places like Mughalbasa (literal meaning being a locality of the Mughals), and Mughalhat (literal meaning a "local market" organized by the Mughals) bear testimony to the Mughal association and past of Rangpur and its hinterland. Later on, Rangpur passed under the control of "Sarker" of Ghoraghat. During the period of the East India Company, Fakir-Sannyasi Rebellion took place.

Rani Hamid : Rani Hamid (b. 1944) is a chess player from Bangladesh. Hamid was born in Sylhet, Bangladesh. She was awarded the FIDE Woman International Master (WIM) title in 1985. She has won the British Women's Championship multiple times and is the only female international master in Bangladesh. Rani Hamid is arguably the most well known and successful female sports personality Bangladesh has produced.

Rani Lakshmi Bai : Rani Lakshmi Bai (born-19 November 1835- died 18 June 1858), also known as Jhansi Ki Rani, was the queen of Jhansi, a Maratha-ruled princely state of northern India, was one of the great nationalist heroes of the Revolt of 1857, and a symbol of resistance to British rule in India.

Lakshmi Bai was born on 19 November 1835 at Kashi (Presently known as Varanasi). Her father Moropanth Tambey was a brahmin and her mother Bhagirathibai was cultured, intelligent and religious. Born Manikarnika, she was affectionately called Manu in her family. Manu lost her mother at the age of four, and responsibility of looking after the young girl fell to her father. She completed her education and martial training, which included horse riding, fencing and shooting, when she was still a child.

She was married to Raja Gangadhar Rao Niwalkar, the Maharaja of Jhansi in 1842, and became the queen of Jhansi. After the marriage she was given the name Lakshmi Bai. The ceremony of the marriage was performed at the Ganesh Mandir, the temple of Lord Ganesha situated in the old city of Jhansi. Rani Lakshmi Bai gave birth to a son in 1851, but this child died when he was about four months old. After this, the couple adopted Damodar Rao as their son. But Maharaja Gangadhar Rao expired on 21 November 1853, when Lakshmi Bai was 18 years old.

Rani Lakshmi Bai started strengthening the defense of Jhansi and she assembled a volunteer army of patriots. Women were also recruited and given military training. Rani was accompanied by her generals Gulam Gaus Khan, Dost Khan, Khuda Baksh, Lala Bhau Bakshi, Moti Bai, Sunder-Mundar, Kashi Bai, Deewan Raghunath Singh and Deewan Jawahar Singh. Many from the local population volunteered for service in the army ranks, with the popular support for her cause on the rise.

When the Revolt of 1857 broke out, Jhansi became a center of the rebellion. A small group of British officials took refuge in Jhansi's fort, and the Rani negotiated their evacuation. When the British left the fort, they were massacred by the rebels. Although the massacre probably occurred without the Rani's consent and she protested her innocence, she stood accused by the British.

In September and October of 1857, the Rani led the successful defense of Jhansi from the invading armies of the neighboring rajas of Datia and Orchha. In March of 1858, the British Army advanced on Jhansi, and laid siege to the city. After two weeks of fighting the British captured the city, but the Rani escaped the city in the guise of a man, strapping her adopted son Damodar Rao closely on her back. She regrouped loyal soldiers in the town of Kalpi where Tatia Tope other patriots joined her. On June 1, she and her allies captured the fortress city of Gwalior from the Sindhia rulers, who were British allies. She died three weeks later at the start of the British assault, when she saw Tatia Tope being attacked. She rode silently towards him when a British came up behind her and hit her on the head with a club, while at the same time another hit her with a spray of bullets. The British captured Gwalior three days later. The 22 year-old Rani's dying words were not to let the British touch her body. Her soldiers put her body on a nearby haystack and put fire to it.

Rani Rashmoni : Rani Rashmoni, founder of the Dakshineswar Kali Temple and numerous charitable works was born into a poor farming family of Kona village,in present day North 24 Parganas on 26th September 1793. Exceptionally beautiful, she was married to Babu Rajachadra Das of Janbazar(Kolkata), a member of a wealthy zamindar family, when she was eleven years old. After her husband's death she took charge of the zamindari and business. She soon proved herself a natural leader. While the prestige of the zamindari grew, Rani Rashmoni, being very pious from child hood, continued to lead an extremely religious and austere life, befitting a widow in Indian society. Rani Rashmoni passed away on 19th February, 1861.

The Rani and her clashes with the British in India had become household tales in her time. By blocking the shipping trade on a part of Ganges she compelled the British to abolish the tax imposed on fishing in the river, which threatened the livelihood of poor fishermen. When Puja processions were stopped by the British on the charge that they disturbed the peace, she defied the orders. The

British had to withdraw the penalty imposed on her in the face of public opposition and rioting in her support.

Rani Rashmoni also had to her credit numerous charitable works and other contributions to society. She oversaw the construction of a road from Subarnarekha river to Pari for pilgrims. She funded the construction of bathing ghats such as Babughat(in memory of her husband), Ahiritola Ghat and Nimtala Ghat for the daily bathers in the Ganges. She donated generously to the then Imperial Library (now National Library of India) and Hindu College (now Presidency College).

Rani Sisodia's Garden and Palace : The terraced garden is located 8 kms from Jaipur on the Agra route. Sawai Jai Singh built it in 1728 for his Sisodia Queen from Udaipur. The beautiful landscaped garden laid in Mughal style have murals of the life of Lord Krishna in the interior apartments.

Ranikhet : Ranikhet is a hill station and tourist resort town in the Kumaon district of India. It gets its name, which mean Queen's meadow in English, from a legend that an Indian queen visited the site and built herself a palace here. There is no palace in the area. In 1869, the British established the headquarters of the Kumaon regiment here and used the station as a retreat from the heat of the Indian summer. It is at an altitude of 1829 metres above sea level and within sight of the western peaks of the Himalayas. Ranikhet is a small town under district Almora of Uttaranchal. It is a peaceful town and with vast forests of Pine and Deodar.

The Himalayan view available from Ranikhet is excellent, it can make you forget every thing else. Ranikhet is a cantonment town and is the home for the Kumaon Regimental Centre (KRC). It is very well maintained by the Army. Ranikhet becomes very cold in the winters and is moderate in summers. One can enjoy the Himalayan view from October to March. The local language of this town is Kumaoni. Ranikhet is well connected by buses from Delhi and Lucknow. The nearest Railway station is Kathgodam which is approximately 80 km from Ranikhet. Ranikhet gets snowfall in the winter season, which can be expected in the months of December, January and February. It has got a vast diversity of flora and fauna. One can see leopards here. Ranikhet has got a natural Golf Ground which views beautiful. It has many Temples. The famous temples here are Jhula Devi temple, Haidakhan temple, Kalika temple, Mankameshwar temple etc. Ranikhet has its own charm and beauty, it is the most peaceful and beautiful town in India.

Ranikot Fort : Ranikot Fort is a large fort in the region of the Kirthar Hills, in Sani, Sindh, approximately 90 km north of Hyderabad in Pakistan. Built by Imran Bin Musa Barmaki, the Governor of Sindh in 836 A.D., it is one of the largest forts in the world. It has an approximate diameter of 9 km. Its walls are on the average 10 meters high. They are made of gypsum and lime cut sandstone and total about 29 km in circumference. While originally constructed for bow and arrow warfare it was later expanded to withstand firearms.

Rann of Kutch : The Rann of Kutch is a seasonally marshy region located in the Thar Desert biogeographic province in Gujarat state of northwestern India and the Sind province of Pakistan. The name "Rann" comes from the Hindi word ran meaning "salt marsh". Kutch is the name of the district wherein it is situated. The Rann of Kutch comprises some 10,000 square miles between the Gulf of Kutch and the mouth of the Indus River in southern Pakistan. The Luni River, which originates in Rajasthan, empties into the northeast corner of the Rann. In India's summer monsoon, the flat desert of salty clay and mudflats, averaging 15 meters above sea level, fill with standing waters, interspersed with sandy islets of thorny scrub, breeding grounds for some of the largest flocks of Greater and Lesser flamingoes.

The area was a vast shallows of the Arabian Sea until continuing geological uplift closed off the connection with the sea, creating a vast lake that was still navigable during the time of Alexander the Great. The Ghaggar River, which presently empties into the desert of northern Rajasthan, formerly emptied into the Rann of Kutch, but the lower reaches of the river dried up as its upstream tributaries were captured by the Indus and Ganges thousands of years ago. Traces of the delta and its distributary channels on the northern boundary of the Rann of Kutch were documented by the Geologic Survey of India in 2000.

This inhospitable salty lowland, rich in natural gas and a resting site for migratory Siberian birds, is part of India and Pakistan's ongoing border dispute concerning Sir Creek. In April 1965, a dispute there contributed to the Indo-Pakistani War of 1965, when fighting broke out between India and Pakistan. Later the same year, British Prime Minister Harold Wilson successfully persuaded both countries to end hostilities and set up a tribunal to resolve the dispute. A verdict was reached in 1968 which saw Pakistan getting 10% of its claim of 3,500 sq. miles. The majority of the area thus remained with India. Tensions spurted again in 1999 during the Atlantique Incident.

The Rann is also famous for the Indian Wild Ass sanctuary, the Little Rann of Kutch, where the last of three species of Asiatic Wild Ass (Equus hemionus khur or khar), the only ones in Asia, still exists along with wolves, foxes, jackals, chinkara gazelles, nilgai antelope and blackbucks. The Rann of Kutch is also the only place in Pakistan and India which plays host to migrating flamingoes. There are 13 species of lark in the Rann of Kutch.

Ranthambore : Ranthambore is a national park and tiger reserve in Rajasthan state of western India. It is located in Sawai Madhopur district of southeastern Rajasthan, about 130 km from Jaipur, which is also the nearest airport. The nearest town and railway station is at Sawai Madhopur, 11 km away.

The park lies at the edge of a plateau, and is bounded to the north by the Banas River and to the south by the Chambal River. It is named for the historic Ranthambore fortress, which lies within the national park. The park covers an area of 392 km^2, and is famous for its tiger population, and is one of India's Project Tiger reserves. Other major wild animals include the leopard, dhole, wild pig, sambar, chital and the gaur.

Major wild animals found in the national park include the tiger, leopard, nilgai, dhole, wild pig, sambar, chital and the gaur. It is also home to wide variety of trees, plants, birds and reptiles.

Ranthambore National Park : Set up in 1955, Ranthambore National park is situated in the district of Sawai-Madhopur, at the function of Aravalis and Vindhyas covering an area of 392sq.km. The nearest town and the railhead from the park is Sawaimadhopur. The nearest airport is Jaipur at a distance of 132km.

The land consists both of steep slopes and gently rolling plateau on the hill top. The forests are dry deciduous dominated by dhok trees interspersed with grasslands. There are scattered pools to provide water to the wild animals. The well forested park harbours diverse fauna which include tiger, leopard, wild boar, caracal, sloth bear, ratel, hyena, civet, jungle cat, sambar, chinkara, nilgai, four-horned antelope, python, cobra, crocodile, partridge, green pigeon, red spur fowl, peafowl, parakeet, teal etc.

Rapid Action Battalion (RAB) : Rapid Action Battalion or RAB is an elite anti-crime and anti-terrorism force in Bangladesh. It is under the jurisdiction of the Ministry of Home Affairs, Government of Bangladesh. RAB was formed on 26 March 2004. It started its operation from 14 April 2004. Initially, it consisted of members of Bangladesh Army, Bangladesh Navy, Bangladesh Air Force and the Police. Since its initiation, RAB has participated in anti-crime drives throughout the country. Its elite commando forces have been able to arrest several notorious criminals and terrorists.

However, RAB has also come under criticism for human rights violations, after several of the criminals arrested by RAB died in cross-fires and ambushes, allegedly by their accomplices. Some human rights organizations claim that these are extra-judicial executions, while RAB has denied the allegation. The initial success in catching the criminals has made RAB very popular among the common people of Bangladesh. Extra judicial killings by the force numbers between 150 and 200 as of December 2005 as the government admits the lower figure and human right organizations support the higher. However, there is a popular consenscious that most of those killed are known criminals though is 2004 the RAB drew flak from the opposition parties after it killed an important witness of the murder of an opposition MP.

Rasa : The Rasa is another dance from Sirmaur, where the dancers form chains (pindi-bandhas) or concentric circles and sing songs depicting love stories. This dance is different from the Rasa dances of Braj and Manipur.

Rasam : Rasam (Telugu: Chaaru; Kannada: Saaru) is a South Indian soup. It is prepared mainly with the juices of tamarind and tomato with pepper and other spices. Lentils are added frequently and other vegetables optionally. It is eaten mixed with rice, or drunk by itself.

In a formal meal, it follows the sambar course and is in turn followed by curd rice. It differs from sambar in that it usually relies on tomatoes for its sourness rather than tamarind, and it is usually much thinner. Rasam contains many spices which are considered beneficial to health

Rashbehari Bose : (1885-1945) was a revolutionary leader against the British Raj in India and was one of the organisers of the Indian National Army. Bose was born in the Subaldaha village of Burdwan, in the province of Bengal. He had his education in Chandannagar, where his father, Vinodebehari Bose, was stationed.

He was involved in revolutionary activities early in his life and was implicated in the Alipore bomb case (1908). After being released from jail, he went to Dehradun and worked there as a head clerk at the Forest Research Institute. At Dehradun, he secretly got involved with the revolutionaries of Bengal, the United Provinces and the Punjab. His involvement in many revolutionary activities aroused the suspicion of the government and ultimately he was obliged to leave the country. He was hunted by the colonial police due to his active participation in the failed bomb throwing attempt directed at the Governor General and Viceroy Lord Charles Hardinge in Delhi (the bomb was actually thrown by Basanta Kumar Biswas, his desciple). But he managed to escape British intelligence and reached Japan in 1915.

Bose was instrumental in persuading the Japanese authorities to stand by the Indian nationalists and ultimately to support actively the Indian freedom struggle abroad. Bose convened a conference in Tokyo on March 28-30, 1942, which decided to establish the Indian Independence League. At the conference he moved a motion to raise an army for Indian liberation. He convened the second conference of the League at Bangkok on June

22, 1942. It was at this conference that a resolution was adopted to invite Subhas Chandra Bose to join the League and take its command as its president.

The Indian prisoners of war captured by the Japanese in the Malaya and Burma fronts were encouraged to join the Indian Independence League and become the soldiers of the Indian National Army (INA), the military wing of Bose's Indian National League. But his rise to actual power and glory was unfortunately terminated by an action of the Japanese military command, which expelled him and his general Mohan Singh from the INA leadership. But though he fell from grace, his organisational structure remained, and it was on the organisational spadework of Rashbehari Bose that Subhash Chandra Bose later built the Indian National Army (also called 'Azad Hind Fauj'). Before his death, the Japanese Government honoured him with the 'Second Order of the Merit of the Rising Sun'.

Rashid Minhas : Rashid Minhas or Rashid Minhas Shaheed (born February 17, 1951 / d. August 20, 1971) was a Pilot Officer in the Pakistan Air Force during the 1971 Bangladesh Liberation War. He was new to the Air Force having been commissioned that year.

On August 20, 1971 Minhas was getting ready to take-off in a T-33 trainer in Karachi when a Bengali pilot, Matiur Rahman forced his way into the back of the plane. Rahman knocked out Minhas with some blunt object and tried to defect to India in order to join the liberation movement for Bangladesh.

Minhas regained consciousness and realized that the plane was heading towards India. What happened next has not been ascertained, but it is widely believed that the ensuing struggle between Minhas and Rahman resulted in the crash of the plane just thirty miles from the border of India.

For his act he was awarded top military honor, Nishan-E-Haider, becomes the youngest man to win the award, and the only member of the Pakistan Air Force to win it. With this award he has become a national hero. The Pakistan Air Force base at Kamra has been renamed in his honor.

Rashogolla : Rashogolla (Rasgulla in Hindi) (pundor balls in sugar syrup) is one of the most widely available and popular sweetmeats in eastern India and Bangladesh. Rasgulla was first made by Haradhan Maira, a confectioner of Phulia district, during the time of Bengal renaissance. These white cottage cheese balls in sugar syrup not only created a revolution in the confectionary industry but also set the trend for the main sweets of today.

Nabinchandra Roy of Bagbazar, Kolkata, was the first person to make 'sponge' Rasgulla in 1868, and is immortalised in the local limerick "Rasgulla got a Columbus/ In Bagbazar's Nabin Das". KC Das of Kolkata was the first to invent the canned version of this highly perishable sweet, which led to much wider availability.

Rashtrakutas : The Rashtrakutas were a dynasty which ruled the Deccan during the 8th-10th centuries. Feudatories of the Chalukyas they rose to prominence after the Chalukyas fell to Dantidurga. The Pratiharas, Vengis, Gangas Cholas and Palas were their contemporaries. They were destined to become a truly formidable political force in South India, and in fact, waves of their imperial expansion went beyond the Vindhyas into North India, where they had occasions to pose as masters. Their dazzling political achievements, however, were adequately matched by some of their impressive contributions to Karnataka and Kannada culture. The period of their rule is considered as the time of "imperial Kannada". Kannada inscriptions have been discovered as far north as Jabalpur, MadhyaPradesh

Rashtrapati Bhavan : Rashtrapati Bhavan is the official residence of the President of India, located in New Delhi, Delhi. Until 1950 it was known as "Viceroy's House" and served as the residence of the Governor-General of India.

During the Delhi Durbar year of 1911 it was decided that the capital of India would be shifted from Calcutta to Delhi. This was announced on December 12 by King George. As the plan for New Delhi took shape, the Governor-General's residence was given an enormous scale and prominent position. The British architect Edwin Landseer Lutyens, a key member of the city-planning process, was also given the prime architectural opportunity of designing the building.

The original plans of the viceroy's house called for something which would be a mixture between western and eastern styles. There were some who wanted the palace to be a classical designed one, in the tradition of the Greeks. This would clearly show western power in India. Others desired a palace which would be modelled on Indian architecture, and designed by Indians. It was also suggested for various degrees of mixing the two styles. The Viceroy declared that the palace was to be classical, but with an Indian motif. This was close to what the design eventually developed into. While Lutyens wanted an almost totally classical building, it was probably due to pressure from others that forced him to include Indian elements in the design. It is thought that Lutyens believed he came to India to bring Western culture to it, rather than to conform to Indian designs. The palace developed very similarly to the original sketches which Lutyens sent Baker from Simla on June 14, 1912.

Rashtriya Janata Dal : The Rashtriya Janata Dal (RJD- "National People's Party") is a political party in India. It is led by Laloo Prasad Yadav. It held power in the Indian state of Bihar, under the Chief Ministers Laloo Yadav and then Rabri Devi, who is also Laloo's wife, but after the elections in February 2005 the state of Bihar came under President's Rule through Governor of Bihar Sardar Buta Singh. Since then, a new election has brought another party to power in the state. The RJD is also a member of India's governing coalition led by the Congress Party. The RJD was formed when Laloo Yadav broke away from Janata Dal in 1997. The mass base of the party has traditionally been comprised of Yadavs and Muslims, two large and relatively disadvantaged segments of Bihar's population.

Rashtriya Rifles : The Rashtriya Rifles is a counterinsurgency force in India. It was raised by General B C Joshi in 1990 specifically for fighting insurgency in Kashmir, to complement the weak local security forces in the area. The main role of the formation is to allow the Indian Army to ensure its primary task of defending the borders and the state's territory unhindered by action from Pakistani-backed terrorists and guerrillas. The Rashtriya Rifles itself comprises 30 battalions, with another 30 formed using regular army battalions. Six new battalions were raised, but their fate is unclear with the Union Financial Ministry yet to sanction the move.

Rashtriya Swayamsevak Sangh (RSS) : The Rashtriya Swayamsevak Sangh (RSS) is an extreme Right Wing Hindu nationalist organization which bases itself on the principles of Hindutva. It was started in 1925 by Dr. K.B. Hedgewar. Since 1925, it has slowly gained prominence and political influence, giving rise to the creation of the Bharatiya Janata Party (BJP, formerly the Bharatiya Jana Sangh, and considered to be the political wing of the Sangh Parivar movement) to head the central government of India. Whilst centered in India the RSS also functions in 34 other countries.

Rasipuram Krishnaswami Narayan : Rasipuram Krishnaswami Narayan (October 10, 1906—May 13, 2001) was an Indian novelist writing in English, whose sensitive, well-drawn portrayals of twentieth-century Indian life were set mostly in the fictional South Indian town of Malgudi.

Many of Narayan's works are rooted in everyday life, though he is not shy of invoking Hindu tales or traditional Indian folklore to emphasize a point. His easy-going outlook on life has sometimes been criticized, though in general he is viewed as an accomplished, sensitive and reasonably prolific writer.

Rastrakutas : The Rastrakutas were a dynasty which ruled the southern and the central parts or the deccan India during the 8th - 10th century. The emergence of the Rashtrakutas heralded a new era in the history of South India. The idiom of a Pan-Indian empire had moved to south. South Indian kingdoms had hitherto ruled areas only south of the Narmada. It was the Rashtrakutas who first forged north to the Gangetic plains and successfully contested their might aginst the Palas of Bengal and the Prathiharas of Gujarat. Their period brought about great contributions from Jaina mathematicians and scholars, particulary in Kannada language. Architecture reached a pinnacle in dravidian style, finest examples of which are seen in Ellora and Elephanta in Maharashtra and the Jain cave temple at Pattadakal in Karnataka, all of which are UNESCO world heritage sites. They also built many fine Jaina monuments in Lokapura and Kuknur in present day Karnataka.

Ratan N. Tata : Ratan N. Tata (born 28th December 1937, in Bombay, now Mumbai) is the present Chairman of the Tata Group. He received a degree in Architecture and Strucutral Engineering from Cornell University, and completed an advanced management programme from Harvard University in 1974-1975. Tata received an offer of employment from IBM, but he turned it down after J. R. D. Tata advised him to do so.

In 1962, Ratan joined the family business. In 1991, he took over as group Chairman from the legendary J.R.D. Tata, pushing out the old guard and ushering in youthful managers. Since then, he has been instrumental in reshaping the fortunes of the most respected conglomerate of India. The Tata Group has the largest market capitalisation in the Indian Share Market.

Ratha Yatra : Ratha Yatra is one of the major festivals associated with Lord Jagannath, Puri, Orissa state, India. It is a large annual festival originating in the city of Puri. Most of the city's society is based around the worship of Lord Jagannath with the ancient temple being the fulcrum of the area. Usually the deities—Jagannath (Krishna), Baladeva and Subhadra are worshipped within the temple, but on this one day they are taken through the streets so that everyone can have the fortune of seeing them. The Rath carts themselves are some 50-60 feet high and are pulled by the thousands of pilgrims who turn up for the event. The festival commemorates Krishna's return to His home in Vrindavan after a long period of separation from the people there.

Ratnagiri : Ratnagiri is a district in Maharashtra, India. Ratnagiri nearly 400 km from Mumbai. It has the distinction of being the native place of three Bharat Ratna awardees, namely Maharishi Karve, Dr. Pandurang Vaman Kane and Dr.B.R. Ambedkar. No other district in India has produced as many Bharat Ratna awardees or more.

The district is in the Konkan region of Maharashtra. This region was under the rule of the Mauryas, the Nalas, the Silaharas, the Chalukyas, the Kadambas, the Portuguese, the Marathas and subsequently the British. In 1948 the independent princely state of Sawantwadi was merged with the Indian union and in 1956 with Bombay Province, thus becoming part of Ratnagiri district. In 1960 with the creation of Maharashtra, Ratnagiri became a district of that state. In 1981 Ratnagiri district was bifurcated and the new district of Sindhudurg was created. Ratnagiri has nine tehsils and eight towns.

Rattanbai Petit : Ruttenbai "Ruttie" Petit ("The Flower of Bombay") (February 20, 1900—February 15, 1929), was the second wife of Muhammad Ali Jinnah—an important figure in the Indian Independence Movement and later founder of Pakistan. She was the only daughter of Sir Dinshaw Petit, who in turn, was the son of Dinshaw Maneckji Petit, founder of the first cotton mills in India. The Petits were textile magnates and one of Bombay's wealthiest Parsi families.

"Ruttie" as she was affectionately called, was bright, gifted and graceful. Although she was only 16 the year she met Mohammad Ali Jinnah, she was intellectually much more mature than other girls her age. She had diverse interests ranging from romantic poetry to politics. With her maiden aunt she attended all public meetings held in Bombay and was familiar with the movement for swaraj (home-rule). She was a fierce supporter of India for Indians and many years later when asked about rumors of Jinnah's possible knighthood and whether she would like to be Lady Jinnah, she snapped that she would rather be separated from her husband than take on an English title.

Rava Dance : Rava dance is from the northern part of West Bengal. These dances are performed mainly by the Rava women. Their dances include Fai Nang Mein or Welcome Dance, Nak Chung Baini or the dances evocative of catching prawn, Baishar Bidan or New Year's Dance and Larai Lunji or War Dance. Dances of Rava Community are colourful and rhythmic accompanied by melodious music. The themes include things connected with their daily lives and joys of various festivals.

Ravi River : The Ravi River (Punjabi:, Urdu:) is a river in India and Pakistan. It is one of the five rivers which give Punjab its name. The Ravi was known as Parushni or Iravati to Indians in Vedic times and Hydraotes to the Ancient Greeks. It originates in the Himalayas in the Chamba district of Himachal Pradesh following a north-westerly course. It turns to the south-west, near Dalhousie, and then cuts a gorge in the Dhaola Dhar range entering the Punjab plain near Madhopur. It then flows along the Indo-Pakistan border for some distance before entering Pakistan and joining the Chenab river. The total length of the river is about 720 km. The waters of the Ravi river are allocated to India under the Indus Water Treaty between India and Pakistan.

Ravi River : The Ravi River is a river in India and Pakistan. It is one of the five rivers which give Punjab its name. The Ravi was known as Parushni or Iravati to Indians in Vedic times and Hydraotes to the Ancient Greeks. It originates in the Himalayas in the Chamba district of Himachal Pradesh following a north-westerly course. It turns to the south-west, near Dalhousie, and then cuts a gorge in the Dhaola Dhar range entering the Punjab plain near Madhopur. It then flows along the Indo-Pakistan border for some distance before entering Pakistan and joining the Chenab river. The total length of the river is about 720 km. The waters of the Ravi river are allocated to India under the Indus Waters Treaty between India and Pakistan.

Ravi Shankar : Ravi Shankar is an internationally known Indian sitar maestro. As an exponent of Indian music and incomparable Sitarist, Pandit Ravi Shankar enjoys great popularity all over the world. Ravi Shankar received training in sitar from Ustad Alaudin Khan. His musical performance have an aesthetic appeal. The first Indian to compose music for foreign films, he has made a notable contribution in popularising Indian music abroad. He opened Kiunara school of music in Los Angeles in 1967.

He wrote and conducted orchestral music for ballet, set to Nehrus's 'Discovery of India' and the 'Festival of India' music with top musicians of Europe and America. During 1949-55 he served as the Director of Music, All India Radio. He also composed music for the welcome song of the IXth Asiad held at Delhi.

Ravi Shankar has received a number of prestigious awards and honours, both national and international. International Music Vensco Award, Silver Bear and Venice Festival Award, Magsaysay award are some of them. In 1976, he was elected a fellow of the Sangeet Natak Academy and in 1962 and 1980 was the recipient of Presidential Awards. He was also awarded Bharat Ratna. Some universities in India as well as abroad have conferred doctorates on him. The government of India honoured him by nominating to Rajya Sabha in 1986. In 1999, he received the International prize for film and media music in Germany. His autobiography "My Life and My Music " is an extremely revealing document of his musical career.

Ravi Shastri : Ravishankar ("Ravi") Jayadritha Shastri (born 1962-05-27 in Mumbai (Bombay), India) is a former Indian cricketer. He was an all–rounder who batted right–handed and bowled left arm spin. His international career started when he was 18 years old and lasted 12 years. He started his career purely as a bowler but gradually became more of a batsman who could bowl.

As a batsman, he was rarely stylish but often effective. He was essentially a defensive batsman, with the flick off the pads being his trademark shot, but could raise his strike rate when required. Due to his above-average height (he stood 6' 3" tall) and an upright stance, he had a limited number of shots against fast bowling, but was able to put the lofted shot to good use against spin bowling. Shastri played either as an opening batsmen or in the middle order.

The highlight of his career was when he was elected the Champion of Champions in the World Championship of Cricket in Australia in 1985. In the same season, he equalled West Indian Garry Sobers's record of hitting six sixes in an over in first class cricket. He was regarded as a potential captain, but his image outside cricket, injuries and tendency to lose form at crucial times meant that he captained India in only one Test match.

In domestic cricket, he played for Bombay and led them to the Ranji Trophy title in his final year of playing. He also played four seasons of county cricket for Glamorgan. He was forced to retire aged 31 due to a recurring knee injury. He is now a noted TV cricket commentator.

In ODI cricket, he is known for his aggressive, dazzling batting style, and does not hesitate to play unorthodox shots. He is at his element in the first 15 overs of the one-day game, dispatching the ball to the fence with ease and panache. It has been noted that his technique is very similar to Sachin Tendulkar, with whom he forms a most dangerous and entertaining opening pair. Sehwag is also a useful spin bowler.

Sehwag has adapted to both the forms of the game. In the longer version of the game, he plays to ensure that he does not lose his wicket quickly although he scores at a rapid rate. His Test debut was in style as he put on a rollicking ton against South Africa after early loss of wickets. Despite not being a specialised Test opener he started to open matches for India scoring 80 & 100 in his first 2 games in England. On March 29, 2004 he became the first ever Indian batsman and only the 4th Asian batsman to score 300 runs in a Test innings, playing against Pakistan at Multan. He scored a total 309 runs in that innings.

Rawalakot : Rawalakot is a city in Azad Kashmir, an area of Pakistan near the border of India. Rawalakot is the capital of the Poonch district of Azad Kashmir. It is in a saucer-shaped valley at elevation 1615 meters (5300ft). It is 76 kilometers (47 miles) from Kohalla, and is also linked with Rawalpindi and Islamabad via the neighboring districts of Azad pattan and Dhalkot, and with Muzaffarabad via Kohalla by asphalt roads. The population is approximately 50,000 people. The town suffered significant damage from the 2005 Kashmir earthquake; although most of the buildings were left standing, many of them were rendered uninhabitable, and most of the population was left homeless.

Rawalpindi : Rawalpindi is a city in the Potwar Plateau near Islamabad, the current capital of Pakistan. It is the military headquarters and also served as the nation's capital while Islamabad was being constructed in the 1960s. The city is home to many industries and factories. Islamabad International Airport is closer to Rawalpindi than to Islamabad, and it serves the city along with the capital. Rawalpindi is located in the Punjab province, 275 km to the north-west of Lahore. It is the administrative seat of the Rawalpindi District.

The population of Rawalpindi is approximately 1,400,000. Rawalpindi, also known as Pindi, has a long history spread over several millennia. Archaeologists believe that a distinct culture flourished on this plateau as far back as 3000 years. The material remains found at the site prove the existence of a Buddhist establishment contemporary to Taxila, but less celebrated than its neighbor.

It appears that the ancient city went into oblivion as a result of the Hun devastation. The first Muslim invader, Mahmud of Ghazni (979-1030), gifted the ruined city to a Gakhar Chief, Kai Gohar. The town, however, being on an invasion route, could not prosper and remained deserted until Jhanda Khan, another Gakhar Chief, restored it and named it Rawalpindi after the village Rawal in 1493. Rawalpindi remained under the rule of the Gakkhars till Muqarrab Khan, the last Gakkhar ruler, was defeated by the Sikhs in 1765. The Sikhs invited traders from other places to settle here. This brought the city into prominence.

Following the British conquest of the Sikhs and their occupation of Rawalpindi in 1849, the city became a permanent garrison of the British army in 1851. In the 1880s a railway line to Rawalpindi was laid, and train service was inaugurated on January 1, 1886. The need for having a railway link arose after Lord Dalhousie made Rawalpindi the headquarters of the Northern Command and Rawalpindi became the largest British military garrison in British India.

In 1951, Rawalpindi saw the murder of the first elected Prime Minister of Pakistan, Liaquat Ali Khan, in Liaquat Garden. Today Rawalpindi is the headquarters of the Pakistani Army and Air Force.

The famous Murree Road has been a hot spot for various political and social events. Nala Lai, famous for its floods, runs in the middle of the city, dividing it into city area and Cantonment area. History describes Nala Lai water pure enough to do washing clothes but now it has become polluted with the waste water from all sources including factories and houses.

It is rapidly developing into a large modern city. It has many good hotels, restaurants, clubs, museums, playgrounds. It has a number of parks, of which the largest is Ayub National Park. Rawalpindi is the nearest major city for the holiday resorts and hill stations of the Galiyat area, such as Murree, Nathiagali, and Ayubia. It is also a common starting point for tourists visiting Abbottabad, Swat, Kaghan, Gilgit, Hunza, Skardu and Chitral.

Rayalaseema : Rayalaseema is an unofficial region of India's Andhra Pradesh state. It generally includes the districts of Kurnool, Cuddapah, Anantapur and Chittoor, parts of Prakasam and often Nellore. Rayalaseema is widely thought to be underdeveloped compared to the Telangana and Coastal Andhra regions of the state. The growing movement in Telangana to secede from Andhra Pradesh, as well as southern India's long drought have caused several movements to coalesce around Rayalaseema's grievances. All of these movements are calling for greater official attention for the region, especially in the form of new water projects to harness the Krishna and Godavari rivers to the aid of the region's beleaguered farmers. If nothing is done in this respect, the secession of Telangana would almost certainly precepitate matters in Rayalaseema, especially if other demands, such as moving the capital of Andhra Pradesh to Rayalaseema, and for a stronger state commitment to regional development, are not met.

Raymangal River : Raymangal river is the Ichamati-Kalindi-Raymangal is the same river known under different names at different places. It flows through the western part of Satkhira district as the Kalindi, further south after entering the Sundarbans it is named as the Raymangal and debouches into the Bay of Bengal. The mouth of the river is like a funnel at the estuary. A steamer service during the British period used to ply on the river from Calcutta to other riverports of Bangladesh via Barisal. The Raymangal is a tide-influenced river and its water is saline

Raymond Textiles : Raymond Textiles is one of India's largest textile companies. It is managed by the famous Singhania family.

Razakar : Razakar is a Persian word which means volunteer. Two volunteer militia armies have used this name, one during the Bangladesh Liberation War of 1971, the other was organised by Qasim Razvi under the Nizam of Hyderabad state in 1947. Razakar was the paramilitary force organized by the Pakistan Army during the Bangladesh Liberation War in 1971. It was composed of mostly Bengali collaborators and Urdu-speaking migrants to erstwhile East Pakistan (now Bangladesh). Initially, the force was under the command of local collaboration committees. But through the East Pakistan Razakar Ordinance (promulgated by General Tikka Khan on 1 June 1971) and a Ministry of Defence, Pakistan, ordinance (promulaged 7 September 1971), Razakars were recognized as members of the Pakistan Army. Razakars were associated with many of the atrocities and genocides committed by the Pakistan Army during the 9-month war.

Razia al-Din : Given name Razia al-Din, "throne name" Jalâlat ud-Dîn Raziyâ. She is usually referred to in history as Razia Sultan or Razia Sultana. She succeeded her father Iltutmish to the Sultanate of Delhi in 1236. Iltutmish appointed her his heir over many of his sons. But when Iltutmush died, Rukn-ud-din Firuz, one of his sons, occupied the throne and ruled for about seven months. Razia Sultana, with the support of the people of Delhi, secured the throne after defeating her brother in 1236.

Razia Sultana established complete law and order in her country. To rule the country, she abandoned the veil.

She used to dress as a man when appearing in public, be it in court or on the battlefield. She made an Ethiopian slave named Jalal-ud-din Yaqut her personal attendant and started trusting him the most. This challenged the monopoly of power claimed by the Turkish nobles. While Razia was trying to suppress a rebellion in Bhatinda, the nobles deposed her and crowned her brother Bahram. Razia married Malik Altuniya, the rebelious Governor of Bhatinda and attempted to recaputure the throne. Defeated by the alliance of Turkish nobles, she was murdered when fleeing from the battlefield. She was the only woman to have ruled Delhi, albeit for four years. Following a revolt by the city's nobles she was killed and is buried in present day 'Old Delhi', next to her sister Saziya.

R Bendre : R. Bendre (Dattatreya Ramachandra Bendre),((1896-1981) who wrote under the pen-name of Ambikatanayadatta, is amongst the most famous of Kannada poets of the Navodaya period. He also made several contributions to Marathi literature. He started off with some amazingly simple and earthly romantic poetry, in fact often using the "spoken" language, thus gaining instant admiration of the masses. His later works dig deeper into social and philosophical matters. He is a recipient of the prestigious Jnanpith Award. He was part of the famous Geleyara Gumpu a grouping of for promotion of study of literature and included famous authors, poets and intellectuals.

R D Tata : Jehangir Ratanji Dadabhoy Tata, was born on July 29, 1904 in Paris. He was the second child of Mr Ratanji Dadabhoy Tata. He spent much of his childhood in France since his mother was French. In 1922, Tata returned to India to join the family business. He inherited most of his grandfather Jamshedji's industrial empire but first became a pioneer in aviation. He had a great personality with a charm and style of his own.

After his father's death in 1926, Tata became the director of the Board of Tata Sons Ltd. Eventually in 1938, he became the chairman of the company. Under his leadership Tata Sons expanded into one of the largest industrial empire in the country- from ironworks and steelworks into chemicals, hotels, engineering and lot of other industries. In 1945, Tata Steel promoted the Tata Engineering and Locomotive Company (TELCO) with an objective to produce locomotives for the Indian Railways. Today Telco has emerged as the country's largest Commercial Vehicle producer.

JRD Tata was the first Indian pilot to qualify for a British private license. He founded Tata Airlines in 1932 and by 1953, it developed and came to be known as Indian Airlines. Till 1978, Tata was the Chairman of the Indian Airlines and Air India.

Tata was an early advocate of family planning and he created the Family Planning Foundation in 1971. His innovations in India's fledgling hotel and tourist industry as well as his contributions to scientific and technical research and corporate management gained public recognition from the Indian Government. He was honoured by India's highest civilian award, Bharat Ratna in 1991 and United Nations Population Award in 1992. In 1991, at the age of 87, Tata retired from Tata Sons. He passed away on November 29, 1993.

Red Fort : The Delhi Fort is located in Delhi, India. It is also known as Lal Qil'ah and the Red Fort.

The Red Fort was the palace for Shah Jahan's new capital, Shahjahanabad, the seventh Muslim city in the Delhi site. He moved his capital from Agra in a move designed to bring prestige to his reign, and to provide ample opportunity to apply his ambitious building schemes and interests. The Red Fort stands at the eastern edge of

Shahjahanabad, and gets its name from the massive wall of red sandstone that defines its eight sides. The wall is 1.5 miles (2.5 km) long, and varies in height from 60ft (16m) on the river side to 110 ft (33 m) towards the city. Measurements have shown that the plan was generated using a square grid of 82 m.

The fort lies along the Yamuna River, that fed the moats that surround most of the wall. The wall at its northeastern corner is adjacent to an older fort, the Salimgarh, a defense built by Islam Shah Sur in 1546. The Red Fort was conceived as a whole, and subsequent modifications have not taken away from the overall unity of the scheme. In the 18th century, however, occupiers and looters damaged some sections of the palace. After the Sepoy Mutiny of 1857, when the Fort was used as a headquarters, the British army occupied and destroyed many of its pavilions and gardens. A program for restoring the surviving parts of the fort began in 1903.

The Red Fort is one of the most popular tourist destinations in Delhi, attracting millions of tourists every year. The fort is also the site from which the Prime Minister of India addresses the nation on August 15, the day India achieved independence from United Kingdom. At one point of time, more than 3000 people lived within the premises of the Delhi Fort complex. But after the First War of Indian Independence, the fort was captured by Britain and was made the headquarters of the British Indian Army. After India achieved independence in 1947, the Indian Army took control over the fort. However, in December 2003, the Indian Army handed the fort over to the Indian tourist authorities.

Red Hills Lake : The Red Hills Lake, located in Ambattur taluka of Thiruvallur district, Tamilnadu, South India, is one of the rain-fed reservoirs from where water is drawn for supply to Chennai. On account of scanty rainfall for last three years (2003-05), the Red Hills Lake looks like a small pond. This lake is also called Puzhal lake

Reddy : Reddy is a caste found mainly in the state of Andhra Pradesh in southern India. They constitute about 11-15% of the Population of Andhra Pradesh. Though there are a number of Reddys with roots in Karnataka and Tamil Nadu, they are predominantly a Telugu speaking farming community from the state of Andhra Pradesh.

Reema Khan : Reema Khan, popularly known as Reema, is a Pakistani film actress. She debuted in the film Bulandi, directed by Mohammad Javed Fazil in 1990, opposite Shaan. In 1990 when Reema started her film career through Javed Fazal's Bulandi, it was the reign of Anjuman, Neeli, Nadra and Shahida Minni.

The great success of Javed Fazal's Bulandi not only helped Reema to stick in Lollywood also gave a lovely pair of Reema and Shan to Lollywood, success key of every film. Reema's early films with Shan, such as, Zherilay, Ishq, Naag Devta, Pyar Hi Pyar, Sailab, Dil, Aag, Shama and Sahiba inspired Pakistani film viewers due to her acting.

Reh Festival—Idu Festival : Reh is one of the most important festivals of the Idus. The Idus believe that they are the sons and daughters of the divine mother 'Nanyi Inyitaya'. But none can get her blessings and keep alive bond of brotherhood and social feeling strong, unless one performs the puja or celebrate the Reh festival. But it is so expensive that only a few people can afford to celebrate the festival for propitiation of the supreme creator, the great mother 'Nanyi Inyitaya'. It is the festival of Arunachal Pradesh. This is celebrated during February-August. The people who inhabit snow fall areas viz. Talo, Amru, and Dri villages of the Dibang valley celebrate it during summer and monsoon i.e. during June-August, when the climate is moderate and shoal of fishes are available in streams and rivers. The Idus in the other parts celebrate the same during February to May.

The festival requires a number of sacrificial buffaloes for offering to the great mother 'Nanyi Inyitaya'. Presents such as money in cash and pigs are given to the relatives. The festival being very expensive, all arrangements and preparations for the festival have to be made four or five years before the actual celebration of the festival. As such a person wanting to celebrate this festival has to take resort to the system locally called 'Ada' which is nothing but collection of mithuns, pigs, cash, money etc., even by way of loan from others. When 'Ada' is completed a tentative year is fixed about one year ahead of the actual celebration. The preparation of rice beer in large scale locally called 'Yunyiphri' is under taken, three to four months before the actual celebration.

After all necessary arrangements and preparations are made, 'Tayi' a form of calendar is served to all kith and kin as an invitation to come to the celebration on scheduled dates. The 'Tayi' is counted by knots on a string and each knot is cut off as a night passes on, one after another. The invited kith and kin arrive at the place of celebration when two knots remain on the string.

Rehman Dheri : A Pre-Harappan Archaelogical Site situated near Dera Ismael Khan in North Westren Province of Pakistan. This is the oldest urbanized center found to date in South Asia. Dated about 4000 BC, site is situated 22 KM north of Dera Ismail Khan. The low mound of this fortified town is visible from Bannu Road. This rectangular mound covering about 22 hectares and standing 4.5 meter above surrounding field. This fortified town of about ten to fifteen thousands inhabitant shows sign of town planning. Pottery, and stone and metal tools were found.

Rehman Sobhan : Rehman Sobhan, a prominent economist, played a significant role in the nationalist movement of Bangladesh. Professor Sobhan along with other nationalist economists contributed to the drafting of six-points programme that became the basis for the struggle for autonomy in the then East Pakistan. The various writings of the young Cambridge trained economist Sobhan on regional disparity between West Pakistan (present day Pakistan) and East Pakistan (present day Bangladesh) played a successful role in fomenting nationalist aspiration. During the liberation war for Bangladesh (March 26, 1971 to December 16, 1971) he was a roving ambassador of Bangladesh lobbying for Bangladesh in the United States.

After the independence of Bangladesh he was made a member of the Planning Commission. He was in self-exile after the military coup of August 1975. Upon his return to Bangladesh, he continued to be active in economic research and policy debates first with Bangladesh Institute of Development Studies (BIDS) and later he founded the Centre for Policy Dialogue, a leading Think Tank in South Asia. He authored over two dozens books and numerous articles both in professional journals as well as popular media. He was also made an advisor of the Caretaker Governemnt in Bangladesh in 1990-91.

Professor Sobhan's cohorts at Cambridge included prominent economists of the Indian subcontinent such as Amartya Sen, Manomohan Singh, and Mahbub-ul Haque. Sobhan continues to play an active role in the civil society movement in South Asia. He is a leading public intellectual in Bangladesh.

Reis Magos Church : The Reis Magos Church was constructed in 1555. It is one of the earliest Churches built in Goa and the first in Bardez Taluka, dedicated to three

Magi-Kings. This Church was once the residence of all dignitaries and also a mission centre of the Franciscan order. There is a fort adjacent to this Church.

Reita Faria : Reita Faria was the first Indian woman to win the Miss World title of 1966, bringing much recognition to her home country. By winning the crown, she led the way for her successors. After her one year tenure, she refused modeling and films and instead, concentrated on medical studies.

Reliance Industries Limited : Reliance Industries Limited is India's largest private sector company with a turnover of 744 billion rupees (US$17 billion) for the fiscal year ending in March 2004. It was founded by Dhirubhai Ambani in the 1970s.

Reliance Infocomm : Reliance Infocomm is an Indian telecommunications company, and is the brainchild of Mukesh Ambani, CMD, Reliance Industries. It is the flagship company of the Anil Dhirubhai Ambani Enterprises Group,comprising the power, financial services, telecom and infocomm initiatives of the Reliance Group. Reliance Infocomm is currently managed by Anil Dhirubhai Ambani.

Religious Affinity : It is a fruitless endeavor, indeed one that Kabir himself disliked, to classify him as Hindu or Muslim, Sufi or Bhakta. The legends surrounding his lifetime attest to his strong aversion to communalism. In fact, Kabir always insisted on the concept of Koi bole Ram Ram Koi Khudai..., which means that someone may chant the Hindu name of God and someone may chant the Muslim name of God, but God is the one who made the whole world. His birth and death are surrounded by legends. He grew up in a Muslim weaver family, but some say he was really son of a Brahmin widow who was adopted by a childless couple. When he died, his Hindu and Muslim followers started fighting about the last rites.

The legend is that when they lifted the cloth covering his body, they found flowers instead. The Muslim followers buried their half and the Hindu cremated their half. In Maghar, his tomb and samadhi still stand side by side. Another legend surrounding Kabir is that shortly before death he bathed in both Ganga and Karmnasha to wash away both his good deeds and his sins

Rengmas : The Rengmas celebrate eight days of Ngadah festival towards the end of November just after harvest in Nagaland. It is the festival of thanksgiving, merrymaking and rejoicing. This festival also marks the end of the year. Ritual are performed along with feasting, dancing, singing to mark the festival. The Sangtams have about 12 festivals spreading over the year including some special functions. Except for certain Gennas, all the festivals are concerned with food production, blessings and prosperity.

Republic Day pf India : Republic Day is the name of a public holiday in India to commemorate the day when it first became a republic.

The Constitution of India was formally adopted by the Parliament, and India declared itself as a "Republic" on January 26, 1950, a date thereafter celebrated annually as Republic Day in India. The Constitution had been prepared by the Constituent Assembly which was set up upon India gaining its independence from the British in 1947. This, in fact, was a deliberate act: the 26th of January was initially India's "Independence Day", one of Gandhi's many symbolic acts during what is termed "The Freedom Struggle", and the adoption of the Constitution on this date was felt able to strengthen its initial meaning, one calling for Indians of all ages to declare their freedom from the Raj. It is one of three annual national holidays in India, the other two being the nation's Independence

Day on August 15 (since 1947) and the birthday of Mohandas K Gandhi on October 2.

To mark this occasion, a grand parade is held in New Delhi, the Capital of India, beginning from Raisina Hill near the Rashtrapati Bhavan (Presidential Palace), along the Rajpath, past India Gate and on to the historic Red Fort in the old quarter of the city. Different infantry, cavalry and mechanized regiments of the Indian Army, the Indian Navy and the Indian Air Force march in formation, decked in all their finery and official decorations. The President of India, who is also the Commander in Chief of the Indian Armed Forces, takes the salute. The parade also includes many traditional dance troupes, to symbolize the cultural heritage of India. It traditionally ends with a colourful fly-past by Air Force jets in a tiranga formation. Similiar parades are held in the capitals of all the states of India, where the Governor of the respective state takes the salute.

Republican Party of India (Athvale) : The Republican Party of India (Athvale) is a political party in India. Since 2004 it has a small representation in the Lok Sabha.

Research and Analysis Wing (RAW) : The Cabinet Secretariat Research and Analysis Wing (RAW) is India's premier external intelligence body. It was created as an independent unit in 1968 from the Intelligence Bureau which at that time handled both internal and external intelligence. It's headquarters are on Lodhi Road in New Delhi. The current director of the organization is P K Hormese Tharakan, who was with RAW from 1989 to 2001, and is an IPS officer. Most available information about the RAW is largely speculative. Relative to other intelligence agencies of comparable size, the RAW maintains a very low media profile and is largely ignored by Indian writers, filmmakers and the general public. It reports directly to the Prime Minister's Office (PMO) and its operations and structure are not revealed to Parliament. Even its name and legal status are rather unusual—unlike the CIA, the RAW is not an "agency", but a "wing" of the Cabinet Secretariat of the Government of India responsible for "research" (gathering of raw intelligence) and "analysis" (organizing information and drawing conclusions for presentation to the PMO).

The RAW's budget and funding are not discussed in public forums. According to some reports, part of its funding comes from "discretionary grants" provided to various government bodies, especially Indian embassies and representatives abroad. Estimates of its annual budget vary wildly among experts—from $16 million to $145 million. One consequence of such a low profile is that it is very difficult to judge RAW's effectiveness and performance. Reports cover the entire range of judgements from "highly effective and professional" to "inadequate and riddled with internal politics".

The cadre for RAW is drawn by deputation from state police forces and other intelligence agencies. The Research Analysis Service instituted during the times of Indira Gandhi is the All India Level Service of RAW. The RAW is rumored to have around 12,000 agents in neighboring countries. Countries that have had past hostilities with India are also watched. It also provides assistance to interest groups that are able to promote India's national interests overseas. The RAW does not determine foreign policy—that is the job of the elected government.

Reserve Bank of India (RBI) : The Reserve Bank of India (RBI) is the central bank of India, and was established on April 1, 1935 in accordance with the provisions of the Reserve Bank of India Act, 1934. Since its inception, it has been headquartered in Mumbai. Though originally privately owned, RBI has been fully owned by the Government of India since nationalization in 1949. RBI is governed by a central board (headed by a Governor) appointed by the Central Government. The current governor of RBI is Dr.Y.Venugopal Reddy (who succeeded Dr. Bimal Jalan on September 6, 2003). RBI has 22 regional offices across India. The Reserve Bank of India was set up on the recommendations of the Hilton Young Commission. The commission submitted its report in the year 1926. However, operations began only on April 1, 1945.

Revolutionary Socialist Party : Revolutionary Socialist Party is a marxist-leninist political party in India. The party got around 0,4% of the votes and three seats in the Lok Sabha elections 1999 and 2004.The party was founded on March 19, 1940 and has its roots in the Bengali liberation movement Anushlian Samiti and the Hindustan Socialist Republican Army. RSP has always had its stronghold in West Bengal, but has branches in a total of 18 states. In Kerala, it is concentrated to the Kollam area, with support amongst fishing communities. Its Kerala branch originates from a split in the Kerala Socialist Party. K. Pankajakshan, the current general secretary, was a KSP member.

Rewa : Rewa is a town in the Indian state of Madhya Pradesh. It is the administrative center of Rewa District and Rewa Division, and was formerly the capital of the eponymous princely state in central India. The town lies about 210 km (131 mi) south of the city of Allahabad, India.

Historical, the Rewa region was divided into two well-defined portions. The northern and smaller division was the plateau lying between the Kaimur range of hills and that portion of the Vindhya Range known as Binjh, which overlook the valley of the Ganges. This plateau was for the most part cultivated and well peopled; two rich harvests were generally obtained every year. Water was generally plentiful; the country is full of large tanks and reservoirs, which however were not used for irrigation: that purpose was met by bunds or mounds of earth raised at the lower ends of sloping fields to retain the rain water for some time after the monsoon rains cease. The country to the south of the Kaimur hills comprised the largest portion of the state. Cultivation here was restricted to the valley between the hills and the Son River. The principal river is the Son, which flows through the state in a northeasterly direction into Mirzapur district. Another important river was the Tons; neither is navigable. The annual rainfall averages about 41 in.

Rewa Kantha : Rewa Kantha was a political agency or collection of princely states in British India, subordinate to the government of Bombay Presidency. It stretched for about 150 miles between the plain of Gujarat and the hills of Malwa, from the Tapti River to the Mahi River crossing the Narmada or Rewa River, from which it takes its name. The number of separate states is 61, many of which were under British jurisdiction. The largest state was Rajpipla. It also included five second-class states entitled Chota Udaipur, Bariya, Sunth, Lunawada, and Balaimor. The total area of the agency was 12877 km^2 (4972 square miles). In 1901 the population was 479,065. Many of the inhabitants were Bhils and Kolis. The political agent, who was also collector of the British District of the Panch Mahals, resided at Godhra.

The states came under British control after the Third Anglo-Maratha War of the early 19th century. After Indian Independence in 1947, the rulers of the states acceded to the Government of India, and the agency was integrated into Bombay State. Bombay state was split along linguistic lines in 1960, and Rewa Kantha became part of Gujarat.

Rewari : Rewari is one of the 19 districts of Haryana state, India. It is located in southren Haryana. It is around 80 km away from the capital city of New Delhi. The Rewari city has historical importance. This city produced great freedom fighters. Rao Tula Ram was the most famous freedom fighter from Rewari. Rewari is famous for its metal work. Particularly Brass work. If anybody needs best brass work in the world, Rewari is the place for him/her. The main markets of Rewari have shops which sell brass utencils and artistic work of brass. Alongwith Moradabad, Rewari is the brass hub of India. Rewari has kept the art of Tilledar Jutti alive. People from various parts come here to purchase tilledar Juttis. Though all of the festivals are celebrated here with great enthusiasm, but festival of Teej has got a special place in the heart of citizans of Rewari. The most colourfull Teej is witnessed by this Indian city, every year.

Ri Bhoi : Ri Bhoi District in Meghalaya, was upgraded from subdivisional level to a full fledged district on 4 June 1992. The new District, was carved out from the erstwhile East Khasi Hills. The District lies between 90°55′15 to 91°16′ latitude and 25°40′ to 25°21′ longitude. It is bounded on the north by Kamrup District and on the East by Jaintia Hills and Karbi Anglong District of Assam and on the West by West Khasi Hills District. There are three C and RD Blocks and one administrative unit at Patharkhmah, and the number of villages is 561.

The density of population is 79 per square kilometer. Literacy rate is 51 % in the year. Ri Bhoi District is one of the Seven Districts of Meghalaya, carved out from the erstwhile East Khasi Hills District. It is bounded in the north by the Kamrup District of Assam, east by the Karbi Anglong District of Assam, south by the East Khasi Hills and west by the West Khasi Hills District. Ri Bhoi District covers an area of 2448 km^2 with a population of 192,795 as per 2001 census.

The headquarters of the District is at Nongpoh located at 53 km away from the state capital Shillong and 50 km from Guwahati. This District is characterized by rugged and irregular land surface. It includes a series of hill ranges which gradually sloped towards the north and finally joins the Brahmaputra Valley. The important rivers flowing through this region includes the Umtrew, Umsiang, Umran and Umiam rivers. The region is still poor in transport and communication facilities. The National Highway No.37 origination from Jorabad to Shillong passes through the District.

Ribandar : Ribandar is an unincorporated town in Goa, in the district (conselho) of Ilhas or Tiswaddi, lying in between the cities of Pangim (or Nova Goa) and Old Goa. It is separated from Pangim by the Rio de Ourem, River of Gold, whose junction with the Mandovi here forms a large, wide marshy estuary. This estuary in traversed by an old causeway built in 1633 under the auspices of one of the Viceroys of Portuguese India, the Count of Linhares, after whom it is called the Ponte de Linhares. This causeway is the sole direct land access Ribandar has with Pangim. The name Ribandar originates from "Rayachem Bandar" meaning the wharves, docks or portage of the Rayas or Kings.

Rich Villa Inn : Rich Villa Inn, also known as the Rich Villa Hotel, was an old European style hotel at the Murree hill station in modern Pakistan that came into existence before the end of the British Raj in 1947. Rich Villa Inn continued to exist at Murree during the 1950's and the 60's. The hotel operated throughout the year, but mostly during the summer season because the roadblocks caused by the deep snowfall in winter affected the hotel business and created a still.

Richard William Timm : Richard William Timm, CSC, also known as Father Timm, is an educator, a zoologist, and the winner of 1987 Ramon Magsaysay Award for International Understanding. He is the Superior of the Order of Holy Cross in Dhaka. He is also one of the founders of Notre Dame College in Dhaka, Bangladesh. Since 1952, Richard Timm has worked in the eduation sector of Bangladesh. He founded the science department of Notre Dame College, and acted as the principal of the college between 1970-1971. He conducted extensive research on the nematodes and discovered 250 new species of nematodes. He has also been influential in disaster management, rural poverty alleviation, and other development activities.

Rigveda : The Rigveda is a collection of hymns counted among the four Hindu religious texts known as the Vedas, and contains the oldest texts preserved in any Indo-Iranian language. Its core is accepted to date to the late Bronze Age, making it the only example of Bronze Age literature with an unbroken tradition: All other texts of similar or greater age, such as the Egyptian "Book of the Dead" are known from archaeological excavations and linguistic reconstructions only.

It consists of 1,017 hymns (1,028 including the apocryphal valakhilya hymns 8.49–8.59) composed in Vedic Sanskrit, many of which are intended for various sacrifical rituals. These are contained in 10 books, known as Mandalas. This long collection of short hymns is mostly devoted to the praise of the gods. However, it also contains fragmentary references to historical events, notably the struggle between the early Vedic people (known as Vedic Aryans, a subgroup of the Indo-Aryans) and their enemies, the Dasa.

The chief gods of the Rigveda are Agni, the sacrificial fire, Indra, a heroic god that is praised for having slain his enemy Vrtra, and Soma, the sacred potion, or the plant it is made from. Other prominent gods are Mitra, Varuna and Ushas (the dawn). Also invoked are Savitar, Vishnu, Rudra, Pushan, Brihaspati, Brahmanaspati, Dyaus Pita (the sky), Prithivi (the earth), Surya (the sun), Vayu (the wind), Parjanya (the rain), Vac (the word), the Maruts, the Asvins, the Adityas, the Rbhus, the Vishvadevas (the all-gods) as well as various further minor gods, persons, concepts, phenomena and items.

Some of the names of gods and goddesses found in the Rigveda are found amongst other Indo-European people as well: Dyaus-Pita is cognate with Greek Zeus, Latin Jupiter (from deus-pater), and Germanic Tyr; while Mitra is cognate with Persian Mithra; also, Ushas with Greek Eos and Latin Aurora; and, less certainly, Varuna with Greek Uranos. Finally, Agni is cognate with Latin ignis and Russian ogon, both meaning "fire".

Rihand : The Rihand is a river in east-central India, a tributary of the Son River. The Rihand's headwaters rise the Bagelkhand region of Madhya Pradesh state, and flow north into Sonbhadra District of Uttar Pradesh, where it joins the Son. The Rihand Dam was constructed across the river in 1962 for hydropower generation; the reservoir impounded behind the dam is called Govind Ballabh Pant Sagar.

Rihand River : The Rihand is a river in east-central India, a tributary of the Son River. The Rihand's headwaters rise the Bagelkhand region of Madhya Pradesh state, and flow north into Sonbhadra District of Uttar Pradesh, where it joins the Son. The Rihand Dam was constructed across the river in 1962 for hydropower generation; the reservoir impounded behind the dam is called Govind Ballabh Pant Sagar.

Risalpur : Risalpur city is located nearly 45km from Peshawar, NWFP, Pakistan. Risalpur has several important educational institutions and industrial plants. The Risalpur Export Processing Zone is situated on the main Nowshera-Mardan road. Pakistan Army's has Risalpur Cantonment and Military College of Engineering. Pakistan Air Force Academy is also located at Risalpur. Pakistan Railways's Pakistan Locomotive Factory is also located at Risalpur.

Rishi Pahar : Rishi Pahar is the Himalayan mountain peak, located in Uttaranchal state in India.It lies in the Pithoragarh district. The altitude of the summit is 6,992 M. Rishi Pahar is situated on the west ridge over Milam Glacier.The peak lies south to Trishuli 7,074 M and Hardeol 7,151 M peaks on the same ridge.The massif forms barrier or divide between Milam and Uttari Rishi Ganga valley.The first ascent to the summit was made in 1975 through western ridge.This peak is situated on the eastern rim of Nanda Devi Biosphere Reserve. Rishi Pahar in Hindi means 'The Peak of Saint'.

Rishi Valley School : Rishi Valley School is one of India's leading boarding schools, and was founded by the well known philosopher Jiddu Krishnamurti. It is located close to the city of Madanapalle (where J Krishnamurti was born), in the state of Andhra Pradesh and is a 3 hour drive from Bangalore. The school teaches students from standards (grades) 4-12 in about 21 hostels. It is well known for focusing on a more holistic approach to education which includes developing an appreciation for nature, art and music. The schools goal is to release sensitive citizens. The school also runs the RIVER program and a rural school and health center.

Rishikesh : Rishikesh (also spelt Hrishikesh, another name for Lord Vishnu), in the state of Uttaranchal, is a holy city for Hindus located in the foothills of the Himalaya in northern India. It is 24 kilometers away from another holy city, Haridwar, and is considered an access point for the cities that form the Char Dham - Badrinath, Kedarnath, Gangotri, and Yamunotri.

The sacred river Ganga (anglicized to Ganges) flows through Rishikesh, adding to its spiritual appeal and natural beauty. In fact, it is here that the river leaves the Himalayas, and flows out into the plains of northern India. Several temples, ancient as well as new, can be found along the banks of the river in Rishikesh. The city attracts thousands of pilgrims and tourists each year, from within India, as well as from other countries. The city has several Yoga centres that also attract tourists. It is believed that meditation in Rishikesh brings one closer to attainment of salvation, or moksha, as does a dip in the holy river that flows through it.

The name Rishikesh is loosely applied to an association of five distinct sections encompassing not only the town but also hamlets and settlements on both sides of the river Ganges. These include Rishikesh itself, the commercial and communication hub; the sprawling suburban Muni-ki-Reti or the "sands of the sages"; Shivananda Nagar, north of Rishikesh; the temple section of Lakshman Jhulla, a little further north; and the assorted Ashrams around Swarg Ashram on the East bank.

Ritwik Ghatak : Ritwik Ghatak (1925—1976) was a Bengali Indian filmmaker. Ghatak's stature among Bengali directors is probably second only to that of Satyajit Ray. Ritwik Ghatak was born in Dhaka in East Bengal (now Bangladesh). He and his family moved to Kolkata just before millions of other refugees from East Bengal began to flood into the city, fleeing the catastrophic 1943 famine and the Partition of India in 1947. Identification with this tide of refugees was to define his practice, providing an overriding metaphor for cultural dismemberment and exile that unified his subsequent creative work.

River Ganga : The Ganga Ma (Mother Ganga), the sacred river flow through Uttar Pradesh. The water of Ganga is believed to have a purifying effect on the soul. India's holiest city Varanasi is on the banks of this sacred river. It is India's fourth largest state with an area of 2,94,413 sq km.

R K Narayan : One of the most famous Indian writers in English Language, R.K Narayan was born in 1906 in Madras. He was educated in Mysore and settled there for over half a century. Narayan created the enchanting fictional world of Malgudi through his several novels and short stories which captivated his readers throughout the world and more recently millions of Indian Television viewers, who saw TV adaptations of many Malgudi stories. His famous works are ' Malgudi days' and ' Swamy and his Friends'. Narayan has a humorous way of presenting life around him.

First Novel ' Swamy and Friends' (1935), and its successor,' Bachelor of Art's (1937) are both set in the enchanting fictional territory of Malgudi. His books are regularly published in USA, UK and India and have also been widely translated into several European and Indian languages. His novel, ' the Guide' (1958) won him the National Prize of the Indian Literary Academy, the country's highest Literary honour. He was awarded the A.C.Benson Medal in 1980 by the Royal Society of Literature and in 1981 he was made an Honoray Member of the American Academy and Institutes of Arts and letters. In addition to 4 collection of short stories-A horse and 2 goats, An Astrologer's Day and other stories, Lawley Road and Malgudi Days- he has published 2 travel books, 4 collection of essays and several other books.

His biography 'R.K. Narayan, The Early Years' provides a splendid insight into the first four decades of his life. The famous cartoonist R.K.Laxman is his brother.

Rock Cut Architecture : Rock cut architecture refers to the practice of creating buildings, temples, etc., by carving living rock. Essentially everything that isn't the structure is carved away until only the desired structure remains. Major examples of rock cut architecture include the so-called 'caves' of many places in India (such as Ellora, Ajanta and Pataleshwar cave), as well as the Nabatean city of Petra and the monolithic churches of Ethiopia.

Rogan Josh : Rogan Josh is a tomato/red pepper based lamb curry dish. It originated in Northern India, and is particularly associated with Kashmir. 'Roghan' means oil in Persian & Urdu, probably indicating the cooking medium (although some argue that it is a reference to red for either the tomatoes or red peppers) and Josh is a corruption of 'Gosht', meaning meat. It's said to have been first made and tasted at the court of the Nawab of Lucknow.

It is typically made with a teacup of oil or ghee (clarified butter), 2 pounds of different cuts of lamb, 1 pound of onions, one pound of tomatoes, a mixture of different spices called 'garam masala' (hot spice) and some other spices depending on where it is being cooked.

The location is important. For example, if cooked in its place of origin, which is Kashmir, India, the tomatoes are added last and aniseed is used, whilst some Kashmiri Brahmins refuse to eat onions or garlic and use large quantities of fresh and powdered ginger in the dish instead. In north India, the meat is cooked in the tomatoes and no aniseed is used. In its place a special concoction of spices called 'meat masala' is used.

Rohilkhand : Rohilkhand is a region of northwestern Uttar Pradesh state of India. Rohilkhand lies on the upper Ganges alluvial plain and has an area of about 25,000 sq. km. (10,000 square miles). It is bounded by the Ganges

River on the south and the west by Uttaranchal and Nepal on the north, and by the Awadh region to the east. The region is named for the Rohilla tribe, and was known as Madhyadesh in the Hindu epic Mahabharata.

Rohillas were Pashtun highlanders (Roh means mountains and Rohilla literally means mountaineer) who belonged to Yousafzai tribe of Pushtuns were awarded the Katehr region in northern India by Mughal emperor Aurangzeb Alamgir to suppress Rajput uprisings. Later it gained fame as Rohilkhand due to large settlements of Rohilla Pushtuns. It is located in modern Uttar Pradesh state.

Rohillas were distingiushed from local people by their tall stature, fair complexation, and by their separate langauge and culture. They used to speak Pashto among each other but gradually lost their langauge. Rohilkhand was invaded by the Marathas after Panipat war. Rohillas requested military help from Nawab of Oudh in exchange of sums. After the defeat of Marathas the Rohillas refused to pay. Nawab of Oudh was not able to fight Rohillas alone so he sought help from Warren Hastings of the British East India Company. Nawab of Oudh promised stipulated sums in return for their military aid. They invaded and defeat Rohillas after fierce war. The Rohillas started a guerilla warfare against the British occupation of Rohilkhand. The Rohillas were hunted down and slaughtered mercilessly by the British and were scattered in the countryside and settled in many small towns. Later British transfered Rohilkhand to British empire in 1774.

Rohin : Perhaps the first folk festival of this land is Rohin in Jharghand. It is a symbolic festival of sowing seeds in the field. Farmers begin sowing seeds from this day. There is no dance or song like other festivals but just a few rituals. There are also some other festivals along with Rohin and they are Rajsawala Ambavati and Chitgomha.

Rohini Space Satellite : Rohini is the name dispatched to a series of satellites launched by Indian space research organisation. The Rohini series consisted of four satellites all of which were launched by SLV although only three made it to orbit. The series were mostly experiemental satellites launched on the experimental launch vehicle SLV.

Rohtak : Rohtak is a district in Haryana, India. It is located in the southeast of Haryana, bound by Jind and Sonipat districts to the north, Jhajjar and Sonipat districts to the east and Hissar and Bhiwani districts to the west. Rohtak is home to the current chief minister of Haryana, Mr Bhupinder Singh Hooda. Rohtak is considered to be the 'Jat' heartland and political capital of Haryana. Quilla road is an upmarket place near the old walled city, where people from all parts of the city and surrounding towns. The city has a major Punjabi touch on account of a large population of Punjabi Community migrated from Pakistan at the time of Partition in August 1947. Through their hard work they have come to own a large number of business establishments in the city.

Rohtang Pass : The Rohtang Pass connects the Kullu Valley with the Lahul and Spiti valleys of Himachal Pradesh, India. The pass (3,978 m. or 13,051 ft.), which is only open from June to September, has a well-deserved reputation for being very dangerous because of unpredictable snowstorms. The pass provides a natural cultural divide between the foothills and wet lowlands of northern India and its primarily Hindu culture, with the dry desert uplands north of the first range of the Himalayas and its mainly Buddhist and heavily Tibetan-influenced culture.

Rohtas Fort : Rohtas Fort in Pakistan is situated approximately 3 miles west off the Grand Trunk Road from Dina. The model village of Khukha is about 2 miles north across the river Kahan. The fort was built in 1541-43 by Sher Shah Suri to protect the area against the Gakhars, who were loyal to the Mughal ruler Humayun, to whom the fort was finally surrendered by a treacherous commander 10 years after Sher Khan's death. The fort was named after the site where Sher Khan defeated the Mughals. After the structure was abandoned by the military in the early 18th century, a village was built inside its walls.

Rokeya Sakhawat Hussain : Rokeya Sakhawat Hussain, often known as Begum Rokeya, was a writer, feminist and social worker in Bengal in early 20th century. She struggled all her life for gender equality and other social issues. She established the first school for Muslim girls. Rokeya was born in 1880 at the village Pairaband, in Rangpur, now in Bangladesh. Her father Jahiruddin Haidar Saber was a local landlord. Rokeya had two sisters, Karimunnesa and Humayra; and three brothers, one of whom died in childhood. Rokeya's eldest brother Ibrahim, and her sister Karimunnesa, both had great influence on Rokeya's life. Karimunnesa wanted to study Bangla. The family disliked this as, first of all, education for women was looked down upon, and secondly Muslims of the time preferred to study Arabic or Persian instead of the native language Bangla. Karimunnesa was made to stop her education and was married off at the age of fourteen.

Rokeya's own fate wasn't very different. She got married at the age of eighteen, to a Bihari widower named Sakhawat Hossain. However, both her husband and her brother encouraged her to learn Bangla and English as well as to write. In 1902, Rokeya started her literary career with a Bangla story named Pipasa (Thirst). In 1909, Sakhawat Hossain passed away. Five months later, Rokeya established a Girl's High School in his memory and named it Sakhwat Memorial Highschool. It was established in Bhagalpur and started out with only five students. Dispute with relatives with her husband forced Rokeya to move the school to Kolkata in 1911. Rokeya remained busy with this school and her writings the rest of her life. She died of heart problems in 1932.

Rollapadu Bird Sanctuary : Rollapadu Bird sanctuary is located 60 Km away from Kurnool near Nandikotkuru. It spreads over an area of 614 sq.Km. This sanctuary is home for the endangered Great Indian Bustard.

Roman Catholic Church in Bangladesh : The Roman Catholic Church in Bangladesh is part of the worldwide Roman Catholic Church, under the spiritual leadership of the Pope and curia in Rome. There are approximately 300,000 Catholics in Bangladesh and the country is divided into six dioceses including one archdiocese. Pope John Paul II visited Dhaka in November 1986.

Romila Thapar : Romila Thapar (born 1931) is a Marxist Indian historian whose principal area of study is Ancient India. She secured her doctorate under A. L. Basham at the School of Oriental and African Studies, London University in 1958. Later she worked as Professor of Ancient Indian History at the Jawaharlal Nehru University, New Delhi, where she is Professor Emeritus today.

Roopa Mishra : In 2004, Roopa Mishra became the first Oriya Lady as well as the first married lady of India to top All India Civil Service Examinaton of 2003. Roopa Mishra, an MBA from Utkal University in Bhubaneshwar, topped the 2003 Civil Services examination while Ms. Ashima Garg from Delhi University stood second amongst the three lakh candidates who had applied for the 2003 Indian Civil Service Examination. She has been selected in the Indian Administrative Service (IAS) in her home cadre of Orissa and is currently (2005-2006) undergoing her district training in Mayurbhanj under Shri. V.K.Pandian, the Collector and District Magistrate.

She was born in Angul, Orissa state on 9th June 1977 and went to various schools in Orissa. She completed her schooling from St. Joseph's Girls High School at Cuttack before studing in DAV Public School at Bhubaneswar. She went on to Ravenshaw College to study Science at the Intermediate Level before doing her Graduation in Commerce from Buxi Jagabandhu Bidyadhar (BJB) College in Bhubaneswar in 1998. Daughter of bureaucrat Shri. Dandanirodh Mishra and academician Dr Usha Mishra, Ms. Roopa Mishra is the third IAS topper from Orissa. The other two toppers have been Shri. Hrushikesh Panda (in 1979) and Shri.

Prafulla Chandra Mishra (in 1982). Roopa says she grew up in a very encouraging environment where she interacted with "leading people from every walk of life." Her husband Dr. Anshuman Tripathy, who is at the IIM Calcutta, encouraged her to take the examination after two years of marriage(which took place in 2000). Ms. Mishra had worked at the Directorate of Distance & Continuing Education of Utkal University for over an year before she decided to quit job and start preparing for this national level examination. An Odissi Dancer since her childhood, she achieved this feat in her first attempt itself and that too by having absolutely two new subjects (Psychology & Public Administration) for the examination.

Roshnai Gate : The Roshnai Gate is one of the thirteen gates of the old Lahore city. The gate has extraordinary height and width because it was designed for the passage of the Emperor's caravan of elephants.

Roshni Fair : The Roshni (lights) Fair is held in Jagranvan from the 14th to the 16th of Phalgun in honour of the Muslim Pir, Abdul Kader Jalani. It is held in the vicinity of his tomb. Although it is a Muslim fair in origin, the Hindus of the area also flock to the site of this shrine. It is called the 'fair of lights' because innumerable devotees who come to visit the place light earthen lamps at the shrine of the Pir. The lights are visible from long distances. It is believed that whatever wish one sincerely makes, at the shrine of this Pir is granted. Young people sing Bolian and perform dances, thus adding to the gaiety and glamour of the fair. It is sheer delight to villagers performing dances and singing songs to the sweet strains of the flute and the one-stringed instrument called Toomba.

Some fairs are held at places associated with the lives of some Sikh Gurus, such as the Masya fair in Taran Taran, and the Muktsar fair in Ferozepur. Small fairs are periodically held here and there all over the Punjab. In Phalgun a fair in memory of Guru Nanak is held on the full-moon night at Dera Baba Nanak. At Jindwal (Navanshehar), a fair is held near a pond on Baisakhi day, at a spot where once Shri Guru Hargobind is believed to have sat. At Nanaksar in Hakeempur (Navanshehar), a fair is held at the place where the seventh Guru, Guru Harirai, stayed for some time.

Roti : Roti is the Hindi, Urdu, Punjabi, Indonesian and Malaysian word for bread. Generically, the word roti may refer to many different kinds of bread, such as chapati and phulka, each with its specific name. In Marathi, roti is often called Chapati or Poli. In Gujarati it is rotli. In Punjabi large roti is often called Phulka. It is usually used to refer to the round flat unleavened breads eaten throughout India and Pakistan, in contrast to the yeasted naan breads originating primarily in the north-west of the South Asia and Central Asia. It is sometimes referred to as the baloon bread by westerners.

Rourkela : Rourkela is an industrial town in the state of Orissa, India. One of the largest steel plants of the Steel Authority of India Limited is situated here. It is surrounded by a range of hills and encircled by rivers. It is situated in an area with the richest deposit of mineral wealth in Orissa. It came into prominence in 1955, with the establishment of the Rourkela Steel Plant. Rourkela also has one of the National Institutes of Technology located in the town. Rourkela also acts a major jumping off point in the tourist itenary to Orrissa. Rourkela has other attractions to offering, including the Indira Gandhi Park, Rourkela which contains a zoo.

Rubab Raza : Rubab Raza (born January 15, 1991) is a Pakistani swimmer from Lahore. At the 2004 Summer Olympics in Athens, Greece she became her country's first female swimmer to compete at the event when she contested the 50 m freestyle, though unable to progress through the first round she undoubtedly opened up the opportunity for future female Pakistani swimmers. Rubab has won a wild card entry for the 2004 Olympics due to her performances in swimming championships around the world.

Rudra Mohammad Shahidullah : Rudra Mohammad Shahidullah was a Bangladeshi poet. Shahidullah was noted for his revolutionary and romantic poetry. In the popular culture of Bangladesh, Shahidullah's most well known contribution is the song Bhalo Achi Bhalo Theko, popular ever since it was written. In 1991, an annual fair called Rudra Mela was started to commemorate the poet.

Rudra Veena : The Rudra Veena is a large, stringed, ancient Indian musical instrument that is played by being plucked. It is one of the three other major types of veena popular today.

The others include Vichitra Veena and Sarasvati Veena. Out of these the Rudra and Vichitra Veenas are used in nothern Indian classical music, while Saraswati Veena is used in South Indian Classical or Carnatic music.

Ruhul Amin : Ruhul Amin (1935-1971) was naval officer and freedom fighter of Bangladesh.. Born at village Bagh-chapra under Begumganj thana of Feni district Ruhul Amin had his early education in Bagh-chapra Primary School and Amishpara High School.

figure ban-E He joined the Pakistan navy in 1953 as junior mechanical engineer, and was elevated to the post of artificer in 1965. While working at the PNS Bakhtiar naval post at Chittagong Ruhul Amin left the post in April 1971 to join the liberation war. He joined the newly formed Bangladesh Navy in September, and was placed as the Chief Artificer at the gunboat styled 'Palas'. Ruhul Amin was burnt to death by a shell thrown from enemy plane into the engine room of the gunboat while attempting to capture the Pak naval post and PNS Titumir at Mangla port on 10 December. In recognition of his chivalry and sacrifice in the war of liberation, Ruhul Amin was awarded the title of Bir-Srestha, the highest honour of the state bestowed upon the freedom fighters.

Rumtek Monastery : Rumtek, Wylie: Rum-theg dGon-pa), also called the Dharmachakra Centre, is a Tibetan Buddhist monastery located in the Indian state of Sikkim near the capital Gangtok. Originally built by the 9th Karmapa Wangchuk Dorje in 1740, Rumtek served as the main seat of the Karma Kagyu lineage in Sikkim for some time. But when the 16th Karmapa arrived in Sikkim in 1959, after fleeing before the Chinese occupation of Tibet, it was in ruins. Despite being offered other sites, the Karmapa decided to rebuild Rumtek. To him, the site possessed many auspicious qualities and was surrounded by the most favorable attributes. For example, flowing streams, mountains behind, a snow range in front, and a river below. With the generosity and help of the Sikkim royal family and the Indian government, it has been built by the 16th Karmapa as his main seat in exile.

After four years, construction of the monastery was completed. The sacred items and relics brought out from Tsurphu, the Karmapa's seat in Tibet, were installed. On Tibetan New Year's day (Losar) in 1966 the 16th Karmapa officially inaugurated the new seat called, "The Dharmachakra Centre, a place of erudition and spiritual accomplishment, the seat of the glorious Karmapa."

The monastery is currently the largest in Sikkim. It is home to the community of monks and where they perform the rituals and practices of the Karma Kagyu lineage. A Golden Stupa contains the relics of the 16th Karmapa. Opposite that building is a college, Karma Shri Nalanda Institute for Higher Buddhist Studies. Rumtek is located 24 km from Gangtok, the capital of the Sikkim, at an altitude of about 1500 m.

Runa Laila : Runa Laila is a popular singer of Bangladeshi origin. Although in her home country, she is best known for her pop songs, she is a very well-known Ghazal singer in the rest of South Asia. She did playback for many movies in Bangladesh and India and, before the independence of Bangladesh, in Pakistan. She is especially know for her song "Dama Dam Mast Kalandar", which has been covered by numerous artists.

Rupali Bank : Rupali Bank is a commercial bank in Bangladesh. It was established as a nationalised bank in 1972 under the Bangladesh Banks Nationalisation Order, through the amalgamation of the branches of Muslim Commercial Bank, Australasia Bank and Standard Bank that were operating in East Pakistan, following the 1971 Bangladesh Liberation War. The bank was denationalised in 1986, and reorganised as a limited company, with the Government of Bangladesh holding 51% shares. However, after the year 2000, the Government divested of its shares, and the privatization of the bank was complete.

Rupnagar : Rupnagar is a town in Punjab, India. It was formerly known as Ropar. The town of Rupnagar is said to have been founded by a Raja called Rokeshar, who ruled during the 11th century and named it after his son Rup Sen. It is also the site of an ancient town of the Indus Valley Civilization. The major cities in Ropar District are Morinda, Kurali, Anandpur Sahib. Morinda is also known as Baghawala The city of gardens. Morinda City is located at Chandigarh-Ludhiana Highway.

Rupnarayan River : The Rupnarayan River is a river in India. It rises as the Dhaleswari (Dhalkisor) in the Chhota Nagpur plateau foothills northeast of Purulia town. It follows a tortuous southeasterly course past the town of Bankura, where it is known as the Dwarkeswar. It is joined by the Silai near the town of Ghatal, where it takes the name Rupnarayan. Finally it joins the Hoogli River. It is famous for the Hilsa fish available in it and also for the West Bengal Power Development Corporation Limited (WBPDCL) Thermal Power plant at Kolaghat, where there is a pair of big bridges for the railway tracks and the road

Rupsa-Pasur River : Rupsa-Pasur river is the Pasur river is a continuation of the Rupsa, which is formed of the union of the Bhairab and Atrai rivers. At present, much of its water is from the Gorai diverted through the Nabaganga. From near Batiaghata upazila the Rupsa changes its name to Kazibacha, which is given up near Chalna in favour of Pasur. Near the Mongla Port, the Pasur receives Mongla river, and near the forest outpost at Chandpai it receives the Mirgamari cross-channel from the Bhola, both on the leftbank. On the rightbank the Manki, Dhaki and Bhadra are connected with the Shibsa system. In the lower delta, the Rupsa-Pasur is second only to the Meghna in size. Formerly it was third, after the Madhumati, but with the considerable diversion of the Gorai flow through Nabaganga, it is now bigger than that river. From its junction with the Mongla, it is no less than a kilometre and a half in width. Thirty-two kilometres from the open sea, it joins the Shibsa to form the five to eight kilometres wide Morzal river, which empties into the Bay of Bengal by the Marjat and Pasur estuaries.

Rustic Plantation : It is situated on the extreme North-East of Goa at Dongurli village, Thane, Valpoi, Sattari. The Plantation is a rejuvenating experience of a lifetime. Nestled in a vallery amidst verdant mountains with grossy expanses, lush green fruit bearing trees and gurling rivulets, Rustic Plantation is the gateway one looks for.

R Vijayaraghavan : Prof. R. Vijayaraghavan (b. 3-Jan-1931) is from an illustrious family of Iyengars. One of his forefathers was the deputy chief minister of Ramnad Samasthanam. His grandfather was Mahawidwan R. Raghava Iyengar a renowned Tamil and Sanskrit scholar of the twentieth century. Prof. Vijayargahavan, after graduating from the Annamalai University in 1951 joined the Tata Institute of Fundamental Research (TIFR) at Bombay as a Research Student, and rose to the position of Distinguished Professor and Dean (Physics Faculty). He formally retired in 1996. He was awarded INSA Senior Scientist position from 1996 to 2001, during which he worked at SAMEER, Mumbai in collaboration with TIFR.

He specialized in the area of condensed matter physics and pioneered active research in the areas of metal physics, magnetic resonance in biophysical systems and fine particle physics, a forerunner to nanoscience. He is a Fellow of several science academies and twice elected as a member of the IUPAP commission in magnetism. He was conferred the prestigious Shanti Swarup Bhatnagar Award in 1976 and received the UGC Raman award in Physical Sciences in 1983. Apart from science, he is well versed in Hindu philosophy and Tamil literature.

Ryali : Ryali is a small village in East Godavari District of Andhra Pradesh in South India. It is very famous for the temple of Lord Jagan Mohini Kesava Swamy. The beauty of the idol of Jagan Mohini Kesava Swamy has to be seen to be believed. The idol is in the form of Kesava Swamy when seen from the front and it is in the form of Jagan Mohini when seen from the back. The priests at the temple show the idol in the light of burning camphor and explain the idol of the god in detail. There is temple of Lord Shiva in front of Lord Jagan Mohini Kesava Swamy temple. Lord Shiva is known as Sri Uma Kamandalesara Swamy here. The Legend of these two temples relates to Samudra manthan.

S

Saadat Hasan Manto : Saadat Hasan Manto (May 11, 1912-1955) was a Urdu short story writer of Kashmiri ancestry who was born in the Punjab. He was arguably one of the best short story tellers of the 20th century, and one of the most controversial as well. He is often compared with D. H. Lawrence, and like Lawrence he also wrote about the topics considered social taboos in Indo-Pakistani Society. His topics range from the socio-economic injustice prevailing in pre- and post- colonial subcontinent, to the more controversial topics of love, sex, incest, prostitution and the typical hypocrisy of a traditional subcontinental male.

In dealing with these topics, he doesn't take any pains to conceal the true state of the affair—although his short stories are often intricately structured, with vivid satire and a good sense of humour. In his own words, "If you find my stories dirty, the society you are living in is dirty. With my stories, I only expose the truth". He was tried for obscenity in Pakistani Courts, but never convicted. Some of his works have been translated in other languages.

Saag : Saag is a curry-like side dish eaten with Indian bread such as roti or naan. Saag can be made from spinach, mustard leaves, or other greens, along with added spices and sometimes other ingredients. A common form of saag is "Saag paneer", which contains a type of cheese known as paneer. Saag is more common in Punjab. There it is eaten more often with Makki di roti. This roti is made of corn flour and is yellow in colour. Though it can also be eaten with other Indian breads. When made with spinach and paneer, a common name for the dish is palak paneer. "Saag gosht" is version of the dish prepared lamb, and spinach. The lamb is usually cooked in a tandoor before being marinated in the other ingredients.

Sabarimala : Sabarimala (72 Km from Pathanamthitta) is a famous pilgrimage centre in Kerala. There is a shrine dedicated to Sri Ayyappan at Sabarimala, high up in the Sahyadhri Mountains at an altitude of 914 m above sea level. Sabarimala Sri Dharmasastha Temple is the most famous and prominent among all the Sastha Temples. The pilgrimage begins in the month of November and ends in January. The temple attracts pilgrims not only from the southern states of India, but also from other parts of the country and abroad.

Non Hindus are also allowed to conduct pilgrimages to the temple. This is one place which has turned out to be a model of communal harmony. There is 'Vavar Nada', a shrine in honour of a Muslim Saint close to the Ayyappa Swami Temple at Sabarimala. Pilgrims to Sabarimala worship here first and then proceed to the main temple.

Women between the age group of 10-50 are not permitted for the Sabarimala pilgrimage. Only pilgrims who have observed 'Vritham' (penance) and carry 'Irumudikkettu' (Pallikkettu) alone are allowed entry through the Holy 'Pathinettampadi' (18 Divine Steps) to the shrine. The steps depict elements, mind, intelligence etc. Those who crosses all these steps is believed to achieve 'Punyadarshan'.

Sabarmati : The Sabarmati is a river in Western India. It is approximately 371 km in length. The Sabarmati originates in the Aravalli Range of Udaipur district of Rajasthan. In its initial course it is also called as Wakal. Most of the river flows in Gujarat state. It empties in the Gulf of Cambay of Arabian Sea.

Ahmedabad and Gandhinagar, the commercial and political capitals of Gujarat were established on the banks of Sabarmati river. The legend is that Sultan Ahmed Shah of Gujarat, resting on the bank of Sabarmati, got inspired with the courage of a rabbit to chase a bully dog to establish Ahmedabad in 1411.

Sabarmati Ashram : Sabarmati Ashram, also known as Gandhi Ashram, is located on the Western banks of Sabarmati River, in Northern Ahmedabad. This ashram originally was established in the Kochrab area of Ahmedabad in 1915. In 1917 it was shifted to the banks of Sabarmati river. It also is known as Harijan Ashram, or Satyagraha Ashram.

Sabeer Bhatia : Sabeer Bhatia, the pioneer in the field of first web based e-mail—The Hotmail, was born in Chandigarh in the year 1969. He grew up in Bangalore and had his early education at Bishops Cotton's School in Pune, then St. Joseph's College in Bangalore. For a short-time he was a student at the Birla Institute of Technology (BITS), Pilani and in 1988 he went to US on a Cal Tech Transfer scholarship to get a bachelor's degree at the California Institute of Technology. He earned a master's degree in electrical engineering from Stanford University.

After graduation, Sabeer briefly worked for Apple Computers as a hardware engineer and Firepower Systems Inc. While working there he was amazed at the fact that he could access any software on the internet via a web browser. His success graph took off exponentially when he, along with his colleague Jack Smith, set up Hotmail on 4th July 1996. Today, Hotmail remains the world's largest e-mail provider with over 50 million registered users. As President and CEO, he guided Hotmail's rapid rise to industry leadership and its eventual acquisition by Microsoft in 1998. Bhatia worked at Microsoft for a little over a year after the Hotmail acquisition and in April 1999, he left Microsoft to start another venture, Arzoo Inc. It's an e-commerce firm with a revolutionary new way to shop on line and may just turn out to be Bhatia's next multi-million dollar winner.

Bhatia's success has earned him widespread acclaim; The venture capital firm Draper Fisher Jurvetson named him 'Entrepreneur of the Year 1997', MIT chose him as one of 100 young innovators who are expected to have the greatest impact on technology and awarded 'TR100', San Jose Mercury News and POV magazine selected him as one of the ten most successful entrepreneurs of 1998 and Upside magazine's list of top trendsetters in the New Economy named him 'Elite 100'.

Sabiha Khanum : Sabiha Khanum was the leading star of the Pakistani cinema in the 1950's and the 1960's.

She played successful character roles later.

Sachal Sarmast : Sachal Sarmast (1739-1829) was a renowned Sindhi Muslim Sufi poet during the Kalhora era. Abdul Haq Farooqi was his real name and "Sachal Sarmast" was the title given to him by his admireres. Such means truth in Sindhi and Urdu and Suchal means truthful. Sarmast means mystic in Urdu and Sindhi. Suchal Sarmast literaly means 'truthful mystic'. Sachal Sarmast was an ardent follower of Wahdat-ul-Wujood, a Islamic Philosophy synonymous with Hamah Oost.

Sachin Tendulkar : The pride of Indian cricket Sachin Tendulkar, was the first batsman to score 10,000 runs in one-day cricket, in a five-day match series against Australia on the 31st of March 2001. He has scored a world record, 28 hundreds and 50 half-centuries in his 10,000 runs.

Sachin Ramesh Tendulkar was born on April 24, 1973, in Mumbai. Young Sachin wanted to be a fast bowler. He even undertook trials at the MRF pace foundation, Chennai, but his short stature proved to be a hindrance for bowling. Meeting Mr. R. Achrekar, his Cricket Coach and changing his school to Shardashram Vidya Mandir in Dadar marked a turning point in Sachin's cricket career.

Sachin at the age of 16, made his International debut in ODI's India v Pakistan at Gujranwala and Tests debut India v Pakistan at Karachi around 1989/90. He then went to England as a part of the national team, and has not looked back ever since. He knows every shot in the book and and makes his own improvisations. His shots have tremendous power and he times the ball perfectly, making him one of the best batsman in the world. He is also an effective bowler and also one of the best fielders.

This all rounder has been the captain of the Indian cricket team twice. On the personal front, Sachin is god fearing and he is married to a doctor Anjali and they have a daughter Sarah. In1998, he won the Coopers and Lybrand Award for 'Player of the year' and has been in the number one position in the Wisden Cricket ratings.

Sacred Fig : The Sacred Fig Ficus religiosa, also known as Bo (from the Sinhalese Bo), Pipal (Peepul) or Ashwattha tree, is a species of banyan fig native to India, southwest China and Indochina east to Vietnam. It is a large dry season-deciduous or semi-evergreen tree up to 30 m tall and with a trunk diameter of up to 3 m.

The leaves are cordate in shape with a distinctive extended tip; they are 10-17 cm long and 8-12 cm broad, with a 6-10 cm petiole. The fruit is a small fig 1-1.5 cm diameter, green ripening purple. The Bodhi tree and the Sri Maha Bodhi propagated from it are famous specimens of Sacred Fig. The known planting date of the latter, 288 BC, gives it the oldest verified age for any angiosperm plant.

This plant is considered "sacred" by the followers of Hinduism, Jainism and Buddhism, and hence the name 'Sacred Fig' was given to it. Siddhartha Gautama is referred to have been sitting underneath a Bo Tree when he found enlightenment and became the Buddha. Until today Sadhus often meditate below this tree.

Sadar Bazaar : Sadar Bazaar is the largest wholesale markets of household items in Delhi, India and is located at the western side of Khari Baoli. This market like all the major markets of Old Delhi is very crowded and busy. Though it's mainly a wholesale market but one can purchase any item in small quantity as well. At present, the market deals not just in household goods but also in various other items like toys, imitation jewelry, stationery etc. The market can be aptly described as chaotic but to experience Delhi in its totality, a visit to the bazaar is definitely required.

Saddle Peak National Park : The park started in Andaman district in 1979, covers an area of 33sq.km. It is at a distance of 5km from Diglipur; the nearest town and 200km from Port Blair, the nearest airport and the capital of Andaman and Nicobar Islands.

The forest land of the islands is covered by luxuriant and lush green and thick tropical rain forests. The vegetation is characterized by humid, warm and wet tropical climate. The fauna of this park comprises Andaman wild pig, water monitor lizard, salt water crocodile. The important birds are Andaman hill mynah and imperial pigeon. The best period for visiting the park is November to March. There are two rest houses.

Saddo Ceremony : In the northern part of Goa, there is a beautiful ceremony called the Saddo. Saddo is the ceremonial cutting of the cloth, normally flowery red, to be worn by the bride in the house after the wedding. A tiny image of child Jesus is placed on the floor mat where the tailor is sitting with the clothes, at their house and two tiny length wise pieces of clothes are cut by him and placed there in the form of a cross. To begin with, there is the 'Nomon' in which blessing of God almighty and especially of the virgin Mary, mother of Jesus are invoked in the form of Zot (a special song peculiar to the occasion sung by an expert song-stress). Then each relative, from the nearest to begin with, followed by others to the accompaniment of references to them made in beautiful metaphor in the form of Zotis, walks up to the spot where lies the Infant Jesus and lays his or her offerings of money from Rs. 2 to Rs. 10 before the image.

Then a piece of betel nut and leaf with calcined lime and some sweets are disturbed to the people present. The elder men are served with liquor, women and children with sweet red wine and soft drinks. The money collected on the occasion is taken by the tailor, apart from his wages. The tailor will later stitch the main wedding dress or gown in milky white colour and other necessary clothes for the bride and near relatives, brides maids etc. The brides gown, ornaments and trousseau are displayed in a special ceremony at which people are invited, and then they are sent to the groom's place for display there.

Sadequain : Sadequain is a world renowned Pakistani painter and artist. Born in 1930 in a Urdu speaking family of Amroha, he was a rare visionary who was able to bridge the gulf between disparate groups in society. At the age of 31, his work won recognition at the 1961 Paris

Biennale. Sadequain had a prolific career and much of his work is displayed in public places. During his life, Sadequain became a cult figure, with a large following from all walks of life. The content of his work has wide appeal, and the early works addressed social evils. In the later decades, Sadequain used the unifying spirit of calligraphy to appeal to the masses, who came in large numbers to see his exhibitions. One of his first patrons was Zaib-un-nissa Hamidullah, who wrote about him in her magazine 'The Mirror' during the fifties. These articles helped him to win fame in his own country, Pakistan.

Sadinuktso (Akas) : Akas is a dance of Arunachal. The Akas have a number of dances and songs for the different socio-religious festivities. One of the well known dance among the Akas is the Sadinuktso. A member from the boy's group comes forward, gives his performance for a short while and recedes. A girl then comes and she also dances all alone. This relation goes on till all the boys and girls of the group have danced. No song is sung with this dance. It is generally performed in marriages, guest, entertainments or on the construction of a new house.

Sadras : Sadras is a fortress town located on India's Coromandel Coast, 70 km south of Chennai in Tamil Nadu state. 'Sadras' is the anglicized form of the ancient town of Chadhuranga Pattinam.

Modern Sadras was established as a Dutch colony in the sixteenth century, and became a center for weaving superfine muslin cloth for export. The magnificient Sadras Fort, built for commercial purposes by the Dutch, is a vast compound enclosing a huge granary, stable and structures used to mount elephants (unfortunately only one of these structures survives). The fortress was raided by the British in 1818 and came under the control of the British East India Company. It is now maintained by the Archaeological

Survey of India in efforts to contain further dilapidation of this great monument.

In recent times, Sadras has found mention due to its proximity to the atomic power plant (Madras Atomic Power Station) and the atomic research centre (Indira Gandhi Centre for Atomic Research—IGCAR) both located at nearby Kalpakkam. The village of Sadras is sandwiched between the power plant and its township.

Sadya : Sadya means big feast in Malayalam. A sadya is a big feast associated with an occasion like marriage, birthday, childbirth or death ceremony. A sadya is traditionally a vegetarian meal served on a plantain leaf, with people eating it sitting cross legged on the floor.

The dishes are mainly cooked rice, many curries, papad, curd or butter milk, banana, banana chips and two or more sweet dishes. The curries are made of different vegetables and are of different tastes. For example, they are made of curd (yoghurt), bitter gourd, mango, jaggery etc. The idea of making many dishes in the sadya is that there will be at least two or three dishes liked by everybody.

Saeed Anwar : Saeed Anwar (b. September 6, 1968) is a former Pakistani cricketer. He is most famous for scoring 194 runs against India in Chennai, the highest in any one day international. He was an opener for Pakistan and generally opened with Aamer Sohail. A top-order batsman capable of demolishing any bowling attack.

He is generally ferocious as an opening batsman in the one day matches and once settled in the Test matches, will score quickly and all over the field. He was named as a Wisden Cricketer of the Year in 1997.

Saeed Khan Rangeela : Saeed Khan Rangeela (1937 - 2005) was a famous Pakistani comedian, who was featured in nearly 300 Urdu and Punjabi-language films. He started his career as a body builder and painter but ended in acting. His movie career started back in the late 1950s. Despite acting in the movies he also directed many of them. He also sung many songs and wrote some scripts.

He was married thrice and a son also tried his luck at acting in some movies but failed. One of his daughters is an elected councilor in Lahore. He belonged to a Pathan family from Afghanistan who came to Peshawar and then settled down in Lahore.

Sagar District : Sagar District is a district of Madhya Pradesh state in central India. Sagar is bounded by Lalitpur District of Uttar Pradesh state to the north, and the Madhya Pradesh districts of Chhatarpur to the northeast, Damoh to the east, Narsinghpur to the south, Raisen to the southwest, Vidisha to the west, and Ashoknagar to the northwest.

Sagar District is an extensive, elevated and in parts tolerably level plain, broken in places by low hills of the Vindhyan sandstone. It is traversed by numerous streams, chief of which are the Sunar, Beas, Dhasan and Bina rivers, all flowing in a northerly direction towards the valley of the Ganges. In the southern and central parts the soil is black, formed by decaying trap; to the north and east it is a reddish-brown alluvium. Iron ore of excellent quality is found and worked at Hirapur, a small village in the extreme north-east. The district contains several densely wooded tracts, the largest of which is the Ramna teak forest preserve in the north.

Sahabzada Yaqub Khan : Sahabzada Yaqub Khan (born 1920) was the International Face of Pakistan for many years. He served as foreign minister of Pakistan from 1982 to 1987 and from 1988 to 1991 during the closing years of the Cold War, and was again foreign minister from 1996 to 1997.

He was a central player in the UN negotiations to end the Soviet involvement in Afghanistan. He was later Pakistan's UN Representative. He also served as the UN's point man in negotiating an end to the Civil War in Nicaragua.

Sahaja Yoga : Sahaja Yoga (Sahaja meaning born with and Yoga meaning union) is a type of meditation, religion and yoga. It claims to be "a unique method of meditation based on an experience called self-realization (Kundalini awakening) that occurs within each human being. The term Sahaja Yoga is also used to refer to the Sahaja Yoga International (Vishwa Nirmala Dharma movement) founded by Nirmala Srivastava (also known by devotees as Shri Mataji) on 5 May 1970 based on this practice.

This non-profit organization claims to offer an experience by which individuals can spontaneously become aware of their subtle system through which they become one with (union) the all pervading power. Sahaja Yoga holds that Kundalini is an energy that exists in every human being, but is dormant. Sahaja Yoga suggests one can feel this power as a cool or warm breeze coming out of the top of one's head and blowing in one's hands, after self-realization. Sahaja Yoga sees Self Realisation as the realisation that we are more than our body, mind or emotions, but the spirit within, due to the awakening of the Kundalini.

Sahara India Pariwar : Sahara India Pariwar is among India's largest private enterprises. The company has interests in media, airlines and housing. It employs more than 50000 people, the largest by any private Indian company. Since the group is rather secretive,an accurate account of its annual turnover or profits are not available.The company is headed by Subrato Roy.Subroto Roy has been away from the public eye for over 6 months and is believed to have suffered from a debilitating stroke which has severely impaired his speech.

Sahara India is basically a para-banking company.It has commercial interests across a range of sectors. Sahara India owns one of the private commercial airlines in India, cable television, media and insurance providers. Sahara India is also a major developer of up-market residential and tourism developments in India. It is not in the pink of financial health.The airlines is bleeding money and the group has engaged a consultant to hive off its airlines business

Saharanpur : Saharanpur is a town in Uttar Pradesh state of northern India, famous for its woodworking industry. It is the administrative headquarters of Saharanpur District. It lies in a very fertile agricultural belt, plentiful in grains and fruits. Even though Dehradun is famous for Basmati Rice, a lot of it is grown in the Saharanpur area. Saharanpur is also rich in industrial wealth: textile, sugar, paper and cigarette factories operate there.

Saheed Minar : This 165 ft high monument similar to Qutab Minar of Delhi was erected by public subscription in 1828, to honour Sir David Ochter Lony, a one- time resident of Malwa & Rajputana. More recently, it has now been renamed 'Shaheed Minar' to honour the martyrs of the freedom struggle. An important landmark in Calcutta. It is located at the Northern end of the Maidan.

Sahibzada Abdul Qayyum Khan : Sahibzada Abdul Qayyum Khan (b. 1863 d. 3, December 1937) hailing from Swabi, Pakistan, was a distinguished educationist and politician from a notable family. He is perhaps best known for establishing the first education institution of Islamia college in Peshawar on the mould of Sir Syed Ahmad Khan's policy of educating Muslims.. Sahibzada Saheb started his career as a civil servant but eventually turned into a great educationist and respected politician.

In 1887, Sahibzada Abdul Qauyum was appointed Naib Tehsildar and subsequently held several administrative portfolios i.e. Tehsildar, Chief Political Officer of Hazara, Revenue Assistant and Treasury Officer, Extra Assistant Commissioner, Superintendent of the Commissioner's Vernacular Office, Assistant Political Officer Khyber, ' Assistant Political Agent' of Chitral, and then of Khyber and 'Political Agent' of Khyber during the period from 1891 to 1919. Sahibzada Abdul Qayyum became the first Chief Minister of NWFP in 1937. But after a few months Dr. Khan Sahib of the 'Congress Party became the Chief Minister after Sahibzada lost a vote of no confidence.

Sahir Ludhianvi : Sahir Ludhianvi, whose real name was Abdul Hayee, (March 8, 1921-October 25, 1980] was a popular Indian poet of Urdu ghazals and nazms but mostly known for being one of the most important Bollywood lyricists. Sahir Ludhianvi is a pen name and It is a common practice for Urdu poets to attach the name of their birthplace in their pen-names (in this case, Ludhiana in India).

Sahir's poetry reflected the mood of the age. His poetry, similar to that of Faiz Ahmed Faiz (who was already an established poet when Sahir came of age), had the same lyricism and forcefulness. Sahir also participated in various mushairas and was a crowd-puller. But while Faiz was to appeal to the intelligentsia, Sahir's poetry was to flower as lyrics in the Bombay film industry where it found the medium that expanded Sahir's audience to far beyond the elite minority. More than 25 years after Sahir's death, his poetry and lyrics remain an inspiration for lyricists of the day. Composers and singers of Sahir's time swear by the depth, intensity and purity in his poetry.

Sahitya Akademi : The Sahitya Akademi is an Indian organisation dedicated to the promotion of literature in the languages of India. It organises national and regional workshops and seminars; provides research and travel grants to authors; publishes books and journals, including the Encyclopaedia of Indian Literature; and presents an annual award in each of the 22 languages it supports. The Akademi was launched on March 12, 1954 and is supported by, though independent of, the Indian government.

Sahiwal : Sahiwal is a growing city in southeastern Punjab province of Pakistan and the administrative centre of Sahiwal District. Founded in 1865, the town was formerly known as Montgomery after Sir Robert Montgomery, then Lieutenant-Governor of India. It took its current name in 1966. Sahiwal lies approximately 180 km from the major city of Lahore. Sahiwal District is included in the former Multan Division and lies between 30-40 north latitude and 73-10 longitude. Its approximate height above the sea level is about 500 feet.

Sai Baba of Shirdi or Shirdi Sai Baba : Sai Baba of Shirdi or Shirdi Sai Baba (?- October 15, 1918), born under an unknown name, was an Indian guru and fakir, who is regarded by his Hindu and Muslim followers as a saint. In his life and teachings he tried to embrace and reconcile both faiths: Sai Baba lived in a mosque, was buried in a Hindu temple, embraced Hindu and Muslim practices, and taught using words and figures that drew from both traditions. One of his well known epigrams says of God: "Sab ka Malik Ek" ("[He] is the Lord of All.")

Sai Baba is among the most popular of Indian saints, and continues to have a large following. His image seems to be everywhere: it may be seen on shrines, lockets, billboards and cars of Hindus and Muslims alike. While he is recognizable throughout India, his devotees are especially numerous in the state of Maharashtra, the place of his birth and in Andhra Pradesh. His samadhi is a well-known place pilgrimage. Many religious teachers, groups and organizations promote his teachings and devotion to Sai. Among the most prominent is the Shri Saibaba Sansthan Trust, which also takes care of the shrines and temples in Shirdi.

Saidpur: Saidpur is a city in the Rajshahi Division of Bangladesh. The city has a population of around 120,000 (1981 estimate). It contains an airport and is important place of railway and train manufacturing. Once Saidpur was under the kingdom of Kamrupa. Alauddin Syed Hussain Shah, king of Gaur, built a fort at Kellabari Hat near Saidpur during his invasion of Kamrupa. The descendants of Hussain Shah lived here.

Saif Ali Khan : Saif Ali Khan is an Indian film star who appears in Bollywood films. He was born August 16, 1970 in New Delhi, India, into the family of the nawabs of Pataudi. His father, Mansoor Ali Khan Pataudi, was not only the nawab of Pataudi but also a former captain of the Indian cricket team.

His mother, Sharmila Tagore, is an Indian film actress of note, and a distant relative (not a direct descendent, as often supposed) of the nobel laureate Rabindranath Tagore. Saif is also related to the late Nafisa Joseph. He won the National Film Award for Best Actor in 2005.

Saif Khan's Mosque : The mosque built by Parwaz Shah, son of Mughal emperor Jahangir located near Harmandir on the banks of river Ganga, is also known as Chimni Ghat, Sangi or Pathar Masjid. The mosque was built during Parwaz Shah's tenure as Governor of Bihar.

Saiful Muluk : Lake Saiful Muluk is located at the northern end of the Kaghan Valley (34:52:37.34 N, 73:41:37.71 E), which is north-east of the Hazara district of Pakistan's North West Frontier Province. At an altitude of 10,578 feet above sea level it is probably one of the highest lakes in Pakistan.

The water is spectacularly clear with a slight green tone. It is accessible by a jeep road during the summer months or can be hiked up from the village below in 4-6 hours. The clarity of the water comes from the multiple glaciers all around the high basin feeding the lake.

Saiful Muluk Lake : Lake Saiful Muluk is located at the northern end of the Kaghan Valley (34:52:37.34 N, 73:41:37.71 E), which is north-east of the Hazara district of Pakistan's North West Frontier Province. At an altitude of 10,578 feet above sea level it is probably one of the highest lakes in Pakistan. The water is spectacularly clear with a slight green tone. It is accessible by a jeep road during the summer months or can be hiked up from the village below in 4-6 hours. The clarity of the water comes from the multiple glaciers all around the high basin feeding the lake.

Saila Dance : Saila is a stick-dance and is popular among the people of Madhya Pradesh. The Saila often comes out with many variations and much buffoonery. Sometimes the dancers form a circle, each standing on one leg and supporting himself by holding on to the man in front. Then they all hop together round and round. Sometimes they pair off, or go round in a single or double line, occasionally, climbing on each other's back. The climax of a day's Saila, is the great Snake Dance. The Saila songs, of which the refrain is the monotonous Nanare nana are usually of a progressive character leading to a highly vulgar conclusion.

Saila comprises over half a dozen varieties. Some of them are named as the Baithiki Saila, the Artari Saila, the

Thadi Saila, the Chamka Kunda Saila, the Chakramar Saila (lizard's dance) and the Shikari Saila. Each variation has a certain theme and distinctive feature of its own. Saila's simple form is the Dasera dance which is always performed by the Baigas before Diwali. Some of the post-harvest dances reach the climax towards the festivities of Diwali. The Diwali dances of the Ahirs and Rawats have enough of vital appeal. Wearing tight-fitting shirts, studded with ghungrus or tiny bells and armlets of ghungurs, the Ahir dancers vigorously perform the Danda dance.

Sailendra Nath Manna : Sailendra Nath Manna is a Mohun Bagan Athletic Club footballer, who has been awarded the Mohun Bagan Ratna award. He is also the holder of the highly prestigious award—"Indian Footballer of the Century".

The name Sailen Manna is incorporated with every nook & corner of Mohun Bagan. In fact the players dressing room of Mohun Bagan was rechristened—The "Sailen Manna Dressing Room", which was inaugurated by the legendary singer Manna Dey, whose other identification is that as an avid Mohun Bagan fan.

Sainik School : The concept of Sainik School was conceived in 1961 by India's leading visionaries led by the Hon. V. K. Krishna Menon, the then Defence Minister, to institute a daring innovative blend of the best traditions of the English Public School system and the leadership qualities & discipline of the Defence Officers of the country, into the minds and education of handpicked privileged few Indian children.

One Sainik School in each of the states of the Republic of India at that time, was started, with the clear objective of nurturing and grooming carefully selected children to become officer-gentlemen who would ultimately lead as officers in the Defence Services of the country.

The sainik schools put emphasis on a variety of other facilities including an athletic track, cross-country track, indoor games, boxing ring, firing range, canoeing club, horse riding club, mountaineering club, trekking & hiking club, obstacles course, fine arts club, craftwork club, music clubs, literary clubs, theatre arts club, philately club, aero-modeling club, ship-modeling club, etc.

Sajjad Ali : Sajjad Ali is one the most popular Pakistani pop singers with a very distinctive high pitch voice that adds in melody and blends in very well with his songs. He became popular after his Album "Sohni Lag Di" which consists of the hit songs "Sohni Lag Di" and "Larri Adda". He is also known for directing the movie "Aik aur love story" which was also successful because of the cast and songs which he took from his own album "Sohni Lag Di". Sajjad Ali later on became a huge success after the song "Teri Yaad" was released which was used as the theme song for a Pakistani drama as well.

S Janaki : S.Janaki, the Melody Queen of South India with her magnificent voice, captured the hearts of millions of people in her reigning days. She was born on 23rd April, 1938, in Pallapatla, Repalle village, Guntur District, Andhra Pradesh.

Janaki showed interest in music at a tender age and started singing at the age of three. She started learning music from Sree Paidiswamy and continued her lessons until she was ten years old. Then she moved to Madras on the advice of her uncle Dr. Chandrashekar who nurtured her talents. She received a second prize from the former President Dr. Rajendra Prasad at the competitions held by AIR (All India Radio) in 1956. Mr. Chandrasekhar, her uncle recommended her for a job as a singer in AVM Studio. She joined and started her career with Tamil films in 1957 in the film 'Vidhiyin Vilayattu' under the famous music director T. Chalapati Rao. Later, she got a chance in a Telugu film MLA. From then on, there was no looking back for her. She has several unforgettable hit songs with the association of the maestros of music.

Janaki has a unique capability to change her voice and sing in a range of tones. She could sing in a child's voice or an old woman's voice or along with a Shenai quite naturally. She is not only a singer but also a good lyricist and a good music composer. She wrote many songs for Tamil and Telugu films. She has sung about 20,000 songs in her career, in almost all languages in South India as well as in Hindi, Simhalese, Bengali, Oriya, English, Sanskrit, Konkini, Tulu, Saurashtra, Baduga, and German. She has given several unforgettable hit songs on her own and with the association of the maestros of music.

She has received many awards for her talent. She won national awards for best singer four times -in 1976 for the song 'Senthoora Poove' in the Tamil Film '16 vayadhinile', in 1980 for the song 'Ettumanoorambalathil' in the Malayalam Film 'Oppol', in 1984 for the song' Vennello godari andham' in the Telugu film 'Sithara', 1992 for the song 'Inji Idippazagha' in the Tamil Film 'Devar magan'. She has won Tamil Nadu state government award 7 times, Kerala state Government awards 14 times, Andhra state government awards 10 times. She was honoured with 'Kalai Mamani' in 1986, 'Sur singar' award in 1987, Cinema 'Achiever Award' by the government of Kerala in the year 2002 and many more.

She has almost retired from the industry after husband Sri.V.Rama Prasad's death. A devotee of Lord Krishna and Shirdi Sai Baba, she spends a lot of time praying and has also released devotional music cassettes on Meera. She lives with her son Murali Krishna, an actor and daughter-in-law Uma Murali Krishna, a classical dancer (Bharatnatyam and Kuchipudi) and two grand daughters

Amruthavarshini and Apsara. Janaki with her magnificent and versatile voice will remain in the hearts of music lovers for ages to come.

Sajjad Ali : Sajjad Ali is one the most popular Pakistani pop singers with a very distinctive high pitch voice that adds in melody and blends in very well with his songs.

He became popular after his Album "Sohni Lag Di" which consists of the hit songs "Sohni Lag Di" and "Larri Adda". He is also known for directing the movie "Aik aur love story" which was also successful because of the cast and songs which he took from his own album "Sohni Lag Di". Sajjad Ali later on became a huge success after the song "Teri Yaad" was released which was used as the theme song for a Pakistani drama as well.

Sajjad Ali Shah : Sajjad Ali Shah was the Chief Justice of the Supreme Court of Pakistan. In 1997, Prime Minister Nawaz Sharif's party was elected with a majority large enough for Sharif to change the Constitution, and to systematically remove the institutional checks and balances on the Prime Minister's power. Shah attempted to preserve the independence of the judiciary. He was forced out of office after the Supreme Court was stormed by Sharif's partisans. His term in office as CJ was one of the most controversial in history of pakistan's judiciary.

Sakal : Sakal is a Marathi language newspaper in Mumbai (Bombay). The name Sakal means "morning" in Marathi. The newspaper is based in Pune. Sakal was founded by Nanasaheb Parulekar around 80 years back. In recent days Sakal has improved its quality a lot compared to other Marathi newspapers like Maharashtra Times and Loksatta. Especially Maharashtra Times owned by Times news group, has become a tabliod news paper.

Sakas : The Sakas are a peoples that lived in what is now Kazakhstan, Uzbekistan, Tajikistan, Afghanistan, Pakistan and north western parts of India, Iran, Ukraine, and Altai and Siberia in Russia, in the centuries before 300 AD. They are considered to be a branch of Scythians by most scholars. Saka is the usual Persian term, while Scythian is a Greek term. Some of their neighbours included the Sarmatians, Issedones and Massagetae. Their language is poorly known, but seems to have originally been a member of the Iranian family (though some question whether this applied to all stratas of their society, or only the ruling class at various times). They were known to the Chinese as the Sai.

S K Pottakkat : S. K. Pottakkat (b. March 14, 1913 _ d. August 6, 1982) A well-renowned author from Kerala whose work Oru Desattinte Katha (The Story of a Land) fetched him the Jnanpith Award in 1980. Sankarankutty or S.K. Pottakkat as he is best known by his readers, was born at Kozhikode as the son of Kunchiraman Pottakkat, an English schoolteacher. After graduating from Zamorin's College, Kozhikode he went on to work as a teacher in a Gujarati local school for a year. It was at this time as if bitten by the travel bug that Pottakkat began his great odyssey that would ultimately take him to many parts of the globe including destinations in Asia, Africa and Europe.

Sakatayana : Sakatayana is an Indian grammarian earlier than the 5th c. BCE. His work is referred by scholars such as Yaska(around 5th c. BCE) and Panini (d. circa 460 BCE), as well as other Sanskrit grammarians, but is lost to us today. One of his views which generated considerable controversy in the Indian tradition, and receives some support in modern etymology, is that most nominal roots are ultimately derived from actions. This refers to the origin of names of things, or nouns. For example, the noun origin derives etymologically from the

Latin originalis, ultimately derived from the verb oriri, "to rise". An example of a morphological derivative might be the noun hitter—derived from the verb hit.

The controversial claim is that all nouns are ultimately derived from some verbal root. This process is reflected in the Sanskrit grammar as the system of of krit-pratyayas or verbal affixes. It is possible that the debate is based on two interpretations of root — as referring to the etymological root (as in origin), as opposed to the morphemic stem (morphological root, as in hitter). However, for many nouns (e.g. the English stem root), it is hard to defend even the etymological claim. A modern interpretation of this claim is that cognitively, most nominal categories are based on behaviours rather than other attributes (e.g. an aeroplane may be made to have the shape of a bird), a point that is reinforced in most cognitive semantics approaches to the lexicon.

Sake Dean Mahomet : Sake Dean Mahomet (or Mahomed; Shaykh Din Muhammad in Arabic) (1759-1851) is thought to have been the first native East Indian to have written a book in the English language. He wrote The Travels of Dean Mahomet, based on his travels in India and Ireland, which was published in 1794. He belonged to a Muslim family of Bengal. Mr Mahomet has been credited with opening the first Indian restaurant in London, Hindoostane Coffee House in George Street, central London. On 29 September 2005 the City of Westminster unveiled a Green Plaque commemorating this.

Sakthan Thampuran : Actual name of Sakthan Thampuran was Raja Rama Varma (1751-1805). He was a king of Cochin and his palace was in Thrissur, central Kerala, south India. Thrissur is the cultural capital of Kerala and Sakthan Thampuran is the very architect of Thrissur. Thrissur Pooram was introduced by him.His palace is located in the heart of Thrissur town and has several well-preserved materials and galleries. The palace is usually know as Vadakkekara Palace, it was reconstructed in Kerala-Dutch style in 1795.

He punished criminals and wrong doers mercilessly. He meted out justice without any mercy. So people called him Sakthan Thampuran which means Powerful king in Malayalam language. He was resposible for the crushing of feaudal lords and hence increasing royal power. Sakthan Thampuran punished thieves and family rivals severely. Also, honesty was the best policy in his rules.

Salankayanas : Salankayanas were one of the two dynasties that succeeded the Ikshvaku around 300-440 AD. The other being the Vishnukundinas, a Kshatriya dynasty. Both Salankayana and Vishnukundina were Vassals under Pallava kings who ruled from southern Telugu and northern Tamil lands. They ruled over a part of the East Coast with Vengi as their capital. During their time the script for Telugu and Kannada began to clearly separating from that of the other South Indian and North Indian languages. They were Brahmins who took their title from their gotra name, which stood for Nandi, the bull of Shiva, which they used as their symbol.

Salar Jung Museum : The Salar Jung Museum is an art museum on the southern bank of the Musi river in the city of Hyderabad, Andhra Pradesh, India. The museum opened to the public on December 16, 1951; it houses the collection of the Salar Jung family, who were important nobles in the courts of the Nizams — Muslim rulers of Hyderabad. The collection of Islamic art from all over Asia includes a variety of illuminated Korans, astrolabes, jewelled swords and daggers, and Persian carpets. The museum also houses fine examples of European painting and sculpture, most famously the "Veiled Rebecca" of Italian sculptor Giovanni Maria Benzoni, as well as Chinese and Japanese pieces. The collection was mostly acquired by Mir Yousuf Ali Khan, also known as Salar Jung III. Some of the items he inherited were collected by his father, Nawab Mir Laiq Khan (Salar Jung II) and his grandfather, Nawab Mir Turab Ali Khan (Sir Salar Jung I). The Indian Parliament has declared the museum an Institution of National Importance.

Salarjung Museum : Salarjung Museum in Andhra Pradesh was constructed by the Prime Minister Salarjung III of the erstwhile Nizams but was later shifted in 1968 to the new imposing building constructed on the southern bank of the river Musi. The museum consists of a vast and varied art mass collected from several countries in the world.

Saleem Raza : Saleem Raza (born 5 July 1964, Lahore, Punjab, Pakistan) is a former cricketer. After playing in eight first-class games for his native Lahore City from 1986-87 to 1987-88, Saleem Raza emigrated to the United Arab Emirates, for whom he competed in the 1994 ICC Trophy. He also played for the UAE in the 1994 Austral-Asia Cup and the 1996 World Cup, in which competitions he played his six one-day internationals.

Salem : Salem is the 5th largest city of Tamil Nadu located in the central part of the southernmost state of India. Almost completely surrounded by hills, Salem is one of the major textile centres in the country. Salem is also the capital of Salem district whose other major locations are Mettur, Omalur and Attur. The district is well connected by rail and road networks. Salem was the largest districts of Tamilnadu before it was bifurcated in to two as Salem and Dharmapuri. Later Salem was again divided with the formation of new districts such as Namakkal. Salem is also at the base of the renowned tourist destination of Yercaud hills, which offers breathtaking views both during the ride up the hill and from the peak. Like all towns of Tamilnadu, there are people from different states of India settled in Salem. Some of them speak Kannada, Telugu, Sowrashtra and a good number of Muslims are also present.

Salim Ali : Salim Ali, Salim Moizuddin Abdul Ali, (November 12, 1896 - July 27, 1987) was an Indian ornithologist and naturalist. Known as the "Birdman of India", Salim Ali was among the first Indians to conduct systematic bird surveys in India and his books have contributed enormously to the development of professional and amateur birdwatching in India.

Salim Ali was orphaned at a young age and was brought up by his maternal uncle, Amiruddin Tyabji, in a middle-class muslim household in Khetwadi, Mumbai. He was introduced to the serious study of birds by W. S. Millard, secretary of the Bombay Natural History Society (BNHS) who helped him identify an unusually coloured sparrow that he had shot for sport. Millard identified it as a Yellow-throated Sparrow, and showed him around the Society's collection of stuffed birds. This was a key event in his life and led to Salim's pursuit of a career in ornithology, an unusual career choice in those days. Salim Ali's cousin Humayun Abdulali also became an ornithologist.

Ali failed to get an ornithologist's position at the Zoological Survey of India due to lack of sufficient academic qualifications. He however decided to study further after he was hired as guide lecturer at the newly opened natural history section in the Prince of Wales Museum in Mumbai. He went on study leave to Germany where he trained under Professor Erwin Stresemann. Salim Ali was very influential in ensuring the survival of the BNHS and managed to save the 200-year old institution by writing to the then Prime Minister Pandit Nehru for financial help.

Although recognition came late, he received numerous awards including the J. Paul Getty International Award, the Golden Ark of the International Union for Conservation of Nature, the golden medal of the British Ornithologists' Union (a rarity for a non-Britisher), the Padma Shri and the Padma Vibhushan from the Indian Government, three honorary doctorates, and numerous other awards. He was nominated to the Rajya Sabha in 1985. Dr. Ali's influence helped save the Bharatpur Bird Sanctuary and the Silent Valley National Park. In 1990, the Salim Ali Centre for Ornithology & Natural History (SACONH) was established at Kalayampalayam, Coimbatore, aided by the Ministry of Environment and Forests (MoEF), Government of India. Dr. Salim Ali died in 1987 at the age of 91 after a prolonged battle with prostate cancer.

Salman Rushdie : Salman Rushdie is a famous writer. He was born in a Kashmiri Muslim Family of Bombay and later migrated to Great Britain. Some of his well known books are 'Rome', ' Midnight's Children', ' Haroun and the sea of Stories' and the 'Moor's Last Sigh'. He commented against India in ' Midnight's Children' and made some critical references about Islam in ' Satanic Verses'. He created a world-wide furore and commotion with the publication of his book ' Satanic Verses'.

Most of the books of Salman Rushdie have been subject to controversies and discussions. The publication of ' Satanic Verses' has raised a storm in the entire Muslim World. This made Iran's spiritual leader Ayatollah Khomeini sentence him to death. So presently he lives in hiding in England. The matter even led to Britain severing diplomatic ties with Iran. Rushdie's work Midnight's Children was awarded the 'Booker of Bookers' prize in 1993, which distinguishes as the best novel to have won the Booker prize over its 25-year history. In 1996 he received the European Union Literary Award in Denmark.

Salsette Island : Salsette is an island in Maharashtra state on India's west coast. The metropolis of Mumbai (formerly Bombay), and the city of Thane lie on this island.The present island was formerly made up of several smaller islands, which were joined together during the 19th and early 20th centuries to form a single island. It is bounded on the north by Vasai Creek, on the northeast by the Ulhas River, on the east by Thane Creek and Bombay Harbour, and on the south and west by the Arabian Sea. The city of Mumbai lies on a peninsula on the southern end of the island, and Mumbai's suburbs cover much of the remainder of the island. The island contains Borivali National Park, also known as Sanjay Gandhi National Park. The city of Thane lies at the island's northeastern corner, on Thane Creek. The coordinates are approximately 20° N and 72° E. Politically, most of the island falls into the municipality of Mumbai. The municipality is divided into two separate districts, Mumbai City and Mumbai Suburbs. The northern portion of the island lies within Thane District, which extends across Vasai and Thane creeks onto the mainland.

Salt Lake Stadium : Salt Lake Stadium (also known as the Yuva Bharati Krirangan) is a multi-use stadium in Salt Lake City, a district of Kolkata, India. It is one of the largest stadiums anywhere in the world. It is currently used for football matches and atheletics. The stadium was built in 1984 and holds 120,000 in a three-tier configuration.

Salt Range : The Salt Range is a hill system in the Punjab Province of Pakistan, deriving its name from its extensive deposits of rock-salt. The range extends from the Jhelum River to the Indus, across the northern portion of Punjab Province. The salt range contains the great mines of Mayo, Warcha and Kalabagh, which yield vast supplies of salt. Coal of an inferior quality is also found.

Salt Satyagraha : The Salt Satyagraha, also known as the Salt March to Dandi, was an act of protest against the British salt tax in colonial India. Mahatma Gandhi led fellow Indians from Sabarmati Ashram to Dandi, Gujarat. The march lasted from March 12 to April 6, 1930.

The effects of the salt march were felt across India. Thousands of people made salt, or bought illegal salt. As the march mobilized many new followers from all of Indian society, it came to the world's attention. Thus, tens of thousands of Indians were arrested for buying and selling salt illegally; however, the Viceroy ordered his troops to arrest Gandhi last. After Gandhi's release from prison, he continued to work towards Indian independence, which was achieved in August, 1947. Dandi was a key turning point in that struggle.

After the second world war Clement Attlee appointing Mountbatten as the Viceroy of India . In his position as Viceroy, Mountbatten oversaw the granting of independence to the Partitioned India as India and Pakistan. He developed a strong relationship with the Indian princes who reposed considerable confidence in him, and on the basis of his relationship with the British monarchy persuaded most of them to accede to the new states of India and Pakistan. This was vitally important in the lead-up to Indian independence, though, of course, ultimately they were betrayed when post-Independence India and Pakistan abolished their prerogatives.

With his strong friendship with Nehru and amicable relations with Mahatma Gandhi but inability to work his famous charm on Jinnah, Mountbatten quickly gave up hope of salvaging a unified independent India, becoming resigned to Partition into a post-Independence Pakistan and Bharath (India).

After Independence (midnight of 14/15 August 1947, celebrated on the 14th in Pakistan and the 15th in India) he remained in New Delhi for ten months, serving as the first of independent India's two governors general until June 1948 (the monarchy being abolished in 1950 and the office of governor general of India replaced with a non-executive presidency.)

Saltoro Kangri: Saltoro Kangri is the highest peak of the Saltoro Muztagh, which is a subrange of the Karakoram. It is one of the highest mountains on Earth, but it is in a very remote location deep in the Karakoram

Salwar Kameez : Salwar kameez is the traditional dress worn by various peoples of South Asia. Salwars are loose trousers and the kameez (similar to chemise or shirt) is a long shirt. It is the national dress for both men and women in Pakistan. It is also popular among women in India and Bangladesh and often worn in Afghanistan. Some versions are sometimes called a Punjabi suit, after the Indus valley area called the Punjab.

Salwars are loose pajama-like trousers. The legs are wide at the top, and narrow at the bottom. The legs are pleated or gathered into a waistband with a drawstring. The pants can be wide and baggy, or they can be cut quite narrow, on the bias. In the latter case, they are known as churidar.

The kameez is a long shirt or tunic. The side seams (known as the chaak) are left open below the navel, which gives the wearer greater freedom of movement. The word kameez is derived from the Latin camisia (shirt or tunic), from which it probably made its way into various European languages and also into Arabic, the likely immediate source for kameez. The kameez is usually cut straight and flat; older kameez use traditional cuts, as shown in the illustration; modern kameez are more likely to have European-inspired set-in sleeves. The tailor's taste and skill are usually displayed not in the overall cut, but in the shape of the neckline and the decoration of the kameez.

When women wear the salwar kameez, they usually wear a long scarf or shawl called a dupatta around the head or neck. For Muslim women, the dupatta is a less stringent alternative to the chador or burqa. For Hindu women (especially those from northern India, where the salwar kameez is most popular), the dupatta is useful when the head must be covered, as in a temple or the presence of elders. For other women, the dupatta is simply a stylish accessory that can be worn over one shoulder or draped around the chest and over both shoulders.

Sam Manekshaw : Field Marshal Sam Hormusji Framji Jamshedji Manekshaw (born April 3, 1914) was the Indian Army Chief of Staff who led the Indian forces during the Indo-Pakistani War of 1971. He is the only the second Indian military officer to hold the highest ceremonial rank of Field Marshal of the Indian Army. His distinguished military career has spanned four decades and through five wars, including World War II.

For his selfless service to the nation, the President of India awarded him a Padma Vibhushan in 1972 and conferred upon him the rank of Field Marshal on 1 January 1973. Manekshaw became the second Indian General to be awarded this prestigious rank, which is mainly honorary (the other was the late Field Marshal Kodandera Madappa Cariappa). Manekshaw retired a fortnight later, on 15 January 1973, after completing nearly four decades of military service.

Samai Dance : Samai Dance is performed with traditional metallic lamps or deepaks from Goa. In southern and middle Goa, Samai dance is performed during the Shigmo Festival. The men and women balance the Samai on their heads and perform various movements.

During religious gatherings the dance is accompanied by slow singing.

Samajwadi Krantikari Sena : Samajwadi Krantikari Sena (Socialist Revolutionary Army), a political front and militia group in the Indian state of Bihar founded in 1980 by Anand Mohan Singh (a Rajput strongman). The group fought against different groups belonging to lower castes. The prime objective of the Sena was to work against reservation quotas for lower castes

Samajwadi Party : Samajwadi Party (Socialist Party) is a political party in India. It describes itself as a democratic socialist party. It was founded on 4 October 1992. It is one of several parties that emerged when the Janata Dal was fragmented. SP is led by Mulayam Singh Yadav. SP is primarily based in Uttar Pradesh, were is currently holds the state government. SP is mainly based amongst the Yadav caste, but also has large support from other groups such as Muslims.

In the 13th Lok Sabha (1999-2004), it was the 5th largest party with 27 members (3 of whom were expelled later). In 2004 Lok Sabha elections, SP decided not to align with neither BJP nor Congress. Instead it ran in alliance with the Rashtriya Lok Dal. Since the elections, SP has provided external support to the Congress-led UPA government, despite sometimes acrimonious relations between its leaders and the Nehru-Gandhi family. In March 2005 Samajavadi Party got a boost as former Karnataka Chief Minister Bangarappa deserted BJP to join SP. When Bangarappa left BJP he resigned from Lok Sabha. In June 2005 Bangarappa was reelected to Lok Sabha in a bye-election in his constituency Shimoga, as an SP candidate. The Samajwadi party faired badly in the October/November 2005 Bihar elections getting only 2 seats out of the 158 seats which they contested but Bihar is not a stronghold of the Samajwadi Party and they were expected to do badly.

Samarth Ramdas : Samarth Ramdas (1608-1681) is considered one of the greatest Hindu saints of Indian history. A contemporary of another Hindu saint, Tukaram, he was a devotee of Lord Hanuman and Lord Rama, the former of which appears in carvings on many of the established mutts (monasteries) he constructed. He was also the spiritual guru of Shivaji, one of the most popular Hindu leaders in history.

Samaveda : The Samaveda (Sanskrit: , samaveda, a tatpurusha compound ot saman "ritual chant" + veda "knowledge"), is third in the usual order of enumeration of the four Vedas, the ancient core Hindu scriptures.

The Samaveda ranks next in sanctity and liturgical importance to the Rigveda or Veda of Recited praise. Its Sanhita, or metrical portion, consists chiefly of hymns to be chanted by the Udgatar priests at the performance of those important sacrifices in which the juice of the Soma plant, clarified and mixed with milk and other ingredients, was offered in libation to various deities.

The Collection is made up of hymns, portions of hymns, and detached verses, taken mainly from the Rigveda, transposed and re-arranged, without reference to their original order, to suit the religious ceremonies in which they were to be employed. The verses are not intended to be chanted, but to be sung in specifically indicated melodies using the seven svaras or notes. Such songs are called Samagana and in this sense the Samaveda is really a book of hymns.

In these compiled hymns there are frequent variations, of more or less importance, from the text of the Rigveda as we now possess it which variations, although in some cases they are apparently explanatory, seem in others to be older and more original than the readings of the Rigveda. In singing, the verses are still further altered by prolongation, repetition and insertion of syllables, and various modulations, rests, and other modifications prescribed, for the guidance of the officiating priests, in the Ganas or Song-books. Two of these manuals, the Gramageyagdna, or Congregational, and the Aranyagana or Forest Song-Book, follow the order of the verses of part I, of the Sanhita, and two others, the Uhagana, the Uhyagana, of Part II. This part is less disjointed than part I, and is generally arranged in triplets whose first verse is often the repetition of a verse that has occurred in part I.

The Samaveda survives in a single shakha or recension, the Kauthuma shakha, with a second shakha, Jaiminiya (or Talavakara), surviving fragmentarily, the Jaiminiya Samhita. From the Jaiminiya shakha, we also have the Jaiminiya Brahmana, the Jaiminiya Upanishad Brahmana and the Kena Upanishad.

Sambalpur : Sambalpur is the western most district district in the state of Orissa, India. It has a total area of 6,702 square kilometers, of which almost 60% of the district is covered in dense forest,and is located in the Mahanadi River basin. The district is surrounded by Deogarh district in the east, Bargarh and Jharsuguda districts in the west, Sundergarh district in the north and Subarnpur and Angul districts in the south. The district headquarters is Sambalpur city.

Sambalpur city is the connecting city between Madhya Pradesh and Orissa. Whereas it used to be known for its importance as a diamond trading centre, nowadays it is mainly known for its textiles. It's a good place from which to explore the surrounding forests and spot some of the rare species still roaming the area in one of the wild life sanctuaries, such as the well-known Badrama sanctuary.

Sambhaji Raje Bhonsle : Sambhaji Raje Bhonsle (Born-May 14th 1657;Died-1689) was the eldest son of the Maratha king Shivaji, and succeeded him as the Chhatrapati i.e a Maratha king, after Shivaji's death in 1680.

Sambhaji was a scholar of Sanskrit and eight other languages. He led the Maratha's fight against the Mughal emperor Aurangzeb. Aurangzeb had invaded the Deccan in 1682 in order to end Maratha raids on Mughal territory, suppress Maratha independence, and to conquer the last of the independent Deccan sultanates. Sambhaji was captured in an ambush by Mughal troops in 1688. He refused to convert to Islam, and shortly thereafter died while being tortured and dismembered; in so doing earned the title of Dharmaweer. He was succeeded as leader of the Marathas by his younger brother Rajaram.

There is some dispute among historians about his ability as a ruler. Some historians have portrayed him as ineffective and/or alcoholic. Other historians, notably S.G. Shevde, portray Sambhaji as a capable ruler. But his claim to fame came in his death. The Prince's single heroic death unleashed an unprecedented unity and heroic spirit among the Marathas who eventually managed to create one of the most powerful empires, the Maratha Empire in India after the weakening of the Mughals.

Sambhar Salt Lake : Sambhar Salt Lake is an India's largest salt lake, sits west of the Indian city of Jaipur (Rajasthan, Northwest India). On the eastern end, the lake is divided by a 5-km long dam made of stone. East of the dam are salt evaporation ponds where salt has been farmed for a thousand years. East of the dam is a railroad, built by the British (before India's independence) that provides access from Sambhar Lake City to the salt works. More importantly, Sambhar has been designated as a Ramsar site (recognized wetland of international importance) because the wetland is a key wintering area for tens of thousands of flamingos and other birds that migrate from northern Asia. The lake is actually an extensive saline wetland, with water depths fluctuating from just a few centimeters (1 inch) during the dry season to about 3 meters (10 feet) after monsoon season. The specialized algae and bacteria growing in the lake provide striking water colors and support the lake ecology that, in turn, sustains the migrating waterfowl.

Sambhulingeswara Kalyanotsavam : The Kalyanotsavam of Sambhulingeswara is celebrated during Mahasivaratri for five days in Andhra. On the first day, Prabhas are taken out in procession. Kalyanam, village procession, Rathotsavam Ponnaseva, Vasantotsavam and Pavalimpuseva are performed on the following days. Cash, silver and gold ornaments, coconuts, fruits and flowers are offered to the Lord. Devotees also offer cows and calves, tying—them to the Dhwajasthambha in fulfillment of their vows. It is believed that childless women who perform puja for five days, wearing wet clothes, would be blessed with children. Fasting and Jagaranam are also observed.

Samiullah Khan : Samiullah Khan (born September 6, 1951) is a former field hockey player from Pakistan, who was nicknamed The Flying Horse. He played as a left winger for his native country in 1970s and 1980s. He was instrumental in Pakistan's bronze medal in the 1976 Summer Olympics in Montreal, and winning gold in Asian Games in Bangkok in 1978. Khan retired from international hockey in 1982 while he was a captain of Pakistan. His brother Kaleemullah Khan also played for the national field hockey team of Pakistan. He later managed the Pakistani team, quitting in 2005.

Samjhauta Express : The Samjhauta Express was a bi-weekly train that ran between India and Pakistan, the only rail connection between the two countries. Up to 2002 it had been running, with just one break of service, since 1976. It was a daily train when the service started, and changed to a bi-weekly schedule in 1994. Earlier the rakes were returned to the home country the same day but later in 2000 the rake remained overnight at that location. Its termini were Lahore in Pakistan and Amritsar in India. The border crossing took place between Wagah in Pakistan and Attari in India. Originally, this was a through service with the same rake going all the way between the termini; later the Pakistani rake stopped at Attari at which point passengers had to change trains. The train service was set up with an agreement between Indian Railways (IR) and Pakistan Railways (PR) to alternately use an Indian and a Pakistani rake and locomotive for the train, six months at a time.

Samkhya : Hinduism preaches that the material world is responsible for all of man's sorrows. Shown here are two men being offered both liberation and bondage. One looks up towards the supreme-consciousness and follows the path towards spiritual wisdom while the other goes behind the material pleasures. Drawn by ropes which are held by the personifications of lust, greed, and anger, he glides towards hell.

Samkhya is widely regarded to be the oldest of the orthodox philosophical systems in Hinduism. Its philosophy regards the universe as consisting of two eternal realities: purusha and prakrti. The purushas (souls) are many, conscious and devoid of all qualities. They are the silent spectators of prakrti (matter or nature), which is composed of three gunas (dispositions): satva, rajas and tamas (steadiness, activity and dullness). When the equilibrium of the gunas is disturbed, the world order evolves. This disturbance is due to the proximity of Purusha and prakrti. Liberation (kaivalya), then, consists of the realisation of the difference between the two.

This was a dualistic philosophy. But there are differences between the Samkhya and Western forms of dualism. In the West, the fundamental distinction is between mind and body. In Samkhya, however, it is between the self (purusha) and matter, and the latter incorporates what Westerners would normally refer to as "mind". Samkhya was originally atheistic, but in confluence with its offshoot Yoga later, it accepted God.

Samkrant : Samkrant or the beginning of a month (in Bikrami era) is regarded as a sacred day by Hindus in Kashmir. Women bathe in rivers and observe a day's fast.

Samma : Samma dynasty ruled in Sindh and parts of Punjab and Balochistan from 1351-1551 A.D. The Samma dynasty declined and was replaced by Arghun Dynasty.

Sammakka Jatara : Medaram is a small village in the forest area of the Mulugu taluk of Warangal district. Here Sammakka Jatara is celebrated once in two years on a very large—scale for three days before Magha. Purnima Sammaka is a tribal goddess and the patrons and the priests are Koyas. All the tribals of Mulugu area and the thousands of other Hindus congregate there during the celebrations. There is no permanent idol of the deity. A Koya tribal boy who gets a vision before the festival roams about in the forest for a week without food and sleep and finally brings the goddess in the farm of vermilion caskets, one representing the main duty sammakka and the other her daughter Sarakka both tied to a piece of bamboo. This is installed on an earthen platform raised under a tree.

Animals are sacrificed and vows are redeemed, intoxicants are widely used. Hundreds of people who are often possessed by the goddess come there dancing ecstatically throughout their journey. The special offering to the deity is jaggery which collects in huge piles. Those who fulfil vows offer jaggery equal to their weight and jaggery is distributed as prasadam. More than lakh of people congregate every day.

Sammi : This is a popular dance of Sandal Bar in Punjab. This is a women's dance and like the Giddha it is danced in a circle. The dancers stand in a ring and swing their hands bringing them up from the sides, right in front, up to the chest and clap. They take the hands down in accordance with a rhythm and a system and clap again. Repeating this gesture, they bend forward and clap again and go round and round in a circle, as the rhythm is maintained with the beat of the feet. Various kinds of swinging movements are performed with the arms. This is a very simple dance. Most of the gestures and confined to the movements of the arms, clicking and clapping. No instrument is required as an accompaniment to this dance. Rhythm is kept up with the beating of feet and clapping. The dance is named after the young heroine of a legend, Sammi, who was madly in love and used to sing and dance as best she could for the sake of her lover.

Samosa : A samosa is a common snack in India and the rest of South Asia. It likely originated in Central Asia prior to the 10th century. It generally consists of a fried triangular-/pyramid-shaped pastry shell with a savory potato, onion and pea stuffing, but other stuffings like minced meat are also used. The size and shape of a samosa, as well as the consistency of the pastry used can vary considerably. It is spicy and is often eaten with chutney, such as mint, coriander or tamarind. Samosa is a favorite snack loved by young and adult alike. It is often savored with tea or coffee. It can also be prepared as a sweet, rather than savory, form.

Samosas are often served in chaat, along with the traditional accompaniments of yogurt, chutney, chopped onions and coriander, and chaat masala. Samosas are so popular in many parts of Africa that people often think of them as native. In East Africa they are regularly sold in shops and restaurants and many housewives make them as a snack. Samosas were presumably introduced (along with other foodstuffs) by Indians brought out to work on the East African Railway. The African form is often called "samousa".

Sampurna Vikas Dal : Sampurna Vikas Dal, a political party in the Indian state of Bihar. SVD was formed by ex-Rajya Sabha MP and former Rashtriya Janata Dal leader Ranjan Prasad Yadav on October 20, 2003. Yadav had differed with RJD leader Laloo Prasad Yadav when the latter appointed his wife, Rabri Devi, as the Chief Minister of the state.

S P Gupta : S.P. Gupta (1931) is a well-known Indian archaeologist and art historian. He has done extensive studies on the Indus Valley Civilization and in South Asia. He was also the editor of several volumes of the Puratattva, the Bulletin of the Indian Archaeological Society, He is the Chairman of the Indian Archaeological Society in New Delhi. He was awarded the Mortimer Wheeler Prize.

Samudragupta : Samudragupta, ruler of the Gupta Empire (c.AD 335—380), and successor to Chandragupta I, is considered to be one of the greatest military geniuses that India ever produced, thus also known as the 'Napoleon of India'. His name is taken to be a title acquired by his conquests (Samudra referring to the 'oceans'). Samudragupta is believed to have been his father's chosen successor even though he had several older brothers. It is therefore believed that after the death of

Chandragupta I, there was a struggle for succession in which Samudragupta prevailed.

The main source of Samudragupta's history is an inscription engraved on one of the stone pillars set up by Ashoka in Kausambi (present day Allahabad). In this inscription Samudragupta details his conquests. This inscription is also important because of the political geography of India that it indicates by naming the different kings and peoples who populated India in the first half of the fourth century AD The inscription or more aptly the eulogy to the Great Gupta's martial exploits states that its author is Harishena, who was an important poet of Samudragupta's court.

The beginning of Samudragupta's reign was marked by the defeat of his immediate neighbours, Achyuta, ruler of Ahichchhatra and Nagasena. Following this Samudragupta began a campaign against the kingdoms to the south. This southern campaign took him south along the Bay of Bengal. He passed through the forest tracts of Madhya Pradesh, crossed the Orissa coast, marched through Ganjam, Vishakapatnam, Godavari, Krishna and Nellore districts and may have reached as far as Kancheepuram. Here however he did not attempt to maintain direct control. After capturing his enemies he reinstated them as tributary kings. This act prevented the Gupta Empire from attaining the almost immediate demise of the Maurya empire of Ashoka and is a testament to his abilities as a statesman.

Beyond doubt Samudragupta was a great military general, but apart from that, his personal accomplishments are equally remarkable. He showed great magnanimity towards all those kings who were defeated. His polished intelligence and good knowledge of scriptures won him many admirers. He gathered a galaxy of poets and scholars and took effective actions to foster and propagate religious, artistic and literary aspects of Indian culture. He had good proficiency in music and was perhaps an accomplished Veena player. This fact is amply demonstrated in his lyrist type coins. Most king took pride in trumpeting their bravery but Samudragupta is the only king in whole of Indian history who showed softer side of his personality. These coins are very special and rare. Samudragupta probably died in AD 380, and was succeeded by his sons Ramagupta and Chandragupta.

Samundri : Samundri is a city in Punjab, Pakistan. It was the tehsil (county) of Jhang District in 1900; later, when lyallpur (faisalabad) was made a district in 1904, Samundri was made its tehsil. Because there were three Hindu temples (mandir) in the locality, the town was first called Sehmandri; the name was subsequently converted to Samundri. In the reign of Sher Shah Suri this area was a link road for transportation.

Sanatan Dharma Maha Sabha : The Sanatan Dharma Maha Sabha is the major Hindu organisation in Trinidad and Tobago. It operates 150 mandirs and over 50 schools. It was formed in 1952 when Bhadase Sagan Maraj engineered the merger of the Satanan Dharma Association and the Sanatan Dharma Board of Control. An affiliated group, the Pundits' Parishad, has 200 affiliated pundits. The organisation's headquarters are located in St. Augustine. The President General of the Maha Sabha is Dr. D. Omah Maharaj, and the Secretary General is Satnarayan Maharaj, son-in-law of the founder, Bhadase Sagan Maraj.

Sanchi : Sanchi is known for its stupas, monasteries, temples and pillars stretching from the 3rd century BC to the 12 century AD in Madhya Pradesh. The most famous of these monuments, the Sanchi Stupa 1,was originally built by the Màuryan Emperor Ashoka. The site is one of the most evocative in India, and a good base for a number of interesting bicycle excursions.

Sanchi Stupa : Sanchi, variously known as Kakanaya, Kakanava, Kakanadabota and Bota-Sriparvata in ancient times, has a singular distinction of having remarkable specimen of Buddhist art and architecture right from the early Mauryan period (c. 3rd century BC to 12th century AD). Sanchi is famous in the world for Stupas, monolithic Asokan pillar, temples, monasteries and sculptural wealth. During Sunga times, several edifices were raised at Sanchi and its surrounding hills. The Ashokan Stupa was enlarged and faced with stones and decorated with Blustrades, staircase and a Harmika on the top. The reconstruction of Temple 40 and erection of Stupas 2 and 3 also seem to date back around the same time.

In the first century BC the Andhra-Satavahanas, who had extended their sway over the eastern Malwa, caused the elaborately carved gateways to Stupa 1. From the second to fourth century AD Sanchi and Vidisha came under the Kushanas and Kshatrapas and subsequently passed on to the hands of the Guptas. During the Gupta period some temples were built and sculptures were added. Shrines and monasteries were also constructed in the Sanchi during seventh and twelfth centuries AD.

Since the fourteenth century Sanchi stupa remained deserted and uncared for till 1818 when General Taylor rediscovered the site, Sir John Marshall, established an archaeological museum in 1919, which was later transformed into the present site museum at Sanchi.

Sandal Bar : A region between river Chenab and river Ravi in Punjab Pakistan spread over almost 80 km in length and40 km in length from north to south. Bar actually means forest area where there is no resources for cultivation like water. This Bar is named after Saandal who is thought to be Father od famous Dulla Bhatti. In old times almost all the area of this bar was part of current district Jhang but nowadays it is devided between ditricts Faisalabad,Jhang and Toba Tek Singh.

Sandspit Beach : Sandspit Beach is situated north west of Karachi. It is very famous tourist spot. The sea here is very calm and quite during the period October to March and very rough in Monsoon. Remarkable variety of marine life-algae, and crabs are found here. The shallow water here are ideal for swimming and sunbathing. It has an unusual rocky formation. Sandspit beach is quite a popular hangout and relaxation spot in the Karachi. Facilities at the Sandspit Beach includes boating and camel riding.

Sandwip : Sandwip is an island along the south eastern coast of Bangladesh. It is situated at the estuary of the Meghna River on the Bay of Bengal. It is separated from the Chittagong coast by the Sandwip channel.

Sangam : The Sangam is a collection of Tamil literature composed between 1,500 and 2,000 years ago. Though the idea that early Tamil literature was fostered in ancient academies on a submerged landmass has been widely discredited, literary historians do still refer to Tamil literature from 200 BCE to 300 CE as Sangam literature. Sangam literature is the oldest known Dravidian literature, written in Tamil, and deals with love, war, governance, trade, eloping, bereavement, and mourning. In contrast to contemporary literary works in Sanskrit and Pali, Sangam literature is surprisingly secular, dealing with day-to-day themes in a unique South Indian context.

The word "Sangam" is probably of Indo-Aryan origin, coming from Sangha, the Buddhist and Jain term for an assembly of monks. In Tamil the word means "assembly" or "academy". According to medieval commentators on older Tamil poetry, assemblies, academies, or learned gatherings called Sangams were founded to foster the

Tamil language. Each was shifted around due to "Piralayams" or "Great Deluges". Three such Sangams, Talaicchangam (the first), Idaicchangam, the middle and Kadaicchangam (the last), had poets, musicians, kings, and nobles as members. According to other accounts, even before the first Sangam, another one with the name of Mahendramalai Tamil Sangam is said to have existed, between 16000 BCE and 14550 BCE. These ideas were first expressed in a commentary to Iraiyanar Akapporul, a medieval work on Akam poetry. While the work itself is dated by K.A. Nilakantha Sastri to c. 750 CE, the commentary dates to the 13th century.

Sangh Parivar : The Sangh Parivar is a loose "family" of organisations, including political parties, which promote the ideology of Hindutva. The word parivar means family in Hindi, so the term Sangh Parivar is used to refer to the family of organisations affiliated to the Rashtriya Swayamsevak Sangh.

Hindutva proponents insist that they stand for more than the Hindu religion; they believe in a Hindu nation or community that includes Sikhs, Jains and Buddhists. Muslims are in general distrusted, unless they accept Hindustan, rather than the Islamic ummah, as their primary identity. Sangh organisations have also been strongly anti-Communist, anti-socialist, and pro-business. They are considered to be on the political "right" wing.

Sanghar : Sanghar is one of the district located on the Indo-Pak border. Sanghar itself a small city lies among Nawabshah, Mirpur Khas, Tando Adam (cities). Basically, it is argiculture town where mostly people engaged with farming profession and businesses related to arigiculture. Majority of Sindhi language speakers people live their and Punjabi people also in second majority population.

Sanghi Temple : The Sanghi Temple is a temple in Sanghi Nagar, which is an industrial suburb and is located about 25 km from the heart of Hyderabad, India. The sacred Raja Gopuram can be seen from several kilometers away which is very tall.

This beautiful temple complex is located on the top of hill Paramanand Giri, which attracts a number of devotees who seek gods blessings. The beauty of the slope around the temple is simply breath taking and beckoning ordent visitors. As you approach the Paramanand Giri, the gateway or Maha Dwaram welcomes the visitors. As you further proceed, the stone elephant is seen at the stairway. There are three Gopurams seen at the foot of the hillock which are so tall and seen as if touching the heavens. On the top of the temple complex one can see the shrine of Lord Anjaneya, the son of Anjana devi, and the son of wind God, who is believed to shower his blessings to his devotees.

Sangrur : Sangrur is one of the districts of Punjab. Sangrur is a district headquarter of the district. It is located on cross section of Delhi Ludhiana and Patiala Bathinda roads. Sangrur was the winter capital of the princely Jind State (Khunga Kothi, a place on the left bank of a canal near Jind was its summer capital). Originally this City belonged to Nabha state but later on the Raja of Jind snatched it from Nabha state. This district gave two chief ministers to present day Indian Punjab and one to the PEPSU(Patiala and East Punjab States Union—This state was later on merged with present day Punjab. It had Patiala as its state capital.)

Sangthang : Sangthang is the Himalayan peak in Kumaon Himalayas in Pithoragarh district of Uttaranchal state of India.It is situated in the easternmost part of Kumaun , lining Byans valley.The peak is situated on Indo-Tibet border.The altitude of the peak is 6,480 m.This peak is near to Jolingkong lake and famous Himalayan passes of Mangshya Dhura and Shin La.The peak climbed for the first time by P.Dasgupta in 1968.

Sangu River : Sangu river has its source at 21°13′N and 92°37′E in the North Arakan Hills, which form the boundary between Arakan and the Chittagong Hill Tracts. It follows a northerly circuitous course in the Hill Tracts up to Bandarban. It enters the district from the east and flows west across the district and finally falls into the Bay of Bengal at the end of a course of 270 km (173 km within Bangladesh territory) at 22°6′N and 91°51′E about 16.09 km south of the mouth of the Karnafuli.

Sania Mirza : The young Indian women tennis sensation Sania Mirza, was born in Mumbai on November 15, 1986. Presently the highest ranked Indian, Sania started playing Tennis at the tender age of six at the Nizam club in Hyderabad

Born to parents, father Imran Mirza a sports journalist and mother Nasima, it was Sania's father Imran who initiated her into the game and who has always encouraged her to be the best. She started practicing under CK Bhupati, India's top tennis player Mahesh Bhupati's father. She learnt the professional game at Sinnet Tennis Academy in Secunderabad before moving to Ace Tennis Academy in the USA. Now she is managed by Mahesh Bhupati's company Global Sports and has a specialist advisor Bob Brett who was Boris Becker's coach earlier.

Sania played her first international tournament in 1999 when she represented India at the World Junior Championship at Jakarta. Mirza's big boost came in 2002 when Paes decided to take her as his mixed doubles partner at the Asian Games. The duo went on to claim the bronze medal. The rise has been steady since then. In 2003, Sania at 16years did India proud by becoming the youngest and first ever Indian to figure in the main draw of the girls' doubles junior Wimbledon tennis championship and winning the Grand Slam title. Sania partnered 13-year-old Russian Alisa Kleybanova and defeated Katerina Bohmova of the Czech Republic and Michaela Krajicek of the Netherlands 3-6, 6-2, 6-3. It was after a long haul of 51 years that an Indian girl figured again in the final of a Grand Slam, the last being Rita Dabur, who had finished runner-up in the singles event in 1952.

A winner of 21 International Tennis Federation (ITF) titles, Sania won over Petra Mandula of Hungary defeating her 6-2, 6-1 in the second round of the women's singles at the Australian Open grand slam. With this victory, she has become the first Indian woman to reach the third round of a Grand Slam event. Sania Mirza outlasted the Ukraine's Alonya Bondarenko to win the Open WTA tour event in her native town Hyderabad and became the youngest and first Indian woman to win a WTA Tour title.

This 20-year-old girl became the brand ambassador of Lotto Sports Italia and the company said that it would soon launch a signature line series. With its launch, Sania would become only the fourth player after Andre Agassi of USA, Germany's Steffi Graf and Stephen Edberg of Sweden to have a signature line of her own.

Sania, is now ranked 77 in her career-high singles after her exploits in the Dubai Open. Mirza's powerful forehand strokes, confidence and positive attitude combined with good looks and charm have floored Indians and attracted sponsors in hordes. On the personal front, Sania likes dancing and listening to Rap, hip-hop and Hindi remix, likes cricket and swimming. She is very religious and never misses her daily prayers and Quran reading. She is now living with her parents and her little sister Anum in the posh suburbs of Jubily Hills, Hyderabad. Mirza, who idolises German tennis great Steffi Graf, has dreams of being the Wimbledon singles champion one day.

Sanjay Gandhi : Sanjay Gandhi (December 14, 1946 - June 23, 1980) was an Indian politician of mixed Kashmiri and Parsi heritage;, he was the younger son of Feroze Gandhi and his wife Indira Gandhi. He was a close political advisor of Indira Gandhi, when she was the Prime Minister. He was accused of abuses during the Emergency and died in a stunt airplane crash shortly after his mother's return to power. He had been elected to the Parliament of India five months before his death.

Sanjay and his elder brother Rajiv Gandhi studied at The Doon School, as well as in England. Sanjay never attended college, but took up an apprenticeship with Rolls-Royce. He was very interested in sports cars, and he also obtained a pilot's license. During his years in England, he was convicted for reckless driving. Many speculate that he along with some brash friends even resorted to stealing cars. The Indian High Commission had to bail him out on several occasions. He did not complete his apprenticeship, returned to India and began living with his mother in Delhi.

While his brother Rajiv was building a career as an airline pilot independent of politics, Sanjay grew close to his mother, and became involved in political affairs. In 1971, Prime Minister Indira Gandhi's Cabinet proposed the production of a "people's car"—a cheap, affordable and efficient indigenious machine that middle-class citizens could afford. While Sanjay had no experience, design proposal or tie-ups with any corporation, he was awarded the contract and the exclusive production license. The criticism that followed this decision was mostly directed at Indira, but the 1971 Bangladesh Liberation War and victory over Pakistan drowned out the issue. India's victory and subsequent Congress landslide in the elections only left Indira Gandhi more powerful.

The Maruti Udyog Ltd., the nation's premier automobiles corporation of today was founded by Sanjay Gandhi, but the company did not produce any vehicles. A test model put out as a showpiece of progress was criticized. Public perception turned against Sanjay, and many began to speculate of growing corruption.

No official and proper investigation has been carried out, but reports of journalists and investigations carried out by them suggest that Sanjay had created a money-laundering empire, handing out kickbacks for fees paid by large corporations that sought to curry favor with the son of the Prime Minister. According to many, Sanjay conducted a campaign of collecting funds, land, capital and production materials from industrialists, who were regarded as currying favour. This is believed to have resulted in substantial personal profit for Sanjay, as well as new political connections, although he produced no vehicles. Several Congress politicians were also suspected of involvement.

In 1974, the opposition-led protests and strikes had caused a widespread disturbance in many parts of the country and badly affected the government and the economy. Prime Minister Gandhi declared a national emergency, enforced martial law, delayed elections, censored the press and suspending some constitutional freedoms in the name of national security. Non-Congress governments throughout the country were dismissed. Thousands of people, including several freedom fighters like Jaya Prakash Narayan and Jivatram Kripalani who were against the Emergency, both ailing old men, were arrested.

In the extremely hostile political environment just before and soon after the Emergency, Sanjay Gandhi rose in importance as Indira's advisor. With the defections of former loyalists, Sanjay's influence with Indira and the government increased dramatically, although he was never in an official or elected position.

It has been suggested that Sanjay's influence with his mother helped to ensure that the Emergency was declared and it is clear that Sanjay only increased his power with the Emergency (1974-1977). Although he had not been elected and held no office, Sanjay began exercising his new-found influence with Cabinet ministers, high-level government officers and police officers. While many Cabinet ministers and officials resigned in protest, Sanjay reportedly appointed their successors.

In one famous example, Inder Kumar Gujral, the future Prime Minister resigned from the Ministry for Information and Broadcasting when Sanjay attempted to direct the affairs of his ministry and give him orders. Gujral is reported to have angrily rebuked Sanjay and refused to take orders from an un-elected person.

Sanjay nevertheless was now openly being groomed as his mother's successor, but it was not to be. Without a permit and against the advice of the civil aviation supervisor at a small airport, Sanjay and his co-pilot crashed nose-down into the ground while flying a special plane in an especially dangerous manoeuvre. He was cremated near the Shantivan. The Congress Party immediately embarked on naming schools, hospitals and parks after him. His brother Rajiv, quickly became its apparrent successor.

Sanjay Gandhi National Park : This park was established in the year 1983 in the district of Thane and Bombay in an area of 86.96sq.km. The nearest town to the park is Borivili just a distance of 3km. This town is also the rail head to visit the park. The nearest airport is Santacruz, Bombay at a distance of 15km.

Most of the forest is dry deciduous type with a few patches of evergreen and semi-evergreen forests towards the Kanheri caves. Plant species are mangrove, jambal, teak. About 1,000 species of flowering plants are present in the park.

Sanjay National Park : Set up in the year1981. The park is spread over an area of 1938sq.km in the districts of Sidhi and Sarguja. The nearest town Sidhi is 60km away from the park, railhead Jora 20km away and airport Khafuraho 270km away.

Sanjay Vijay Manjrekar : Sanjay Vijay Manjrekar (born 12 July 1965 in Mangalore, Mysore) is an Indian cricketer who never quite lived up to his potential at the highest level, averaging 37.14 in his 37 Tests between 1987/88 and 1996/97, as opposed to an overall first-class average of 55. He is the son of Vijay Manjrekar.

Manjrekar's favourite team to bat against was Pakistan, whom he had a Test average of 94 and two Test centuries. He made his double-century against Pakistan in Lahore. Manjrekar is currently a commentator for ODI and Test Cricket matches.

Sanjeev Kapoor : Sanjeev Kapoor (b. April 1964) is one of the top chefs in India. He has authored many books and is the host of Khana Khazana a popular cookery program shown on Zee TV ever Sunday since 1993. The show has completed 450 episodes.

He started out in the hospitality industry in 1984 with a diploma in Hotel Management from iihm pusa, Catering Technology & Applied Nutrition. he started his career in the ITDC under their kitchen management scheme. He was a topper in his batch. After working in many hotels, he became the Executive Chef of the Centaur Hotel in Mumbai (Bombay). His television show won the Best

Cookery Show award given by the Indian Television Academy (ITA) in 2001. He is also the recipient of the Best Executive Chef of India Award by H & FS and the Mercury Gold Award at Geneva, Switzerland by IFCA. He hopes to make Indian cuisine the most popular cuisine in the world.

Sanjukta Panigrahi : Noted Odissi danseuse died on 24 June 1997 at the age of 53. Born in a respectable and orthodox family, Sanjukhta was the first Oriya girl to embrace this classical dance at an early age and ensure its grand revival. She started performing Odissi at the age of six under the guidance of Guru Padma Bhusan Kelu Charan Mahapatra and bagged the first prize in the International Children's Film Festival in 1952.

Panigrahi resurrected Odissi dance from obscurity and made it famous the world over. She was the first woman artiste to be allowed to perform in the Shankatmochan temple festival some years ago. She also founded the Kalinga Kalakshetra to impart training in Odissi dance and promote performing arts.

Sanjukta was the first ever artiste who choreographed and performed the non-traditional lyric within the limits of the Odissi style and her experiment with the Surdas Padmavalli, Tagore songs, Bhagwad Geeta and Tulsi Ramayan were highly successful. Being the exponent of both Bharatnatyam and Odissi, she took great interest and initiative in explaining the originality of the Odissi style and established it as an independent style of Indian classical dance. She was awarded Padma Shri in 1975.

Sankarni : In Nagaland, one of the major festivals of the Zemis is the Sankarni Puja which coincides with Shivaratri. Single boys and girls join in the Sankarni puja which lasts over a week. Chanting songs, they smoke, eat and drink to their hearts content. Contribution in money and kind is welcome from the participant families as well as visitors. The Chakhesang Khilunyie and Rengma Ngadah are both harvest festivals.

Sankethi : Sankethi is distinct from Tamil and is now an independent language according to Dravidian linguists such as Hampa Nagarajaiah. Many still call it a dialect of Tamil in keeping with tradition. It is to be noted that Sankethi can hardly be understood by native Tamil speakers.

This language clearly separated from Tamil around the same time as Malayalam did and is unique in that no contact was retained with the country of origin. Thus the language grew independently. It has certaily been influenced by and borrowed from Kannada and Sanskrit but has some unique characteristics. It shares similarities with Malayalam as well, as the land from which the Sankethis migrated is on the Kerala-Tamilnadu border and they must have spoken a similar tongue in the days gone. Some of the words used in Sanketi are more similar to classical Tamil vocabulary. Sankethi has also retained the proto-Dravidian elements in some places.

S Anwarul Haq : Anwarul Haq is a former Chief Justice of the Supreme Court of Pakistan, who gave legitimacy to General Zia ul-Haq's martial law and upheld the decision of Lahore High Court which sentenced Zulfikar Ali Bhutto to Death in a sham trial of a murder case. Four Supreme Court judges headed by Chief Justice Anwarul Haq ordered the hanging of Pakistan's first elected Prime Minister Zulfikar Ali Bhutto to, as some suggest,please the military dictator General Zia ul-Haq.

The community of international jurists described the 4-3 judgement of the Supreme Court as judicial murder since there had been no precedent in judicial history to hang a man on a split verdict. Sharifuddin Pirzada

(Attorney General) threatened Justice Anwarul Haq with dismissal and thus got him to grant Gen. Zia the power to amend the constitution.

Sanskrit : Sanskrit is an an Indo-European classical language of India and a liturgical language of Hinduism, Buddhism, and Jainism. It has a position in India and Southeast Asia similar to that of Latin and Greek in Europe, and is a central part of Hindu tradition. It is one of the oldest Indo-European languages in the world and boasts a rich tradition of poetry, literature, and philosophical and religious texts. Sanskrit is one of the 22 official languages of India. It is being revived as a vernacular in the village of Mattur near Shimoga in Karnataka.

Today Sanskrit is mostly used as a ceremonial language in Hindu religious rituals in the forms of hymns and mantras. Its pre-Classical form of Vedic Sanskrit, the liturgical language of the Vedic religion, is one of the earliest attested members of the Indo-European language family, its most ancient text being the Rigveda. It is also the language of Yoga. The scope of this article is that of Classical Sanskrit as laid out in the grammar of Panini, roughly around 500 BC. Most Sanskrit texts available today were transmitted orally for several centuries before they were written down in ancient/medieval India.

Sant Ravidas Nagar District : Sant Ravidas Nagar District is a district of Uttar Pradesh state in northern India. The city of Gyanpur is the district headquarters. This district is situated in the plain of the Ganges River, which forms the southwestern border of the District. The Ganges, Varuna and Morva are the main rivers. The district is bounded by Jaunpur District to the north, Varanasi District to the east, Mirzapur District to the south, and Allahabad District to the west. The district has an area of 1055.99 km^2. Sant Ravidas Nagar District was created on June 30,

1994 as 65th district of the state. The district is famous for its carpets in India and abroad.

Santal : Santal is an ethnic group in Bangladesh. Mainly living in the Himalayan sub-mountain region in different districts of Rajshahi division. Their principal home is in Radha (in West Bengal), the forests of adjacent Bihar (Jhadkhand) and Orissa, and Chhota Nagpur. The British government assigned a special territory for their living and named it Santal Pargana. It is difficult to definitely say when and why they settled in the East Bengal region. But the census of 1881 shows that there were Santal settlements in the districts of Pabna, Jessore, Khulna and even in Chittagong. A survey of the Santal population of present Bangladesh area conducted in 1941 recorded their number as 829,025. The censuses organised after the Partition of Bengal (1947) did not count Santals as a separate group of people, and consequently, their exact number in East Pakistan could not be determined. According to an estimate made by Christian missionaries in the 1980s, the Santal population in northern Bangladesh was over one hundred thousand. According to the 1991 census, the Santal population was over two hundred thousand.

Santali : Santali is a language in the Munda subfamily of Austro-Asiatic, related to Ho and Mundari. It is spoken by about six million people in India, Bangladesh, Nepal, and Bhutan. Most of its speakers live in India, in the states of Jharkhand, Assam, Bihar, Orissa, Tripura, and West Bengal. It has its own alphabet, known as Ol Cemet', but literacy is very low, between 10 and 30%. Santali is spoken by the Santhals.

Santhal Pantheon : Religion is in extricably woven into the social life of the Santhals in Bihar. It has strengthened the social unity of these tribal people, inspired in them a sense of social responsibility and endowed them with a strong consciousness of the righteousness. They have no temples or idols for purposes of worship. They look up on natural objects like hills and dales, trees and groves with great reverential awe. The Santhal Pantheon is essentially hierarchical in character. Singbonga is the Supreme Being and the omnipotent deity who ranks highest in this hierarchy. He is believed to be the creator and destroyer of all creatures inhabiting both the visible and invisible world. There is no idol to represent him nor any temple or shrine for his worship.

Inferior in status to Singbonga is the deity called Marang-Baru, the guardian of the Santhal village who is invoked on all ceremonial occasions. Other deities are Jaher-Buri and deities known as 'five and six'. All the deities are worshipped by the Naik, village priest. He is held in high esteem by the villagers and enjoys a number of privileges denied to common folk. The Santhals have an extra priest called Kadam Naik who performs such functions as are entrusted to him by the chief priest. The Mati or Ojha is a spirit doctor possessing knowledge of the herbs as well as other malevolent spirits.

Santiniketan : Santiniketan was founded by Maharshi Debendranath Tagore, the father of Rabindranath Tagore. In 1901 Rabindranath Tagore started an experimental place of learning with a 'class room' under the trees, and a group of five pupils. This class room that he started later became the 'Vishva Bharati University in 1921. This university attracts pupil from all over the world and aspires to be a spiritual meeting ground in a serene environment. It has the faculties in all major disciplines like humanities, agriculture, cottage industries, Indian Music and Drama, performing arts, Philosophy, Sanskrit and art. An interesting feature of this university is that the sculptures, paintings, murals and frescoes are found around the campus. It has the paintings of Rabindranath and Nandalal Bose and sculptures of Ramkinkar.

Santoor : The santoor is a trapezoid-shaped hammered dulcimer often made of walnut, with seventy strings. The special-shaped mallets (mezrab) are lightweight and are held between the index and middle fingers. A typical santoor has two sets of bridges, providing a range of three octaves.

In Sanskrit Santoor means "one hundred strings" called the Shata-tantri Veena or "a hundred-stringed lute". Presumably, the itinerant musicians and gypsies carried this instrument in their wanderings across Asia and Europe, giving rise to a variety of similar instruments.

The Indian santoor is more rectangular and can have more strings than the original Persian counterpart. The santoor as used in Indian classical musician is played with a pair of curved mallets made of walnut wood and the resultant melodies are similar to the music of the harp, harpsichord or piano. The sound chamber is also made of walnut wood and the bridges are made of local wood and painted dark like ebony. The strings are made of steel from Germany and England. Notable Santoor players of present days are Pandit Bhajan Sopori , Pandit Shivkumar Sharma.

Santoor is made of a box of wood, trapezoid in shape. Over this there are thirty bridges, arranged in fifteen rows, two in each row. A set of four strings of metal tuned to the same note is stretched over each pair of bridges, thus the total number of wires is sixty. The length and thickness of strings vary according to the octave, the strings are thickest in the lower octave. It is played with a pair of flat wooden pieces curved at the striking end.

Saptak Music Festival : A festival of Indian classical music usually conducted on the First week of January in Ahmedabad every year. This festival was inaugurated by Pt. Ravi Shankar in 1980. The musical event is organised by a public charitable trust which runs the Saptak School of Music. This festival which spans the first 11 days of January, showcases the best talents and presents as many as a hundred plus musicians with sincere commitment to standards.

All leading vocalists as well as instrumentalists participate on this platform regularly. Some of the innovative features of this festival have been instrument and dance ensembles, Tala Vadya Kacheri, Rajasthani and Punjabi folk music. Saptak also tries to keep alive the fading traditions of vocal music like Thumri and Dhrupad, and instruments like Sarangi and Pakhawaj by inviting the older generation of artists specializing in these fields. The students of Saptak also perform in the presence of renowned musicians, musicologists and a large appreciative audience.

Saqib Malik : Saqib Malik is one of the most established directors in Pakistan, known primarily for his avant-garde videos and advertisements. He has directed numerous successful videos for many Pakistani pop acts, the more notable among them being Fuzon's Khamaj and Ali Azmat's Na Re Na.

Saqlain Mushtaq : Saqlain Mushtaq (born December 29, 1976) is a Pakistani cricketer and member of the Pakistani cricket team since 1995. He was born in Lahore, Punjab. He made his international debut against Sri Lanka at Peshawar. His bowling style is off spin.

He has taken over 200 Test wickets. His ODI figures are 288 wickets at an average of 21.78. He last played Test cricket for Pakistan against India at Multan, in 2004. He has taken over 500 first class wickets. He won many matches for Pakistan.

Saraghrar : Saraghrar massif is the fourth highest in High Hindu Kush, a 600km long mountain chain located at the North frontier of Pakistan with Afghanistan. Tirich Mir, 7708m, is the highest peak of High Hindu Kush chain, whose numerous valleys are often difficult to reach. Saraghrar massif is a huge, irregular stretched plateau (7000m), lying above vertical granite and silver ice faces, which protect it all around. Its distinct summits are poorly identified and information gathered from expeditions, which visited the area are often misleading. The main summits are: NE summit (7349m), NW summit (7300m), SW summit (7148m), S summit (7307m) and SE summit (7208m). To date (2005) NW summit is the only unclimbed peak.

Sarail Hatkhola Mosque : Sarail Hatkhola Mosque is located in the heart of Sarail thana Bazar (hat), about 11.5 km due north of Brahmanbaria district headquarters. Although now in a good state of preservation, the mosque has suffered much due to unplanned restoration and repairs done by the people of the locality.

The original building can now be viewed only from its rear because of the recent addition of a flat masonry veranda on the north, east and south sides. The mosque still bears an inscription recording its erection by the wife of Nur Muhammad, son of Majlis Shahbaz, during the reign of aurangzeb in 1670 AD.

An important aspect of the Sarail mosque is that it provides, like many others in the country, example of a happy blending of two different art traditions – the Sultanate style and the Mughal style. The former is best represented by bent cornices and terracotta ornamentation, while the latter is represented by the use of panels on the exterior surface of walls and the surface plastering, the use of drum under the domes, and the extension of the corner towers much beyond the parapet.

S R Ranganathan : Shiyali Ramamrita Ranganathan (August 9, 1892, Shiyali, Tamil Nadu - September 27, 1972,

Bangalore) was an innovative mathematician and librarian from India. His most notable contributions to the field were his five laws of library science and the development of the first major analytico-synthetic classification system, the Colon classification. He is considered to be the father of library science in India.

One of the most progressive information scientists of the twentieth century, and the man believed to have coined the phrase "library science," was born of middle-class, educated parents in the state of Tamil Nadu in southern India. S. R. Ranganathan earned B.A. and M.A. degrees in mathematics at a local college in order to realize his ambition to teach. While a young professor of mathematics at the University of Madras, he was chosen from 900 applicants for a new position as University Librarian. Neither he nor any of the other applicants were formally trained as librarians. Ranganathan reluctantly took the position and was soon sent to London to earn a graduate degree in library science at University College. His grades were only a bit above average, but he immersed himself in the problems of decimal classification and began to formulate a new system of classification that would become known as Colon Classification for the colons used to separate the fields.

Ranganathan's biographers claim that when he returned to India to take up the position of librarian, he dedicated the rest of his life to all aspects of his new profession, working long days with no time off for the next 20 years and writing and promoting the cause of libraries in India during his spare time. Over the next few years Ranganathan, ever the rationalist and a disciple of the scientific method, contributed his deceptively simple and yet incredibly profound "Five Laws of Library Science.

Another of Ranganathan's many contributions to the discipline of modern information science is his method of faceted classification. Also known as the analytico-synthetic method, Ranganathan's system of classifying library materials, although never widely used in traditional libraries, has greatly influenced classification theory. Colon Classification is based on the idea that traditional systems such as the Dewey Classification System and the Library of Congress Classification System set up categories into which individual objects must be fitted. Ranganathan's system starts with the individual object itself and arranges the categories around the salient aspects (facets) of that object. According to classification researchers, this method is a more flexible and precise means of classification.

Sarangi : Sarangi is one of the most important bowed instrument of India. Sarangi is suitable both for solo playing and group performances.

Sarangi is about 2 feet long and made by hollowing out a single block of wood and covered with a parchment. A bridge is tied on the belly in the middle. The sides of the sarangi are pinched to facilitate bowing. Four tuning pegs are fixed to the hollow head, one on each side. The instrument usually has 3 main strings of guts. But in some type a fourth string made out of brass is used for drone.

When played, sarangi is positioned in such a way that the uppermost part (head) is placed on the lap and the other end rests against the left shoulder. It is played with a horse hair bow which is held in the right hand. The finger of the left hand is used for stopping the strings. The most notable aspect is that strings are stopped with the sides of finger nails and not by the balls of fingers.

Modern sarangis generally have 35 to 40 sympathetic strings running under the main strings. These are fastened to small pegs on the right side of the finger board and also on the top of the head. The other members of sarangi family are the Dotara, the Dhad sarangi of Punjab and the Chikara of Uttar Pradesh.

Sarasvati River : The Sarasvati River is an ancient river that is mentioned in Hindu texts. The Nadistuti hymn in the Rig Veda mentions the Sarasvati between the Yamuna in the east and the Sutlej in the west, and later texts like the Mahabharata mention that the Sarasvati dried up in a desert. The largest concentration of Indus Valley sites appears to be east of the Indus, at and near the dried-up Ghaggar-Hakra riverbed. There is also a small present-day Saraswati River that joins the Ghaggar river and appears to be one of the branches of the ancient river.

Saraswat Brahmins : The Saraswat Brahmins claim descent from a Brahmin caste mentioned in ancient Hindu scriptures as inhabiting the Saraswati River valley, the geographic location of which is unknown. The actual origins of this community and the circumstances of its relocation to the areas that they now inhabit are shrouded in mystery. It is said that one of the offshoot of this community merged into the Brahmkshatriyas. Mostly after Sri Parshu Ram carved the community out of the 5 sons of Raja Ratten Sen. A few Brahmkshtriyas i.e. Kapoors, Malhotras/Mehras and Chopra, retain the Brahmin Gotras, such as Bharadwaj, Angiras, Bhargav, Atri and Kashyap. They fell under the Kshatriya Varn, but were considered the Highest among them.

Saraswat brahmins are found in north and south-west India. The majority of the Brahmins of Kashmir, Punjab, Himachal Pradesh and Haryana are Saraswat Brahmins. Other saraswat brahmins such as those found along the western coast of India also claim to be originally from Kashmir and through migration have settled in various parts of India.

Saraswati : Saraswati is the Sakti, the power and consort of Brahma the creator. Hence she is the mother of the entire nation. She is considered as the personification of all knowledge -arts, science, crafts and skills. Hence she is depicted as pure white in colour. Clad in spotless white apparel and seated on a lotus seat, she holds in her four hands a Veena (lute), Akshamala (rosary) and pustaka (book).

Though these are most common, there are several variations. Some of the other objects shown are: pasa (noose) Ankusa (goad), padma (lotus) Trisula (trident) Sankha (conch) chakra (discus) and so on. Occasionally she is shown with five face or with eight hands. Even three eyes or blue neck are not uncommon. In this case she is the Mahasaraswati aspect of Durga or Parvati.

Dr. Sarvapalli Radhakrishnan : Dr. Sarvapalli Radhakrishnan was born on 5 September, 1888 in Tirutani, a well-known religious center in the Madras State. He was the second son of Veera Samayya, a tehsildar in a zamindari. It was a middle-class, respectable Hindu Brahmin family. Indeed, the place, the time and the family were most suitable, from every point of view, for the advent of a new philosopher-statesman, so directly needed in those turbulent days of the awakening of a very ancient and glorious nation, drowsy and dormant in its own ignorance and indolence, for reasons well known to all.

As usual in those days, Radhakrishnan was married in 1906, at the tender age of 18 and while still a student, to Sivakamamma, and spent a happy conjugal life with her for half a century before she died in 1956. Bright and brilliant, with a scholarly disposition and a serene and saintly demeanor, from the very beginning, Radhakrishnan spent the first eight years of his life happily and fruitfully in his home town with his parents. The peaceful and exhilarating atmosphere of that well-known and well-loved place, as well as the benign influence of his parents who, as was common in the South, were intensely religious in the traditional sense, went far in moulding his character and sowing a lively seed of religiousness and moralism in him.

It was, indeed, an indubitably significant fact that Radhakrishnan's parents, though orthodox, thought it fit to send their beloved son to Christian Missionary schools and colleges: Lutheran Mission School, Tirupathi (1896-1900), Vellore College, Vellore (1900-1904), Madras Christian College (1904-1908).

The wonderful far-sightedness, open-heartedness and broad-mindedness of his revered and beloved parents, which enabled them, in those days of blind prejudices and equally blind social taboos, to send their son to well-known, well-managed, well-disciplined Christian educational institutions—stood him in good stead throughout, making it possible for him to acquire specially Occidental qualities like a sense of duty, punctuality, discipline, sobriety and the like, together with specially Oriental qualities of religiosity, calmness, patience, faith in God and men.

Radhakrishnan's choice of Philosophy as his main or Honours subject in his B.A. degree course was due to a very fortunate accident. At that time, he was really rather baffled as to what particular Honours subject to choose from amongst the possible five, viz., Mathematics, Physics, Biology, Philosophy and History. Then, purely accidentally, and out of a mere boyish curiosity, he read three well-known works on Philosophy, passed on to him by one of his cousins who had that year obtained the B.A. degree with Philosophy Honours; and that definitely decided his future course of studies.

He studied Sanskrit and Hindi also; and had a good deal of interest in the traditional languages of India. He read also the Vedas and the Upanishads with great care and reverence. In fact, Radhakrishnan was, and is, still today, a reader and a digester in the true sense of the terms. For, what he read—and he read widely and lovingly all kinds of good books—did not remain an external acquisition, an ornamental decoration, with him; but blossomed forth in him in fullest glory and grandeur.

It is not always that in this strange world of ours inner worth is accompanied by outer success. But Radhakrishnan is a glorious exception in this regard. For, all throughout his brilliant career, honour after honour was showered on him. The following are some of the main posts held by him most fittingly and efficiently: Lecturer in Philosophy, Presidency College, Madras, in the Madras Provincial Educational Service, after graduation; Assistant Professor of Philosophy in the same College for five years; Professor of Philosophy, Mysore University (1918-1921); King George V Professor of Philosophy, Calcutta University (1921-1931) and again (1937-1944); Vice-Chancellor of the Andhra University (1931); Spaulding Professor of Eastern Religion and Ethics, Oxford University (1932-1953) —first Indian to be so appointed; and Vice-Chancellor of the Banaras Hindu University (1942).

Among the cultural posts held by him may be mentioned: Leader of the Indian Delegation to UNESCO many times (1946-1950); Chairman of the University Education Commission (1948) appointed by the Government of India; Chairman of the Executive Board of UNESCO (1948); President of UNESCO (1952); Delegate to the P.E.N. Congress (1959); Vice President of International P.E.N.; Honorary Fellow of the British Academy (1962); Representative of the Calcutta University at the Congress of Philosophy, Harvard University, U.S.A. (May 1962).

Saraswati Puja : Saraswati Puja is the festival of Sikkim. This festival falls in the month of January and honours the Hindu Goddess of knowledge "Saraswati". School children place their study books in front of the statue and seek blessings for doing well in their studies.

Sarbul (Sarhul) : It is a summer dance of the Oraon tribe.

Sardar Abdur Rab Nishtar : Sardar Abdur Rab Nishtar (13 June 1899 - 14th February 1958) Muslim League stalwart and Pakstan movement activist Sardar Nishtar was born in Peshawar, NWFP. He completed his early education mission school and later Sanatan Dharram High School in Peshawar. He dropped out of King Edward Medical College but later on completed his Bachelor of Arts degree from the Punjab University. He later went to Aligarh and received an LL.B with honours from Aligarh Muslim University in 1925.

A man of deep religious convictions he also had a deep interest in Islamic mysticism, a fact which probably reflects the influence of his associate Maulana Ali. Sardar Abdur Rab Nishtar remained member of Indian National Congress 1927-31, was elected Municipal Commissioner, Peshawar Municipal committee, successively from 1929-38, joined All India Muslim League became a confidante of Pakistan's founder Muhammad Ali Jinnah.

In 1932, remained a member AIML Council, 1936, member NWFP legislative Assembly 1937-45, Finance Minister NWFP 1943-45, member AIML Working Committee, 1944-47, represented the AIML at Simla Tripartite Conference 1946. Abdur Rab Nishter died on February 14, 1958 in Karachi. Nishtar Medical College in Multan and Nishtar Park in Karachi are named after him.

Sardar Ataullah Khan Mengal : Sardar Ataullah Khan Mengal, popularly known as Sardar Ataullah Mengal, is a well known political figure of Pakistan hailing form

Balochistan.He has been campaigning nationalist and separatist movement in Pakistan for a long time. He is also the Chief of his Mengal tribe. He was Chief Minister of Balochistan during Zulfiqar Ali Bhutto's Premiership from May 1, 1972 to February 13, 1973.

Sardar Bahadur Khan Women University : Sardar Bahadur Khan Women University is located in Quetta, Balochistan, Pakistan. Sardar Bahadur Khan Women University was established in 2004. It offers degree programs in Arts and Sciences. It is named for the former Agent to the Governor General and Chief Commissioner of Balochistan Sardar Bahadur Khan.

Sardar Farooq Ahmad Khan Leghari : Sardar Farooq Ahmad Khan Leghari (b. May 29, 1940) was President of Pakistan from November 14, 1993 until December 2, 1997. Leghari was born in Choti Zareen, a village of Dera Ghazi Khan, on May 29 of 1940.

He comes from a political family that has been active in politics in this part of the world since the pre-colonial days. His father Sardar Muhammad Khan Leghari and grand father Sir Nawab Muhmammad Jamal Khan Leghari had both been ministers.

After his initial schooling at the "Eton" of Pakistan, Aitchison College, Lahore where he was the head boy and declared the Best Leaving Student of 1957. He graduated with honours from the Forman Christian College, Lahore where again he was amongst the best students, he went on to study at Oxford University. After returning to Pakistan he joined the Civil Service and served for quite sometime in East Pakistan. On the death of his father he resigned from service and came back to his roots to look after the tribal affairs of his tribe. He is the head of the Leghari tribe.

He joined the Pakistan Peoples Party, and was made the leader of that party upon the imprisonment of Zulfiqar Ali Bhutto. However, later Leghari was also imprisoned during the military regime of General Muhammad Zia-ul-Haq, only to be freed upon the death of the General.

In 1993, with the express support of his leader, he ran for President and won the election against Wasim Sajjad. During this time, his relationships with Benazir Bhutto and her husband Asif Ali Zardari gradually deteriorated, and reached their lowest level in November 1996, when he dismissed Benazir Bhutto's government on the pretext of lawlessness and extra judicial killings. The true reason of their falling out is believed to be more of a personal nature. The 1997 general elections brought Nawaz Sharif to power. Leghari and Sharif soon had a falling out and a personal power struggle ensued between them. Shortly after Nawaz Sharif's supporters ransacked the Supreme Court, Farooq Leghari was forced to resign.

Instead of retiring from politics, he went on to create his own political party, the Millat Party, which entered into a coalition of 7 parties, known as National Alliance, to participate in the general elections of 2002. The National Alliance, however, failed to appear as a dominant force in the elections, and won just 13 seats in the National Assembly. The political atmosphere of the time helped him in entering in a coalition with the majority party to form a government, and his son Awais Ahmed Leghari was made a federal minister for Telecom and IT, as a consequence.

Sardar Sarovar Project (SSP) : Sardar Sarovar Project (SSP) also known as the Narmada Dam Project, is a project involving the construction of a series of large hydroelectric dams on the Narmada River in India. The project was first conceived of in the 1940s by the country's first prime minister, Jawaharlal Nehru. The project only took form in

1979 as part of a development scheme to increase irrigation and produce hydroelectricity. The Narmada dam is India's most controversial dam project and its environmental impact and net costs and benefits are widely debated. The Narmada Dam has been the center of controversy and protest since the late 1980s.

Local protests taking the form of a genuine peoples movement, known as the Narmada Bachao Andolan (Save Narmada Movement) have been led by Medha Patkar. The World Bank was a funder of the SSP, but withdrew after an independent review in 1990. Indian writer Arundhati Roy has protested the Narmada Dam project.

Sardar Vallabhbhai Patel : Sardar Vallabhbhai Patel (31 October 1875—15 December 1950) was an Indian freedom fighter, senior political leader and statesman. In India and across the world, he is known as Sardar Vallabhbhai Patel, where Sardar stands for Chief or Leader in many languages of India. Inspired by the work of Mohandas Gandhi, Patel organized the peasants of Kheda and Bardoli in Gujarat in satyagraha—non-violent mass civil disobedience—against the oppressive tax policies imposed by the British Raj. He served as the President of the Indian National Congress in 1931, and rose to the forefront of rebellions and political events—helping lead Indians into the Salt Satyagraha and the Quit India movement. Patel was regarded by many Indians and British alike as the second-most powerful Indian leader after Gandhi. He was imprisoned by the British for many years with Gandhi in the early 1930s, and from 1942 to 1945 with the entire Congress leadership.

Historians consider that Patel's most important contribution to India came on the eve of independence. Becoming the first Home Minister and Deputy Prime Minister of India, Patel took charge of the task to forge a united India from a plethora of semi-independent princely states, colonial provinces and possessions. Patel employed an iron fist in a velvet glove diplomacy — frank political negotiations backed with the option (and the use) of military action to weld a nation that could emancipate its people without the prospect of divisions or civil conflict.

His leadership obtained the peaceful and swift integration of all 565 princely states into India. Patel also used force against Hyderabad state and Junagadh to preserve India's unity, security and future when their respective rulers indulged ambitions for independence and subsersive activities against the will of their people. Patel's initiatives spread democracy extensively across India, and re-organized the states to help transform India into a modern federal republic with states autonomy. Historians consider Patel almost single-handedly responsible for overseeing the unification of India, and his admirers called him the Iron Man of India for his resolute and principled leadership during the freedom struggle and the early years of a nascent India.

He was officially awarded the Bharat Ratna, the nation's highest civilian honor, posthumously in 1991

Sardul Singh Caveeshar : Sardul Singh Caveeshar (1886 in Amritsar - 1963) was an Indian newspaper editor, and a major figure in the Indian independence movement. Educated in Lahore, Caveeshar began his public career in 1913, when he launched the English-language newspaper Sikh Review. An early article in the Sikh Review criticized the demolition of an external city wall during the construction of New Delhi, as the wall had been part of a historic Sikh gurdwara; this led to widespread Sikh agitation until the outbreak of the First World War, at which point that particular issue was considered to be of lessened priority. After the war, however, Caveeshar renewed his calls for action, with the result that he was expelled from Delhi. He moved to Lahore and began another newspaper, the New Herald. In 1919, he was arrested and imprisoned for writing against the Rowlatt Act.

In 1921, he issued a public call for 100 Sikh volunteers to rebuild the gurdwara's demolished wall, at the cost of their lives if need be. 700 volunteers (including Caveeshar himself) turned out; however, before they could leave Lahore for Delhi, word arrived that the Delhi city government had rebuilt the wall. The next month, he was arrested, charged with sedition, and imprisoned for four years for having written about a massacre of Sikh reformists.

In 1933, he became acting president of the Congress after his predecessor was arrested for participating in civil disobedience. In 1935, he openly opposed the Congress's participation in the Government of India Act, and in 1937 chose to resign his membership in the party after they accepted office in the provinces where they had earned a majority.

In 1939, he joined Subhash Chandra Bose's All India Forward Bloc faction; when Bose left India in 1941, Caveeshar became the Bloc's president. As a result, he was arrested, and imprisoned for four years. After Indian independence, Sardul Singh Caveeshar retired from active politics in 1948.

Sargodha : Sargodha is the eighth largest city of Pakistan, 175 kilometres north-west of Lahore, in Sargodha District. It is called "Shaheeno Ka Shahar" (City of Eagles) because of the presence of the largest airbase of the Pakistan Air Force,Which is now been given the name of Mushaf AirBase Sargodha,as a tribute to the genius Air Marshal of Pakistan,Mushaf Ali Mir. It is an agricultural city, wheat, rice, and sugarcane being its main crops.It is an amazing thing that Sargodha has the largest production of Citrus as compared to its size,in the world.So the city and region reknowned for citrus fruit,all over the country; kino is a newly developed variety.

Sarhul Festival : The Sarhul festivals is the worship of the village deity who is supposed to be the protector of the tribes in Jharghand. Unless the deities of their village are pleased on them they can not be safe and prosperous. The festival is very popular for its festive mood. The whole region is highly charged with dance and song, food and drinks. It is celebrated in the spring season when the sprouting Sal gets greener and Sal trees blossoms with its flower called Shalony or Shalai.

This is the symbolic flower of Sarhul. The village deities are worshipped with this flower. The Shalai is also a symbol of friendship and brotherhood which the tribal priest distribute in every house of the village. The Prasad or offering of this festival is known as Hadia or Diang, immensely popular wine made of stale rice. Men & women get absorbed in nature with gay and over whelm with joy.

Sari : A sari (also spelled saree) is the traditional garment worn by many women in the Indian subcontinent. The garment is known by different names in various Indian languages; in Hindi, Gujarati and Marathi, it is known as Saadi; in Kannada as Seere; in Telugu as Cheera and in Tamil as Podavai.

The sari is long strip of unstitched cloth, ranging from five to nine yards in length, which can be draped in various styles. The most common style is for the sari to be wrapped around the waist, with one end then draped over the shoulder. The sari is usually worn over a petticoat (called lehenga/Ghagra in northern India and Pavada/Pavadai in the south) and a low-cut, short-sleeved, midriff-baring blouse known in north India as a choli.

Sariska National Park : The park was set up in 1982 in the district of Alwar covering an area of 274sq.km. The nearest town and the rail head is Alwar at a distance of 36 km from the park, Jaipur is the nearest airport at a distance of 110 km. The tract of the park is mainly hilly with two plateaus. The forests are dominated by dhok.

The fauna of the park comprise tiger, leopard, panther, wild boar, hyena, jungle cat, civet, four horned antelope, sambar, cheetah, ratel, caracal, chinkara, nilagi, partridges, green pigeon and pea fowl. The park can be visited round the year except in July, August, and September. It has rest houses.

Sariska Tiger Reserve : The Sariska Tiger Reserve is an Indian National Park located in the Alwar District of the state of Rajasthan. Originally a hunting preserve of the erstwhile Alwar state, the area was declared a wildlife reserve in 1955. In 1978 it was declared a Tiger Reserve and is now a part of India's Project Tiger scheme. The present area of the park is 866 km^2. The park is situated 107 km north east of the state capital Jaipur.

Some of the wildlife found in the Sariska Tiger Reserve include the tiger, leopard, jungle cat, hyena, jackal, chital, sambar, gaur, langur, wild boar and several species of birds.

The tiger reserve is also the location of several archeological sites such as the Neelkanth and Garh Rajor temples from the 9th and 10th centuries and the Kankwadi fort. The Kankwadi fort, located near the centre of the park is where, in the 17th century, Mughal Emperor Aurangzeb briefly imprisoned his brother Dara Shikoh in the battle for succession of the Mughal throne. The area also has historical buildings associated with the Maharajas of Alwar.

Sariska Tiger Reserve : The Sariska Tiger Reserve is an Indian National Park located in the Alwar District of the state of Rajasthan. Originally a hunting preserve of the erstwhile Alwar state, the area was declared a wildlife reserve in 1955. In 1978 it was declared a Tiger Reserve and is now a part of India's Project Tiger scheme. The present area of the park is 866 km^2. The park is situated 107 km north east of the state capital Jaipur.

Some of the wildlife found in the Sariska Tiger Reserve include the tiger, leopard, jungle cat, hyena, jackal, chital, sambar, gaur, langur, wild boar and several species of birds.

The tiger reserve is also the location of several archeological sites such as the Neelkanth and Garh Rajor temples from the 9th and 10th centuries and the Kankwadi fort. The Kankwadi fort, located near the centre of the park is where, in the 17th century, Mughal Emperor Aurangzeb briefly imprisoned his brother Dara Shikoh in the battle for succession of the Mughal throne. The area also has historical buildings associated with the Maharajas of Alwar.

Sarit Sarak : Sarit Sarak is a deadly form of martial arts, which is relatively unknown outside of its place of origin—the north east Indian state of Manipur. This form of art was much in vogue with the people of Manipur a few generations back.It was taught much for defending rather than attacking.

Sarnath : Sarnath (formerly also Mrigadava, Rishipattana, Isipatana), located 13 kilometres from Varanasi, Uttar Pradesh, India, is the deer park where Gautama Buddha first taught the Dharma, and where the Buddhist Sangha was founded. The Buddha went to Sarnath from Bodh Gaya after his enlightenment. He was seeking his five former companions. Having found them he taught them and they also became enlightened, and hence the Sangha, or community of the enlightened ones, was founded. The Buddha spent the next rainy season in Sarnath at the mulagandhakuti vihara. The Sangha having grown to 60 in number, the Buddha sent them out in all directions to teach the Dharma. Buddhism flourished in Sarnath in part because of kings and wealthy merchants based in Varanasi. By the third century Sarnath had become an important center for the arts, which reached its zenith during the Gupta period (4th to 6th centuries CE). In the 7th century by the time Xuan Zang visited from China, he found 30 monasteries and 3000 monks living at Sarnath.

Sarnath became a major centre of the Sammatiya school of Buddhism, one of the Nikaya or Hinayana schools. However, the presence of images of Heruka and Tara indicate that Vajrayana Buddhism was also practiced here. At the end of the 12th century Sarnath was sacked by Turkish Muslims, and the site was subsequently plundered for building materials. All of the ancient buildings and structures at Sarnath were damaged or destroyed by the Turks. However, amongst the ruins the Dhamekh Stupa is an impressive 128 feet high and 93 feet in diameter. The Dharmarajika Stupa is one of the few pre-Ashokan stupas remaining, although only the foundations remain. The decaying ruins of the Mulagandhakuti vihara mark the place where the Buddha spent his first rainy season while to the east is the modern Mulagandhakuti Vihara with its beautiful wall paintings and behind it the Deer Park.

The Ashoka pillar was broken some time ago but the base still stands. The lion capital, which miraculously survived its 45 foot drop to the ground, became a symbol on the Indian flag, and is still on display at the Sarnath Archeological Museum which also houses some of the greatest treasures of Indian Buddhist art including almost 300 images. There is also a Bodhi tree planted by Anagarika Dharmapala which was grown from a cutting of the Bodhi tree at Bodh Gaya. For Buddhists, this is one of four pilgrimage sites designated by Gautama Buddha, the other three being Kushinagar, Bodh Gaya, and Lumbini.

Sarod : The sarod is an Indian classical musical instrument which probably originates from the Senya rebab, an Indio-Persian instrument played in India to the 19th century. It is a 25-stringed lute-like instrument, whose body is hand carved from a single block of tun (Indian Mahogany) or teak wood, with a steel fretless finger board. The bridge rests on the belly of the instrument which is covered in goat skin. It is played with a plectrum or jaba made of coconut. Four of the strings are melody or playing strings, three are rhythm strings, and the rest are sympathetic and jawari strings, all made of metal.

The lack of frets and the tension of the strings makes it very technically demanding to play, as the strings must be pressed hard against the finger-board. There are two schools of sarod playing, one where the tip of the finger nails are used to stop the strings, thus certain strength and stiffness of the finger nails is a prerequisite for accuracy of pitch, and the other using the fingers to stop the strings against the finger-board. The technique which uses the finger nails produces a ringing tone to the sarod as against the flatter tone produced by the finger technique.

Sarod representations have been found in carvings of the 1st century in Champa temple and also in paintings in the Ajanta caves. It is similar to the Rabab of Afghanistan and Kashmir. The instrument was modified by Amir Khusru in the 13th century. Ustad Ali Akbar Khan also changed the shape to improve the tonal quality.

Sarojini Naidu : Sarojini Naidu (February 13, 1879 - March 2, 1949) was known as Bharatiya Kokila (The

Nightingale of India) and was a freedom fighter and poet. Naidu was the first Indian woman to become the President of the Indian National Congress and the first woman to become the governor of a state in India. She was born in Hyderabad, India as the eldest daughter of scientist-philosopher, Aghornath Chattopadhyaya, and Barada Sundari Devi, a poetess. At the age of 19, she married Dr. Govindarajulu Naidu.

She joined the Indian independence movement, in the wake of the aftermath of partition of Bengal in 1905. From 1915 to 1918 she lectured all over India on welfare of youth, dignity of labour, women's emancipation and nationalism. After meeting Jawaharlal Nehru in 1916, she took up the cause of the indigo workers of Champaran. In 1925 she was elected as the President of the Congress, the first Indian woman to hold the post.

In March 1919, the British government passed the Rowlatt Act by which the possession of seditious documents was deemed illegal. Mohandas Gandhi organized the Non-Cooperation Movement to protest and Naidu was the first to join the movement which the government worked to suppress. In July 1919, Naidu became the Home Rule League's ambassador to England. In July 1920 she returned to India and on August 1, Mahatma Gandhi declared the Non-Cooperation Movement. In January 1924, she was one of the two Indian National Congress delegates at the East African Indian Congress. Naidu arrived in New York in October 1928 and was concerned with the unjust treatment of the African Americans and the Amerindians. Upon her return to India she became a member of Congress Working Committee.

On January 26, 1930 the National Congress proclaimed its independence from the British Empire. On May 5, Mohandaș Gandhi was arrested. Naidu was arrested shortly thereafter and was in jail for several months. She, along with Gandhi, was released on January 31, 1931. Later that year, they were again arrested. Naidu was eventually released due to her poor health and Gandhi was released in 1933. In 1931, she participated in the Round Table Summit, along with Gandhiji and Pundit Malaviyaji. In 1942, she was arrested during the "Quit India" protest and stayed in jail for 21 months with Gandhiji. Naidu shared a warm relationship with Mohandas Gandhi, even calling him "Mickey Mouse".

On August 15, 1947, with the independence of India, Naidu became the Governor of Uttar Pradesh, India's first woman governor and she died in office in 1949.

Sarpo Laggo Glacier : The Sarpo Laggo Glacier (Sarpo Laggo: young husband) is a glacier in Pakistan, in the Karakoram mountain range of the Himalayas.

Sarva Shiksha Abhiyan (SSA) : The Sarva Shiksha Abhiyan (Hindi: The 'Education for All' Movement, sometimes referred to as "each one teach one") is a flagship programme of the Government of India for achievement of universalization of elementary education in a time bound manner, as mandated by the 86th amendment to the Constitution of India making free and compulsory education to children of ages 6-14 (estimated to be 205 million in number in 2001) a fundamental right. The programme aims to achieve the goal of universalization of elementary education of satisfactory quality by 2010.

The programme seeks to open new schools in those habitations which do not have schooling facilities and strengthen existing school infrastructure through provision of additional class rooms, toilets, drinking water, maintenance grant and school improvement grants. Existing schools with inadequate teacher strength are provided with additional teachers, while the capacity of existing teachers is being strengthened by extensive training, grants for developing teaching-learning materials and strengthening of the academic support structure at a cluster, block and district level. SSA seeks to provide quality elementary education including life skills. SSA has a special focus on girl's education and children with special needs. SSA also seeks to provide computer education to bridge the digital divide.

Sasaram : Sasaram is the administrative headquarters of Rohtas District, Bihar state, India. Sasaram is sometimes also spelled as Sahsaram. It is an ancient city and is believed to derive its name from Sahasrabahu, an ancient king and Parsuram, the warrior sage.

Sasaram is located on a major rail and road junction. Sasaram Railway station is located on the Grand Chord line of the Indian Railways, connecting Calcutta and Delhi. The famed Grand Trunk Road passes through Sasaram town. It also has a fertile agricultural hinterland. Sasaram is also famous for the red sandstone mausoleum of Emperor Sher Shah Suri, built during 1540-45 AD stands magnificently in the middle of an artificial lake.

Saser Kangri : Saser Kangri (or Sasir Kangri) is a Himalayan mountain located in the Saser Muztagh region of the Karakoram range.

Sasthamkotta Lake : Sasthamkotta Lake, is a large freshwater lake in Kerala state of southern India. It is located near Sasthamkotta in Kollam District, 30 kilometres from Kollam. The lake is surrounded on three sides by hills, and on the south side a bund separates the lake from the neighboring rice fields. Sasthamkotta lake provides water supply to entire Kollam District. The Sastha Temple is situated on the banks of Sathamkotta Lake.

Satara : Satara is a town located in the Satara District of Maharashtra state of India. The name is derived from the seventeen walls, towers and gates which the town was supposed to possess. The town is 2320 ft. above sea-level, near the confluence of the Krishna River (Kistna) and its tributary the Venna, 56 mi south of Pune.

The city of Satara was the seat of the former Maratha Maharajas, the nominal rulers of the Maratha empire until its conquest by Britain in 1818. The Maratha empire was founded by Shivaji in the 17th century. His descendants had lost effective control of the Maratha state by the mid-18th century, which had passed to the Peshwas, who moved the capital to Pune in 1749. After their victory in the Third Anglo-Maratha War in 1818, the British annexed most of the Maratha territory to Bombay Presidency, but restored the titular raja Pratap Singh, and assigned to him the principality of Satara, with an area much larger than the present district. As a result of political intrigues, he was deposed in 1839, and his brother Shahji Raja was placed on the throne. This prince, dying without male heirs in 1848, Satara was annexed by the British government, and added to Bombay Presidency.

Satavahanas : The Satavahanas, also known as the Andhras, were a dynasty which ruled in Southern and Central India starting from around 230 BCE. Although there is some controversy about when the dynasty came to an end, the most liberal estimates suggest that it lasted about 450 years. Long before that their kingdom had disintegrated into successor states. The Satavahana dynasty belongs to Andra Maval, a region in western Maharashtra. Their first capital was Junnar, near Pune. From the area where they lived they are referred to as Andhras.

Present day Andhra Pradesh got its name from this dynasty. In the Puranas and on their coins the dynasty is variously referred to as the Andhras, Andhrabhrityas, Satakarnis and Satavahanas. They have been variously thought of as originating from present day Maharashtra or Andhra Pradesh, and were probably of Aryan origin. The Satavahanas started out as feudatories to the Mauryan Empire but declared independence soon after the death of Ashoka (232 BCE).

Satavahanas : The Satavahanas, also known as the Andhras, were a dynasty which ruled in Southern and Central India starting from around 230 BCE. Although there is some controversy about when the dynasty came to an end, the most liberal estimates suggest that it lasted about 450 years. Long before that their kingdom had disintegrated into successor states.

The Satavahana dynasty belongs to Andra Maval, a region in western Maharashtra. Their first capital was Junnar, near Pune. From the area where they lived they are referred to as Andhras. Present day Andhra Pradesh got its name from this dynasty. In the Puranas and on their coins the dynasty is variously referred to as the Andhras, Andhrabhrityas, Satakarnis and Satavahanas. They have been variously thought of as originating from present day Maharashtra or Andhra Pradesh, and were probably of Aryan origin. The Satavahanas started out as feudatories to the Mauryan Empire but declared independence soon after the death of Ashoka (232 BCE).

Satellite Launch Vehicle : Satellite Launch Vehicle or SLV was a project started in the early 1970s by Indian Space Research Organisation to develop the technology needed to launch satellites. The project leader was Dr. APJ Abdul Kalam who is the present President of India. SLV was intended to reach a height of 400 km and carry a payload of 40 kg. SLV is a four stage rocket with all solid-propellant motors. The first launch of the SLV took place in Sriharikota on 10 August 1979. The last launch of the SLV took place on 17 April 1983. SLV formed the basis of the ASLV.

Sathya Sai Baba : Sathya Sai Baba (born Sathya Narayana Raju with the family name Ratnakaram, November 23, 1926 or October 4, 1929) is a popular, controversial Indian guru and miracle worker, who has millions of followers. According to the Sathya Sai Organisation, there are an estimated 1,200 Sathya Sai Baba Centers in 130 countries world-wide.

Sathyanarayana was born into a poor agrarian family in the remote village of Puttaparthi (located in Andhra Pradesh, India), as the son of Pedda Venkama Raju and mother Easwaramma. In the 1940s he claimed to be the reincarnation of Shirdi Sai Baba and subsequently took the fakir's name. He says that he is an avatar (incarnation) of Shiva and Shakti and an embodiment of love with divine powers such as omniscience and omnipotence.

Sathyamangalam : Sathyamangalam or Satyamangalam is a town in Tamil Nadu state of southern India. It lies on the north bank of the Bhavani River, a tributary of the Kaveri. The Bannari Betta is the seat of the temple of Bannari Amma, a Hindu deity. Although desolate during most parts of the year, the temple draws huge crowds during the annaul car festival. Sathyamangalam forms a taluk (subdistrict) of Erode District. Sathyamangalam was formerly part of Coimbatore District, but became part of Erode District when the district was constituted in 1979.

Satish Dhawan : Satish Dhawan (25 September 1920–3 January 2002) was born in Srinagar, India and was educated in India and the United States. He is considered by the Indian scientific community to be the father of experimental fluid dynamics research in India and one of the most eminent researchers in the field of turbulence and boundary layers. He succeeded Vikram Sarabhai, the founder of the Indian space programme, as Chairman of the Indian Space Research Organisation (ISRO) in 1972.

He was also the Chairman of the Space Commission and Secretary to the Government of India in the Department of Space. In the decade following his appointment he directed the Indian space programme through a period of extraordinary growth and spectacular achievement.

Satish Dhawan Space Centre (SDSC) : The Satish Dhawan Space Centre (SDSC) is the launch centre for the Indian Space Research Organisation (ISRO). It is located in Sriharikota, Andhra Pradesh, in India,. The centre is roughly 100 kilometres north of Chennai in South India at 13°47' North 80°15' East. It was originally called as Sriharikota Range (SHAR), and was sometime known as Sriharikota Launching Range. The centre was renamed in 2002 after the death of the ISRO's former chairman Satish Dhawan. The space centre has kept the title SHAR during these name changes. Centre became operational in October 1971 when on October 9 and October 10 three Rohini rockets were launched.

The SHAR facility now consists of two launch pads, with the second one being recently built. The second launch pad was used for launches beginning in 2005 and is a universal launch pad, accommodating all of the launch vehicles used by ISRO. The two launch pads will allow for multiple launches in the year, which was not possible earlier. India's lunar orbiter Chandrayaan 1 will be launched from this launch location in 2007-2008.

Satkoshia Gorge Sanctuary : In Orissa, this sanctuary was established in 1976 and, including a 22 kilometre long gorge where the Mahandi river cuts through the Eastern Ghats, the total sanctuary area is about 796 square kilometres. Dhenkanal is situated to the south of the gorge and to its north is Phulboni district.

Satpura National Park : Satpura National Park is located in district Hoshangabad of Madhya Pradesh in

India. It gets the name from Satpura hill ranges (Mahadeo hills). It covers an area of 524 km^2. Satpura National Park, and along with the adjoining Bori and Panchmarhi Sanctuaries, provides 1427 km^2 of unique Central Indian Highland ecosystem. It was set up in 1981. The terrain of the national park is extremely rugged and consists of sandstone peaks, narrow gorges, ravines and dense forests. The altitude ranges from 300 m to 1352 m. It has Dhoopgarh peak as high as 4500 feet (1400 m) and the almost level plains of Churna. The nearest town to the national park is Pachmarhi and the nearest railhead is Piparia at a distance of 55 km. The state capital Bhopal is situated at a distance of 210 km.

Satpura National Park, being part of a unique ecosystem, is very rich in biodiversity. The fauna comprises of tiger, panther, sambar, chital, Bhedki, nilgai, four-horned antelope, chinkara, bison (gour), wild boar, wild dog, bear, black buck, fox, porcupine, flying squirrel, mouse deer, Indian joint squirrel etc. There are a variety of birds. Hornbills and peafowl are the common birds. The flora of the national park consists of mainly sal, teak, tendu, aonla, mahua, bel, bamboo, and a variety of grasses and medicinal plants.

Satpura National Park : The park is located in the district of Hoshangabad covering an area of 502sq.km. The nearest town is Pamchamarhi. The nearest railhead is Piparia at a distance of 55 km and the nearest airport is Bhopal at a distance of 210 km. The fauna comprise leopard, tiger, barking deer, Sambar, nilgai and bison. Hornbill and peafowl are the common birds.

Satpura Range : The Satpura Range is a range of hills in central India. The range rises in eastern Gujarat state near the Arabian Sea coast, running east through Maharashtra and Madhya Pradesh to Chhattisgarh. The range parallels the Vindhya Range to the north, and these two east-west ranges divide the Indo-Gangetic plain of northern India and Pakistan from the Deccan Plateau to the south. The Narmada River runs in the depression between the Satpura and Vindhya ranges, and draining the northern slope of the Satpura range and running west towards the Arabian Sea. The Tapti River drains the southern slopes of the western end of the Satpura Range. The Godavari River and its tributaries drain the Deccan plateau, which lies south of the central and eastern portions of the range, and the Mahanadi River drains the easternmost portion of the range. The Godavari and Mahanadi rivers flow into the Bay of Bengal. At its eastern end, the Satpura range meets the hills of the Chota Nagpur Plateau.

Sattal : Sattal, meaning The Seven Lakes, is part of the lake district in India. Mostly it is a popular tourist spot. Travellers to the hill resort of Nainital occationally head for both Bhimtal or Sattal. Sattal lies to the north of the Indian capital Delhi and is only a few hour's rail journey away. Tourists often prefer to stay in outdoor camps. However travellers are warned that in the rainy season leeches are abundant and it is advisable to keep a packet of salt handy.

Sattar, (Justice) Abdus : He was the President of Bangladesh. Born in 1906 at village Daraka of Bolpur in Birbhum district of West Bengal Abdus Sattar obtained his MA in Political Science (1928) and B.L degree (1929) from Calcutta University, and joined the Calcutta Judge Court Bar. At the same time he joined politics as an activist of Krishak Praja Party of Ak Fazlul Huq. He joined Calcutta High Court Bar in 1941. He was the councillor of Calcutta Corporation (1939), Assessor-member of Calcutta Improvement Tribunal (1940-42), and Chief Executive Officer of Calcutta Corporation (1945). After the partition of India he moved to Dhaka (1950), and joined the Dhaka

High Court Bar. After the floating of Krishak Sramik Party (1953) headed by AK Fazlul Huq he joined the party. He was elected a member of the Pakistan Constituent Assembly in 1955. He was the Minister of Home and Education in the central cabinet of Pakistan headed by I. I. Chundrigarh (1957), Justice of Dhaka High Court (1957-68), Justice of Pakistan Supreme Court (1968-69), and Chief Election Commissioner of Pakistan (1969-72).

Sattriya Dance : Sattriya dance or Sattriya Nritya is one among the eight principal classical dance traditions of India. The others are Bharatanatyam, Kathakali, Mohini Attam, Kuchipudi, Odissi, Kathak and Manipuri. The dance has its origin in Assam. According to historians Sattriya dance is a creation of the great Vaishnavite (bhakti) guru Srimanta Sankardeva considered the lead architect of Assamese literature and culture. He created this mangificent Sattriya dance to accompany the Ankiya Naat (a form of Assamese one-act play, another creation of Sankardeva) which was usually performed in Satras (Assamese monastries). Since the dance developed and grew within the Satras, it is named after these religious institutions.

The content of Sattriya Nritya has usually been mythological stories. This dance is an attractive way to present mythological teachings in front of common people in an enjoyble form. Sattriya dance is accompanied by classical raga based compositions called borgeets (yet another creation from Sankardeva) and music. Instruments that accompany a performance are khols (drums), taals (cymbals), flute and violin etc. The ornaments and costumes used in this dance have a very distinct Assamese flavour. Traditionally, Sattriya dance is performed by bhokots (male monks) in monastries as part of their daily rituals or special festivals. Today, in addition to this practice, Sattriya dance is performed on stage by men and women who are not part of the Satras. Dances are performed either solo or in groups.

Satya Pir : Satya Pir is a belief system found in Bengal created by the fusion of Islam and local religions. Experts maintain that the muslim Satya Pir and the Hindu Satya Narayan essentially represent the same beliefs and rituals.

Satyagraha : Satyagraha is the philosophy of nonviolent resistance most famously employed by Mohandas Gandhi in forcing an end to the British Raj and also against apartheid in South Africa. Satya is Sanskrit for Truth, and Agraha is used to describe an effort, endeavor. The term itself may be construed to mean any effort to discover, discern, obtain or apply Truth. The word is rooted in Sanskrit, Hindi and Gujarati.

Satyajit Ray : He (May 2, 1921—April 23, 1992) was an Academy Award winning Indian film director whose films are perhaps the greatest testament to Bengali and Indian cinema. He is mostly known for his Apu trilogy—the films Pather Panchali (Song of the Road), Aparajito (The Unconquered), and Apur Sansar (The World of Apu)—but has a large collection of works that are widely acclaimed. He has been called one of the four greatest directors of cinema in the world.

In 1985, Ray won the Dadasaheb Phalke Award for lifetime contribution to Indian cinema. He received the Academy's Lifetime Achievement Award in 1992, one of only two Oscar winners from India. He was also awarded the Bharat Ratna in 1992.

Satyam Computer Services Limited : Satyam Computer Services Limited is a consulting and information technology services company. Satyam was founded by Ramalinga Raju in 1988. Satyam offers a variety of IT services to many different types of businesses. Satyam's network spans 46 countries, across six continents, and the company employs over 30,000 IT professionals, who work in development centers in India, the United States, the United Kingdom, the United Arab Emirates, Canada, Hungary, Singapore, Malaysia, China, Japan and Australia and serve over 410 global companies, 148 of which are Fortune 500 corporations. Satyam has strategic technology and marketing alliances with over 50 companies.

Satyam Computer Services Limited : Satyam Computer Services Limited is a consulting and information technology services company. Satyam was founded by Ramalinga Raju in 1988. Satyam offers a variety of IT services to many different types of businesses. Satyam's network spans 46 countries, across six continents, and the company employs over 30,000 IT professionals, who work in development centers in India, the United States, the United Kingdom, the United Arab Emirates, Canada, Hungary, Singapore, Malaysia, China, Japan and Australia and serve over 410 global companies, 148 of which are Fortune 500 corporations. Satyam has strategic technology and marketing alliances with over 50 companies.

Satyam is headquartered at Hyderabad, India and also has development centres in India at Bangalore, Pune, Chennai, Mumbai, Kolkata and Bhubaneswar.Satyam also has development centres in USA and in Europe.

Satyananda Saraswati : Paramahamsa Satyananda Saraswati (born 1923), is an important yoga master and guru in both his native India and the West. He was born in the small Himalayan town of Almora, Uttar Pradesh. At the age of nineteen he met his spiritual master, Swami Sivananda, in Rishikesh and lived in his circle for the following twelve years. For the next eight years he wandered through India, Afghanistan, Nepal, Burma and Ceylon, extending his knowledge of spiritual practices. In 1943 he took sannyasa and served his guru Swami Sivananda and The Divine Life Society in Rishikesh.

A respected master of Yoga Nidra and tantra, Swami Satyananda founded the International Yoga Fellowship in 1963 and the Bihar School of Yoga in the following year. He toured extensively, teaching yoga globally for the next twenty years, and authored a number of books. Hundreds of yoga teaching centres have been establishing under his name. In 1988 he retired from active involvement in yoga teaching and is now a patron of charitable institutions.

Bihar Yoga Bharati, the world's first university of yoga, was established under his guidance by his disciple Swami Niranjanananda in 1994. Swami Satyananda has trained thousands of yoga teachers and sannyasins all over the world and is a well respected author of over 80 books of yoga and spirituality. Swami Satyananda's system of yoga is considered to be Integral yoga. In 1988, he passed on the worldwide coordination of Satyananda Yoga to his disciple, Swami Niranjanananda.

Saugor and Nerbudda Territories : The Saugor and Nerbudda Territories was a region of British India, located in central part of present-day Madhya Pradesh state in central India. It includes the present-day districts of Sagar (Saugor), Damoh, Jabalpur, and Narsinghpur. The Saugor and Nerbudda Territories were captured from the Marathas at the conclusion of the Third Anglo-Maratha War in 1818.

Saugor was the seat of a Maratha governor, and the northern portion of the territory was ceded by the Maratha Peshwa, the southern portion, which included Jabalpur and the upper Narmada River valley, was ceded by the Bhonsle maharaja of Nagpur. The Saugor and Nerbudda Territories were attached to the North-Western Provinces, which included the British Dominions in the southern portion of present-day Uttar Pradesh state. In 1861 the Saugor and Nerbudda Territories were combined with Nagpur

Province, which the British had annexed in 1853, to form the Central Provinces.

Saundarya Lahari : The Saundarya lahari is a famous literary work written by Adi Shankara. Its hundred shlokas (verses) eulogize the grace and munificance of Goddess Parvati / Dakshayani, consort of Shiva. The Saundarya lahari actually contains 103 shlokas. It also gives many yantras, almost one to each shloka; describes tantric ways of performing devotion connected to each apecific shloka; and details the results ensuing therefrom. There are many interpretations and commentaries but best of these are arguably those that provide word-to-word translations, as also the yantras, the devotion to be performed and the results of the devotion.

Saurashtra : Saurashtra (also Soruth and Sorath) is a region of western India, located on the Arabian Sea coast of Gujarat state. It shares a peninsula with Kathiawar which occupies the north, Saurashtra or Sorath forming the southern portion. Sorath was the former name of the Muslim-ruled Princely State of Junagadh ("Junagarh" or the "Old City"). In 1947, Junagadh's Muslim ruler desired to accede his territory to Pakistan, but the predominantly Hindu population rebelled, and while he fled to Pakistan, a plebiscite was conducted as a result of which the kingdom was merged into the Indian Union.

During British rule, Junagadh and its neighboring princely states were supervised by the Western India States Agency (WISA). After India's independence in 1947, 217 princely states of Kathiawar and Saurashtra, including the former kingdom of Junagadh, were grouped together to form the province of Saurashtra. The capital of Saurashtra was Rajkot. On November 1, 1956, Saurashtra was merged into Bombay state. In 1960 Bombay state was divided along linguistic lines into the new states of Gujarat and

Maharashtra. The territory of Saurashtra, including that of the former kingdom of Sorath or Junagadh is now part of the state of Gujarat.

Sawai Gandharva Sangeet Mahotsav : Savai Gandharva Sangeet Mahotsav is celebrated with great fervor in Pune usually in December. It is held in commemoration of Pandit Rambhan Kundgolkar, the eminent Khyal singer. Pandit Bhimsen Joshi his student conducts the festival for the past three decades to observe his Gurus death anniversary. The festival nearing its 50th year of origin is an institution by itself with participation of eminent classical music artists from all over the Country. Pandit Joshi also performs at the concluding session of the festival.

Sawi Mosque : Sawi mosque is supposed to be one of the oldest mosques, which still exists though it has no roof now and most of its decorations have been damaged. Some portions of this mosque are still intact which indicate that glazed blue tiles were profusely used for ornamentation.

Sawlakin : Another popular dance is *Sawlakin*. This was originally a Lakher dance, but now it has been adopted by all the Mizas. Sawlakia means spirit of the slain. The dance was led by the warrior who had hunted a big game or killed a man. He would wear his best clothes and a plume of red feather. He would wield a gun or dao and a shield. He would be followed by other dancers in a row, who would also carry weapons, or cymbals or gongs. Some boys would stand in a group beating drums or blowing bugles. The dancers would move forward and slowly go round the head. While dancing weapons and shields would be wielded keeping time with drum or gong beats. All the time dancers would be plied with Zu by the women. This dance is a popular dance now. The modifications now are that there is no head in the circle and no Zu.

Sayyid Abul A'la Maududi : Sayyid Abul A'la Maududi was one of the most influential Muslim theologians of the 20th century and the founder of Jamaat-e-Islami (Islamic Party), an Islamic political party in Pakistan.

Maulana Maududi's philosophy, literary productivity and tireless activism contributed immensely to the development of Islamic political and social movements around the world, but also, more controversially, many militant Islamic organisations regard Maulana Maududi as an inspiration. Maulana Maududi's ideas profoundly influenced Sayyid Qutb of Egypt's Jamiat al-Ikhwan al-Muslimun ("Muslim Brotherhood") another leading Muslim philosopher of the 20th century. Together, Maududi and Qutb are considered the founding fathers of the global Islamic revival movement.

Sayyid Dynasty : The Sayyid dynasty were rulers of India's Delhi sultanate as successors of the Tughluq dynasty until displaced by the Afghan Lodis; this family claimed to be sayyids, or descendants of Muhammad. The central authority of the Delhi sultanate had been fatally weakened by the invasion of Timur (Tamerlane) and his sack of Delhi in 1398. For the next 50 years, North India was virtually divided.

Scheduled Castes and Tribes : Scheduled Castes and Scheduled Tribes are communities that are accorded special status by the Constitution of India. These communities were considered 'outcastes' and were excluded from the Chaturvarna system that was the social superstructure of Hindu society in the Indian subcontinent for thousands of years. These castes and tribes have traditionally been relegated to the most menial labour with no possibility of upward mobility, and are subject to extensive social disadvantage and discrimination, in comparison to the wider community.

The Scheduled Caste people are also known as Dalits; Scheduled Tribe people are also referred to as Adivasis. Gandhi used the terms Harijan and Girijan respectively.

Scottish Church College : The Scottish Church College, which is located at 1 & 3 Urquhart Square, Calcutta 700006 is the oldest continuing Missionary administered liberal arts and sciences academy in India. It is affiliated with the West Bengal Board of Secondary Education (for the Scottish Church Collegiate School), the West Bengal Council of Higher Secondary Education, and the University of Calcutta for the awarding of baccalaureate, post baccalaureate and undergraduate degrees.

Se Cathedral : Most imposing of all churches at Old Goa. Its vaulted interior overwhelms the visitors by sheer grandeur.

This Cathedral has five bells of which one is the famous Golden bell, the biggest in Goa and one of the best in the World.

Second Anglo-Sikh War : The Second Anglo-Sikh War (1848–1849), resulted in the subjugation of the Sikh kingdom and absorption of the Punjab into lands controlled by the British East India Company.

On April 19, 1848 Vans Agnew of the civil service and Lieutenant Anderson of the Bombay European regiment, having been sent to take charge of Multan from Diwan Mulraj, were murdered there, and within a short time the Sikh troops and sardars joined in open rebellion. Governor-General of India Lord Dalhousie agreed with Sir Hugh Gough, the commander-in-chief, that the British East India

Company's military forces were neither adequately equipped with transport and supplies, nor otherwise prepared to take the field immediately. He also foresaw the spread of the rebellion, and the necessity that must arise, not merely for the capture of Multan, but also for the entire subjugation of the Punjab. He therefore resolutely delayed to strike, organized a strong army for operations in November, and himself proceeded to the Punjab. Despite the brilliant successes gained by Herbert Edwardes in the Second Anglo-Sikh War with Mulraj, and Gough's indecisive victories at Ramnagar in November, at Sadulapur in December, and at the Battle of Chillianwala on January 13, 1849, the stubborn resistance at Multan showed that the task required the utmost resources of the government. At length, on January 22, the Multan fortress was taken by General Whish, who was thus set at liberty to join Gough at Gujrat. Here a complete victory was won on the February 21 at the Battle of Gujarat, the Sikh army surrendered at Rawalpindi, and their Afghan allies were chased out of India.

After the victory at Gujerat Lord Dalhousie annexed the Punjab for the East India Company in 1849. For his services the Earl of Dalhousie received the thanks of the British parliament and a step in the peerage, as marquess. The Sikh Wars gave the two sides a mutual respect of each other's fighting prowess. The Sikhs would fight loyally for the British in the Indian Mutiny and in many other campaigns and wars up to Indian Independence in 1947.

Second Battle of Panipat : The Second Battle of Panipat took place on November 5, 1556. Akbar, who was crowned in the year 1556 due to his father's death, defeated Muhammad Adil Shah and his Prime Minister Hemu (Hemchandra). This defeat of Adil Shah and Hemu marked the end of Afghan power in India and perhaps gave the signal of the beginning of a glorious reign by Emperor Akbar.

On 24 January 1556 Mughal ruler Humayun slipped while climbing down the steps of his library and fell to his death. His son Akbar was only thirteen years old when he ascended the throne. At the time of Akbar's accession to the throne, the Mughal rule was confined to Kabul, Kandhahar, and parts of Punjab and Delhi. Akbar was then campaigning in Punjab with his chief minister Bairam Khan. On February 14, 1556, in a garden at Kalanaur, Akbar was enthroned as emperor. Hemu (Hemchandra) was a military chief of the Afghan King Muhammad Adil Shah who had established himself at Chunar and was seeking to expel the Mughals from India. Taking advantage of Humayun's death, Hemu marched to Agra and Delhi in October and occupied it without difficulty, and became the ruler under the title 'Raja Vikramaditya'.

To counter this, Bairam Khan (Akbar's guardian) marched towards Delhi. On November 5 both the armies met at Panipat. Hemu with a large army including 1,500 war elephants had initial success. There was a pitched battle and Hemu was on a winning spree when a stray arrow struck him in the eye. He fell unconscious. As in many other battles, the loss of the leader caused panic among the troops and turned the tide of the battle. The Mughals won the battle. Shah Quli Khan captured the Hawai elephant with its prize occupant, and took it directly to Akbar. Hemu was brought unconscious before Bairam and Akbar. Among much self-congratulation Akbar then severed the head of unconscious Hemu with his saber.

Some historians claim that Akbar did not kill Hemu himself, but just touched the infidel's head with his sword and his associates finished Hemu off. After the battle Hemu's head was sent to Kabul as a sign of victory to the ladies of Humayun's harem. Hemu's torso was sent to Delhi for exposure on a gibbet. Iskandar Khan chased Hemu's fleeing army and captured 1500 elephants and a large contingent. Hemu's wife escaped from Delhi with the treasure. Pir Mohammad Khan's troops chased her caravan without success. This battle, known as Second Battle of Panipat was an epoch-making event in the history of India as it resulted in re-establishment of the Mughal empire in India.

Secunderabad : Secunderabad is the twin city of Hyderabad, India, and is separated by the man made lake, Husain Sagar, from the capital of Andhra Pradesh. Secunderabad was founded in the 18th century as a British cantonment, and to this date has a large Army presence. Named after Sikandar Jah, the third Nizam of the Asaf Jahi dynasty, Secunderabad had its own municipality and city government, until recently when it was merged with Hyderabad, the district. In common parlance however, Secunderabad is seldom used these days outside the twin cities. Instead Hyderabad is used normally. The population of Secunderabad Cantonment is 204,182 (2001 census}.

Seemantam : This sacrament is performed in the fourth month of pregnancy of women in Kerala (only in the case of first pregnancy). Seemantam is conducted for the protection of the mother at the critical period of gestation. If the child is still born, this has to be prepared during the next pregnancy. Fragrant oil was poured on the mother's head and a line or parting (sumanta) was drawn 3 times through her hair from the forehead upwards with 3 stalks of 'Kusa' grass bound together. Three sacred words called 'Vyathiris' (Bheer, Bhavar, Svar) and the hallowed syllable OM uttered during each operation.

Seetharkundu : Seetharkundu is a small place at Nelliampathy in Palakkad District of Kerala state, south India. it offers a fantastic view of the valley below. The 1000 meters high water falls is one of the major attractions. It is believed that Rama, Lakshmana and Sita of the epic

Ramayana had lived in the place and Sita used to offer worship with the water from a small stream. Seetharkundu got its name from the legend that Sita devi during the vanavasa period with Rama, took a bath here. Far away, the dams at Chulliar and Meenkara and the town of Kollengode can be seen.

Sehra : In Indian and Pakistani Muslim traditions, especially in Uttar Pradesh and Hyderabad (Deccan), there is a social ritual where the sisters of the groom sing a sehra, a poem in praise of the groom and pray to God for his future wedded life. The groom follows this by giving cash to his sisters. There are no specifications for a sehra except that it should rhyme and be of the same meter. Sehras are generally written by individuals praising their brothers, so they are very varied in style and nature. A good sehra appears in the Urdu Film Razia Sultan; however, this particular sehra was sung by males, quite contrary to the current tradition.

Sehwan : Sehwan is located in Sindh province of Pakistan. Sehwan town is of unimpeachable antiquity, Sehwan, some eighty miles north-west of Hyderabad lay on the opposite bank of the Indus. Most historians have accepted the link between Sehwan and the Greek settlement of Siwistan. It was significant enough during the 8th century to be conquered by Muhammad bin Qasim in 711 CE, and two centuries later by Mahmud of Ghazni. An abortive attempt was made by the Mughal emperor Humayun to capture it on his way to Umarkot but it finally fell to his son Akbar. Apart from the remnants of the ruins scattered about its environs, the most famous monument in Sehwan remains the shrine of Hazrat Lal Shahbaz Qalandar.

Sehwan Sharif : Sehwan Sharif is located in Sindh, Pakistan. The city is known for its Muslim patron saint

Hazrat Lal Shahbaz Qalandar who lived here in 13th century CE. The mausoleum

Sei : In Mizoram, Lakher counterpart of the Lushai bawi was Sei. Unlike the Lushais among whom only the chiefs could have bawis, the Lakhen custom allowed anyone to keep one's captive as a Sei. A Sei was sometimes allowed to set up his own house hold. But the obligation was hereditary. A Sei could acquire property of his own, but his master could always take a share of the crops or animals of the sei.

With the British administration prohibiting raids by the chiefs, the custom of tuklut bawi, sal and sei ceased to have new entrants. The custom was of mutual assistance, help and obligation and not of slavery. The bawi was after treated as a part of the family and could be adopted in the family by the saphun (adoption) ceremony. The bawi custom gradually died. The administration liberally allowed freedom of the bawis on usual cash payment. A bawi was allowed to leave at will and the chief only had the remedy to sue for the compensation.

Sekrenyi : In Nagaland, this festival is celebrated in February by the Western Angamis and in December by the Southern Angamis. The festival is to ensure the health and well being of the community during the coming year. It is an occasion of great merry making, enormous quantities of rice-beer, beef and pork are consumed. An interesting feature of the festival is that the men have to prepare a separate hearth and abstain from any sexual relation for the first two days.

Semmangudi Srinivasa Iyer : Dr. Srinivasa Iyer (1908 - October 31, 2003) was one of the great Carnatic vocalists of the twentieth century. He was the youngest recipient of the Sangeetha Kalanidhi awarded by the Music Academy in 1947, has received many awards including

Padma Bhushan and Padma Vibhushan from the government of India. He was affectionately addressed as "Semmangudi Maama" (Semmangudi Uncle) by later generations. He is also considered the "Pitamaha" or the grand sire of modern Carnatic Music.

He was born on July 25, 1908 in Tirukkodikaval, Thanjavur District as the third son of Radhakrishna Iyer and Dharmasamvardhini Ammal. At the age of eight he started learning music from Narayanaswamy Iyer, and underwent musical apprenticeship with Maharajapuram Viswanatha Iyer. In 1926, he performed his first music recital at Kumbakonam. He was known for producing soulful music, highly creative and yet very orthodox, despite a recalcitrant voice. He was instrumental, along with Harikesanallur Muthiah Bhagavathar, for his woek on the krithis of Maharaja Swathi Tirunal.

Semmangudi was widely renowned for his virtuosity as a concert performer. He was famous for the meticulous planning that he put into every concert, including the choice of krithis, raagas and duration. He was also widely acknowledged as a master of improvisation, particularly in the form of niravals. His singing style has been widely followed and his prominent disciples include at least three Sangeetha Kalanidhis, M. S. Subbulakshmi, T. M. Thyagarajan and violinist, Prof. T. N. Krishnan.

Senate of Pakistan : The Senate of Pakistan is the upper House of the bicameral Parliament of Pakistan. The Constitution does not give the President of Pakistan the authority to dissolve the Senate (unlike the National Assembly). If the office of the President of Pakistan becomes vacant, or the President is unable to perform his functions, the Chairman of the Senate acts as President until a President is elected. There are one hundred senatorial seats. There are 18 women Senators; Pakistani Law requires that there be atleast 17 women Senators.

Seraiki : The Seraiki people (also Saraiki people) are an ethnic group from the southern areas of Pakistani Punjab. There is much dispute over whether the Seraiki language is a separate language or a Punjabi dialect. The Seraikis are based mainly in the former Princely state of Bahawalpur, though they live in surrounding areas of Punjab, Sindh, Balochistan and North West Frontier Province. The Serakis maintain that they have a separate language and culture, whilst many Punjabis view Seraiki as merely a dialect of Punjabi.

Seraikistan : Seraikistan is the region of southern Punjab (Pakistan) inhabited by Seraiki speaking people. The Seraiki nationalist movement wish to separate the Seraiki speaking region into a new province of Seraikistan. The Seraiki region is bordered by Punjab (Pakistan), Sindh and Balochistan provinces.

Sethu Samudram : Sethu Samudram is a Tamil name, that translates as Setu Sea. This sea separates Tamil Nadu from Sri Lanka. The sea is composed of the Gulf of Mannar, and the Palk Strait, and a shoal of islands and bays that separate them, Rama's Bridge. Both parts of the name are derived from Sanskrit, setu for bridge, and samudra for sea. The name may also be written as Sethu Samudram and Sethusamudram.

The sea is quite shallow, with a depth of less than 10 meters across most of its extent. Much of its seabed consists of limestone rock. It formed part of a land bridge that joined Sri Lanka to the continent of Asia during the last ice age. It became newsworthy in 2005 with the launch by the government of India of the Sethusamudram Shipping Canal Project.

Sethusamudram Shipping Canal Project : The Sethusamudram Shipping Canal Project proposes linking the

Palk Bay and the Gulf of Mannar between India and Sri Lanka by creating a shipping canal through the shallow sea sometimes called Setu Samudram, and through the island chain of Rama's Bridge. This would provide a continuous navigable sea route around the Indian Peninsula. The project involves digging a 44.9 nautical mile (83 km) long deepwater channel linking the shallow water of the Palk Strait with the Gulf of Mannar. Conceived as early as 1860 by Alfred Dundas Taylor, it recently received approval of the Indian government.

Possibly conceived in 1860 by Commander A. D. Taylor of the Indian Marines, the project has been reviewed many times over the years but no decision was ever made. It was part of the election manifestos of all political parties during elections. The Union Government of India appointed the Sethu Samudram Project Committee in 1955, headed by Dr. A. Ramasamy Mudaliar, which was charged with the duty of examining the desirability of the project. Vaiko , the General Secretary of MDMK, whose continuous efforts made this project come true. He wrote letter to the then Prime Minister Atal Behari Vajpayee when he was jailed under POTA as followup. He has shown great interest on Sathusamudram Project. After evaluating the costs and benefits, this committee found the project feasible and viable. Several reviews of the proposals followed. Finally, the United Progressive Alliance Government of India headed by Prime Minister Manmohan Singh announced the inauguration of the project on June 2, 2005.

Sevagram : Mahatma Gandhi established his Sevagram Ashram in 1933, where he spent 15 years. It is believed that this place had the honour of being the headquarters of the social service programmes that Gandhiji conducted. It gets its name thus. Accommodation is available at Yatri Niwas, MTDC and also has a beautiful resort at Wardha.

Shaan : Shaan is one of the most popular film stars in Pakistan.

He is the son of actress Neelo and the film director Riaz Shahid.

Shabad : Shabad is the term used by Sikhs to refer to a hymn or paragraph or sections of the Holy Text that appears in their several Holy Books. The main holy scripture of the Sikhs is the Sri Guru Granth Sahib also shortened to SGGS. The first Shabad in the SGGS is the Mool Mantar. The text used for the Shabad is in the holy book is Gurmukhi.

Shabana Azmi : The famous and versatile film actress, Shabana Azmi, is one of the icons of Indian Cinema. She was born on September 18th 1950 in Mumbai, Maharashtra. Her mother, Shaukat was a well-known theatre actress, and her father late Kaifi Azmi, a well known Urdu poet and lyricist. After completed her degree in Psychology at St.Xavier's College, Mumbai, she took a Diploma in Acting at the Film and Television Institute in Pune, India in 1972.

She made her film debut as Lakshmi in Shyam Benegals 'Ankur'(1974), for which she received the National Award as Best Actress. Azmi then went on to star in the films of all of India's most prominent art directors like Satyajit Ray, Mrinal Sen, Shyam Benegal and Gautam Ghose. She dominated the art/parallel film scene in the 70's and 80's. At the same time, she appeared in commercial Hindi cinema and gave hits like 'Amar Akbar Anthony', 'Fakira' and in- between films such as the more recent Mrityudand(1997), Godmother(1999) etc. She was one of the few actress in India, who could alternate with Indian Art films, as well as the commercial cinema with her natural and intensive acting. A perfectionist, she would go to great lengths to bring alive her characters on screen, even putting on weight if the character needed it. She reflects every inflection in moods and feelings with her intense portrayal. She has proved her mettle and won rave reviews in theatre also with her performance in 'Tumhari Amrita' which ran to packed audience for five long years.

She was acknowledged for her powerful performances with many awards. She is the winner of five National Awards for Best Actress for the films Ankur (1974), as the betrayed wife in Arth (1983-also received Filmfare award), as the tragic protagonist in Khandhar (1984), as a slum dweller in Paar (1985), and Godmother (1999) and also won international awards for best actress at the Taormina Arte Festival in Italy for Gautam Ghose's 'Patang' (1994), Silver Hugo Award at the 32nd Chicago Film Festival and the Los Angeles Out fest for a controversial role as Radha in Deepa Mehta's 'Fire' (1996). International Award for Best Actress for Gulzar's 'Libaas' in North Korea in 1993.

Shabana Azmi is also a committed social and political activist. She has undertaken campaigns and made public statements over issues close to her heart, particularly social justice such as the rights of women, plight of slum dwellers etc. She is a leading advocate of AIDS awareness in India. She has also addressed students and faculty of several universities in India and abroad, including MIT, Boston, University of Chicago and University of London. For her sincerity and commitment in social activism, Shabana Azmi won the Rajiv Gandhi Award, Yash Bhartiya award from the government of the state of Uttar Pradesh, India and the Padma Shri in 1988 from the Government of India. Shabana was a former member of the Rajya Sabha. Shabana Azmi, married to poetith utmost sincerity. Her niece Tabbu is also an actress in Indian Cinema.

Shabnam : Shabnam was an actress active in the Pakistani film industry during the late 1960s and much of the 1970s. She is considered a romantic heroine by many South Asian movie fans.

Shabnam is actually her film-name. Her real name is Jharna Bashak. Shabnam is married to Robin Ghosh, a musician. Shabnam was originally from East Pakistan, now Bangladesh. After the countries were partitioned, Shabnam settled in Lahore to pursue her movie career. The well-known Indian actress Madhubala once said that she took inspiration from Shabnam. During the conservative era of 1960s and 1970s, her heavy breathing style and mannerism were considered extremely erotic. Fans in the South Asia would often wait in long lines outside theaters to see her.

Shad Nongkrem : Another folk dance of the Khasis, Shad Nongkrem is associated with Ka Pomblang Nongkrem in Meghalaya. Like all other ceremonies of the Meghalayans, it is performed to propitiate the all powerful Goddess Ka Blei Synshar for a rich bounteous harvest and prosperity of the people (subject). There is no fixed date for this festival. It is generally celebrated in November of every year.

The Syiem of Khyrim accompanied by the high priest performs the Pomblang ceremony. He offers oblation to a Lei Shyllong; the god of Shyllong peak by sacrificing a cock. Goats are killed during the ceremony. The Nongkrem dance is associated with the Pomblang Nongkrem. When the ceremony has been performed by the Syiem and the high priest, the Nongkrem dance starts. At drawn-break on that day a maiden dance is held in which virgins from the Syiem house take part and the Syiem Sad shaded by an umbrella, dance with great solemnity.

This is called an opening dance or royal dance which is generally done by the Syiem before the dance starts. When the royal dance is finished, youngsters and damsels of the Khyrim Syiemship enters the field and the *dance of U Khun U Raiot* (subjects) of the Hima Khyrim (Khyrim Syiemship) starts. The dance lasts for three days, the last day or the third day is the biggest of all. Unmarried males and females from four corners of the Khyaim Syiemship take part in the dance.

Another dance among the Khasis is Doregata in which the women try to knock off the turbans of their male partners, using their heads. Another dance that the performer dangles a pomelo or any other fruit on a cord tied to his waist and then whirls it round and round after the initial impetus with a barely perceptible movement of his hips. Some experts can control two separate pomelos in this way. The Garos have traditional dance called *Do Dru-su'a* in which two women dance like doves pecking each other.

Shad Sukmynsiem : The Shad Sukmynsiem (Dance of the Blissful Heart) is popularly known as Shad Weiking. It is so called after the name of the ground where the dance used to be held every year. A thanksgiving festival, Shad Suk Mynesiem is a symbolic offering of salutations to God, homage to their ancestors and proclamation of unity of the Khasi people of Meghalaya. There is no fixed date for this dance. It used to be held during the month of April of each year. This is the most popular dance among the Khasis. It is organised by the Seng Khasi (Khasi Religion). The dances last for three days. Only unmarried men and women are allowed to take part in the dance. Youngsters and damsels from different part of Khasi hills participate in the dance.

The Shad Sukmynsiem welcomes the whole of the Khasi community to take part in the dance. There was no bar for any one to take part in the dance since it is the traditional dance of the Khasis. Christians or Hindus as long as they belong to Khasi community could take part in this dance. Young lads brilliantly clad in colourful silk dhotis, coat and a plumed turban and adorning glittering ornaments look like Rajput Princes. They dance around with a sword or spear in one hand and a plume in the other.

Pretty maidens in magnificent many-splendoured silk-robes and elaborately decked in priceless intricately designed ornaments of gold and silver and wearing a silver crown emerge before use as apsaras from the world beyond. These 'angels' move in an inner circle in two's and three's in tiny steps while the lads form a protective ring around them and flashing their weapons. The embroidery on the girl's apparel and the workmanship of their ornaments, many of them handed down for generations as heirlooms, can made even an aristocratic millionaire envious.

It is difficult to see how the European missionaries could so heartlessly condemn these fine expressions of blissful hearts as 'barbaric'. The dancers dance rhythmatically making regular movements and keeping time with the beat of the drum and pipe (Tanguari). Damsels (unmarried) dressed colourfully in their very originality and making tiny steps in the centre while men folks with swords and sometimes with shields in their hands encircling them.

Shah Abdul Latif Bhittai : Shah Abdul Latif Bhittai (1689-1752), was a great Sufi scholar and saint, and is considered as the greatest poet of the Sindhi language. He settled in the town of Bhit Shah in Sindh, Pakistan. His most famous written work is the Shah Jo Risalo. His shrine is located in Bhit and attracts hundreds of pilgrims every day. He is most famous Sindhi poet and Sufi. He was not just adored for his poetry alone. People from far and near respected and loved this man as a saint, a sufi and a spiritual guide. Not much is known about the early life of this noble son of Sindh from written records. Most of the information that has come down to us has been collected from oral traditions. A renowned Sindhi scholar, educationist, and a foremost writer of plays, dramas and stories, Mirza Kalich Beg, has rendered a yeoman service to Sindhi literature by collecting details about the early life of Shah Bhitai, from the dialogues that he has constantly held with some of the old folks, still living at that time, who knew these facts from their fathers and grandfathers for they had seen Shah Latif in person and had even spoken to him.

He was born sometime around 1689 CE (1102 A.H.) at a small village called Bhainpur near Khatian. Shah Abdul Latif's lineage has been traced back directly to Prophet Mohammad, through Imam Zain-ul-Abideen, son of Imam Hussain, grandson of the Prophet. His ancestors had came from Herat in Central Asia, and settled at Matiari. Shah Abdul Karim 1600 CE, whose mausoleum stands at Bulri, about 40 miles from Hyderabad, a mystic Sufi poet of considerable repute, was his great, great grand father. His verses are extant and his anniversary is still held at Bulri, in the form of an Urs.

In 1742, Shah Abdul Latif decided to settle in Bhit, meaning "The Sandy Mound". Having a great passion for music, one day he ordered the musicians to play music. They played continuously for three days. When they stopped playing from pure exhaustion, they found the poet dead. He died in 1752, and is buried in Bhit. A mausoleum was later constructed there. Ir was built by the ruler of Sindh, Ghulam Shah Kalhoro. His name literally means, 'the servant of the Shah'. He, along with his mother, had adored and revered Shah Latif and were his devoted disciples. The work of the construction of the mausoleum was entrusted to the well-known mason, Idan from Sukkur. The mausoleum, as well as the mosque adjoining it, were later repaired and renovated by another ruler of Sindh, Mir Nasir Khan Talpur. A pair of kettle drums, that are beaten every morning and evening even till today by the fakirs, jogis and sanyasis, who frequent the mausolem, were presented by the Raja of Jesalmeer.

Before his death, fearing that people might ignore his poetry, he destroyed all his writings by throwing them in the Kiran Lake. But at the request of one of his disciples, the sufi poet asked his servant, Mai Naimat, who had memorized most of his verses, to rewrite them. The message was duly recorded and compiled. A copy of the compilation known as "Ganj" was retained at the mausoleum. The original copy disappeared sometime in 1854. It was in 1866, 114 years after the poet's death, that Ernest Trumpp, a German scholar who knew Sindhi as well as many other languages, compiled "Risalo", a complete collection of Shah Abdul Latif's poetry, along with two other Sindhi scholars. Shah Abdul Latif Bhitai is always remembered for his great poetry with love and reverence.

Shah Amanat International Airport : Shah Amanat International Airport serves Bangladesh's southeastern port city of Chittagong. It was formerly known as MA Hannan International Airport, but was renamed on April 2, 2005 by the Government of Bangladesh. The move was controversial since the previous name honored a member of the Awami League, while the new name honors an Islamic saint. Flights from the airport chiefly serve South Asia and the Middle East. Airlines serving Shah Amanat include Biman Bangladesh, GMG Airlines, Phuket Airlines, and Thai Airways.

Shah Azizur Rahman : Shah Azizur Rahman (1925 - 1988) was the prime minister of Bangladesh from 1978 to 1982. During this period he headed the government formed by the Bangladesh National Party, which first came to power in the elections for the second parliament held on 18 February 1978. The party was formed, and the election called, by Ziaur Rahman who had then come to power through a military coup. Rahman continued to be the prime minister after Zia was assassinated in a failed military coup in 1981 and Abdus Sattar became the president. When Sattar was overthrown by the army chief, Hossain Mohammad Ershad, in March 1982, the government led by Rahman was dismissed.

Shah Jahan : Ghiyasuddin Shah Jahan, January 5, 1592 – January 22, 1666) was the ruler of the Mughal Empire in India from 1628 until 1658. He is best known as the builder of the Taj Mahal, a shrine to his Persian second wife, Arjumand Bano Begum, popularly known as Mumtaz Mahal whom he married on May 10, 1612, at the age of 20.

Shah Jahan was born with the name Prince Khurram to Jahangir and the Hindu Rajput Princess Manmati, and was reportedly close to his grandfather Akbar as a child. Khurram raised an army against Jahangir in 1622, but the insurgency failed. He was forgiven and accepted back into the fold but two of his sons, Prince Aurangzeb and Dara Shikoh, were sent to Jahangir's court against the possibility of Prince Khurram revolting again. After Jahangir's death in 1627, Khurram captured power after a fratricidal war against his weaker brother, Shahryar, who was supported by Jahangir's powerful widow Nur Jehan with the help of Abdul Hassan Asaf Khan. It was shortly after this that he took the rule name Shah Jahan, February 4, 1628.

Although his father's rule was generally peaceful, the empire was experiencing challenges by the end of his reign. Shah Jahan reversed this trend by putting down a Muslim rebellion in Ahmednagar, repulsing the Portuguese in the

Bengal, capturing the Rajput kingdoms of Baglana and Bundelkhand to the west, and the kingdoms of Bijapur and Golconda in the Deccan and the northwest beyond the Khyber Pass. Shah Jahan's military campaigns drained the imperial treasury. Under his rule, the state became a huge military machine and the nobles and their contingents multiplied almost fourfold, so did the demands for more revenue from the peasantry. However, his political efforts encouraged the emergence of large centers of commerce and crafts—such as Lahore, Delhi, Agra, and Ahmadabad—linked by roads and waterways to distant places and ports. He moved the capital from Agra to Delhi, the traditional seat of Muslim power.

Under Shah Jahan's rule, Mughal artistic and architectural achievements reached their zenith. Shah Jahan was a prolific builder with a highly refined aesthetic. He built the legendary Taj Mahal in Agra as a tomb for his beloved wife, Mumtaz Mahal. Among his surviving buildings are the Red Fort and Jamia Masjid in Delhi, the Shalimar Gardens of Lahore and buildings at the Lahore Fort. Although the empire's financial expenditures were excessive when resources were shrinking, by the end of Shah Jahan's reign, the empire was again expanding.

In September 1657, Shah Jehan fell ill. The physicians were not hopeful about his recovery. He even made his last will and testament. As soon as the news of his illness reached his four sons, Dara Shikoh, Shuja, Aurangzeb and Murad, they all started making preparations to capture the throne. Aurangzeb who succeeded in his efforts, kept his aged father imprisoned until his death, allowing one of his sisters to look after him. Shah Jehan died in 1666. He was laid to rest beside his beloved wife, Mumtaz Mehal.

Shah Nawaz Bhutto : Shah Nawaz Bhutto was a well known feudal lord and politician hailing from Larkana in

Sindh province of Pakistan. Before the partition of India, he was the Dewan of Junagadh. He was the father of the 1st elected Prime Minister of Pakistan, Zulfikar Ali Bhutto. He was married to Khursheed Begum. Sir Shah Nawaz Bhutto, one of the wealthiest and most influential landowners of Sindh, was a good friend of Governor General (later President) Iskander Mirza. Mirza had been a regular guest for the annual hunt in Larkana, staying at Al-Murtaza (the Bhutto family home). In the winter of 1955-1956, he brought General Ayub Khan along to Larkana for the hunt, and both generals enjoyed the hospitality of the Bhutto family.

Shah Paran : Shah Paran (R) was a renowned Sufi belonging to the Suhrawardiyya and Jalalia sects. It is said that he was the son of a sister of Hazrat Shah Jalal (R) and was born in Yemen. He, with his uncle, took part in the expedition of Sylhet (1303 AD). After the conquest of Sylhet he established his Khanqah at Khadim Nagar in Dakshingarh Pargana, about 7 km away from Sylhet town, and started spiritual ascetic practice there. He played a significant role in propagating Islam and establishing Muslim rule in Sylhet region.

Even now a large number of people daily visit his tomb. On the 4th, 5th and 6th day of Rabi-ul-Awal, the Urs of Hazrat Shah Paran (R) takes place. His grave is located in a high hillock and it is carefully preserved at a place which is built with bricks and surrounded by walls. On the northern side of the grave there is an old tree, the branches and branchlets of which are extended above the entire tomb.

The name of the tree is 'Ashagachh' (a tree of hopes). From a close observation of the leaves of the tree, it appears that the tree has grown out of a mixture of the fig, mango and some other tree. People eat the seeds of the figs devotionally in the hope of getting rid of diseases. Mangoes are also eaten with utmost respect as Tabaruk. There is an ancient mosque by the side of the tomb. The mosque has been modernised in 1989-91. About 1500 devout Muslims in a body can now say their prayers there.

Shahabuddin Ahmed : Shahabuddin Ahmed (b. 1 February 1930) is a former president and Chief Justice of Bangladesh. He served as acting president of Bangladesh in 1990 following the resignation of Hossain Mohammad Ershad in a popular uprising. After the resumption of democracy, he returned to his duties as the Chief Justice. Later, he served as president from 1996 to 2001.

Justice Shahabuddin Ahmed was born in 1930 in village Pamal of Kendua in the greater Mymensingh district. After passing the Matriculation and intermediate examinations he took admission into the Dhaka University in 1948, obtained B.A. (Hons) in Economics in 1951 and M.A. in International Relations in 1952 as a resident student of Fazlul Haq Hall. He entered the Civil Service of Pakistan (CSP) in 1954 through a competitive examination, completed training in the Lahore Civil Service Academy and in the United Kingdom.

Mr. Shahabuddin was transferred to the judicial branch in1960. He worked as Additional District and Session Judge of Dhaka and Barisal, and as District and Sessions Judge of Comilla and Chittagong. He also served as Registrar of the High Court of the then East Pakistan. He was elevated to the Bench of the High Court on 20 January 1972. Acted on deputation at the Labour Appellate Tribunal for two years, 1973 and 1974. He was appointed a Judge of the Appellate Division of the Supreme Court of Bangladesh on 7 February 1980 and was confirmed in this office on 15 April 1981. He reputed to be a strong disciplinarian and hardworking officer all through and his disposal of cases in all branches of law is one of the highest in the country.

As Chief Justice he attended the International Appellate Judges Conference in Washington DC in September 1990. Justice Shahabuddin took charge as Acting President of Bangladesh on 6th December 1990. He resigned on 9 October,'91. He resumed as Chief Justice on 10 October 1991. Chief Justice Mr. Shahabuddin Ahmed retired from service on 1 February 1995. On 23 July 1996 Mr. Justice Shahabuddin Ahmed was elected unopposed as the President of the country. He was sworn-in the office of the President on 9 October 1996.

Shahbaz Qalander : Shahbaz Qalander (1177-1274) CE was a Sufi in the regions of South Asia that now lie in Sindh province of Pakistan. Lal Shahbaz Qalandar was born as Usman Shah in Marwand in Afghanistan in the twelfth century and he is also known as Shaikh Usman Marvandi. His annual Urs [birthday] celebrations are held on the 18 Sha'aban—the eighth month of the Muslim lunar calendar. Usman Shah migrated to Sindh and settled in Sehwan and was buried there.

It is believed that Lal Shabaz Qalandar was so named because of the red robe he wore all his life, and that he turned into a falcon to pick up his friend Shaikh Farid Shakar Ganj from the gallows. The famous Qawwali, Muslim religious songs, 'Lal Meri Pat Rakhiyo...' is in honour of Shahbaz Qalander. This famous mystic often quoted the teachings of Maulana Jalal ad-Din Rumi. A book detailing his life is called "Solomon's Ring" by Gul Hasan.

Shaheed Chandu Stadium : Shaheed Chandu Stadium is a stadium located in Bogra, in northwestern Bangladesh. It became a Test cricket venue on 8 March 2006, when it hosted a test match between Sri Lanka and Bangladesh.

Shaheed Dibash : Shaheed Dibash The 21st day of February (ekushey february) is being officially observed as the Shaheed Dibash (Martyrs' Day) since the emergence of Bangladesh. On this day in 1952, students and youths, rose in protest against the imposition of Urdu by the then government as the lone state language of Pakistan. This was viewed by the Bangali people as a conspiracy against their culture. When the students brought out a procession on the day in violation of official prohibitory order, the police fired on the demonstrators killing a number of students and members of the public. abul barkat, abdus salam, abdul jabbar, rafiq uddin ahmed and a number of unknown others lost their lives. The subsequent mass upsurge was so tumultuous that the Pakistan government had to yield to it and recognise Bangla as one of the state languages of Pakistan. This event was the first significant victory of the Bangalis against attempts of cultural subversion by the Pakistani ruling clique. Since then, the occasion has inspired the Bangalis in their struggle for autonomy, and later independence. The day has also been accorded recognition by the UNESCO as the international mother language day in 1999, and the day is being observed accordingly throughout the world since 2000 AD.

Shaheed Minar : The Shaheed Minar is a national monument in Dhaka, Bangladesh, established to commemorate the martyrs of the Language Movement of 1952. On February 21, 1952, dozens of students and political activists were killed when the Pakistani police force opened fire on Bengali protesters who were demanding equal status to their native tongue, Bangla. The massacre occurred near Dhaka Medical College and Ramna Park in Dhaka. A makeshift monument was erected the same night by students of University of Dhaka and other educational institutions, but soon demolished by the Pakistani police force. The Language Movement gained momentum and after a long struggle, Bangla was given equal status as Urdu. To commemorate the martyrs, the Shaheed Minar was designed and built by Hamidur Rahman, a Bangladeshi sculptor.

The monument stood in its solemn glory until the Bangladesh Liberation War in 1971, when it was demolished completely during Operation Searchlight, a genocide carried out by the Pakistani Army resulting in an estimated 50,000 civilian deaths. After Bangladesh gained independence, it was rebuilt. Today, the Shaheed Minar is the centre of cultural activities in Dhaka. Every year, the Language Movement is remembered with due respect at the monument.

Shaheen Air International : Shaheen Air International is an airline based in Karachi, Sindh, Pakistan. It operates scheduled services between the main cities of Pakistan and to the Gulf. Its main base is Quaid-e-Azam International Airport (KHI), Karachi, with a hub at Islamabad International Airport (ISB), Islamabad

Shahenshah-e-Jazbaat : Shahenshah-e-Jazbaat, i.e. The King of Emotions, Mohammad Ali (1928 – March 19, 2006), popularly known as Ali bhai, started his career at Radio Pakistan Karachi in the early 1960s. In 1968, he married the renowned actress Zeba.

He was known in the film circle for his command as a passionate actor and his ease in dramatic situations as well. He is the winner of 7 Nigar Awards for Best Actor one for Best Supporting Actor, and one special award for the film Dooriyaan.

Shahi Dynasty : The Shahi dynasty ruled portions of eastern Afghanistan, northern Pakistan, and northwestern India from the mid-seventh century to the early eleventh century. The Hindu Shahi were the last Hindu dynasty to rule Afghanistan and the western Punjab before the

Muslim conquest of the tenth and eleventh centuries. They are usually described as descendants of the Indo-Sassanians and Indo-Hephthalites. Archeological sites of the period, including a major Hindu Shahi temple north of Kabul and a chapel in Ghazni, contain both Buddhist and Hindu statuary, suggesting that there was a close interaction between the two religions.

The Hindu Shahis owe their origins to Lalliya, a Brahmin minister in the service of Kabul's Buddhist kings. Lalliya took control of the state, which at its height extended from the Hindu Kush to the Himalaya, including Kabul and the Khyber Pass region of western Afghanistan, the Punjab region of northern India and Pakistan, and Himachal Pradesh in the Himalayas. Their kingdom was bounded on the north by the Hindu kingdom of Kashmir, on the east by Rajput kingdoms, on the south by the Muslim kingdom of Sind, and on the west by the Abbasid Caliphate. In 870, Kabul was captured by the Muslims, and the Shahi capital shifted east to Hund or Ohind, near Attock in the Punjab. The initial Hindu Shahi dynasty was Brahmin but was later assumed from Bhim Dev by the Janjua Raja Jayapala, son of Asatapala. This occurred at some point in the late 10th century before the campaigns of Sabuktigin began. In the 980's, Sabuktigin, the Turkic ruler of Ghazni, defeated the Shahis and captured the Khyber Pass region as far as the Indus River. His son and successor, Mahmud of Ghazni, waged several campaigns against the Shahi, capturing most of the kingdom in 1008. The Shahi retained a small territory in the eastern Punjab until 1013, when it too was captured by Mahmud.

Shahi Mohalla : Shahi Mohalla, also known as Hira Mandi (literally "Diamond Market"), is today known for being the red-light district of Lahore, Pakistan. It was originally the center of the city's tawaif culture in the Mughal era. It is located in the northwest corner of the

Walled City of Lahore, next to Roshnai Gate, Badshahi Masjid, Lahore Fort, and Hazuri Bagh.

Shahid Afridi : Sahibzada Mohammad Shahid Khan Afridi (born March 1, 1980 in Mardan to Pashtun parents of the Afridi tribe) popularly known as Shahid Afridi is a Pakistani cricketer who has represented Pakistan since 1996 in international cricket.

He made his ODI debut on October 2, 1996 against Kenya at Nairobi and his Test debut on October 22, 1998 against Australia at Karachi. He has scored over 4,500 ODI runs at a strike rate of more than 107 runs per 100 balls, and has taken over 160 ODI wickets.

Shahidul Alam : Shahidul Alam was born in 1955 in Dhaka, Bangladesh. Studied and taught chemistry in London where he obtained a PhD from London University. Started photography in 1980 while hitch hiking through the USA and Canada. Nominated the best photographer of the year by the London Arts Council in 1983. He Became the president of the Bangladesh Photographic Society in 1989. Alam set up Drik Picture Library, Bangladesh Photographic Institute and Pathshala and South Asian Institute of Photography. He is also a director of Chobi Mela, the festival of photography in Asia.

Dr. Alam had been jury member of numerous international photographic competitions including World Press Photo where he has been a judge on four occasions. He was the first Asian person to chair the international jury in World Press Photo history. He was awarded the Andrea Frank Foundation Award and the Howard Chapnick Award in 1998. He has also been awarded the Honorary Fellowships of the Bangladesh Photographic Society and later, the Royal Photographic Society in 2001, for his contribution to photography. He is on the advisory board for the Eugene Smith Memorial Fund and the National Geographic Society.

Shahidullah Kaiser : Shahidullah Kaiser (1927-1971) was a Bangladeshi novelist and writer. He was born on 16 February 1927 in the Mazupur village in what is now the Feni District, Bangladesh. Kaisar was active in politics and cultural movements from his student days. Following the formation of Pakistan in 1947, he became a member of the provincial Communist Party of East Pakistan. He started working as a journalist in 1949 with the Ittefaq in Dhaka. In 1952, he participated actively in the Language Movement. For his political role in the movement for protection of Bengali language, Kaiser was arrested on 3 June 1952. He was later jailed for three and a half years. Right after his release in 1955, he was again arrested and jailed on a political crackdown on activists. A few years later he was released. In 1958, Kaiser joined as an associate editor of the Daily Sangbad—a Bengali language daily—where he worked for the rest of his life. When the Military coup of 1958 put Ayub Khan in power, and martial law was proclaimed, Kaiser was arrested again on 14 October 1958 and remained in jail for four years till his release in September 1962.

Shahjalal University of Science and Technology (SUST) : Shahjalal University of Science and Technology, commonly known with its initials SUST, is a state supported technical university located in Sylhet, Bangladesh. This is the first science and technology in Bangladesh. SUST was established in 1987. The campus is at around five kilometers distance from the town heart. The place is known as Kumargaon. The Sunamganj highway passes by the university. The local BDR sector headquarter is just beside the university boundary.

Shahmukhi : Shahmukhi is a script used to record the Punjabi language. It is based on the Nasta'liq style of the

Persian script and has traditionally been used by the Punjabi Muslims of India and Pakistan. The Gurmukhi script is also used to write Punjabi. The text is written in the right to left direction and from right page to left page.

Shahriar Nafees Ahmed : Shahriar Nafees Ahmed (born January 25, 1986 in Dhaka) is a Bangladeshi Cricketer. Nafees, a left-handed opening batsman, first played in the national team in Bangladesh's maiden English Tour (2005).

Shahryar Rashed : Shahryar Rashed (1948–1998) was a Pakistani English language poet. He was the son of the 'father of modern Urdu poetry,' Noon Meem Rashed. Rashed attended Aitchison College, Lahore; Karachi Grammar School; and the United Nations International School in New York. After attending Drew University, Shahryar returned to Pakistan to complete his masters in English from Punjab University. He joined the Ministry of Foreign Affairs in 1971. His diplomatic postings took him to Europe, West Africa, Tokyo and Bombay. At the time of his death in 1998, he was ambassador to Uzbekistan

Shaikh Alaul Haq : Shaikh Alaul Haqa saint of pandua and a disciple of Shaikh akhi sirajuddin usman. His father, Umar bin Asad Khalidi, claimed his descent from the famous Arab general Khalid bin Walid, and was an inhabitant of Lahore. After the establishment of Muslim rule in Bengal he settled at Pandua where his son Alaul Haq was born. The boy, given proper education, grew up into a learned scholar.

Shaikh Ayaz : Shaikh Ayaz was one of the major Sindhi poets of Pakistan. He is the second best Sindhi poet after Shah Abdul Latif Bhittai. By profession he was a lawer but he also served as the Vice Chancellor of University of Sindh. The people of Sindh province, in Pakistan, admire his poetry greatly. In Sindhi poetry he is considered like Pablo Neruda to the Latin America. His poetry brought new trends in Sindhi literature. His poetry has high aesthetic value. He is the author of more than fifty books.

Shaivism : Shaivism is a branch of Hinduism that worships Siva as the Supreme God. Followers of Saivism are called Saivas or Saivites. Saivism is a form of nondual spiritual practice and philosophy originating in India. Saivites believe that the entire creation is both an expression of conscious divinity and is non-different from that divinity which they call "Siva". Because he is simultaneously the created and the creator, Siva is both immanent and transcendent. This concept contrasts with many semitic religious traditions in which God is seen as fundamentally different from the creation and transcendent, or "higher" than the creation. As in all Hindu denominations, Saivism acknowledges the existence of many other deities. These deities are expressions of the Supreme One. This type of spiritual view is called Monistic Theism: the cosmos is a "monad" or single consciousness that expresses itself dualistically, but is fundamentally one.

Saivism is a very deep, devotional and mystical denomination of Hinduism. As a very broad religion, Saivism encompasses philosophical systems, devotional rituals, legends, mysticism and varied yogic practices. It contains monistic, dualistic and ultimately aetheistic traditions. Saivites believe God transcends form, and devotees often worship Siva in the form of a lingam, symbolizing all universe. God Siva is also revered in Saivism as the anthropomorphic manifestation of Siva Nataraja.

Shaji N. Karun : A graduate in cinematography from the FTII, Pune, Shaji N. Karun started working with notable directors like G Aravindan, K G George and M.T.Vasudevan Nair as a cinematographer. His camerawork, especially the films of Aravindan from Kanchana Seeta to Chidambaram, for some defines the look of Kerala's New Wave Cinema.

Shaji made his directorial debut with Piravi ("The Birth",1988), which won him the prestigious 'Camera-d'Or' at the Cannes Film Festival. While Piravi was about the grief of a father who loses his son, Shaji's second film, Swam (1994) continued with the theme of grief. Swaham was selected to the competition section of Cannes Film Festival. *Vaanaprastham* ("The Final Dance", 1999) dealt with the identity crisis faced by actor. Mohanlal played the lead role in this critically acclaimed film.

Shakidor : The Shakidor dam is located near Pasni, in the Balochistan province of south west Pakistan, 1,900 km (1,180 miles) from Islamabad and has a length of about 148 meters (485 feet). It was built in 2003 to provide irrigation water to the nearby farms. On February 10, 2005, it burst under the pressure of a weeks' worth of rain, killing at least 70 villagers and dragging their bodies to the Arabian Sea. The Pakistani military was sent into emergency Search and Rescue operations, saving 1,200 people but still having to account for over 400 missing.

Shakti Peethas : The Shakti Peethas are places of worship consecrated to the Goddess 'Shakti', the female principal of Hinduism and the main deity of the Shakta sect. This Goddess is often associated both with Gowri / Parvati, the Goddess of marital felicity and longevity, and with the virgin Goddess Durga, Goddess of strength and valour.

Shaktism : Shaktism is a denomination of Hinduism that worships Shakti, or Devi Mata — the Hindu name for the Great Divine Mother — in all of her forms whilst not rejecting the importance of masculine and neuter divinity (which are however deemed to be inactive in the absence of the Shakti). In pure Shaktism, the Great Goddess, or Devi, is worshiped as nothing less than the highest divinity, Supreme Brahman Itself, the "one without a second," with all other forms of Divinity, female or male, considered to be merely her diverse manifestations.

Shaktism as we know it today developed between the 4th and the 7th centuries CE in India. It was during this development that the many religious texts, known as the Tantras, were written. In a certain sense, one could consider oneself a Shakta (a devotee of Shakti), a Shaiva (a devotee of Shiva), and a Vaishnava (a devotee of Vishnu) all at the same time. This form of Hinduism is strongly associated with Vedanta, Samkhya and Tantra Hindu philosophies and is ultimately monist, though there is a rich tradition of Bhakti yoga associated with it. The feminine energy (Shakti) is considered to be the motive force behind all action and existence in the phenomenal cosmos in Hinduism. The cosmos itself is Brahman, the concept of the unchanging, infinite, immanent and transcendent reality that is the Divine Ground of all being, the "world soul". Masculine potentiality is actualized by feminine dynamism, embodied in multitudinous goddesses who are ultimately reconciled in one.

Shakuntala Devi : Shakuntala Devi is generally known as a 'Human Computer' because of her extraordinary talents in solving complex mathematical problems without any mechanical aid. She also found her place in the Guinness book of records as a result of her extraordinary talents. Nowadays, apart from solving mathematical problems, she is utilising her amazing talent in the field of astrology.

She was born in 1939 in Bangalore, Karnataka. Manifested with an extraordinary love for numbers at the age of 3, she became an expert in complex mental arithmetic at the age of five. On 18 June 1980, Shakuntala Devi gave the product of two, thirteen digit figures after multiplying them within 28 seconds. Many countries have invited Shakuntala Devi to demonstrate her extraordinary talent. Today, she is acclaimed as an accomplished mathematician.

Shalimar Gardens : The Shalimar Gardens were built by the Mughal emperor Shah Jahan in Lahore, Pakistan. Construction began in 1641 A.D. (1051 A.H.) and was completed the following year. The project management was carried out under the superintendence of Khalilullah Khan, a noble of Shah Jahan's court, in cooperation with Ali Mardan Khan and Mulla Alaul Maulk Tuni.

The Shalimar Gardens are laid out in the form of an oblong parallelogram, surrounded by a high brick wall, which is famous for its intricate fretwork. The Gardens measure 658 meters north to south and 258 meters east to west. The Gardens have been laid out from south to north in three descending terraces, which are elevated by 4-5 metres (13-15 feet) above one another.

Shalimar Gardens : The Shalimar Gardens, sometimes written Shalamar Gardens, were built by the Mughal emperor Shah Jahan in Lahore, Pakistan. Construction began in 1641 A.D. and was completed the following year. The project management was carried out under the superintendence of Khalilullah Khan, a noble of Shah Jahan's court, in cooperation with Ali Mardan Khan and Mulla Alaul Maulk Tuni.

Shams-ud-Din Iltutmish : Shams-ud-Din Iltutmish, or Altamash, was the third Sultan of Delhi, and the only other significant ruler, besides the founder Qutb ud din Aibak, of the Slave Dynasty. After the establishment of the Delhi Sultanate, Multan became its western frontier. In the beginning it was governed by Nasir-ud-Din Qabacha, then captured by Jaial-al-Din Manakabarni and finally annexed by Shams-ud-Din Iltutmish. Iltutmish was the first king to appoint a woman as his official successor named Razia Sultan. He completed the famous Qutub Minar in Delhi, started by the founder of the dynasty, Qutb ud din Aibak.

Shamsul Hoque Chowdhury: Shamsul Hoque Chowdhury (born July 23, 1957 in Chittagong) is the Secretary General of Chittagong Abahani Limited and Managing Director of Richie Group of Companies. He is one of the renowned sports organiser,businessman & politician.

Shamsur Rahman : Shamsur Rahman is a Bangladeshi poet. Rahman has more than sixty books of poetry to his credit, and there is little dispute that he is the greatest living poet in Bangladesh. Shamsur Rahman was born in Dhaka. Fourth of thirteen children, he studied at Pogos School and later at Dhaka College. Rahman started writing poetry after graduating from Dhaka College at the age of eighteen. Shamsur Rahman studied English literature from Dhaka University. He had a long career as a journalist and was the Editor of a national daily, Dainik Bangla.

Shan and Shabu Dances : These are two popular dances of the Lahaul valley people and are danced at the Buddhist Gompas in the memory of the Buddha. Shan means a song of prayer for the Buddha. Dances danced to these songs are known as Shan dances. It is a tribal dance which is performed at the completion of the harvesting of crops. The instrument played in this are drums, *shehnai* and a stringed instrument like a violin. A similar dance known as Shabbo is performed at festivals. It depicts the feelings and beliefs of the people in this area. These dances are linked to the local religious festivals.

Shanti Swaroop Bhatnagar : Dr. Shanti Swaroop Bhatnagar is known as 'The Father of Research

Laboratories'. He is remembered for having established various chemical laboratories in the country. He was born in Bera, Punjab. After completing his M.Sc in India he went to England on a fellowship. On his return he served as a professor in Benaras Hindu University. He used to spent all his spare time in his laboratory doing research.

He was awarded the title 'Sir' by the British in recognition of his service to Science, in 1941. As Nehru was much in favour of scientific development after Independence, Council of Scientific and Industrial Research was set up under the chairmanship of Dr. Bhatnagar. Later, he was awarded 'Padma Bhushan'. He became the first director-general of the Council of Scientific and Industrial Research (CSIR) in 1940. After his death, CSIR established a Bhatnagar Memorial award for eminent scientists in his honour.

Shandur Top : Shandur Top is a high mountain pass that connects Chitral to Gilgit. Shandur Top is 12,200 feet high. However, the top is flat, a plateau. For this reason, it is safe to cross throughout the year. This contrasts with Lowari Top which is only 10,230 feet high but is very dangerous because of avalanche.

Shangla : Shangla is a district in the North-West Frontier Province of Pakistan that contains the town of Alipuri the district headquarters and tehsil Puran. Shangla has the lowest Human Development Index in the province. Shangla, previously a sub-division of Swat district, was upgraded to the status of a district on July, 1, 1995 by the then Chief Minister Aftab Khan Sherpao.

Shankaracharya Temple : Shankaracharya Temple is situated at a height of 2611 metres above sea level on a hill near Dal Lake in Kashmir. There is a Shivling in this temple.Thousands of visitors and piligrims go by bridle path or by road to visit this holy shrine.

Dr. Shankar Dayal Sharma (1918-1999) : Dr. Sharma received his education at St. John's College, Agra, Allahabad University, Lucknow University, Fitzwilliam College, Cambridge University, Lincoln's Inn and Harvard Law School. He took his M.A. Degrees in English Literature, Hindi and Sanskrit standing first in the University. He obtained his LL.M. from Lucknow University once again standing first in the University. He obtained his Ph.D. in Law at Cambridge. Dr. Sharma was awarded the Chakravarti Gold Medal for Social Service by Lucknow University.

Dr. Sharma taught Law at Lucknow University and at Cambridge University. While at Cambridge, Dr. Sharma was Treasurer of the Tagore Society and the Cambridge Majlis. Called to the Bar from Lincoln's Inn, he was later a Fellow at Harvard Law School. He has been elected Honorary Bencher and Master of Lincoln's Inn and Honorary Fellow, Fitzwilliam College, Cambridge. The University of Cambridge has honoured him with degree of Doctor of Law (Honoris Causa).

Dr. Sharma started his legal practice in 1940 in Lucknow. Dr. Sharma participated in the historic Quit India Movement during the national struggle for freedom, and in the merger Movement in Bhopal, and underwent imprisonments.

Dr. Sharma was Chief Minister of the erstwhile Bhopal State (1952-1956), Cabinet Minister, Government of Madhya Pradesh, holding the portfolios of Education, Law, Public Works, Industry and Commerce, National Resources and Separate Revenue (1956-1967) and was thereafter Union Minister for Communications (1974-1977).

Dr. Sharma was Vice-President of India and Chairman of the Council of States (Rajya Sabha) from September 3, 1987 till he assumed office of the President of India in

1992. Earlier he has been the Governor of three States: Andhra Pradesh, Punjab and Maharashtra.

Dr. Sharma was the President of the Indian National Congress in 1972-1974. Dr. Sharma was Member, Bhopal Legislative Assembly (1952-1956); Madhya Pradesh Legislative Assembly (1956-1971); Fifth Lok Sabha (1971-1977) and Seventh Lok Sabha (1980-1984). His participation in matters concerning Parliament was resumed when he assumed office as Vice-President of India and ex-officio Chairman of the Council of State (Rajya Sabha), and continues in his office as President of India.

Dr. Sharma led several official delegations to International Conferences including a Parliamentary Delegation to the Inter-Parliamentary Union Conference at Oslo in 1980; a Special Delegation of veteran freedom fighters to Moscow in August, 1987 for the celebrations of the 40th Anniversary of India's Independence during the Festival of India in USSR, also led a Special Delegation of veteran freedom fighters to Jalalabad (Afghanistan) to pay homage to Khan Abdul Ghaffar Khan in 1988.

The title of 'Rashtra Ratnam' (Jewel of the Nation) has been conferred upon Dr. Sharma by His Holiness the Shankaracharya of Sringeri. The title of "Dharmaratnakara' has been conferred on him by the Pontiff of Shravanbelagola. The International Bar Association has presented to Dr. Sharma the Living Legends of Law Award of Recognition for his outstanding contribution to the legal profession internationally and for commitment to the Rule of Law.

Shankha Ghosh : Shankha Ghosh (1932-) is an Bengali Indian poet and critic. Ghosh was born on February 6, 1932 at Chandpur of what is now Bangladesh. Shankha Ghosh is regarded a leading authority on Rabindranath in addition to being one of the most prolific writers in Bangla.

Shanti Bahini : Shanti Bahini is the name of the military wing of Jana Shanghati shamiti in Chittagong Hill Tracts, Bangladesh. It has now abandoned militancy and its members have returned to normal life following the peace treaty signed by the government and the Shamiti in 1999.

Sharada Script : The Sharada script is an abugida writing system of the Brahmic family of scripts, developed from ca. the 8th century. It is closely related to and predates Devanagari. Originally more widespread, its use became later restricted to Kashmir, and it is now rarely used at all. The name sharada means "autumnal". The Sharada script is also known as Sarada, Sarda, and Sharda.

Sharat Chandra Chattopadhyay : Sharat Chandra Chattopadhyay, also known as Sharat Chandra Chatterjee (15 September 1876 - 16 January 1938) was a popular Bengali novelist of early 20th century India.

He was born at Devanandapur, Hooghly, India and received his education in the city of Bhagalpur. His work represented rural Bengali society and he often wrote against social superstitions, malpractice and oppression. He died in Kolkata of liver cancer in 1938.

Sharavati : Sharavati is a river flowing through Karnataka state, India. It originates from the Western Ghats and flows for about 95 km before reaching the Arabian Sea at Honavar. The power projects Mahatma Gandhi Hydroelectric Power Station and the Sharavati Valley Project, are built on this river. The Sharavathi river basin in rich in biodiversity. In a survey conducted in the basin, 23 amphibians belonging to the families of Bufonidae, Ichthyophiidae, Microhylidae, Ranidae and Rhacophoridae were recorded. Out of these 23 amphibians, 15 species are endemic to the Western Ghats.

Sharbat : Sharbat is a popular Indian "juice" that is prepared from fruits or flower petals. It is sweet and served chilled. It can be in concentrate form and eaten with a spoon or mixed with water to create the drink. It was popularised by the Mughal rulers one of whom sent for frequent loads of ice from the Himalayas to get a cool refreshing drink.

Shardha Ram Phillauri : Shardha Ram Phillauri is almost unknown, although his composition Jai Jagdish Hare is recited everyday by millions of Hindus throughout India and everywhere in the world. He is also regarded to be the first novelist of the Hindi language. having written Bhagyavati, published in 1888. Pandit Shardha Ram Phillauri was born in a Brahmin family at Phillaur in 1837. He was a dedicated scholar and proponent of traditional Hinduism Sanatana dharma. He studied Hindi, Sanskrit, Persian, astrology and music. He died in 1881 at Lahore.

Shari-Goyain River : Shari-Goyain river is one of the trans-boundary rivers of Bangladesh, originated from the hilly areas of the Meghalaya State of India. The Shari-Goyain enters Bangladesh through northern part of Jaintiapur upazila in Sylhet district. Flowing southwestward of Sylhet district through Jaintiapur, Gowainghat, Sylhet Sadar and Chhatak upazilas, the river meets the Surma near Chhatak Bazar. The river receives flow from the Goyain river at Gowainghat upazila. The Shari-Goyain is a flashy hill river and it transports a huge amount of Sediments from the upstream. The average width of the river is about 100 metres. Sylhet, Chhatak are important places on the banks of the river. The Chhatak Cement Factory is located on the bank of the river. The river also transports a lot of Boulders and coarse sand from its upstream. Hundreds of labourers are engaged in collecting boulders daily and their livelihood thus depends on the Shari-Goyain river.

Sharmin Murder Case : The Sharmin murder case is one of the most notorious criminal cases in the history of Bangladesh. Munir Hussain, a wealthy industrialist, killed his wife Sharmin Rima on April 9, 1989 as the culmination of a long-running affair with his mistress Hosne Ara Khuku. Both Munir and Sharmin came from prominent families — Munir was the son of Dr. Meherunnessa, a renowned physician, while Sharmin was the daughter of an intellectual who had been martyred in the 1971 war of independence.

The murder investigation and the subsequent trial received blanket coverage in the press. Every new revelation was greeted with dramatic headlines, and the details of the case kept the entire nation gripped for months. Indeed, it may be argued that the Sharmin murder case was the most sensational criminal trial in contemporary Bangladeshi history.

The trial concluded on 21st May, 1990. Munir and Khuku were both found guilty, and both were condemned to death. Two years later, in July 1992, an appellate court overturned Khuku's sentence and acquitted her of all charges. Munir's death sentence was upheld in the face of successive legal appeals. On 3rd and mercy petitions. He was hanged on either July 3, 1993 or July 27, 1993.

Shashanka : Shashanka is often attributed with creating the first unified political entity in Bengal. He reigned in 7th century A.D., and some historians place his rule approximately between 600 AD and 625 AD. He is the contemporary of Harshavardana.

Shashi Tharoor : Shri Shashi Tharoor, is a well-known Indian English writer, scholar and international civil servant. He was born in London in 1956 to father, a newspaper executive and mother a housewife, with their roots in Palakkad, a town in Kerala, India.

Tharoor mostly grew up in India did his schooling and under graduation in cities such as Bombay, Calcutta and Delhi. He completed his honors degree in History from the prestigious St. Stephen's College in Delhi and won a scholarship to Tufts University in Boston. As a student he took part in debates, quiz contests and also tried his hand in theatre. In the mid 1970's, he went to the United States and acquired two master's degrees and a Ph.D. in Diplomacy from the Fletcher School of Law & Diplomacy at Tufts University, all by the age of twenty-two.

Tharoor joined the United Nations in May 1978 in the office of the U.N. High Commissioner for Refugees (UNHCR) in Geneva and has been with the organisation since then. He became the head of UNHCR Singapore office (1981-1984) at the peak of the Vietnamese "boat people" crisis. Then he served as Special Assistant to the Under-Secretary-General for Peacekeeping Operations from 1989 to1996 at UN headquarters in New York, towards the end of the term from 1991 to 1996, he led the team responsible for peacekeeping operations in the former Yugoslavia. He served as the Executive Assistant to UN Secretary General Kofi Annan (1997-1998) and as the Director of Communications and Special projects in the office of the Secretary-General from 1998 to 2001. In January 2001, he was appointed as interim head of the Department of Public Information (DPI) by Kofi Annan, and after a year and a half was confirmed as the Under-Secretary-General for Communications and Public Information of the United Nations. In this capacity, he is responsible for the communication strategy, enhancing the image and effectiveness of the organisation. In 2003, the Secretary-General appointed him United Nations Coordinator for Multilingualism.

As a journalist, Tharoor has written many articles, short stories, literary reviews and commentaries in such publications as the New York Times, the Washington Post, the International Herald Tribune, the Times of India, the Indian Express, and Foreign Affairs. As a writer, he is very much an Indian expatriate. Shashi Tharoor has explored the diversity of culture in his native India. By exploring the themes of India's past and its relevance to the future, he has produced both works of fiction and nonfiction. He is the winner of several journalism and literary awards, including Commonwealth Writers' prize. In 1998, the Association of Indians in America (AIA) and the Network of Indian Professionals (NetIP) awarded him the Excelsior Award for Excellence in Literature. He was named by the World Economic forum in Davos as a Global Leader of Tomorrow. He received the honorary degree of Doctor of Letters in International Affairs from the University of Puget Sound in May 2000.

Mr. Tharoor is also the author of several books, including 'Reasons of State' (1982), a scholarly study of Indian foreign policy; 'The Great Indian Novel (1989)', a modern ironic adaptation of the 2000-year-old Indian epic 'Mahabharata' which is narrated from a 20th century viewpoint; 'The Five-Dollar Smile & Other Stories' (1990); a second novel, 'Show Business' (1992) filmed in 1994 under the title 'Bollywood' which is a satire on the Indian film industry, which received a front-page accolade from The New York Times Book Review; 'India: From Midnight to the Millennium' (1997), published on the 50th anniversary of India's independence; 'Riot. A Love Story'(2001) which is about a married American government official who have a secret love affair and 'Nehru, the Invention of India'. He has also published a collection of short stories. On the personal front, he has separated from his journalist wife Tilottama who lives with their twin sons, Ishaan and Kanishk. Though Shashi Tharoor has been out of India since he was a teenager, he retains a strong attachment to his Indian roots. This versatile personality now lives in

New York, balancing his career at the UN as well as his life as an author with equal brilliance and ease.

Shaukat Aziz : Shaukat Aziz, born March 6, 1949 in Karachi, Pakistan is the current Finance Minister and Prime Minister of Pakistan.

Shaukat Aziz is the son of Aziz Ahmed the former minister and senior bureaucrat of Pakistan. He became Finance Minister in November 1999 and was nominated for the position of Prime Minister after the resignation of Zafarullah Khan Jamali on June 6, 2004. He became Prime Minister on August 28, 2004.

Shaunaka : Shaunaka (a patronym of Shunaka "little dog", the name of a Rishi) is the name applied to teachers, and to a Shakha of the Atharvaveda. He is claimed as the teacher of Katyayana and especially of Ashvalayana, and is said to have united the Bashkala and Shakala Shakhas of the Rigveda. In legend, he is sometimes identified with Gritsamada, a Vedic Rishi. According to the Vishnu Purana, Shaunaka was the son of Gritsamada, and invented the system of the four Hindu castes.

Shaurya Chakra : Shaurya Chakra is an Indian military decoration awarded for valor, courageous action or self-sacrifice away from the battlefield. It may be awarded to civilians as well as military personnel, sometimes posthumously. It is the peacetime equivalent of the Vir Chakra. It is third in order of precedence of peacetime gallantry awards and comes after Ashoka Chakra and Kirti Chakra. Before 1967, the award was known as the Ashoka Chakra, Class III.

Shawkat Osman : Shawkat Osman (1917-1998) (also Shaukat Osman) was a Bangladeshi novelist and short story writer. He was born in 1917 in the district of Hughli, West Bengal. Born what was then West Bengal, Shawkat

Osman came to Bangladesh (at that time East Pakistan) after the partition of India in 1947. He died in Dhaka in 1987.

Shayama Shastri : Shayama Shastri is among the most renowned composers of Carnatic music; indeed, he was the senior-most of the Trinity of Carnatic music, along with Tyagaraja and Muthuswamy Dikshitar. He was born Venkatakrishna, in Tiruvarur on April 26, 1762, into the scholarly and priestly Tamil Brahmin family of Viswanatha Iyer; a family not particularly interested in music. Though Shyama Shastri attained scholarship in Telugu and Sanskrit at a young age, he got no further than the elementary stages in music education, in spite of his melodious voice. When he was eighteen years old, his family moved to Tanjore.

Over the years, Shyama Shastri became a well-known and respected musician, scholar and a composer. He was quite admired and respected by Tyagaraja and it appears that the two of them often held scholarly and lengthy discussions on their latest compositions. Shyama Shastri, like his father was the archaka (priest) in the Bangaru Kamakshi Temple in Tanjore.

Shyama Shastri, like Tyagaraja and Dikshitar, was well-versed in astrology. Like his great contemporaries, he too correctly predicted the time of his passing. He passed away on February 6, 1827, six days after, his devoted wife passed away. Although he did not compose as many kritis as his two prolific contemporaries, Shyama Shastri's compositions are equally well known. It is said that he has composed about three hundred pieces in all. He did not have too many disciples to propagate his compositions, nor was the printing press an easy convenience during his time! More importantly, the scholarly nature of his compositions was not appealing to the layperson; they needed to be studied to be savoured.

Shaykh Abdur Rahman: Shaykh Abdur Rahman, also known as Abdur Rahman Shaykh, is the spiritual leader and the administrative head of the banned terrorist organisation Jagrata Muslim Janata Bangladesh (English: Awakened Muslim Masses of Bangladesh). Rahman was educated in Islamic fiqh and law at Saudi Arabia. After being highly critical of the Jamaat-e-Islami Bangladesh for what he deemed as its patronisation of secularism and sacrilege of Islamic values and principles, he soon formed the JMJB, taking initiatives to form an all-Islamic state based upon only the Qur'an and the Sunnah, similar to the ideals espoused by the radicalist Taliban movement of Afghanistan. However, the group soon gained notoreity because of its radical fundamentalist activities, including murder and torture of opponents. On August 17, 2005, this group claimed responsibility for more than 500 bombings across Bangladesh. The Government of Bangladesh banned the organisation, and declared awards for the capture of Rahman. In late 2005, Rahman has been blamed for masterminding several more bomb attacks, including the first suicide bombing in Bangladesh.

Shaykh Muhammad Amir : Shaykh Muhammad Amir was nineteenth century artist working with the East India Company. Like other indigenous company artists Shaykh Muhammad Amir of Karraya drew in a realistic manner the portraits of native and European people of different professions, as well as pictures of his European master's mansion, retainers, equipment, carriage, horses, dogs etc. Under the patronage of his master Thomas Halroyd, the artist visited every nook and corner of European area of Calcutta and drew sketches of their buildings, domestic animals, pets etc. He made excellent tinted drawings of horses and dogs by applying European perspective. One such noteworthy painting is "Two Dogs in a Meadow Landscape" (1840-50).

Shaykh Muhammad meticulously drew in European watercolour style abandoning the Mughal qalam of gouache technique. His colourful paintings in European style reflect European realism, perspective and knowledge of anatomy. Some of his paintings are now preserved in the India Office Library, London.

Sheesh Mahal : The Sheesh Mahal, literally "Palace of Mirrors", is one of the most lavish rooms within the Lahore Fort (in present-day Pakistan). The walls and ceiling are covered with small pieces of colored mirror. The Sheesh Mahal was constructed by the Mughal Emperor Shah Jahan in 1631

Shehnai : The shehnai is an aerophonic instrument which is thought to bring good luck, and as a result, is widely used in North India for marriages and processions. This tube-like instrument gradually widens towards the lower end. It usually has between six and nine holes. It employs two sets of double reeds, making it a quadruple reed woodwind. By controlling the breath various tunes can be played on it.

The shehnai was created by improving upon the pungi. There are two common stories. In the first, a Shah banned the playing of the pungi in his court due to its shrill sound. A barber, belonging to a family of musicians, improved on it and created the shehnai. As it was played in the Shah's court and giving due reference to the 'nai' or barber, it was called shehnai.

Shehzad Roy : Shehzad Roy is one the very famous Pop singers hailing from Karachi, Pakistan. He became a huge hit when he debuted in 1995 with a boisterous and revolutionary approach to Pakistani Pop. In the late 1990s, he became one of the most popular singers in South Asia.

Sheikh Abdur Rehman : Sheikh Abdur Rehman was born on June 4, 1903. He did his MA from University of

Punjab, BA Hons from Oxford and Ph.D. in Law from Cairo. Dr. S.A. Rehman entered Indian Civil Services in 1926. He served in the capacity of Assistant Commissioner and District and Sessions Judge in various Districts of Punjab. He was appointed as Judge Lahore High Court in 1946. In 1947, he was appointed as the Member of Bengal Boundary Commission. From 1947-52 he acted as the Custodian of Evacuee Property Punjab. Dr. S.A. Rehman remained the vice-chancellor of Punjab University Lahore from 1950 to 1952. He became the Chief Justice of Lahore High Court in 1954. He was elevated as the Chief Justice West Pakistan High Court in 1955. In 1958 he was made the Judge, Supreme Court of Pakistan. He replaced Justice A.R. Cornelius as the Chief Justice of Supreme Court of Pakistan. He retired as the Chief Justice on June 3, 1968. He also acted as Chief Election Commissioner in 1964, 1965, 1966, and 1967.

Sheikh Hasina Wajed : Sheikh Hasina Wajed (born September 28, 1947) was the Prime Minister of Bangladesh from 1996 to 2001. She has been the President of the Awami League, a major political party in Bangladesh, since 1981. She is the eldest of five children of Sheikh Mujibur Rahman, the nationalist leader and first president of Bangladesh.

Sheikh Hasina's political career started as a student activist in Dhaka University in 1960's. However, she was mostly under the shadow of her father until her family was killed in a coup d'état on August 15, 1975. She and her sister Sheikh Rehana, who were in West Germany at the time, were the only surviving members of the family. She later moved to the United Kingdom, and then was in self-exile in New Delhi, India before returning to Bangladesh, and Bangladeshi politics, on 17 May 1981.

While living in self-exile in India, Sheikh Hasina was elected the president of Bangladesh Awami League in 1981.

Sheikh Hasina and her party Awami League participated in the 1986 Parliamentary elections held under General Hossain Mohammad Ershad. She served as the leader of opposition between 1986-1987. The first democratic elections were held in 1991 after long dictatorial rule. A caretaker government, headed by Shahabuddin Ahmed, the outgoing chief justice, oversaw the elections. Bangladesh Nationalist Party won the election, and Hasina's Awami League emerged as the largest opposition party.

The next parliamentary election was held under a caretaker government headed by Justice Habibur Rahman on June 30, 1996. Awami League won 148 seats in the 1996 parliamentary elections. The support of the Jatiya Party and a few independents were enough for the 150+ seats needed for the required majority. Hasina took the oath as the prime minister of Bangladesh. The Awami League succumbed to a landslide defeat in the 2001 Parliament elections. It won only 62 seats in the Parliament, while the Four Party Alliance led by the Bangladesh Nationalist Party won more than 200 seats, giving them a two-third majority in the Parliament. Sheikh Hasina and the Awami League rejected the results, claiming that the election was rigged with the help of the President and the Caretaker government. However, the international community was largely satisfied with the elections and the Four Party Alliance went on to form the government.

Sheikh Mohammed Abdullah : Sheikh Mohammed Abdullah known as Sher-e-Kashmir' (the Lion of Kashmir) (1905–1982) was one of the most important political figures in the modern history of Jammu and Kashmir.Sheikh Abdullah became the Prime Minister of Kashmir soon after its Provisional accession (limited to Defence, Foreign Affairs and Finance and subject to ratification by plebiscite that has till now not taken place) to India. Sheikh Abdullah was a charismatic leader, and had the following of a huge majority of Kashmiris.

Sheikh Mujibur Rahman : Sheikh Mujibur Rahman (March 17, 1920 – August 15, 1975), also known as Sheikh Mujib, was a nationalist leader in the former East Pakistan and one of the founder of the independent Bangladesh. He was born at the Tungipara village in Gopalganj, Bengal (now in Bangladesh).

His political career began almost immediately with Pakistan's independence, as co-founder of the East Pakistan Muslim Students' League, a student organization affiliated with the Muslim League. His secular and nationalistic ideals led him to found the Awami League (party of people) in the 1950s. A follower of H.S. Suhrawardy, Sheikh Mujib was a popular Bengali Muslim leader who was far removed from the ideologies of the feudal leaders that dominated the political landscape at that time. Mujib is also referred to as "Bangabandhu" (Friend of Bangladesh) in recognition of his role in the country's struggle for emancipation from West Pakistani rule.

Sheikh Riaz Ahmad : Justice Sheikh Riaz Ahmad was Chief Justice of Pakistan Supreme Court in Islamabad from February 1, 2002 to December 31, 2003.

The former Chief Justice Sheikh Riaz Ahmad had banned entry of press photographers in premises of building of the apex court when the controversy between the judiciary and lawyers community was on the rise on the issue of extension in the age of judges of superior courts under Legal Framework Order. Since then no press or other form of media is allowed on the premises of the Supreme Court.

Sheikhupura : Sheikhupura or Shaikhupura is an industrial city in the province of Punjab, in Pakistan. It is known for its historical places, and is commonly known locally as Qila Shaikhupura, because of the fort in the city, constructed by the Mughal Emperor Jahangir. It is approximately 35 km from Lahore.

Sheila Dikshit : Sheila Dikshit (sometimes rendered Shiela and Dixit) (born March 31, 1938) is the Chief Minister of Delhi since 1998. She is from the Indian National Congress. A Punjabi Khatri, she is married in to a prominent Brahmin family from Uttar Pradesh.

In early 1970s, she was chairperson of the Young Women's Association and was instrumental in the setting up two of most successful hostels for working women in Delhi. Championing the cause of women at various fora, she represented India at United Nations Commission on Status of Women for five years (1984-1989). During the period between 1984 and 1989, she represented Kannauj Parliamentary Constituency of Uttar Pradesh. As a member of Parliament, she served on the Estimates Committee of Lok Sabha. She also chaired the Implementation Committee for Commemoration of Forty Years of India's Independence and Jawaharlal Nehru centenary. She has also served as a Union Minister during 1986-1989, first as the Minister of State for Parliamentary Affairs and later as a Minister of State in the Prime Minister's Office.

She took over as Chief Minister of Delhi on December 3, 1998 after the Congress, led by her in Delhi, swept the assembly polls. The first woman to become CM of Delhi, she is an experienced politician representing Gole Market constituency in the Delhi Assembly. She was reelected in the 2003 elections, after the Congress again obtained a majority in the assembly polls.

Sher Shah Suri : Sher Shah Suri also known as Sher Khan and as The Lion King, was founder of the Sur Dynasty of northern Indian rulers. He was born into an Afghan family in Punjab in 1472. His given name was Farid. His father was the jagirdar of Sasaram, Bihar. Ill-treated by his stepmother, he left home at the age of 22 and went to Jaunpur, where he set himself to serious study and there he acquired good command over the Arabic and Persian languages. Because of his administrative abilities and vision, he was soon appointed by his father to manage the family Jagir. But again because of his stepmother, he left his father's Jagir and went to Bihar where he later joined the service of Babur.

In 1522, he served for Bahar Khan then governor of Bihar. His master was impressed by his service and devotion. Bahar Khan conferred on him the title of Sher Khan for having shown gallantry in killing a tiger single-handed. Later, Sher Khan was appointed Vakil (deputy governor) and also a tutor of Bahar Khan's son Jalal Khan.

Jealous of Sher Khan's success, his enemies poisoned his master's mind and he was thus deprived of his father's jagir. He joined the Babur camp where he served from April 1527 to June 1528. But soon, he left Babur and returned back to Bihar and took over his old job as a guardian of Jalal Khan. Jalal Khan being a minor, Sher Khan became the virtual ruler of Bihar. In 1531, Sher Khan asserted his independence from Humayun, Babur's successor. The unexpected rise of Sher Khan made the Lohani Afghans and Jalal Khan impatient. They even entered into an alliance with Muhamud Shah, the king of Bengal. Sher Khan defeated the Bengal king on the Kiul River in 1534. Later, he invaded Bengal and Muhamud Shah handed over him a large sum and territory to make amends. He then became the independent ruler of Bihar and Bengal.

In October 1537, Sher Khan again invaded Bengal and besieged the city of Gaur. Humayun realising the strength of the Afghan, marched to oppose Sher Khan in December 1537, and besieged Chunar. However, the army of Sher Khan baffled all the attempts of the assailants for six months, which gave enough time to Sher Khan for reduction of Gaur, which was achieved by April 1538. In

1539, when Humayun marched towards Bengal, Sher Khan cleverly went and occupied the Mughal territories in Bihar and Jaunpur. In 1539, Sher Khan was able to defeat Humayun in the Battle of Chausa. Again in 1540, he defeated Humayun in the Battle of Kannauj, and went on to capture Delhi and Agra.

Sher Khan built the Rohtas Fort in 1541-43 to crush the Gakhars, who were loyal to Humayun, to whom the fort was finally surrendered by a treacherous commander 10 years after Sher Khan's death. Meanwhile, in Marwar the Rathores were becoming very powerful. The Rathore king Rao Maldeo had extended his territory to within a couple of hundred kilometers of Delhi. In 1544 Sher Khan attacked Maldeo. Maldeo came with a force of 40 thousand and Sher Khan had 60 thousand. In the evening Sher Khan sent forged letters to Maldeo's camp. In these letters it was depicted as if some generals from Maldeo's army were buying arms from Sher Khan's army. This caused great consternation in Maldeo's camp who thought that some of his generals had crossed over to Sher Khan, and he left with 20,000 men. Later events proved that there was no crossing over by Maldeo's generals. When the Rathore generals Kumpa (his progeny are Kumpawat rathores) and Jaita (his progeny are Jaitawat rathores) found out what happened they did not lose their cool, and decided they would not leave the field even though they just had 20 thousand men and had to face Sher Khan's 60 thousand Pathans. In the ensuing battle of Sammel Sher Khan emerged victorious, but several of his generals lost their lives and his army suffered heavy losses. After this he commented that "for a few grains of bajra [a grain crop that grows in Marwar] he had almost lost the entire kingdom of India". Sher Khan continued to expand his empire, subjugating Bengal, Malwa, Raisen, Sindh and Multan. In the Battle of Raisen, Sher Khan attacked the fort of the Rajput ruler Puran Mal. After it became apparent that defending the fort would be too tough, Puran Mal agreed to surrender the fort on the condition that his troops, their wives and children, be allowed to leave unmolested. Sher Khan agreed. But as Puran Mal and his family were leaving the fort they were attacked by Sher Khan's Pathans. The Rajputs of Puran Mal died fighting to the last man.

In a very short time, Sher Khan had extended his kingdom from the Indus in the west to Bengal in the east. He then besieged the strong fort of Kalinjar in Bundelkhand, where he later died in an accidental explosion of gunpowder in May 1545. He adopted the self-appointed title of Shah during his rivalry with Humayun in anticipation of power, so his name was again changed from Sher Khan to Sher Shah. In his reign, Sher Shah conquered a large portion of India.

Sherbaz Mazari : Sherbaz Mazari, respected Pakistani politician hailing from Baloch background in the Dera Ghazi Khan area of Pakistan. He served as leader of the National Democratic Party from 1975 to 1985, a former friend of Zulfiqar Bhutto he became one of his main political opponents in the Pakistan National Alliance.

Sherwani : A sherwani is a long coat-like garment worn by men, very similar to an achkan. It is worn over the Kurta and Churidaar pyjama or Khada pyjama. The origins of the sherwani are unclear, but it was associated with the court of the Nizam of Hyderabad prior to the Independence. It is the national dress of Pakistan for men, as it is not specifically associated with any of the provinces. Most government officials wear the formal Black sherwani on state ocasions.

This sherwani coat fits close to the body, fastened in the front with buttons, and extends to slightly below knee-length. Sherwanis are usually embroidered or detailed in some way. Many Pakistani grooms wear them at their weddings. The sherwani is named after the Sherwani family, a large muslim family of mixed arab and South Asian descent in Pakistan, some of whose members are settled mainly around the Aligarh (UP) and Malerkotla (Punjab) areas in India.

Shetrunjaya Hill : High up, on Shetrunjaya Hill in Gujarat, western India, is the abode of the Jain Tirthankaras—a set of 24 gods, including Adinath. A cluster of 863 shrines, 600 meters above the town of Palitana, the architecture of the temples reflects centuries and generations of grandeur, wealth, religious leanings, aesthetic values. It is an arduous climb, anywhere between 3500-4000 steps—but in miles, a mere 2.5. Standing atop at the summit, it is possible to view the Shetrunjaya River below. Devout Jains refrain from eating during their uphill climb, which may begin at dawn, as well as when they are descending just before dusk; they may sip on some boiled water. Non-violence in any form is the prime maxim of Jainism; it is an austere religion with practises that are hard to follow. Jains and others should not carry any goods, including wallets, nor wear footwear crafted from leather, especially when they are on the pilgrimage or visiting the temples on Mount Shetrunjaya.

Shibli Nomani : Mowlana Shibli Nomani was a famous Indian Muslim scholar (1857 - 1914). His six volumes biography of Muhammad, the prophet of Islam, in Urdu language, Sirat un Nabi, is very famous. Mowlana Syeed Suleman Nadvi, a close friend, completed the last volume of this biography after his death. He established an Islamic academy called the Dar al-Musannifin, or the House of Writers, and dedicated himself to the development of this academy. In the later years of his life, it became a high class research facility, and was renamed the Shibli Academy. Several renowned professors and 'ulama' of India spent time at this research academy, and benefited from their work there. In 1914 Allama Shibli Nomani died in Azamgarh.

Shibli was a profound and versatile scholar in Arabic, Persian and Urdu. He was also a versatile poet and in his early life he wrote many poems in Urdu and Arabic. But his genius found its real expression in the Urdu language and literature and he is remembered now as a great writer of Urdu. Shibli was a great supporter of Pan-Islamism. He wrote several poems and articles decrying the British and other Western powers when Turkey was defeated in the Balkan war and he urged the world Muslims to unite. In 1913, when the British Administration in India stormed the Cawnpur Mosque, Shibli stood against the British and wrote many poems condemning them for which he was harassed. Shibli was well aware of the progress of science and education in the West. He wanted to inspire the Muslims to make similar progress by having recourse to their lost heritage and culture, and warned them against getting lost in Western culture. In keeping with this goal, he wrote his famous books, As-Sirat al-Numan, al-Faruq, al-Ma'mun, al-Ghazzali, Mawlana Rumi and the immortal Sirat an-Nabi.

Shigi Hunnive : This is observed on the 14th and 15th day of Aswija in Karnataka. It is one of the important festivals in the village and a local fair in honour of god Vithappa, is also associated with it. This fair, which was started about 200 years back, lasts for about three days.

Shigmo : Shigmo is a social festival with a religious core. It is the Goan counterpart of the Holi in the rest of India. On the Holi day, Puja is performed of the stems of the Teflam fruits or betel nut, struck on the ground before the temple and a little grass put at their feet is then burnt. There are a number of dances which burst forth on this occasion in the spirit of plenty that marks the harvesting season when the barns are full and a sense of satisfaction and mirth is bubbling all around Gokulashtami, Mahashivratri and Brahmotsava are celebrated at the temples of Goa with great splendour, when thousands of devotees from all over Goa gather to pay homage to the deity. A famous fair known as Jatra festival is held in the temple of goddess Lairai, situated in the village of Sirigao in Bicholim Taluka where thousands of people from all over Goa come to pay their homage to the goddess. A special feature of this Jatra is walking on burning coals by certain devotees of the goddess popularly known as Dhonds.

Shikaripur Ranganatha Rao : Shikaripur Ranganatha Rao (born 1922) is an Indian archeologist who led teams credited with the discovery of a number of Harappan sites including the famous port city of Lothal in Gujarat. Shikaripura Ranganatha Rao completed his education from the Mysore University. He worked in the Archaeological Department of Baroda State and subsequently served the Archaeological Survey of India in various capacities. Dr. Rao has led excavations of many important sites such as Rangpur, Amreli, Bhagatrav, Dwaraka, Hanur, Aihole, Kaveripattinam and others. One of his most important works were leading the research and excavations at Lothal, the earliest known port in history and the most important Indus-era site in India. Dr. Rao was the recipient of Jawaharlal Nehru Fellowship and a doctorate of literature from Mysore University.

Rao had supervised excavation of several historic sites across the country in the West and South. He was also associated with conservation of monuments such as Taj Mahal and forts. Despite officially retiring in 1980, Dr. Rao was requested to work for the ASI Director General in leading Indian archaeological projects. It was under the initiative of Dr Rao that the NIO opened a marine archaeology research centre in 1981, under the stewardship of then director Dr S. Z. Quazim, which grew into a world recognised body. He was the founder of the Society of Marine Archaeology in India. Rao has been at the forefront of Indian archaeology for many decades—he was involved in extensive research into India's ancient and often mythical past, from the sites of the Indus Valley Civilization to excavations pertaining to the Kurukshetra War.

Shikarpur : Shikarpur is the capital of Shikarpur District in Sindh province of Pakistan. It is situated about 29 km from the right bank of the Indus, with a railway station, 37 km NW. of Sukkur. Shikarpur has always been an important place as commanding the trade route through the Bolan Pass, and its merchants have dealings with many towns in Central Asia. It is famous of Pickle and Sweets too.It has a large market and manufactures of carpets, cotton cloth and pottery. Because of its rich history, Shikarpur is known as Old Paris.

Shillong : Shillong is the capital of Meghalaya, one of the smaller states in India. It is also the district headquarters of East Khasi Hills District and is situated at an altitude of 4,908ft (1,496 m) above sea level. The city has a population of approx. 260,000 according to the 2001 census. Shillong has steadily grown in size and significance in its own traditional way from a mere village as it used to be when it was made the new civil station of Khasi and Jaintia Hills in 1864 by British. It remained the summer capital of Eastern Bengal and Assam for many years. In 1874, on the formation of Assam as a Chief Commissioner's Province, it was chosen as the headquarters of the new administration because of its convenient location between the Brahmaputra and Surma Valley and more so because the climate of Shillong was much cooler than tropical India. Shillong remained the capital of undivided Assam until the creation of the new state of Meghalaya in January 21, 1972 when Shillong became the capital of Meghalaya.

Shimla : Shimla is the capital of the state of Himachal Pradesh, India. It is a popular hill station in Northern India. It was also the Summer Capital of India during the British Raj. During this time, the British spelled the name Simla.Scottish civil servant Charles Kennedy built Shimla's first British summer home in 1822, and by the latter half of the 19th century the city had become the summer capital of the British Raj. Many British soldiers, merchants, and civil servants moved there for roughly half of each year due to heat and disease at India's lower altitudes. Many others, like author Rudyard Kipling, went there for the active social life, which Kipling found both exciting and scandalous. Shimla is also etched in history of Indo Pak relations as it was witness to the Shimla Agreement signed by the two nations following Pakistan's surrender in the Indo-Pakistani War of 1971.

Shimoga : Shimoga is a city in west-central Karnataka state, India. Shimoga is the administrative seat of the surrounding Shimoga District. It is situated 275 km northwest of Bangalore, the capital of Karnataka. The name of the city is derived from the term Shiva-Mukha, literally meaning Face of Shiva. An alternative etymology is that the name is derived from the term Sihi-Moge, meaning Sweet Pot. The district formed the southern tip of Emperor Ashoka's Mauryan Empire in the third century BCE. It was ruled in later centuries by the Kadambas (4th century CE), Chalukyas (6th century), Gangas, Rashtrakutas (8th century), Hoysalas (11th century), and the Vijayanagara rulers (15th century). The city got an independent identity under the Keladi Nayakas in the 16th century, reaching its pinnacle under the rule of Shivappa Nayaka. From the late 17th century onwards, the city was a part of the Kingdom of Mysore until the independence of India in 1947, when Mysore merged into the Republic of India.

Shipra : The Shipra, also known as the Kshipra, is a river in Madhya Pradesh state of central India. The river rises in the Vindhya Range north of Dhar, and flows south across the Malwa Plateau to join the Chambal River. It is one of the sacred rivers in Hinduism. The holy city of Ujjain is situated on its right bank. Every 12 years, the Kumbh Mela festival takes place on the city's elaborate riverside ghats, as do yearly celebrations of the river goddess Kshipra.There are hundreds of hindu shrines along the banks of the river Shipra. Shipra is a perennial river. Earlier there used to be plenty of water in the river. Now the river stops flowing after a couple of months after the monsoon.

Shirdi : Shirdi is a town in the Ahmednagar district of the state Maharashtra in India. It is located at 19° 45' N, 74° 25' E, 83 km north of the city of Ahmednagar and at a distance of 15 km from the town Kopargaon. It has acquired fame as a pilgrimage center because the Shri Shirdi Sai Baba lived there and is buried there.

Shirdi Saibaba : The Saibaba of Shirdi has millions of devotees from different sects and religions across the world. To his devotees 'Sai' is the human form of the 'Supreme Being' (*Paramatma*).

Sai Baba, born under an unknown name, was an guru and fakir, who is regarded by his Hindu and Muslim followers as a saint. In his life and teachings he tried to embrace and reconcile both faiths: Sai Baba lived in a mosque, was buried in a Hindu temple, embraced Hindu and Muslim practices, and taught using words and figures that drew from both traditions. One of his well known epigrams says of God: "Sab ka Malik Ek" ("One Lord of All.")

There is no clear record of Sai's given name, nor of his origins. Sai arrived at the village of Shirdi in Maharashtra state when he was about sixteen years old. He took up residence in a Khandoba temple, where a villager (Mahalsapathi) at worship first called him Sai ("Saint"). He fostered an extremely simple and aescetic life: living in the village as a mendicant monk, and sleeping on the floor in the temple, and later in a dilapidated mosque.

Sai soon began to attract followers who addrssed him by the name Baba ("Father"). He worshipped both at Hindu temples and Muslim mosques, and encouraged tolerance between the faiths. Numerous miracles were attributed to him. He did not discourage such attributions, and his fame spread. Many pilgrims came for his blessings, and he attracted large crowds for the most mundane of his activities. Sai remained in Shirdi all his life. Baba attained samadhi on Dussehra day in 1918. Today Shirdi is one of the most important pilgrime centre. Millions of devottes are coming to Shirdi to every year.

Shiromani Akali Dal : Akali Dal, also termed as Shiromani Akali Dal (Akali Religious Party), is a Sikh political party mainly based in Punjab, India. It was formed in the 1920s after the formation of SGPC (Shiromani Gurudwara Prabandhak Committee), a religious body formed as a result of movement to secure Sikh Gurdwaras from corrupt priests. So in a sense Akali Dal considers itself as a religio-political party and principal representative of Sikhs. Baba Kharak Singh was the first president of the Akali Dal but it was under Master Tara Singh that Akali Dal became a force to reckon with. They launched Punjabi Suba agitation to get a Sikh majority state made from undivided Punjab based on language under the leadership of Sant Fateh Singh. In 1966, Punjab was formed but its division led to bitter conflict as neither parties were satisfied. Akali Dal came to power in Punjab but many a times their governments were dismissed by the Congress Party ruling at the federal level.

In the 1980s, the Akali Dal was torn when a young fundamentalist priest Jarnail Singh Bhindranwale began a militant group, demanding an independent Sikh state. For a while, the Dal sought to appease Bhindranwale and his extremism to preserve the support of Sikh conservatives with the main party, but Bhindranwale's militant acts wrecked the Dal's credibility with the rest of the nation. The Akali Dal however retained calls for greater autonomy, more support and attention from central authorities. It severely criticized the Operation Bluestar, which flushed out and killed thousands of armed followers of Bhindrawale and Bhindranwale himself from the sacred Golden Temple in Amritsar. It supported thousands of angry Sikh demonstrations, strikes and displays of outrage, and attacked the Government as well. But its credibility and respect had been severely eroded by its failure to take a decisive stand on the crisis that had caused havoc to peace and life in Punjab. Its failure to stop Bhindranwale from misusing the shrine, its failure to stop the Army from using force to eject and kill the innocents, and its failure to stop the harsh anti-terrorist police operations that followed only weakened the Dal.

The Dal's chief opponent in the state is the Indian National Congress. Its political ally in the state and at the Centre is the Hindu nationalist Bharatiya Janata Party. Since Punjab is only about 60% Sikh, the SAD needs the support of as many Hindus as the BJP can get to form lasting administrations, and the BJP needs the SAD to bring as many parliamentary seats from Punjab as it can to form a Union government. The BJP's cultural Hindu nationalism strikes a common fiber with Sikh conservatives, though their alliance is purely political.

Shiromani Gurdwara Prabhandak Committee : The Shiromani Gurdwara Prabhandak Committee is a Sikh religious organisation responsible for the upkeep of gurdwaras. It is also responsible for the Harmandir Sahib in Amritsar which is the holiest site in Sikhism. The committee takes care of all the historical Gurdwaras in Punjab as well as in adjoining states. Gurdwaras at Delhi are under the responsibility of the Delhi Gurdwara Prabhandak Committee. These committees have officials picked through regular elections at Harmandir Sahib in which all Sikhs may participate. The SGPC has a chairman, treasurer and general secretary. The SGPC maintains all the physical, financial and religious aspects of Gurdwaras as well as keeping archeologically precious and sacred artifacts belonging to the Sikh Gurus, which include weapons, clothes, books and writings of the Sikh Gurus.

Shirshendu Mukhopadhyay : Shirshendu Mukhopadhyay is a famous writer in Bengali language. His fictions aimed at younger readers are as famous the ones for the grown ups. Shirshendu Mukhopadhyay was born in Mymensingh district,now in Bangladesh.He spent his childhood in many places of Bengal accompanying his father,who worked in the railways.He passed Intermediate from the Victoria College,Calcutta and then took an Master's in Bengali from the Calcutta University. Shirshendu is on the staff of the Ananda Bazar Patrika at Calcutta.

Shishunaga Dynasty : Shishunaga dynasty of north India ruled the Magadhan Empire from 684 BCE to 424 BCE. Shishunaga (also called King Sisunaka) was the founder of the dynasty. He established Magadha empire (in 684 BC), and this empire with its original capital in Rajgriha, then shifted to Pataliputra (both currently in the Indian state of Bihar), was one of the largest empires of the Indian subcontinent. Accounts of this dynasty, as also references to Magadha and the Magadha Empire find elaborate mention in Hindu texts like Puranas, and Jain and Buddhist texts.

Shispare : Shispare is one of the high peaks of the Batura Muztagh, which is the westernmost subrange of the Karakoram range. Alternate forms of the name of this peak are Shispare Sar and Shisparé Sar. Shispare lies east of the Batura Wall, which is the highest part of the Batura Muztagh. The Hunza River curves around the southwest, west, and northwest sides of the Batura Muztagh, and Shispare towers above the western bank of the river. In turn, the Hunza Valley lies in the Gilgit District of the Northern Areas of Pakistan.

Shitala Temple : This white temple is dedicated to Shitala, the smallpox goddess. It is situated at Shitala Ghat in Uttar Pradesh. The Santoshi Mata (Mother of Contentment) shrine is added to this temple.

Shitalakshya River : Shitalakshya river originates from the Old Brahmaputra and bifurcates into two courses at Toke in Gazipur district. One of the courses named the Banar flows southwest and at Lakpur is renamed as the Shitalakshya. It then flows east of Narayanganj town. The Shitalakshya falls into the Dhaleshwari near Kalagachhiya. The length of the river is about 110 km and the width near Narayanganj is about 300 m but reduces to about 100 m in the upper reach. Its highest discharge has been measured at 2,600 cumec at Demra. The river is navigable throughout the year and shows little erosional tendency.

Shitla Ashtami : Shitla Ashtami, which falls on eight day after Holi, is devoted to the goddess of small-pox, followed by Ram Navami on Chaitra Sudi Navami, commemorating the birth of Lord Rama; Baisakhi Purnima, a big bathing day; Bargadee Amavasya in Jaistha Dussehra, another great bathing day; Guru Purnima in Asadh when

Vyas Puja is held and Nag Panchami dedicated to the worship of the Snake God, Shesha.

Shiv Sena : Shiv Sena (Army of Shiva) is a political party in India founded on June 19, 1966 by Bal Thackeray, who is the president of the party. It is a Hindu party, though it is strongly associated with Maratha identity. In the 13th Lok Sabha (1999-2004), it had 15 (out of 545) members. During that period, the party was part of the government coalition at the national level. Manohar Joshi, a Shivsainik, was the Speaker of Lok Sabha 2002-2004. Shiv Sena has its employment cell Shiv Udyog Sena. Bharatiya Kamgar Sena ("Indian Worker's Army"), a labour union, is affiliated to the Shiv Sena. The Akhil Bharatiya Vidyarthi Sena ("All India Students' Army") is the student wing of SS.

Although the party is mainly based in Maharashtra, it has in recent years started to form branches all over India. That work has however, had rather limited success. A sister party in Nepal, Nepal Shiv Sena, has also been founded. Maharashtra has always been the main stronghold of the party. The party has ruled the state in coalition with the Bharatiya Janata Party. The SS-BJP did however lose the 2004 state assembly election. SS is now the main opposition party in the state. The BJP-SS combine governs the Brihanmumbai Municipal Corporation. Traditionally the main strongholds of SS have been Mumbai and the Konkan coastal areas. However, in the 2004 Lok Sabha elections the result was reversed. SS made inroads in the interior parts of the state, while suffering losses in Mumbai

Shivaji Bhonsle : Shivaji Bhonsle, also known as Chhatrapati Shivaji Raje Bhonslé was the founder of the Maratha empire in western India in 1674 which was instrumental in the downfall of the Mughal Empire. He is also remembered for being the only secular king in medieval India.

Using guerrilla tactics superbly suited to the rugged mountains and valleys of the region, he annexed a portion of the then dominant Mughal empire. He is still considered a hero in the present-day state of Maharashtra, and stories of his exploits have entered into folklore. He was one of the pioneers of commando actions, though the term is modern.

Shivanasamudra : Shivanasamudra (or Shivanasamudram) is a small town in southern Karnataka, India near Mysore. The town is situated near the river Kaveri in Malavalli taluk, Mandya District. Near the town is the famous Shivanasamudram (also known as the Siva Samudram) waterfall. The Kaveri River splits here around a small island resulting in two cascades flowing into the same pool. The western cascade is known as Gaganachukki and the eastern cascade is known as Bharachukki. This spectacular waterfall is surrounded by hill forests of the Cauvery Wildlife Sanctuary. The waterfall is 98 m tall, and has a maximum recorded flow of 667,000 cubic feet per sec. One of Asia's oldest hydro-electric power stations, still functional, is located at the waterfall. This is where electricity was first produced in Asia and the electricity thus produced was used in the Gold Mines of Kolar and thus Kolar Gold Fields became the first city in Asia to get electricity.

Shivaram Karanth : K. Shivaram Karanth is a major Kannada writer, social activist, environmentalist, Yakshagana artist and thinker. Shivaram Karanth was born in Kota in Dakshina Kannada district of Karnataka on October 10th 1902. He was an intellectual and environmentalist who has tremendously contributed to art and culture of Karnataka. His contribution to revival of Yakshagana will forever be remembered. He was the winner of Padmabhushana and Jnanapeetha awards. He along with Shri Bhairappa are considered as the greatest Kannada novelists of this century.

Shivaram Wildlife Sanctuary : Shivaram Wildlife Sanctuary is a wildlife preserve in India located 10 km from Manthani, 80 km from Karimnagar and 50 km from Mancherial. This 37 km^2 riverine forest mixed with teak and terminalia is home to marsh crocodiles of the river Godavari. It also harbours panthers, sloth bears, nilgari, black buck, cheetah, python, and langoor. The undulating natural terrain adds to the beauty of the sanctuary

Shivraj Singh Chauhan : Shivraj Singh Chauhan (born 5 March 1959) is the current Chief Minister of Madhya Pradesh. He replaced Babulal Gaur as the chief minister on 29 November 2005.

Shivraj Singh Chauhan was a gold medallist in M. A. (Philosophy) from the Bhopal University. He joined the RSS in 1977. He belongs to the Bharatiya Janata Party and has been the president of its Madhya Pradesh state party unit in the recent past. He has been a five-time Member of Parliament, representing Vidisha in the Lok Sabha since 1991.

Shoaib Akhtar : Shoaib Akhtar (born 13 August 1975 in Rawalpindi, Punjab) is a Pakistani cricket player. He is known for his ability to bowl at great speeds that even the best batsmen find difficult to handle and his talent in swinging the ball at high speeds, whether it be conventional (outswing or inswing) or reverse swing. He is capable of match winning displays and his fast bowling can bring a lot of excitement into the game whenever he plays, he has been labeled by some as the "Rawalpindi Express," after his home town. Rather than his bowling, it has been his fitness and discipline issues that have kept him away from cricket at certain periods in his career.

He is the world's fastest bowler and as of early 2004, he has bowled the fastest recorded ball in Test cricket. He has also bowled over 100 mph (160 km/h) twice in one dayers, with his fastest recorded delivery being clocked at 161.4 km/h, the fastest delivery recorded in modern day cricket.

Shobhana : Shobhana Chandrakumar (born March 21, 1966) is an exponent of the Bharatanatyam dance and a leading actress of South Indian motion pictures. She has won the coveted National Film Award for Best Actress two times.

Shobhana is an equally accomplished dancer of Bharatanatyam, an elaborate dance from South India. She did her dance training at the Chidambaram academy in Chennai, Tamil Nadu. Her gurus included legendary Bharatanatyam dancers Chitra Visweswaran and Padma Subramaniam. Shobhana is famed for her *Abhinaya,* a pivotal element in the South Indian dance of Bharatanatyam. She performed in Kuala Lumpur before the King and Queen of Malaysia. Shobhana's skilled execution of dance movements and her extraordinary beauty has led many people to consider her as the most beautiful South Indian actress from the 1980s through the 1990s. She is often equaled to the curvaceous beauty of South Indian sculptures. Shobhana has founded a school for classical Bharatanatyam dance in Chennai. In 2006 January, Indian government honored Shobana with Padmashree title for her significant contributions to cinema and bharatanatyam.

Shola : Shola is a type of high-altitude stunted evergreen forest found in southern India. Patches of shola forest are usually separated from one another by undulating grassland. Together the shola and grassland form the shola-grassland complex or shola-grassland mosaic. Shola forests are found only in the southern portion of the Western Ghats mountains of Karnataka, Kerala and Tamil Nadu states, in the South Western Ghats montane rain forests ecoregion. The word 'shola' is probably derived from the Tamil word solai, meaning 'thicket' or 'bamboo clump'. Due to its altitude and evergreen character, it is home to some of the most threatened and endemic species. Some of the species found here have close relatives only in the distant evergreen forests of northeast India or those in Southeast Asia. Some others are found nowhere else in the world.

Shompen : The Shompen are one of the indigenous peoples of the Nicobar Islands, part of the Indian union territory of Andaman and Nicobar Islands. Current population is estimated at approximately 400 members and located on Great Nicobar island. They practice a hunter-gatherer subsistence economy. Six members were reported to have died in the Great Sumatran Earthquake and tsunami disaster of December 26, 2004.

Shramik Karyakarta Vidyapith : 'The Worker's University' or the 'Shramik Karyakarta Vidyapith' is a path breaking and visionary idea by Baba Amte of Agro-based education, which is still fresh and aromatic after forty years. The renowned and internationally acclaimed social worker, Baba Amte had observed that traditional university graduates when their minds were too well trained became alienated from the village,thus depriving agriculture of its best talent. At Somnath (a site of one of his leprosy rehabilitation and agricultural based development project in the Chandrapur Distrcit, Maharashtra), Baba Amte hoped to establish a workers' university where students would "dig the soil as well as sharpen pencils" and upon graduation return to the villages to share knowledge with their peers.

Shravan Mondays : Every Monday in the month of Shravan is considered as a festival day in the villages in Karnataka. People offer special worship at the temple of Shidlingappa. They carry the deity in a palanquin in a procession accompanied by music on all the Mondays in Shravana and offer special worship. Many of them observe partial fasting on these days. On the last Shravana Monday they arrange special festivities. They arrange bhajans near the Patrappa tree and feed about 100 people next day.

Shravanbelagola : Shravanbelagola, located 51 km south-east of Hassan in Karnataka is one of the most important Jain pilgrim centres of India. The Statue of the Jain saint Gommateshwara (AD 981)carved out of a mountain, said to be one of the tallest and most graceful statues in the world, is situated in this small town atop the Indragiri hills. The colossal monolithic statue is 58 ft high, naked, with 26 ft wide shoulders, 10-ft of its feet. Starkingly simple, the beautifully chiseled features of this statue embody serenity. Nearly 1,800 years old, the statue which is reached by climbing 700 steps carved in the steep granite slope, is symbolic of the renunciation of worldly possessions. It was sculpted by Aristanemi in 981 AD and Chamundaraya, a general and minister of the Ganga King Rachamatta installed it in 983 AD.

Lord Gomatesheshwara was the Jain prince Bahubali. During a war with his greedy elder brother, Bharata who sought to usurp his kingdom, Bahubali accepted defeat at the moment of his victory when he realized the futility of it all. He renounced the world and his rights to his own kingdom, much to the severe repentance of Bharata and left to lead a life of penance and meditation, attaining Nirvana.

Thousands of devotees congregate here to perform the 'Mahamastakabhisheka' (sacred anointment), a spectacular ceremony which is the focus for Jain pilgrims across India, held once in 12 years. Hundreds of pots containing curds, milk, honey, vermilion, coconut water, turmeric paste and even gold and precious jewels are poured over the statue's head by priests.

Shri Jagannath Dev Temple : More than a hundred years old and named after lord jagannath, the temple has a legend. It is believed that in the 18th century one pujarii family passing through here performed pujas for the ailing ruler, which cured him. The pujari had said that if the ruler recovered he would build a jagannath temple here. The family was requested by the ruler to stay back. In this Yatra Lord Balbhadra, Devi Subhadra and Lord Jagannath are taken in different chariots (raths), which are pulled by the devotees. The yatra goes on for 15 days. On full moon day the rathyatra goes back to the Jagannath temple. There is a myth that those who see lord Jagannath, lord Balbhadra and Devi Subhadra during this rathyatra achieve "moksh" (nirvana) and people not only from raipur but from nearby cities come to be a part of this festival.

Shri jagannath Sanskrit Vishvavidyalaya : Shri jagannath Sanskrit Vishvavidyalaya, the third Sanskrit university in India was established on 7.7.1981 at Puri (Act, 1981-Orissa Act 31 of 1981) by the State Government of Orissa, with initiative of the Chief Minister, Pragnan Vacaspati Dr. Janaki Ballav Pattnaik, beloved son of Orissa and a great lover of Sanskrit and Indian Culture. This Vishvavidyalaya has made very significant contributions to the world of knowledge and in the building up of skills, having been located in a natural setting of the scenic beauty, being ideally built for serious study and research in the field of the most ancient language (sanskrit) science and culture of the world. Its majestic edifice of library symbolises the leadership and commitment to seek through the highest truth, to upset the old dogmas in the society by means of valid knowledge, to be the torch bearer to lead its youth on right path to achieve almost all humanstic goals.

Shri Neelam Sanjiv Reddy : Shri Neelam Sanjiva Reddy was born on May 18, 1913 and died on June 1, 1996. Neelam Sanjiva Reddy, the sixth President of India, was a veteran statesman and administrator. He held many eminent positions in public life both before and after independence. Born in a peasant family at Illuri village in the Anantapur District (Andhra Pradesh) on May 19, 1913, Shri Sanjiva Reddy had his early education at the Theosophical High School at Adyar in Madras and later joined the Arts College at Anantapur.

In 1931, the young Sanjiva Reddy gave up his studies to take part in the freedom movement. His student days were marked by Youth League and other nationalist activities. In fact, he first came into limelight when he participated in a student satyagraha. At the age of 25, Shri Reddy was elected Secretary of the Andhra Pradesh Provincial Congress Committee and remained in that office for 10 years. He was in prison for a greater part of the period 1940-1945. In March 1942,he was released for a while but in August, the same year he was re-arrested and kept in Amraoti jail in Madhya Pradesh along with Shri Prakasam, Shri Satyamurti, Shri Kamaraj, Shri Giri and others till 1945.

In 1946, Shri Reddy was elected to the Madras Legislaltive Assembly and became the Secretary of the Madras Congress Legislature Party the following year. In 1947, he became a Member of the Indian Constitutent Assembly. From April 1949 to April 1951, he was Minister for Prohibition, Housing and Forests in the composite state of Madras. In 1951, he resigned this office to contest the Election for the Presidentship of the Andhra Pradesh Congress Committee which he won. It was during this period that Shri Reddy suffered a terrible tragedy in the death of his five year old son in a motor accident. This shocked him so deeply that he resigned the APCC Presidentship. Later, however, he was prevailed upon to withdraw his resignation.

In 1952, he was elected Member of the Rajya Sabha. In 1953, he accepted the post of Deputy Chief Minister in the Cabinet of the late Shri T. Prakasam, even though he was elected the Leader of the Congress Legislature Party. He was again elected to the Legislative Assembly in 1955 and became Deputy Chief Minister in Shri B. Gopala Reddi's cabinet.

Shri Reddy became the first Chief Minister to the new State of Andhra Pradesh which was formed following the reorganization of the States in October, 1956. In 1959, he resigned the Chief Ministership to take over the Presidentship of the Indian National Congress. On the expiry of his term of office in March, 1962, he again became the Chief Minister of Andhra Pradesh. In February 1964, he voluntarily resigned the office of Chief Minister in order to set high standards of public life. He was, however, re-elected as the leader of the Congress Legislature Party but he recommended to the Governor to invite Shri K. Brahmananda Reddy, a colleague of his to form a new Ministry.

On June 9, 1964, Shri Reddy was appointed a Member of the Union Cabinet formed by Shri Lal Bahadur Shastri and took over the portfolio of Steel and Mines. He was elected to the Rajya Sabha in November, 1964. Shri Reddy was Union Minister of Transport, Civil Aviation, Shipping and Tourism from January 1966 to March 1967 in the Cabinet formed by Shrimati Indira Gandhi. In the General Elections in 1967, he was returned to the Lok Sabha from Hindupur constituency in Andhra Pradesh. He was elected Speaker of the Lok Sabha on March 17, 1967, an office that won him unprecedented acclaim and admiration.

Shri Reddy resigned the Speakership of the Lok Sabha on the 19th July, 1969 to contest the Presidential election on the basis of his nomination as a nominee of the Congress filed by Shrimati Indira Gandhi. It is now common knowledge that after filing this nomination Shrimati Indira Gandhi subsequently organized his defeat in the elections by unethical means. After 1969, Shri Reddy devoted his time to agriculture, which has always remained his first love. However, on May 1, 1975 he entered active politics again by addressing a public meeting at Hyderabad along with Shri Jayaprakash Narain. In March 1977, he fought the Lok Sabha election from Nandyal constituency in Andhra Pradesh as a Janata Party candidate. He was the only non-Congress candidate to get elected from Andhra Pradesh.

Shri Reddy was unanimously elected Speaker of the Lok Sabha on March 26, 1977. He relinquished this office on July 13, 1977 to file his nomination for the Presidentship of the Indian Union. He was unanimously sponsored as the consensus candidate for the Presidentship by all political parties, a rare even in recent political history. He was declared elected unopposed on July 21, 1977. The degree of Honorary Doctor of Laws was conferred on Shri Sanjiva Reddy by the Sri Venkateshwara University in 1958. Shri Sanjiva Reddy married Shrimati Nagarathnamma on June 8, 1935 and they had one son and three daughters.

Shrikhand : Shrikhand is a dessert made of strained yogurt. The yogurt is tied and hung until all the water has drained off, the result being a thick and creamy yogurt. Dried fruits and fresh fruits such as mango are also added. Other ingredients include sugar, cardamom powder, and saffron. Shrikhand is popular in western India. The dish is prepared by placing the strained yogurt and sugar in a deep bowl and mixing it thoroughly. You can use a hand mixer. The cardamom powder and saffron are then added and mixed. The dish is serve chilled. A popular variation is the Amrakhand, which is Shrikhand mixed with mango pulp. Shrikhand is usually paired with Poori.

Shrilal Shukla : Shrilal Shukla (b. 1925), Hindi writer notable for his satire. Also worked as an IAS officer. His other works include "Umraonagar men Kuchh Din" and "Suni Ghati ka Suraj". Shukla has highlighted the falling moral values in the Indian society in the post independence era through his novels. His writings expose the negative aspects of life in the rural and urban India in a satirical manner. His novel "Rag Darbari" has been one of the greatest Hindi best sellers.

Shruti : Shruti (Sanskrit , "what is heard") is a canon of Hindu scriptures. They do not date to a particular period, but span the entire history of Hinduism, beginning with the earliest texts known, with some late Upanishads reaching down into modern times. Shruti is said to have no author; rather, it is believed to be a divine recording of the "cosmic sounds of truth", heard by rishis.

Some sub-divisions within the scriptures, such as the Aranyakas, Brahmanas, and Upanishads, belong to the set of works distinctly labeled as Shruti. In addition, the Mahabharata (an Itihasa, or History, also part of the "friendly scripture" class) is considered by some to be Shruti and is sometimes called the 'fifth' Veda. Sometimes the Bhagavad Gita, a chapter within the Mahabharata, is separately considered as worthy of the Shruti status.

Shudra : Shudra or Sudra is the fourth caste or varna in the traditional four-caste division in Indian society. Their role in Vedic India was that of labourers. These four castes are Brahmin, Kshatriya, Vaisya, and Shudra. Whilst the origins of the other varnas can be traced to Indo-Aryan words, the root of the word is not clear at all. (A threefold division of societies can be found in ancient Iran that matches the Brahmin, Kshatriya and Vaisya varnas.) It has been proposed that the Shudras were same as Dasas and Dahyus, who are portrayed as enemies of the Aryans in the Vedas, and who it is said were enslaved by the Aryans. But the latter groups are also encountered in the Avestan texts and no subjugation is mentioned, though enmity is. The ancient texts of India betray no such subjugation by conquest resulting in servile group of people, but merely assume that the Shudras are part of society, even if not the most exalted. There is no etymology of the word as well, it just emerges suddenly in the purusha-sukta of Rig-veda. The numerical strength of this varna is also not clear from the Vedic corpus as tasks attributed to Shudras later are done by Vaisys in the era represented by these texts.

The Jati (derived from the Sanskrit word for birth) is the full blown expansion of the theoretical and the original varnas carried to its extreme in the ages following the 'Vedic' period. Every Jati claimed to belong to some Varna. Local variations of Jati sub-castes exist within the Shudra caste. A sub-caste is a local endogenous group practicing a particular occupation, which may vary from place to place due to variations in language and occupations in various parts of India.

Shwetamber Jain Temple : Shri Shwetamber Iain shri sangh did the pratistha of "Shri Rishab Dev" in Raipur here. The temple has 3 prasadas, 3 devkulikayes & 8 gavashas. Apart from this there is a beautiful statue of Chandraprabhu Swami, which is adorned with gems. The temple has all the statues of the 24 jain tirthankars.

Shyam Benegal : Shyam Benegal is a prolific Indian director, born 14 December 1934 in Alwal, Hyderabad, British India Andhra Pradesh. Benegal originated what has come to be called "middle cinema". He was initially involved in the advertising industry and produced over 900 advertisements before his interest turned to films. His film directorial debut was Gher Betha Ganga in 1962. Benegal shot to fame with Ankur 1973, which introduced Shabana Azmi, who also starred in Nishant 1975. He was awarded the Padma Shri in 1976 and the Padma Bhushan in 1991.

The success that New India Cinema enjoyed in the 1970s and early 1980s could largely be attributed to Shyam Benegal's quartet Ankur (1973), Nishant (1975), Manthan (1976) and Bhumika (1977), which were artistically superior yet commercially viable films. Tapping fresh talent mainly from the FTII and NSD like Shabana Azmi, Naseeruddin Shah, Om Puri, Smita Patil, Kulbhushan Kharbanda and Amrish Puri, Benegal has made several sensitive and stimulating films.

Siachen Glacier : The Siachen Glacier is located in the East Karakoram/Himalaya, at approximately 35.5° N 76.9° E. It is one of the five largest glaciers in the Karakoram, situated at an average altitude of 5,400 meters above sea level. The Siachen glacier lies South of the great watershed that separates Central Asia from the Indian subcontinent, and Pakistan from China in this region. The 78 km long Siachen glacier lies between the Saltoro ridge line to the west and the main Karakoram range to the east. The Saltoro ridge originates from the Sia Kangri peak in the Karakoram range and the altitudes range from 5500 to 7300 m (18,000 to 24,000 feet). The major passes on this ridge are Sia La at 6100 m (20,000 ft) and Bila Fond La at 5800 m (19,000 ft).

Sialkot : Sialkot is a city in Pakistan, located in the province of Punjab. The population of Sialkot is approximately 3,000,000. It is a major industrial center and is well-known for its leather products, surgical instruments, sports goods and other light manufactures. It is only a few miles from the border of Jammu and Kashmir and is home to a base of the Pakistani Army. The new Sialkot International Airport has been built and it will serve the Sialkot region.

Sialkot District : The Sialkot district lies south of the Gujrat district, the state of Jamu, and Kashmir, while Narowal district is to the southeast and Gujranwala district is situated to the west. The sialkot district is spread over an area of 3,016 square kilometres comprising of the following four tehsils : 1. Sialkot 2. Daska 3. Pasrur 4. Sambrial

Sibi : Sibi is a district in the center of Balochistan province of Pakistan. Sibi district was established in 1903. It was subdivided to create Nasirabad and Kohlu districts in 1974, Dera Bugti District in 1983, and Ziarat District in 1986. The Sibi district has two sub-divisions, Sibi and Harnai, which are further organised into tehsils and sub-tehsils : Sibi, Harnai, Kutmandi and Sangan.

Siddha : Siddha is one of the oldest system of medicine practiced in India. This system was developed in the state of Tamil Nadu in India. It is supposed to have been conceived by the Siddhas or evolved souls (numbering 18) who lived in the past. The word 'Siddha' comes from 'Siddhi' which means an object to be attained or perfection of heavenly bliss.

Siddhas or Siddhars were great doctors of medicine, philosophers, men with deep knowledge of anatomy and chemistry and savants noted for their wide travel, simple living and high thinking. The Siddhas have their own manuscripts or basic works, written in secret code. Some of the treasured treatises on medicine are poems in palm leaf manuscripts which are now preserved in the Saraswathi Mahal Library, Tanjavur in Tamil Nadu. They were the pioneers in the use of metals and minerals in the treatment of diseases.

The systems of Siddha and Ayurveda are very much similar. In both systems, the basis of treatment is the three element theory or 'tridosha' (three humours). The three humours are Vatha (air), Pitta (bile) and Kapha (phlegm). It is believed that without these humours an individual cannot exist and imbalance of these may cause diseases.

There are number of medicines common to both Siddha and Ayurveda. In both systems medicines are prescribed to set right the imbalance in the three life factors. In Siddha, diseases are diagnosed mainly with the help of signs and symptoms of diseases. Other factors that help to diagnose diseases are touch, examining the pulse, tongue, colour, speech, eyes, faeces and urine. The main aim of Siddha is to assure a healthy life to man kind.

Siddha Yoga : Siddha Yoga is a spiritual group teaching traditional Hindu or yogic practices both in India and in the West. The group has an organizational foundation by the name of SYDA Foundation (a domestic not for profit corporation registered in in New York State), founded by the second guru of the Siddha Yoga lineage, Swami Muktananda (1908 - 1982). The guru who is the latest in the lineage of teachers of Siddha yoga is a woman, Gurumayi Chidvilasananda (born June 24, 1955). The group has its U.S. headquarters at a large country ashram called Shree Muktananda Ashram composed of two former resort hotels in South Fallsburg, New York State. Its original home remains the ashram called Gurudev Siddha Peeth at Ganeshpuri in rural Maharashtra, India.

Siddham Script : Siddham (Sanskrit, accomplished or perfected) — referred to in Japanese as bonji— is the name of a North Indian script used for writing Sanskrit. Descended from the Brahmi script via the Gupta script, which also gave rise to the Devanagari script as well as a number of other Asian scripts such as Tibetan script.

Siddham is an abugida or alphasyllabary rather than an alphabet because each character indicates a syllable. If no other mark occurs then the short 'a' is assumed. Diacritic marks indicate the other vowels, the pure nasal, and the aspirated vowel. A special mark can be used to indicate that the letter stands alone with no vowel which sometimes happens at the end of Sanskrit words.

The writing of mantras and copying of Sutras using the Siddham script is still practiced in Shingon Buddhism in Japan but has died out in other places. It was Kukai who introduced the Siddham script to Japan when he returned from China in 806, where he studied Sanskrit with Nalanda trained monks including one known as Prajña. Sutras that were taken to China from India were written in a variety of scripts, but Siddham was one of the most important. By the time Kukai learned this script the trading and pilgrimage routes over land to India, part of the Silk Road, were closed by the expanding Islamic empire of the Abbasids. Then in the middle of the 9th century there were a series of purges of "foreign religions" in China. This meant that Japan was cut off from the sources of Siddham texts. In time other scripts, particularly Devanagari replaced it in India, and so Japan was left as the only place where Siddham was preserved, although it was, and is only used for writing mantras and copying sutras. Siddham was influential in the development of the Kana writing system, which is also associated with Kukai — while the Kana shapes derive from Chinese characters, the princlple of a syllable-based script and their systematic ordering was taken over from Siddham.

Siddhivinayak Ganapti Mandir : The Shree Siddhivinayak Ganapti Mandir is a Hindu temple located in Prabhadevi, Mumbai, Maharashtra originally built by Mr.Laxman Vithu and Mrs.Deubai Patil in November 19th, 1801. The temple has a small mandapam (hall) with the shrine for Siddhi Vinayak (Spiritual Ganesha). The wooden doors to the sanctum are carved with images of the Ashtavinayak (the eight manifestations of Ganesha in Maharashtra). The inner roof of the sanctum is plated with gold, and the central statute is of Ganesha portrayed with four arms, bearing respectively, a lotus, an axe, modakas (sweet deep-fried dumplings) and a garland of beads. Ganesha is flanked by two of his three consorts (wives), Siddhi and Riddhi.

Siddi Dance : The Siddis present tribal dances during marriages and other festive occasions. Their dances depict the tribal warfare of their home land in all its ferocity. Armed with shining sword and matchlock and dressed in their exotic primitive costumes, they dance with vigour and force. In rural Andhra some folk dance forms are confined to certain regions, some dance forms are common to all the regions.

Siddique ul-Islam : Siddique ul-Islam, known popularly as Bangla Bhai (The Bengali Brother), also known as Aziz ur-Rahman, is a Bangladeshi pseudo-Islamic terrorist and the military commander of the radical pseudo-Islamist organisation Jagrata Muslim Janata Bangladesh (Awakened Muslim Masses of Bangladesh), known in popular usage as the JMJB. Most active in the north-western section of Bangladesh around the Rajshahi region, Bangla Bhai has gained a nationwide and worldwide notoreity for the nationa-wide bombings and other terrorist activities.

Siddique ul-Islam fought in Afghanistan in the 1980s as a Mujahedin fighter. Upon his return to Bangladesh, he taught Bengali language for some time. Formerly a member of the Islaami Chattra Shibir, student wing of the Jamaat-e-Islami Bangladesh, Islam joined the ranks of the JMJB and became the commander of military affairs and an acting member of the Majlis-e-Sura, its decision-making committee. Bangla bhai became infamous for the torture and intimidation of the opponents of JMJB and the minorities. On August 17, 2005, JMJB, under Islam's leadership, launched a nation-wide attack by exploding 500 makeshift bombs. Along with Shaykh Abdur Rahman, Islam is alleged to have masterminded the bombing. In late 2005, a series of suicide bomb attacks rocked Bangladesh. JMJB and Jamaat-al-Mujahedin Bangladesh have claimed responsibility of these attacks. The Government of

Bangladesh proclaimed a large prize for the capture of Bangla bhai. On 6 March 2006, Bangla bhai was captured by police and Rapid Action Battalion in Mymensingh District .

Siege of Multan : The Siege of Multan was fought on January 22, 1849 between British forces and the Sikhs. The British were led by General Whish, and they successfully took the fortress

Siju Caves : The famous limestone caves of Siju are located near Naphak Lake in Meghalaya and the Simsang stalactites in these caves resemble those of the Blue Grotto in the Isle of Capri.

Sikander Abu Zafar : Sikander Abu Zafar, (1919-1975) litterateur and journalist, was born at Tentulia in Satkhira (greater Khulna) on 19 March 1919 where his grandfather Syed Alam Shah Hashemi had settled after coming from Peshwar in Pakistan. His full name is Syed Al Hashemi Abu Zafar Muhammad Bakht Sikander.

Abu Zafar was one of the champions of the cultural movement that propagated Bengali nationalism in East Bengal in the 1960's. During the War of Liberation in 1971, he composed a number of lyrics of patriotic and revolutionary nature to encourage the people of his country. His song 'Amader sangram chalbei' (Our struggle must continue) inspired people through out the country during the liberation war.

Sikander Hyat Khan : Sikander Hyat Khan was an Indian Muslim political leader in the province of Punjab, when India was a part of the British Empire. He was the leader of the Unionist Muslim League, a Muslim political party formed to represent the concerns and issues of India's Muslims, however opposed to the political separatism and demand for Pakistan of the All India

Muslim League, led by Muhammad Ali Jinnah. Khan led his party in the elections under the Government of India Act 1935 held in 1937. He governed the Punjab as Chief Minister in coalition with the Sikh Akali Dal and the Indian National Congress. He was widely respected by Punjab's Sikhs and Hindu communities.

Khan had opposed the Quit India Movement of 1942 and backed the British during World War II. While politically cooperating with the British, Khan never gave up his desire for the independence of India and the unity of Punjab. Khan was a very popular Punjabi leader who fought for greater Muslim rights and representation while opposing Jinnah's demands for Pakistan. His death in 1942, historians agree, created a vacuum of leadership for Punjab's Muslims, which increased the popularity of Jinnah, and resulted in the 1946-47 communal violence that killed thousands of people. Punjab was partitioned in 1946, creating the heavily Muslim province of West Punjab, which became the largest and most populated province of Pakistan on August 14, 1947. However, Khan still remains a respected figure in both India and Pakistan.

Sikh Regiment : The Sikh Regiment of the Indian Army is presently headquartered in Ramgarh Cantonment, 30 km from the city of Ranchi, capital of Jharkhand state, India. From Ramgarh, as and when required, the Sikh Regiment has moved on to a number of locations and participated in several actions. The Sikh Regiment came into existence on 1 August 1846, when elements of erstwhile armed forces of Maharaja Ranjit Singh were reorganized into a distinct force of combatants by the then British rulers of India. Over its life of more than 150 years, the Sikh Regiment has emerged as the most decorated segment of the Indian army, and have participated into armed action in India and also outside India, including action during First World War and the Second World War.

The Sikh Regiment is one of the oldest and highest decorated Regiments of the Indian Army. The Regimental Centre is located at Ramgarh, South Bihar. With 73 Battle Honours, the largest collection of Victoria Crosses-Param Vir Chakras and equivalent, the Saga of Saragarhi, the young soldiers of the Sikh Regiment are proud to wear the regimental colours of India's highest decorated regiment. Since it is raising more than 150 years ago, the regiment has been in the vanguard of various actions and operations both in the pre and post-independence era in India and abroad.

Sikhism : Sikhism, is a monotheistic religion based on the teachings of ten Gurus who lived in northern India during the 16th and 17th centuries. It is one of the world's major religions with over 23 million followers. The two core beliefs of Sikhism are:

— The belief in One God. The opening sentence of the Sikh scriptures is only two words long, and reflects the base belief of all who adhere to the teachings of the religion:—Ek Onkar or "One Creator"

— The followers of Sikhism are ordained to follow the teachings of the Ten Sikh Gurus and other saints as scripted in their 1430 page holy scripture the Guru Granth Sahib.

The Guru Granth Sahib is a sacred text considered by Sikhs to be their eleventh and final Guru. Sikh philosophy is characterised by logic, comprehensiveness, and a "without frills" approach to both spiritual and material concerns. Its theology is marked by simplicity. Sikhism shares some similarities in philosophy with that of Bhakti movement and Sufism. Some consider Sikhism to be a syncretic religion, although this is not a widespread belief held by Sikhs; the Sikh Gurus maintained that their message had been revealed directly by God.

Sikki Works : The sikki grass articles made by the women of North Bihar are entirely different from anything else you see in any other part of the country. Sikki seems to grow almost anywhere in this region, even by the road side, tall and rush with a lovely golden shade, it is most attractive. It is out only once after the rain and the cut pieces are stored for use throughout the year. As it is intimatily connected with important ceremonies and rituals, it has evidently come down from very ancient times.

The coiling technique, which is the oldest, used in sikki. The common long grass is wired and stitched together with the Pasikki, dyes in several different shades, using a thick needle called Takua. Espacially in constructing the sclespturelque a forms, the whole build up is made by the coils. There are human figures, animals, birds. Tasels are used for extra embellishment and brilliantly hoed wings of the betle or coloured buttons to emphasise eyes and ears. Every functional item such as a box for keeping cloths, spices toilet articles are all wrought out of sikki in multitude of shapes in dazzling colours.

Sikkim : Sikkim is a landlocked Indian state nestled in the Himalayas. It is the least populous state in India, and the second smallest in area after Goa. Sikkim was an independent state ruled by the Chogyal monarchy until 1975, when a referendum to make it India's twenty-second state succeeded. The thumb-shaped state borders Nepal in the west, the People's Republic of China to the north and east, and Bhutan in the south-east. The Indian state of West Bengal borders Sikkim to its south. The official language is Nepali, and the predominant religions are Hinduism and Vajrayana Buddhism. Gangtok is the capital and largest town. Despite its tiny size, Sikkim is geographically diverse, owing to its location at the Himalayan foothills. Terrain ranges from tropical in the south to tundra in the north. Kanchenjunga, the world's third highest peak, is located in Sikkim, straddling its northern border with Nepal. Sikkim has become one of India's most visited states owing to its reputation for untouched scenic beauty and political stability.

Sikkim Manipal University : The Sikkim Manipal University of Health, Medical and Technological Sciences, established in 1995, is the first government-private initiative in the region. It is recognized by the University Grants Commission and approved by the Government of India. It is located 8 km (5 miles) before (below) Gangtok, on the National Highway (NH) 31A, at a place called Tadong 5 mile. It is about 4 km after (above) Ranipool, overlying the river Ranikhola. It is one of the most well known universities in India imparting distance education in various disciplines.

Sikri : This is a women's dance performed during the Suhi Fair held in the Spring Season. The accompanying song tells of the beauty of flowers and the season, especially the flowering of the Marua flower. Silent Valley National Park : Set up in the year1984, this park is located in the district of Palghat, spread over an area of 89.52 sq.km along the Kunthi river valley. Located 40 km from Mannarkkad, Silent valley is extremely fragile, a unique preserve of tropical evergreen rain forests, totally undisturbed, lying above the equator and the forest strip which causes the summer rains during June- July in Kerala. The local name for the park is Sairandhrivanam (the forest in the valley) which is also the last representative of tropical evergreen forests in India. The park which is remote has difficult terrain and is surrounded with Attappadi Reserve Forests in the east, and vested forests of the Palghat and Nilambur divisions in the west and south. In the North, the park is an extension of the Nilgiri Forests. The park which has never had human habitation is in the core area of the Nilgiri Biosphere Reserve.

Silhara Dynasty : The Hindu Silhara dynasty ruled the region around present-day Mumbai between 810 and 1240. They were split into three branches; one branch ruled North Konkan, the second South Konkan (between 765 to 1029), while the third ruled what is now known as modern districts of Satara, Kolhapur and Belgaon between 940 to 1215 after which they were overwhelmed by the Chalukya.

The dynasty originally began as vassals of the Rashtrakuta dynasty which ruled the Deccan plateau between the 8th and 10th centuries. Govinda II, a Rashtrakuta king, conferred the kingdom of North Konkan (modern districts of Thane, Mumbai and Raigad) on Kapardin (Sanskrit: Wearing the kaparda, a peculiar braid or knot of hair—also a term for Hindu god Shiva) I, founder of the Northern Silhara family, around 800. Since then North Konkan came to be known as Kapardi-dvipa or Kavadidvipa. The capital of this branch was Puri, now known as Rajapur in the Raigad District.

Siliguri : Siliguri is a rapidly developing metropolis in the Indian state of West Bengal. It is strategically located in the Chicken's Neck — a narrow strip of land linking mainland India to its north eastern states. Besides, it is also the transit point for air, road and rail traffic to the neighbouring countries of Nepal, Bhutan and Bangladesh. The town hosts over 500,000 domestic and 15,000 foreign visitors annually. It is the commercial nerve centre of North Bengal. Siliguri is situated in Darjeeling district, and though it is the district's largest city, the district headquarters is located at Darjeeling. The Indian army has a large base here. The Assam Rifles — an Indian paramilitary wing — is located just north of the city and includes an airport within its cantonment area.

Sillanwali : is a town now upgraded as a tehsil headquarter of Sargodha District. It is situated in the southern area of Sargodha, bordering with the Jhang districh areas the famous Bhatiore area. The town existed before partition as a business hub called mandi in local language and most of the population was Hindu Khatris who migrated to india after partition and their property was taken over bu the muslim Sheikhs (having Khatri Origin) mostly belonging to Karnal district of Haryana state of which was then part of united Punjab.

Silvassa : Silvassa is the capital of the Indian Union Territory of Dadra and Nagar Haveli sandwiched between the states of Maharashtra and Gujarat. It is one of the smallest union territories. The city has a large number of factories and industries providing significant government revenue and contributing to the city's low taxes.

Silver Beach : Silver Beach is a beach on the southeast coast of India. It is located 2 km from downtown Cuddalore, however it is untouched by the busy life of the city. It is the second longest beach on the east Indian coast and one of the longest beach in the entire Asia. To the south of the beach the South Cuddalore Bay area appears as if it were a separate island. The backwater separating the main beach from the island-like structure is a safe place for water sports. Boats are available to rent. To the west a river flows into dense mangrove forest teeming with birds.

Simla Agreement : The Simla Treaty, popularly known as the Simla Pact or the Simla Agreement, was signed between India and Pakistan on July 2, 1972. The treaty followed from the war between the two nations in the previous year that had led to the independence of East Pakistan as Bangladesh. The agreement laid down the principles that should govern their future relations. It also conceived steps to be taken for further normalization of mutual relations. Most importantly, it bound the two countries "to settle their differences by peaceful means through bilateral negotiations". It also cemented the Line of Control as something close to a permanent border. "In Jammu and Kashmir, the Line of Control resulting from the cease-fire of December 17, 1971 shall be respected by both sides without prejudice to the recognised position of either side. Neither side shall seek to alter it unilaterally irrespective of mutual differences and legal interpretations. Both sides further undertake to refrain from threat or the use of force in violation of this Line." The agreement also paved the way for diplomatic recognition of Bangladesh by Pakistan. As a gesture of goodwill India decided not to try the 200 odd Pakistan Prisoners of War (of the total 93,000 PoWs) for war crimes and released them.

The treaty has been the basis of all subsequent bilateral talks between India and Pakistan, though it has not prevented the relationship between the two countries from deteriorating to the point of armed conflict (most recently in the Kargil War). The treaty was signed in Simla, India, by Zulfiqar Ali Bhutto, the President of Pakistan, and Indira Gandhi, the Prime Minister of India.

Simlipal National Park : In Orissa, the Simlipal National Park nature has epitomized the beauties of a pulsating tropical forest – its hypnotic rhythm of rolling hills and rich valleys, its sylvan glory on red and saffron soil, its playful brooks and amid rocky glens, its perennial rivers with crystal pools, cascading rapids and gorgeous falls, and its azure blue sky are unmistakably picturesque and awe-inspiring. The perennial water regime owes itself to the unique geological and geomorphological qualities, unique in the country.

Simon Commission : The Indian Statutory Commission was a group of seven British Members of Parliament that had been dispatched to India in 1927 to study constitutional reform in that colony. It was commonly referred to as the Simon Commission after its chairman, Sir John Simon. Ironically, one of its members was Clement Attlee, the

British Prime Minister who would oversee the granting of independence to India and Pakistan in 1947.

Since the 1970s Srivastava has traveled across the world spreading Sahaja Yoga. She is the founder of Sahaja Yoga International or "Vishwa Nirmala Dharma", an organization for teaching the Sahaja Yoga Meditation. Nirmala Srivastava has delivered lectures around the world, given television and radio interviews, and has been the subject of newspaper articles. She also has spoken at the Royal Albert Hall in London during conferences on Sahaja Yoga.

Sindh : Sindh (Sind) is one of the four provinces of Pakistan and is home to the Sindhis, Muhajirs and various other groups. Neighbouring regions are Balochistan to the west and north, Punjab in the north and Rajasthan (India) to the east. To the south are the Arabian Sea and Gujarat (India). The main languages are Sindhi and Urdu. Known by various names in the past, the name Sindh comes from the Indo-Aryans whose legends claimed that the Indus River flowed from the mouth of a lion or Sinh-ka-bab. In Sanskrit, the province was dubbed Sindhu meaning an ocean. The Assyrians (as early as the seventh century BCE) knew the region as Sinda, the Persians Abisind, the Greeks Sinthus, the Romans Sindus, the Chinese Sintow, while the Arabs dubbed it simply Sind, which is what the province is now known as.

Sindh River : The Sindh is a river of Madhya Pradesh state in central India. The Sindh originates on the Malwa plateau in Vidisha District, and flows southwest through Madhya Pradesh to join the Yamuna River in Uttar Pradesh state, near its confluence with the Chambal River. The Pahuj River is a tributary.

Sindhi : Sindhi is the language of the Sindh region of South Asia, which is now a province of Pakistan. It is an Indo-Aryan language spoken by approximately 35 million people in Pakistan, and 2.8 million in India; it is also a recognised official language in both of these countries. Although the language is predominantly Aryan, it also shows up signs of Dravidan influence, making it unique in its importance and identity. Most Sindhi speakers in Pakistan are concentrated in Sindh. The remaining speakers are found spread throughout the many areas of the world to which members of an ethnic group migrated when Sindh became a part of Pakistan during the partition of British India in 1947. The language is written using the modified Arabic script. In 1948, the govt. of India implemented Devanagari script for the Sindhi language that did not get wide acceptance.

Sindhi Memons : Sindhi Memons are an ethnic group residing in Sindh Province of Pakistan. They speak an Indo-European language called Sindhi. They are primarily involved in agriculture, unlike other Memons who tend to be businessmen. Their origins are doubtful. The word Memon came from "Meimana" which means right side and referred to the right flank of Moh Bin Qasim's army. This word may also be derived from Arabic word Momin meaning faithful.

Singhalila National Park : Singhalila National Park located at a very high altitude of more than 7000ft from sea level (between 2400 m to 3650m) is the highest National Park in West Bengal. It is situated in the extreme north western boundary of Darjeeling District and extends on an area of 78.60sq.km.

Singpho : The Singpho tribe of Arunachal Pradesh inhabit in the district of Lohit and Changlang and the Kachin State of Myanmar. Comprising a population size of 7,200 in India, they live in 12 villages, namely Dibang, Ketetong, Pangna, Ulup, Ingthem, Mungbhon, Pangsun,

Hasak, Katha, Bisa, Namo and Kumsai. They are a tribe belonging to the Kachin of Burma and are ethnically related to the Jingpo of China. In contrast to the Jingpo, they speak separate languages. The Singphos are divided into a number of clans, each under a Chief known as Gam. The principal Gams include the Bessa, Duffa, Luttao, Luttora, Tesari, Mirip, Lophae, Lutong and Magrong. The Singpho are also divided into four classes, namely Shangai, Myung, Lubrung and Mirip.

Sinhagad : Sinhagad ("Lion Fort" in Marathi) is a fort located near the city of Pune, India, situated on a hill which rises 800 metres above the surrounding countryside. The fort's location has been strategically important since at least the 14th century and has been the site of many important battles. One of the more famous battles was the recapturing of the fort by Tanaji Malusare, a general for Shivaji in March of 1670. In the ensuing battle, Tanaji was killed, but the fort was successfully captured by his troops. During the 20th century, Lokmanya Tilak, the Indian freedom fighter, built a bungalow atop the fort and Gandhiji is said to have asked for water from it whenever he was imprisoned in the nearby town of Pune. During World War II, the location was temporarily used as a camp for German prisoners of war.[1] The once extensive fortification is now in ruins, but visitors can still get a sense as to how the fort may have appeared while as an active military outpost. It is a popular weekend destination for many residents of Pune. The site also houses a memorial to Tanaji as well as the tomb of Rajaram, Shivaji's younger son, who also died here.

Sinjawi : Sinjawi is a small town (population 80,000) in Ziarat district in the Balochistan region of Pakistan. It is located about 32km from Loralai, and 160 miles from Quetta. It is famous for its apples, annar, and many other kinds of fruits. The tribes over here are Dummer, a sub cast of Kakar. There are also many other tribes. It is a mountanous area, and its tallest mounatain is called TOR GHAR.

Sinla Pass : Sinla pass or Shin la is the high altitude Himalayan mountain pass located in the eastern Kumaun in Pithoragarh district of Uttaranchal state in India. This pass is located at an altitude of 5,495 M. This pass connects Bidang in Darma valley to Jolingkong Lake in the Kuthi Yankti valley. This pass is steep on both the sides and rocky. Chhota Kailash Peak is visible from here on clear sunny day. This pass was the part of ancient trade route of Bhotiyas to Tibet.The route is under heavy blanket of snow all the year round.

Sino-Indian Border War : The Sino-Indian Border War, was a war, declared from September 1962, triggered by a dispute over the Himalayan border in Aksai Chin between the People's Republic of China (PRC) and the Republic of India. The war ended with the Chinese unilaterally declaring a ceasefire on November 21, 1962 after defeating India in Aksai Chin. The disputed area was claim to be strategic for the PRC, as it enabled a western connection (China National Highway G219) between the Chinese territories of Tibet and Xinjiang. The Sino-Indian War remains one of the largest military conflicts fought at such a high altitude, with combat taking place at over 14,000 feet (4267 meters).

Siraiki : Siraiki (also known as Seraiki, Multani and Southern Punjabi) is a language mostly spoken in central Pakistan by approximately 14 million people. It is an Indo-European language of the Indo-Iranian subfamily. Siraiki shows resemblance to both Sindhi and Punjabi languages. The geographic area where it is spoken is primarily located between the provinces of Sindh and the Punjab in Pakistan. It is widely spoken and understood as a second language in northern and western Sindh down to the suburbs of Karachi and in the Kachhi plain of Balochistan. It is also known as Derawali in Derajat area. The word Seraiki comes from the Sindhi word for North, as Siraiki is spoken to the north of Sindhi. According to the archaeologist and historian A.H. Dani of Pakistan, the word Saraiki appears to be derived from Sauviraki, the language of Sauvira, the latter being the name of lower (southwestern) Punjab in prehistoric times of Ramayana and Mahabharata.

Siraj Ud Daulah : Siraj-Ud-Daulah, (1729 - July 2, 1757) was the last independent Nawab of Bengal, Bihar and Orissa. The end of his reign marks the start of British East India Company rule in India. Mahmud Siraj had at one time become impatient to succeed his maternal grandfather Ali Vardi Khan. He turned to open rebellion and besieged Patna. His co-conspirators were quickly killed off in the struggle and with characteristic lack of determination, Siraj quickly surrendered. Ali Vardi Khan forgave his errant grandson and in 1753 officially made him the successor to the throne, creating no small amount of division in the family and the royal court.

Mahmud Siraj succeeded Ali Vardi Khan as the Nawab of Bengal in April 1756 at the age of 27, and took the name Siraj-Ud-Daulah. He resented British presence in Bengal and managed to capture Kolkata from the British in June 1756. During this time, he is alleged to have put 146 British subjects in a 20 by 20 foot chamber, in what is now known as the Black Hole of Calcutta; only 23 were said to have survived the overnight ordeal. The account of this incident by one survivor—Howell—obtained wide circulation in England and helped gain support for the East India Company's continued conquest of India.

After Siraj-Ud-Daulah lost Battle of Plassey to the British because of the treachery of his former army chief Mir Jafar he escaped to Murshidabad and then to Patna by boat. He was eventually arrested by Mir Jafar's soldiers. After few days Siraj Ud Daulah, the last independent ruler of Bengal, was brutally executed on July 2, 1757 by Mohammad Ali Beg under orders from Mir Jafar.

Sirajganj : Sirajganj is a district in the Rajshahi division of Bangladesh. With an area of 2497.92 sq km, the district is bounded by Bogra district on the north, Pabna district on the south, Tangail and Jamalpur districts on the east, Pabna, Natore and Bogra districts on the west. Main rivers are Jamuna, Baral, Ichamati, Karatoa and Phuljuri. About 10% area of the Chalan Beel is located in the Tarash upazila of this district. Annual average temperature: maximum 34.6 C, minimum 11.9 C; annual rainfall 1610 mm. Sirajganj subdivision was established in 1845 and was included in Pabna district. It was turned into a district in 1984. The district consists of 4 municipalities, 42 wards, 9 upazilas, 117 mahallas, 79 union parishads, 1467 mouzas and 2006 villages. The upazilas are Belkuchi, Chauhali, Kamarkhanda, Kazipur, Raiganj, Shahjadpur, Sirajganj Sadar, Tarash and Ullahpara.

Sirajul Islam : Nawab Sirajul Islam (1845-1923) was a lawyer and social-worker. He was born at Pearakandi, a flourishing village under Nabinagar upazila of Brahmanbaria district. His father Kazi Mohammad Kazem was said to have been a Sadr Amin (revenue-judicial officer) under the company government. Sirajul Islam graduated from Dhaka College in 1867 and started his career as an Assistant Headmaster of Pogose School, a famous Armenian institution in Dhaka. Later, he obtained the BL degree and joined the Calcutta High Court Bar in 1873. In 1885, he was elected an Assistant Secretary of the Central National Muhamedan Association. Earlier, he had been elected a Commissioner of the Calcutta Municipality in 1875. In 1893 and 1902 he worked as a nominated member of the Bengal Legislative Council. Sirajul Islam was an honorary member of the Bengal Provincial Educational Conference, in those days an influential forum for moulding public opinion. He was also a nominated member of the Calcutta University Syndicate.

Sirajul Islam was originally against the Partition of Bengal, 1905 and condemned it in a meeting organised by the Central National Muhamedan Association held in 1904 in Calcutta. However, he changed his mind about the partition subsequently. In appreciation of his services to his community and to the British Raj he was conferred the title of 'Nawab' in 1911. Earlier, he had received the title of 'Khan Bahadur' in 1887. Nawab Sirajul Islam died in 1923 in Calcutta and is buried there.

Sirkap : Sirkap is the name of an archeological site on the bank opposite to the city of Taxila, Punjab, Pakistan. The city of Sirkap was built by the Greco-Bactrian king Demetrius after he invaded India around 180 BC. Demetrius founded in the northern and northwestern Indian subcontinent an Indo-Greek kingdom that was to last until around 10 BC. Sirkap is also said to have been rebuilt by king Menander I.

Sirmaur : Sirmaur is the most south-eastern district of Himachal Pradesh, India. It is largely mountainous and rural, with 90% of its population living in villages. The area is popular with tourists, particularly those on pilgrimages. It includes the towns of Nahan (its capital) and Paonta Sahib, as well as the Shivalik Fossil Park at Saketi, where fossils of over 85 million years old have been found. This district has a common border with Uttaranchal.

Sirohi National park : Sirohi National park was established in 1982 in the east district in an area of 41sq.km.The nearest town in Ukhril at a distance of 5km. The nearest airport is Julilal 50km from the park. The railhead serving the park is at Dimapur at a distance of 270kms. The fauna includes tiger and leopard. The birds mainly found include tragopans and pheasants. January to March are the best month to visit the park.

Siron Molo Sochum—Nishi Festival : The biggest festival of the Nishi is called Siron Molo Sochum and is celebrated in the Nishi month of 'Ram Po-Lo' every year in Arunachal Pradesh. Before this festival all houses and granaries are rebuilt and all the crops like dry paddy, millet, maize are harvested and stored in the granaries. For the festival, house holders cook rice, meat and prepare apeng and entertain guests and receives blessing for more abundant crops next year. It is believed by the Nishis that the more guests are satisfied with food and drink, the more crops will grow in the coming year.

On the day of the festival, all singers of the village sing old history of the Nishi people. In the song, it is described that the God Nima Teni did not worship the goddess of crops and goddess therefore moved away to the land of summer and entreated the goddess of crops and ultimately married her. Nima Teni got all kinds of seeds from the goddess and learnt the method of cultivation from her. Prayers are offered to the goddess of crops requesting her not to go away but to fill the granaries with the crops. If some food-stuffs disappears over night or food prints of sóme animals are seen, it is believed that the goddess came to the people and the crops will be abundant.

Sirpur : The old name of the Sirpur was Sripur. It is in Chattisgarh. It used to be the capital of the southern Kosal in the 5th & 6th century. In the 7th century Heuin Tsang visited this place. The Laxman temple that was built here in the 6th century AD. It was the first of its kind to be built with bricks in India. The temple was built by the widow of Somvanshi King Harsh Gupta Queen Basata. Similarly there are temples depicting the life style of Somvanshi dynasty. The place also has Buddha Maths & Vihars. Every year during Shivratri a three day fair is organised at the place.

Sirsi : Sirsi is a town in North Canara, Karnataka, a hill station populated with around 65,000 people. This town is surrounded with lush green forests & numerous waterfalls. Hubli being the nearest commercial city, business opportunities are plenty. Supari (Arecanut) is the primary business of the people. People own Arecanut farms in acres & are satisfying the needs of the people all over India & Abroad. Sirsi is famous for the Marikamba temple, built in 1688. The fabulous Marikamba fair takes place every alternate year. Millions of devotees rush in from all parts of the country to attend this magnificent fair of Sri Marikamba.

SisGanj Gurudwara : The ninth Sikh Sri Guru Tegh Bahadur was beheaded in Delhi in 1675 by the order of Mughal King Aurangzeb, for espousing the cause off freedom of worship for the Hindus, against whom the Emperor had unleashed a war of extermination. Guru Tegh Bahadur opposed it and thereby sacrificed his life. At the place of his martyrdom stands Gurdwara SisGanj as a symbol of unique sacrifice made by the sage prophet.

Sita Ram Goel : Sita Ram Goel (1921 - 2003), author and publisher, is an important figure amongst late 20th century Hindu thinkers. Sita Ram Goel was born in 1921 in Haryana. He studied history in Delhi university. As a student, he was a social activist, and did work for a Harijan Ashram in his village. During the Great Calcutta Killing of 16 August 1946 that was organized by the Muslim League shortly before Partition of India, Goel and his wife and first son narrowly escaped with their lives.

Sita Ram Goel had strong marxist leanings during his student days and was on the verge of joining the Communist Party of India in 1948. He later came under Ram Swarup's influence who converted him out of communism, and was strongly influenced by him and his writings.

A poet and a novelist, in his later career he emerged as a commentator and critic on Christianity, Islam, and Communism in the Indian context. Goel has also criticized the work and research methods of Marxist historians like Romila Thapar. His work has been criticized by writers like Meera Nanda. He published books in English and Hindi. He also translated George Orwell's 1984, three Dialogues of Plato, Denis Kincaid's book "The Great Rebel" about Shivaji and other books into Hindi.

Sitanadi Wildlife Sanctuary : Sitanadi Wildlife Sanctuary in Chattisgarh was established in 1974 Under Wildlife Protection Act of 1972 and Biogeographical province 4.8.4 (Indus-Ganges Monsoon Forest). The Sanctuary is spread in area about 553 sq km. mainly undulating and hilly terrain. Altitude ranges from 327-736m.. Moist peninsular sal forest. The dominant species is sal Shorea robusta mixed with Terminalia, Anogeossis, Pterocarpus, bamboo and others are the main vegetation. Tiger Panthera tigris, Leopard, Pardus, Jackal Canis aureus, sloth bear Melursus Ursinus, Indian wild dog Cuon Alpinus, Chital Axis Axis, Sambar Cervus unicolor, Nilgai Boselaphus tragocamelus, Gaur Bos Gaurus, Muntjac Muntiacus Muntjak, wild boar Sus Scrofa and others. The main considerable interruption is Grazing of cattle and collection of minor forest produce by the villagers.

Sitapur : Sitapur is a town and district in the state of Uttar Pradesh, India. It is in the Lucknow Division of Uttar Pradesh. The town is on the river Sarayan, half-way between Lucknow and Shahjahanpur, on the Lucknow-Delhi National Highway No-24 and on the Lucknow-Bareilly railway, 89 km. N.W. from the state capital Lucknow. In British India it was a cantonment, garrisoned by a portion of a British regiment. The tradational origin for the name is said to be from Lord Ram's wife Sita. It is the location of the Sitapur Eye Hospital.

The district is traversed by meter gauge railway from Lucknow to Bareilly and on broad gauge train network connecting Gorakhpur and Delhi via Gonda,Burhwal. The history of Sitapur is closely associated with that of the rest of Awadh. The district figured prominently in the Indian rebellion of 1857, when the native troops quartered in the cantonments fired on their officers, many of whom were killed, as were also several military and civil officers, with their families, in attempting to escape.

Sitar : Sitar is one of the common stringed instrument of Northern India. The invention of the Sitar is commonly credited to Amir Khusrau, the great musician and statesman at the court of the Khilji. The name Sitar is derived from the Persian expression 'Seh-tar' meaning 'three strings'.

In appearance Sitar is very much similar to Tambura. The body of Sitar is more or less spherical gourd at the lower end. The gourd is almost flat, like the back of a tortoise. Such a Sitar is called 'Kachchawa'. The finger-board of the Sitar is about three feet long and three inches wide, hollow and deeply concave, covered with a thin piece of wood. There are sixteen to twenty-two slightly curved frets of brass or silver which are secured to the finger-board by pieces of gut.

The Sitar originally had only three strings, but the modern one's has a total number of seven strings which are fastened to pegs on the neck and the sides. These include the side strings (Chikari). Side strings are used both for the drone and rhythmic accompaniment. There are eleven or twelve sympathetic strings (Tarab) which runs almost parallel to the main strings under the frets. These tarabs are secured to small pegs fixed at the side of the finger-board. These strings are tuned to produce the scale of the melody.

The Sitar is played by means of wire plectrum (Mizrab) worn on the forefinger of the right hand. All the styles peculiar to instrumental music namely; alap, jod, meend etc. can be played on this instrument with marked effect. Artists such as Ravi Shankar have well known this instrument around the world.

Sitara Devi : Sitara Devi is a living legend known the world over as the 'Kathak Queen'. She took her training in dance from her father Sukhdev Maharaj, Shambhu Maharaj and Acchan Maharaj. By the age of ten, Sitara was on stage as a professional solo dancer.

When she was about 12, Niranjan Sharma, a film producer and dance director chose her for a three-month contract in *Usha Haran* and Sitara became a dancer with the Sagar Studios. Fame followed close behind and *Allehlal, Nagina* and *Roti* made her a movie sensation; Vatan made her a superstar. Sitara Devi was honoured with the Sangeet Natak Akademi Award in 1970.

Siva : Siva, last deity of the Trinity is responsible for the dissolution of the Universe. Literally, Siva is one in whom the Universe 'sleeps' after destruction before the next cycle of creation.

Iconographically Siva may have two, three, four, eight, ten or even thirty-two hands. Some of the various objects shown in the hands are :Trisula (trident), Chakra (discus), Parasu (battle axe), Damaru (drum), Aksamaba (rosary),

Mrga (deer), Pasa (noose), Danda (staff), Pinaka or Ajagava (bow), Khatvanga (magic wand), Pasupata (spear), Padma (lotus), Kapala (skull-cap), Darpana (mirror), Khadga (sword) and soon.

The icon of Siva is never worshipped as the Mulamurti (original, installed in the sanctum sanctorum), but only as an Utsavamurti (the icon used during festivals for taking out in a procession). Lord Siva is a great master of dance (Nataraja). It is believed that all the 108 modes of dancing known to the treatises on dancing have come from him. Siva's consort is Parvati (also known as Uma, Sati, Kali and Durga). His vehicle is bull (Nandi). Ganapati and Subrahmanya are his son's.

Sivaji Ganesan : Sivaji Ganesan (October 1, 1927 - July 21, 2001) was a famous Indian actor and politician. His real name was Villupuram Chinnaiahpillai Ganesan. Ganesan was born in Sirkali, Thanjavur district, Tamil Nadu, India. His parents were P. Chinniah Mandraayer and Rajamani Ammal.

At the age of 9, Ganeshan was so interested in stage plays that he ran away from home to pursue a career in theatre. His mother helped him get into a famous drama troupe. Ganesan's first film was Paraasakthi in the year 1952. He has acted in about 300 movies, including nine Telugu movies, two Malayalam movies and two Hindi movies.

Sivakasi : Sivakasi is a town in the state of Tamil Nadu,India. It is most famous for its fireworks factories with at least 300 manufacturers based there. Sivakasi is also known for printing industry and match boxes and its highly industrious nature and was fondly called Little Japan by Mr.Jawaharlal Nehru. (He called it "Kutty Japan". 'Kutty' in Tamil means Mini/little.) During early 1960's India was under great famine and lots and lots of people are unemployed and it was the time, the people of Sivakasi came in hand in hand with each other to promote themselves with out expecting any aid from the Government and stood on their own to achieve self reliant, high industrial growth rate (especially Matches, Fireworks, Printing and sub industries related to those industries.) Sivakasi is leader for Printing, Fireworks, Safety matches Production. So the name was given to Sivakasi. This happened only because of the people of Sivakasi, who are more dedicated committed to hard work and their togetherness to achieve attitude.

Siwalik Hills : The Siwalik Hills (sometimes spelled Shiwalik, Shivalik, or Sivalik) are a sub-Himalayan mountain range running 1,600 km long from the Tista River, Sikkim, through Nepal and India, into northern Pakistan. The range runs parallel with the Himalayan system from Hardwar on the Ganges to the banks of the Beas, and though only 16 km wide in places, the hills have an average height of 900 to 1,200 m. The Siwalik Hills are chiefly composed of low sandstone and conglomerate hills, the solidified and upheaved detritus of the great range in their rear, the intermediate valley lying between the outer hills and the Mussoorie. Ramapithecus was among many fossil finds in the region.

Siwalik River : Siwalik river is also known as the Indo-Brahm River. The Himalayan Mountain system and its various sub-systems, viz Naga-Lusai of Assam and the hills of the Chittagong and Chittagong Hill Tracts had emerged and the Tethys sea completely disappeared from the subcontinent as a consequence of the violent orogenesis of the mid-Miocene time (approximately 10 million years before present). With the emergence of the Himalayas, a foredeep was also formed on its front. This foredeep was extended from Assam in the east up to Patwar of Pakistan in the west.

Six Point Movement : Six Point Movement was a Bengali nationalist movement in East Pakistan spearheaded by Sheikh Mujibur Rahman, which eventually resulted in the liberation of Bangladesh. The movement's main agenda was the realization of the 6 demands put forward by the East Pakistan Awami League, to end the exploitation of East Pakistan by the West Pakistani rulers.

Sixty Pillar Mosque : The Sixty Pillar Mosque (the Shatgumbad) is a mosque located in Bagerhat, south Bangladesh. It has more than sixty pillars and is one of the oldest mosques in the country.

Skardu : Skardu is the capital city of Baltistan, a subdivision of the Northern Areas of Pakistan. It is also the name of a district in Gilgit-Baltistan. It is located in the wide (10 km) and long (40 km) Skardu Valley, in the very place in which the Indus River receives the Shigar River waters. Quite high (near 2500 m o.s.l.), the town is surrounded by gray-brown coloured mountains, which hide the 8,000 metre peaks of the nearby Karakoram range.

Skeleton Lake : Skeleton Lake is a Himalayan lake in Roopkund in Uttaranchal (itself formerly part of Uttar Pradesh), India, the location of about three to six hundred skeletons. The location is uninhabited and is at an altitude of about 5,029 metres (16,500 ft.). The skeletons were discovered in 1942 when stumbled upon by a park ranger. At that time it was believed that the people died from an epidemic, landslides or a blizzard. The carbon dating from samples collected at that time in the 1960s vaguely indicated that the people were from the 12th century to the 15th century.

Skil Brum : Skil Brum is a mountain in the Karakoram region of Pakistan. In 1957, Marcus Schmuck and Fritz Wintersteller made a flash first ascent of Skil Brum, in pure Alpine style. Starting from base camp of Broad Peak at

4,950 metres, they camped at 6,060 metres, made the summit the next day, then camped again at 6,060 metres, and then returned to base camp the next morning.

Slave Dynasty : The Slave dynasty served as the first Sultans of Delhi in India from 1206 to 1290. The founder of the dynasty, Qutb-ud-din Aybak, was a Turkish ex-slave of the Aybak tribe who rose to command the armies and administer the territory of Muhammad Ghori in India. After Muhammad's death in 1206 without an heir, Qutb-ud-din fought off rivals to take possession of Muhammad's Indian empire. He established his capital first at Lahore, and later at Delhi, where he started building the Qutb complex.

Qutb-ud-din died accidentally in 1210, and after a succession struggle, Iltutmish, another Turkish ex-slave, emerged as Sultan. Iltutmish married Qutb-ud-din's daughter, and all but one of the later sultans of the dynasty were his descendants, including his daughter, Razia, who reigned for four years. Sultan Balban was also an ex-slave, who commanded the armies of Sultan Nasir ud din, and kept the Mongols at bay, eventually securing the throne for himself. After the brief reigns of Balban's grandson and great-grandson, the Slave dynasty was overthrown by Jalal-ud-din Feroz Khalji of the Khalji dynasty, who had established themselves in Bihar and Bengal in Muhammad Ghori's reign.

Smartism : Smartism is a denomination of the Hindu religion. This term is usually used to denote a certain category of Brahmins. Smartas consider the Vedas supreme. The majority of members of Smarta community are followers of Advaita. In practicality, Smarta and Advaita have become almost synonymous because of the prevalence of Advaita philosophy among Smarta Brahmins. But not all believers in Advaita are Smartas. In ancient times, all Brahmins who specialized in the Karma Kanda of the

Vedas, and who followed the Vedas and Shastras (both Smriti and Shruti) came to be known as Smartas. They therefore should not be confused with followers of Advaita philosophy who may not or need not come from this family tradition.

Smiling Buddha : The Smiling Buddha was the first test fission explosion by India on May 18, 1974. On September 7, 1972, Prime Minister Indira Gandhi gave authorization to the scientists at the Bhabha Atomic Research Centre (BARC) to manufacture the nuclear device they had designed and prepare it for a test. Throughout its development, the device was formally called the "Peaceful Nuclear Explosive", but it was usually referred to as the Smiling Buddha. The head of the development team was Raja Ramanna. Other key members were P.K. Iyengar, Rajagopala Chidambaram, and Dr. Nagapattinam Sambasiva Venkatesan. The project employed no more than 75 scientists and engineers from 1967 - 1974.

The device used a high explosive implosion system developed at the DRDO Terminal Ballistics Research Laboratory (TBRL) in Chandigarh based on the American design from WWII. But the Indian design was simpler and less sophisticated than the American system. The 6 kg of Plutonium came from the CIRUS reactor at BARC. The neutron initiator was a Polonium-Beryllium type (again like those used in early U.S. bombs) code-named "Flower." The complete core was assembled in Trombay before transportation to the test site. The fully assembled device had a hexagonal cross section, 1.25 m in diameter and weighed 1400 kg. The device was detonated at 8.05 a.m. in a shaft 107 m under the army Pokhran test range in the Thar Desert, Rajasthan. Officially the yield was reported at 20 kT, but 8 kT is more likely. The CIRUS reactor used to produce the plutonium was a research reactor based on the NRX design and donated by Canada in 1960, with heavy water supplied by the US ("CIRUS" = Canada-India Reactor U.S.). The Smiling Buddha test caused a public outcry in Canada, and the Canadian government cut off exchange of nuclear materials and technology with India in the wake of the test.

Smita Patil : Smita Patil (1955 – 1986) was a leading actress of the 1970s and 1980s Hindi and Marathi cinema. Her unconventional beauty and arresting screen presence made her the undying symbol of the New Wave cinema in India. Smita Patil was also a women's rights activist.

Smita Patil belongs to a generation of actresses, including Suhasini Mulay and Shabana Azmi, strongly associated with a radically political cinema of the 1970s. Her work includes films with parallel cinema directors like Shyam Benegal and Mrinal Sen and the more commerical Bollywood cinema of Bombay. She was an alumna of the Film and Television Institute of India, Pune. In 1977, she won the National Award for 'Best Actress' for her performance in the Bengali film *Bhumika*.

In her films, Patil's character often represents an intelligent femininity that stands in relief against the conventional background of male-dominated cinema (films like *Bhumika, Umbartha,* and *Bazaar*). In her more commercial films, her glamorous roles reveal the permeable boundaries between 'serious' cinema and 'Bollywood' in the Hindi film industry (films like *Shakti* and *Namak Halaal*). Patil worked as a TV news reader before transitioning to film, and was also an accomplished photographer. She was married to the Hindi film actor Raj Babbar. She died in 1986 due to complications from the birth of her son.

Smriti : Smriti (Sanskrit, "that which is remembered") refers to a specific canon of Hindu religious scripture. Smriti also denotes non-Shruti texts generally, seen as secondary in authority to Shruti. Categorization of the

Smriti has been a contentious issue, even the names of proposed categories are debated. Such categorization is arguably unnecessary.

Soan Culture : The oldest evidence of human life in Pakistan was found in the Soan River valley of Pothar (Pothohar) region of Punjab. Along the River Soan in Rawalpindi Division hundreds of men made tools can be found. These tools dated 500,000 to 300,000 years ago. On Adiyala and Khasala about 16 km from Rawalpindi terrace on the bend of the river hundreds of edged pebble tools were discovered. At Chauntra hand axe and cleaver were found. Due to the peculiarity of the tools to the valley archaeologist named this human activity the Soan Culture. No men skeleton of this antiquity has been found yet. In Soan River Gorge many fossil bearing rocks are exposed on the surface. The 14 million years old fossils of gazelle, rhinoceros, crocodile, giraffe and rodent have been found here. Some of these fossils are in display at Natural History Museum of Islamabad.

Sohail Abbas : Sohail Abbas (born June 9, 1977 in Karachi) is a field hockey defender from Pakistan, and one of the most prolific hockey player from the Asian nation. He is specialized in penalty corners. Abbas holds the world record for most goals scored by an individual. The defender scored 274 international goals surpassing the 22-year-old record of legendary Dutch penalty corner specialist Paul Litjens. He retired in Decemeber 2004, just after the Champions Trophy in Lahore, when he was only 27 years of age. He has left his mark with a bright international career and his record will be there for a long time. Since the summer of 2005 he is playing for Dutch club Rotterdam.

Solanki : The Solanki is a Hindu Rajput dynasty of India, who ruled the kingdom of Gujarat from the 10th to the 13th centuries. The Solanki are a branch of the Chalukya clan of Kshatriyas and whose oldest known area of residence may be in present-day Karnataka. In Gujarat, Anhilwara (modern Siddhpur Patan) served as their capital. Gujarat was a major center of Indian Ocean trade, and Anhilwara was one of the largest cities in India, with population estimated at 100,000 in the year 1000. The Solankis were patrons of the great seaside temple of Shiva at Somnath Patan in Kathiawar; Bhima Dev helped rebuild the temple after it was sacked by Mahmud of Ghazni in 1026. His son Karandev conquered the Bhil king Ashapall or Ashaval, and after his victory established a city named Karnavati on the banks of the Sabarmati River, at the site of modern Ahmedabad.

Solung—Adi festival : The 'Solung' is the main festival of 'Adis' and is a manifestation of the Adis festival cult in Arunachal Pradesh. There are various stories about its origin, but the most commonly accepted one is that the Adis were asked by Kine-nane, the Goddesses of wealth and prosperity to perform the Solung Puja. The story goes like this. One 'Doying-Bote' (god of heaven) came in contact with Kine-nane and become sexually excited.

When he was about to copulate with her two monsters Totel-Mone and Dubeng-Mone, intervened and snatched off his testicles to destroy it and in the process scattered the divine sperms over different places from some of which sprouted paddy plants. This was found by Kine-nane. Finding human beings starving for want of food, she sent the paddy seeds through a dog. Since then men have been producing paddy in plenty to meet their requirement of feed. Kine-nane asked the men so helped by her to offer Puja in the name of Solung which they were only too willing to do. Kine-name also helped them to acquire Mithun, and pig, the two animals which are sacrificed at the time of Solung.

In the Solung they try to propitiate both Doying-Bote and Kine-nane and if they are pleased and satisfied the former will appear in the form of clouds and rains and latter will appear in the form of great fertility of soil. They land together on the surface of the earth where ultimately their union take place. It is believed that their successful union will lead to high yields of crops, more animals like mithun, pigs etc and ultimately wealth and prosperity for men. Solung celebration continues for five days, first day is called, 'Solung-Gidi Dogin' or the day of preparations, second and the main day of the celebration is called Doreph-Long (the day of animal sacrifice), third day is 'Binnayat Binam' or worshipping the goddess of plenty and prosperity. Fourth day is Yaktor of Ekoph when the villagers remains busy preparing bows and arrows and other weapons of war. On the fifth day the Miri (religious leader or priest) is given a ceremonial send off when the girl's sing and dance.

During Solung festival, every evening the Miri sings 'Solung Abung' and through the song he relates the stories about the origin of man, animals and plants, ancestry of the Adis, lives and deeds of the Adi Heroes. Solung is celebrated in the month of August or September but there is no fixed date for it. Now-a-days in some places, the festival is celebrated with a three day programme. Solung is celebrated to reap a rich harvest after sowing of seeds and transplantation of paddy plants, to raise more mithuns and pigs and also to be free from natural calamities, fire, accidents, diseases etc.

Soma : Soma (Sanskrit), or Haoma (Avestan) was a ritual drink of importance among the early Indo-Iranians, and the later Vedic and Iranian cultures. It is frequently mentioned in the Rigveda, which contains many hymns praising its energizing or intoxicating qualities. It is described as prepared by pressing juice from the stalks of a certain mountain plant, which has been variously hypothesized to be a psychedelic mushroom, cannabis, or ephedra. In both Indian and Iranian tradition, the drink is identified with the plant, and also personified as a god, the three forming a religious or mythological unity.

Somapura Mahavihara : Somapura Mahavihara was among the best knwon Buddhist viharas in India. The excavations at Paharpur has been identified with the Somapura Mahavihara, built by the Dharmapala (c 781-821 AD). The Pala rulers were devout Buddhists and they founded a number of viharas in their domain. The monastery was renovated during the rule of Mahipala I (c 995-1043 AD). The Tibetan text Pag Sam Jon Zang mentions that that the same king used to visit Somapura Vihara to offer his homage. Somapura Mahavihara gradually declined and was finally abandoned during the 13th century, when the region was conquered by the Muslims.

Many Tibetan monks visited the Somapura during 9th and 12th century AD. Atisha Dipankar Srijnan stayed here for many years and translated the Madhyamaka Ratnapradipa into Tibetan. His spiritual preceptor, Ratnakara Shanti, and several other famous scholars like Mahapanditacharya Bodhibhadra Kalamahapada, Viryendra and Karunashrimitra were associated with this vihara.

Somarama : Somarama is one of the Pancharama Kshetras which is located in Ramachandrapuram Taluk in East Godavari District of Andhra Pradesh in South India. Lord Shiva is known as Someswara Swamy here. The temple is situtated on the bank of Godavari River. The consort of Lord Someswara is Sri Rajarajeswari Ammavaru. The Sivalinga at this place is installed and established by Lord Chandra. Maha Shivaratri and Sarannavarathri are the main festivals celebrated at this temple.

Someshwar : On the way to Gangapur dam, there is a beautiful nature spot called Someshwar in Maharashtra. There is a temple of Lord Shiva and Lord Hanuman on the banks of the river Godavari. The area is covered with greenery all over, with a pleasant climate. Tourists can can enjoy swimming and boating in the river.

Somnath Temple : The Somnath Temple in the Prabhas Kshetra in Saurashtra, on the western coast of Gujarat, India is one of the twelve Jyotirlings (golden lingas) symbols of the God Shiva. It is mentioned in the Rig Veda. The Somnath Temple is known as the Shrine Eternal as it has withstood the shocks of time and the attacks of the destroyers. It has risen like a Phoenix each time it was destroyed or desecrated.

The first temple of Somnath is said to have existed before the beginning of the Christian era. The second temple, built by the Maitraka kings of Vallabhi in Gujarat, replaced the first one on the same site around 649. In 725 Junayad, the Arab governor of Sind, sent his armies to destroy the second temple. The Pratihara king Nagabhata II constructed the third temple in 815, a large structure of red sandstone. Mahmud of Ghazni attacked this temple in 1026, and looted it of gems and precious stones. He then massacred the worshippers and had the temple burnt. It was then that the famous Shiva lingam of the temple was entirely destroyed. During his campaign mahmud was challanged by Ghogha Rana, who at the ripe age of 90, sacrificed his own clan fighting against this icnoclast.

The fourth temple was built by the Paramara King Bhoj of Malwa and the Solanki king Bhima of Gujarat (Anhilwara) between 1026 and 1042. The wooden structure was replaced by Kumarpal who built the temple of stone. The temple was razed in 1297 when the Sultanate of Delhi conquered Gujarat, and again in 1394. The Mughal Emperor Aurangzeb destroyed the temple again in 1706. The present temple is the seventh temple built on the original site (A mosque present at that site was shifted few miles away). Sardar Vallabhbhai Patel, then Home Minister & the first Deputy Prime Minister of India took a pledge on November 13, 1947 for its reconstruction which was completed on December 1, 1995 when the President of India, Dr. Shankar Dayal Sharma dedicated it in the service of the nation. The present temple was built by the Shree Somnath Trust which looks after the entire complex of Shree Somnath and its environs. The Present temple, Kailash Mahameru Prasada, is built in the Chalukya style of temple architecture and reflects the skill of the Sompuras, Gujarat's master masons.

Son : The Son River of central India is the largest of the Ganges' southern tributaries. The Son originates in Chhattisgarh state, just east of the headwaters of the Narmada River, and flows north-northwest through Madhya Pradesh state before turning sharply eastward when it encounters the southwest-northeast-running Kaimur Range. The Son parallels the Kaimur Range, flowing east-northeast through Uttar Pradesh and Bihar states to join the Ganges just above Patna. Geologically, the lower valley of the Son is an extension of the Narmada Valley, and the Kaimur Range an extension of the Vindhya Range. Its length is 784 kilometres (487 miles). Its chief tributaries are the Rihand and the Koel.

The Son has a steep gradient (35-55 cm per km) with quick run-off and ephemeral regimes, becoming a roaring river with the rain-waters in the catchment area but turning quickly into a fordable stream. The Son, being wide and shallow, leaves disconnected pools of water in the remaining part of the year. The channel of the Son is very wide (about 5km at Dehri) but the floodplain is narrow, only 3 to 5 km wide. The river has been notorious for its changing courses in the past, as it traceable from several old beds on its east, but has been tamed squarely with the anicut at Dehri, and now more so with the Indrapuri Barrage, a few km upstream.

Son River : The Son River of central India is the largest of the Ganges' southern tributaries. The Son originates in Chhattisgarh state, just east of the headwaters of the Narmada River, and flows north-northwest through Madhya Pradesh state before turning sharply eastward when it encounters the southwest-northeast-running Kaimur Range. The Son parallels the Kaimur Range, flowing east-northeast through Uttar Pradesh and Bihar states to join the Ganges just above Patna.

Geologically, the lower valley of the Son is an extension of the Narmada Valley, and the Kaimur Range an extension of the Vindhya Range. Its length is 784 kilometres (487 miles). Its chief tributaries are the Rihand and the Koel. The Son has a steep gradient (35-55 cm per km) with quick run-off and ephemeral regimes, becoming a roaring river with the rain-waters in the catchment area but turning quickly into a fordable stream. The Son, being wide and shallow, leaves disconnected pools of water in the remaining part of the year. The channel of the Son is very wide (about 5km at Dehri) but the floodplain is narrow, only 3 to 5 km wide. The river has been notorious for its changing courses in the past, as it traceable from several old beds on its east, but has been tamed squarely with the anicut at Dehri, and now more so with the Indrapuri Barrage, a few km upstream.

Sona Glacier : Sona Glacier is the Himalayan glacier situated in the eastern part of Uttaranchal in the Pithoragarh district of India.Sona Glacier is located at the base of five peaks of Panchchuli in the Lassar Yankti—Darma valley.With Meola glacier it forms the famous Panchchuli glacier as mixed glacial system. One can reach here as glacial trek through Tawaghat-Bailing-Son—Duktu-

.Sona glacier and Meola glacier serves the route to climb Panchchuli peaks from east facing direction. Sona glacier is situated north to Meola Glacier. It is situated just below peaks like Ngalaphu 6,410 M and Panchchuli I.It is divided into Upper and Lower. The direction of the glacier is south west to north east.

Sonali Bank : Sonali Bank is a state-owned commercial bank in Bangladesh. It is the largest bank of the country. Sonali Bank was established in 1972 under the Bangladesh Banks (Nationalisation) Order, through the amalgamation and nationalisation of the branches of National Bank of Pakistan, Bank of Bhowalpur and Premier Bank branches located in East Pakistan until the 1971 Bangladesh Liberation War. When it was established, Sonali Bank had a paid up capital of 30 million taka. In 2001, its authorised and paid up capital were Tk 10 billion and Tk 3.272 billion respectively. The bank's reserve funds were Tk 60 million in 1979 and Tk 2.050 billion on 30 June 2000.

Sonali Bank has a total of 1186 branches. Out of them, 488 are located in urban areas, 696 in rural areas, and 2 are located overseas. It also operates the Sonali Exchange Company Inc. in USA and Sonali Bank (U.K.) Ltd., United Kingdom, to facilitate foreign exchange remittances.

Sonal Mansingh : Sonal Mansingh has been on stage since 1964. Her role as a social activist, thinker, researcher, orator, choreographer and teacher combines admirably with her dancing. She founded the Centre for Indian Classical Dances (CICD) in 1977 in Delhi and has trained many young men and women, some of who have earned critical acclaim already.

A leading exponent of Odissi, with a background of decades of training in Bharata Natyam, *Chhau* and Indian music, she has made original choreographic works based on Indian mythology as well as contemporary issues. She is a recipient of several honours and awards which include Singar Mani from Haridas Sangeet Sammelan, Mumbai (1967), Medal of Friendship Vietnam (1983), Natya Kala Ratna from National Cultural Organization (1985), Nrityakala Kaumudi Kala Priya, Nellore, Andhra Pradesh (1986), Rajiv Gandhi Excellence Award (1991), Padma Bhusan (1992), Indira Priya Darshini Award (1994) and the Medal of Friendship Cuba State Council (1995). She has widely traveled all over India and the world and participated in numerous festivals.

Sonargaon : Sonargaon is the ancient capital of Isa Khan's kingdom in Bengal. It is located near the current-day city of Narayanganj, Bangladesh. The great Muslim traveller Ibn Battuta visited it in the 14th century. It is the eastern terminus of the Grand Trunk Road, which was built by Sher Shah Suri in the 16th century, and which extends approximately 2500 kilometres across northern India and Pakistan to Peshawar in Pakistan's North-West Frontier Province.

Sonbhadra : Sonbhadra or Sonebhadra is the largest district of Uttar Pradesh, India. The district has an area of 6788 km^2 and a population of 1,463,468 (2001 census), with a population density of 216 persons per km&sup2:. It lies in the extreme southeast of the state, and is bounded by Mirzapur District to the northwest, Chandoli District to the north, Bihar state to the northeast, Jharkhand state to the east, Chhattisgarh state to the south, and Madhya Pradesh state to the west. The district headquarters is in the town of Robertsganj.

The Son River flows through the district from east to west, and its tributary the Rihand River, which rises to the south in the highlands of Chhattisgarh and Madhya Pradesh, flows north to join the Son in the center of the district. The Govind Ballabh Pant Sagar, a reservoir on the Rihand, lies partly in the district and partly in Madhya

Pradesh. The district has historic, cultural, and ecological affinities with the Bagelkhand region, but the Uttar Pradesh government has included the district in Purvanchal region for administrative purposes.OBRA a power project is located in this city. The famous duo of javed and adnan belong to this place.

Sonia Gandhi : Sonia Gandhi (born December 9, 1946), is an Italian-born Indian politician, the President of the Indian National Congress (Congress Party) and the widow of former Prime Minister of India, Rajiv Gandhi. She is currently the Chairperson of the ruling United Progressive Alliance in the Lok Sabha. She was named the third most powerful woman in the world by Forbes magazine, next to Condoleezza Rice and Wu Yi in the year 2004. Born into a family of modest means in an Italian village on the banks of a river 57 years ago, Sonia Maino, now Sonia Gandhi, has weaved a dramatic way to a place in history by becoming the President of India's century-old Congress party.

Being the third woman of foreign origin to hold the prestigious post after Annie Beasant and Nelli Sengupta, Sonia Gandhi also became the fifth from the Nehru family to take over the Congress reins. The other four were Motilal Nehru, Jawaharlal Nehru, Indira Gandhi and Rajiv Gandhi. She also is the eighth person of the foreign origin to be the Congress president. On 28th May 2005 Smt. Sonia Gandhi was elected as President of the Indian National Congress by overwhelming support from across the country from all states. Now not only Sonia is in the thick of politics, but her children, Rahul and Priyanka, too are in great demand in the Congress circle for taking over the Youth Congress.

Sonia Rupai Wildlife Sanctuary : This wildlife sanctuary, 175 Sq. Kms. in area, is situated in the Sonitpur District of Assam extending along the Himalayan foothills it offers magnificent view of both scenic beauty and wildlife. The sanctuary is the home of Elephant, Indian Bison, Deer and a variety of hill birds.

Sonipat : Sonipat is one of the districts of Haryana state, India, and Sonipat town is the district headquarters. The district touches Delhi on one end, Panipat District on the other, and the Yamuna River acting as a border in one direction and Rohtak on the other side. On the south of sonipat if we cross delhi, there is a city called SONa and On the north of sonipat there is a city called paniPAT. If we combine these names, it becomes SONa+paniPAT. In spite of a+pani,I was included to give special identity to the city.So, a new name was formed viz SON+i+PAT. Thus came into existence a good city named Sonipat.

Sonipat was earlier known as Sonprastha, which later on became Swarnprastha, meaning the "golden city": derived from two Sanskrit words, Swarn (gold) and Prastha (place). Over a period of time, the classical name Swarnprasth's pronunciation degerated into Swarnpat, and then to its current form of Sonipat. The earliest reference of this city comes in the epic Mahabharata, and at that time it was one of the five villages demanded by the Pandavas in lieu of the kingdom of Hastinapur.

Sonitpur : As varied and lovely as any, the centrally situated Sonitpur district of Assam, comprises of some 5000 sq km of variegated landscape along the mighty Brahmaputra upto the picturesque foothills of Arunachal Pradesh, Known to legend as Sonitpur, Tezpur is the ancient seat of culture, Mythology and romance and is located 181 Kms north east of Guwahati. It is a quality tea growing area with multiple ethnicity. The underlying warmth, concern for the welfare of every guest and the age old tradition of hospitality pervades the atmosphere. The tea garden community and the other ethnic groups present a poly-cultural spectrum with exotic customs and rites. They celebrate these with dance and song which are at one with the lush green vegetation, the enchanting hills, the purling streams and the surging Brahmaputra.

Sonmiani : Sonmiani is a coastal town in the southeast of Balochistan province in Pakistan, approximately 45 kilometres northwest of Karachi. The area hosts a 2 square kilometre flight test range for sounding rockets at 25°12'N 66°45'E that has been operated since 1962 by the Space and Upper Atmosphere Research Commission (SUPARCO). It is also used by the Pakistan Atomic Energy Commission's National Defence Complex to test solid-fueled ballistic missiles such as the short- and medium-range Hatf-III/Ghaznavi (M-11) and Hatf IV/Shaheen-I (possibly M-9) missiles.

Sony Entertainment Television : Sony Entertainment Television in India is a television channel operating in India. Popularly known as only Sony TV or SET, the channel also has its network TV channels SAB for light hearted general entertainment programming targeted towards male audiences and MAX for movies, special events & cricket. Sony Entertainment Television, India's No. 2 Hindi general entertainment television channel, is, backed by Sony Pictures Television International (SPTI).

Sony Entertainment Television is focused at providing quality and innovative entertainment. It combines international expertise and Indian values to create world class programming, which tugs at the heartstrings of viewers of over 33 million households in India. It offers a distinct viewing alternative differentiated in both content and format. The programming covers the entire gamut of genres—habit forming dramas, light hearted comedies, thrillers, Bollywood blockbusters and prestigious events.

Sony Entertainment Television in India is the first venture of Sony Pictures Entertainment, the biggest entertainment powerhouse of America. As part of the Sony family, the channel has access to a wide variety of international software from film and television divisions of Sony Pictures Entertainment. Sony Entertainment Television partners more than 715 brands. It partners brands in the truest sense of the term. In addition to offering significant reach to advertisers, it provides customized promotions to build their brands. All programming & marketing initiatives are focused on the core demographic: women & Men, 25—34 yrs, SEC ABC, the most significant target market in terms of consumption of brands & services.

Being a global brand, Sony Entertainment Television can be seen throughout India, Pakistan, Sri Lanka, Bangladesh, Middle-East, Canada, USA, UK & Eire, Western Europe, Africa, Russia, Australia & New Zealand. Though, the programmes are hardly in any other language, but Hindi.

Soomra Dynasty : Soomra dynasty or Soomro Dynasty was established by Soomro tribe in Sindh, Pakistan. Soomro ruled Sindh (when it was part of Hindustan, currently a province of Pakistan), from 1026-1351 AD a period of nearly 300 years. Soomro dynasty had both Arab and local Sindhi heritage. The early Soomra rulers were Fatimid Shia Ismailis, owed allegiance to Fatmid Khalifas of Cairo, sent them tribute and read their names in the Friday Khutba in mosques. Sultan Mahmud of Ghazni a Orthodox Sunni Muslim in his campaign to defeat heterodox Shia Ismaili sect conquered Soomro capital Mansura. The Soomro shifted their capital to Tharri, nealy 14 km eastwards of Matli on the Puran. Puran was later abandoned due to changes in the course of Puran river. Then Thatta was the capital from about 95 years until the end of their rule in 1351 AD. The Soomra was defeated by the Samma Dynasty, Jams of Lasbela or currently known as the Alianis.

Soon Valley : Soon Valley is located in Khushab, Punjab, Pakistan. Soon Valley starts from Padhrar village and end to Sakesar that is the highest peak of Salt Range. Sakesar is 5010 feet high from the sea level. Soon Valley is situated in the north west of Khushab. The length of Soon Valley is 35 miles and average width is 09 miles. The area of Soon Valley is 300 square feet. There are some special features of this valley that distinguish it from other areas, without knowing about them it is very hard to understand its importance.

Sopanam : Sopanam is a form of Indian classical music developed in the temples of Kerala in the wake of the increasing popularity of the Jayadeva's 'Gita Govinda' or 'Ashtapathi'. Sopanasangitham is sung by the side of the steps (Sopanam) of Temple, with the accompaniment of the drum called 'Idakka'. The sopanasangitam in its traditional form is seen at its best among the Marars and Poduvals, who were hereditary Ambalavasi Brahmins engaged to do the same.

The structure of the Sopanam music is believed to reflect the experience of the devotee in ascending the heights of devotion. Sopanam music developed and became popular through the practice of singing invocatory songs in front of the 'Kalam' of Kali (floor drawing of Kali) and later on at the sanctum of the temple. There are a few powerful schools connected with the temples like Pazhoor, Tiumandhamkunnu, Guruvayoor, Ramamangalam. In these temples, this music had been hereditarily practiced by temple singers. Neralattu Rama Poduval of Tirumandhamkunnu bani, Janardhanan Nedungadi of Guruvayoor, Damodara Marar belonging to the Mudiyettu bant of Pazhoor are some of the most effective experts.

Sopanam music as it is practiced in different schools, maintains its rustic nuances with the feeling of devotion as its basic quality. From the temple sanctum this music has taken many diversions and grown as dance music in Ashtapadiyattam; the mould of which was later adopted by Krishnanattam, devotional music in Kalam pattu and dramatic music in Mudiyettu and Kathakali.

Sorpotel : Sorpotel is a dish from Goa, India usually served at festivals and made from pork. The dish requires the use of the pork along with the liver, the heart and the kidney of the pig which is cooked in a very spicy sauce. The taste improves from day to day. It is sometimes said that sorpotel boasts as many versions as there are cooks in the state of Goa. Each family proudly flaunts its version of the must-have Christmas dish—although it is prepared and served whenever the need for a special meal arises.

Souls : Souls is a pop-music band from Bangladesh. It was established in Chittagong in 1972, and later moved to the capital city Dhaka. Former members include Tapan Chowdhury, Ayub Bachchu, Naseem Ali and Partho Barua. It is one of the oldest pop bands in Bangladesh and has performed more than 4000 concerts all over Bangladesh and also abroad. As of 2005, Souls has released 7 albums. The first album was released in 1982 and the last one was released in 2001.

Sourav Ganguly : Sourav Ganguly the former Captain of the Indian Cricket team is an aggressive left-handed batsman in the middle order and also bowls right-handed military medium pace.

Ganguly was born in an affluent family in Kolkata on 8th July 1973. As a young boy, Sourav's first interest was football and he played in the school football team for four years. But later he shifted to cricket and joined a cricket coaching club. Young Sourav made a century in an under-15 cricket match and another century in the 1991 Duleep Trophy which earned him a place in the Indian Cricket team touring Australia in 1991-92. Although this gave a start to his international career he was made to play only one One-Day International Match because of his inability to play onside strokes. He faced criticism for his attitude and inability. But after a gap of four years, he came back in style in the 1996 tour to England at Lord's; his test debut, scoring centuries and wickets and winning the Man of the Series Award and in the Sahara Cup, Toronto 1997 set a new World Record for 5 consecutive Man of the Match Awards.

From then Sourav has come a long way and achieved a lot—he along with Tendulkar forms the 4th Best Opening Pair in the History of One-day cricket and were involved in a World Record Opening Partnership of 252. Ganguly was named Sport star Person of the Year 1998 and won the Arjuna Award in the same year. Personally Sourav is a quiet, unassuming, undemonstrative man with nerves of steel. He is deeply religious and observes a fast every Tuesday. He is married to Dona, his next-door-neighbour, who is a classical dancer. He has accomplished a top place in Indian Cricket as a batsman and bowler by excelling both in One-Day Internationals and Test Matches.

South Asia : The term South Asia is often considered synonymous with the term Indian subcontinent, and includes these neighboring states: India, Pakistan, Bangladesh, Nepal, Bhutan, Sri Lanka and Maldives. All of these countries are members of the South Asian Association for Regional Cooperation (SAARC). Geographically, the Indian subcontinent would additionally include some disputed territory currently controlled by China and Myanmar. It covers about 4,480,000 km^2 (1,729,738 mi^2), or 10 percent of the Asian continent. However, its population accounts for about 40 percent of Asia. Some or all of Afghanistan is sometimes considered part of the region of South Asia because Afghanistan has shared many historical currents with the region, but is not located on the subcontinent.

South Asian Association for Regional Cooperation (SAARC) : The South Asian Association for Regional Cooperation, or SAARC, proposed by Ziaur Rahman, the then-president of Bangladesh, was established on December 8, 1985. SAARC is an association of eight countries of South Asia: Bangladesh, Bhutan, India, Maldives, Nepal, Pakistan, Sri Lanka, and most recently admitted, Afghanistan. These countries comprise an area of 5,127,500 km^2 and a fifth of the world's population.

SAARC encourages cooperation in agriculture, rural development, science and technology, culture, health, population control, narcotics control and anti-terrorism. SAARC has intentionally stressed these "core issues" and avoided more divisive political issues, above all the Kashmir dispute which bitterly divides the two largest member states, India and Pakistan. However, political dialogue is often conducted on the margins of SAARC meetings. In 1993, SAARC countries signed an agreement to gradually lower tariffs within the region. Nine years later, at the 12th SAARC summit at Islamabad, SAARC countries devised the South Asia Free Trade Agreement which created a framework for the establishment of a free trade zone covering 1.4 billion people. This agreement went into force on January 1, 2006.

South Breeze School : South Breeze School is an educational institution located in Dhaka, Bangladesh. The medium of instruction is the English language. Founded in 1986 by principal Zeenat Chowdhury, the original campus was located in Dhanmandi. In 2000, the campus was relocated and in 2004 a new additional section was opened in Uttara. The schools follows the British syllabus and the students are taught for Ordinary level (O'level) examinations conducted by Edexcel International. The school has been one of the leading ones in Bangladesh in terms of O'level results since 1990, when the first batch of student graduated from the school. Till date, three of the graduates have been selected as the valedictorians of the annual Daily Star Award ceremony that recognises the best O'level result-holders in the nation

South Deccan Plateau Dry Deciduous Forests : The South Deccan Plateau dry deciduous forests is an ecoregion of southern India. The ecoregion lies in the eastern foothills of the Western Ghats; the dry forests lie in the Ghats' rain shadow, and receive considerably less rainfall than the North Western Ghats moist deciduous forests and South Western Ghats moist deciduous forests that lie to the west. The ecoregion covers the southern portion of Karnataka's Malnad region, extending south into the Kongu Nadu region of eastern Tamil Nadu.

The South Deccan Plateau dry deciduous forests receive most of their rainfall with the June-September southwest monsoon, and are characterized by tall trees that drop their leaves during the dry winter and spring months. Much of the forest has been degraded through over-use, and thorn forests and shrub thickets are common. To the north and east, the dry deciduous forests transition to the Deccan thorn scrub forests. The ecoregion includes the cities of Bangalore and Mysore in Karnataka, and Coimbatore, Karur, and Salem in Tamil Nadu.

South Garo Hills : South Garo Hills is an administrative district in the state of Meghalaya in India. The district headquarters are located at Baghmara. The district occupies an area of 1850 km² and has a population of 99,105

South Goa : South Goa is one of the two districts that make up the state of Goa, India. The district has an area of 1966 km² and a population of 586,591 (2001 census).

It is bounded by North Goa District to the north, Utara Kannada District of Karnataka state to the east and south, and by the Arabian Sea to the west. The administrative headquarters of the district is Madgaon. The district is divided into three subdivisions, Margao, Mormugao, and Quepem, and five taluks, Salcete, Mormugao, Quepem, Sanguem, and Canacona.

The Portuguese established a colony in Goa in 1510, and expanded the colony to its present boundaries during the 17th and 18th centuries. Goa was annexed by India on December 19, 1961. Goa and two other former Portuguese enclaves became the union territory of Goa, Daman and Diu, and Goa was organized into a single district in 1965. On 30 May 1987 Goa attained statehood (while Daman and Diu became a separate union territory), and Goa was reorganized into two districts, North Goa and South Goa.

South India : South India is a geographic and linguistic-cultural region of India. Geographically, South India traditionally includes the entire Indian Peninsula south of the Satpura and Vindhya ranges and Narmada River, encompassing the Deccan plateau (from the Sanskrit word dakshina, meaning south), the Eastern and Western Ghats, and the coasts between the Ghats and the sea. As a linguistic-cultural and political region, South India consists of the five south Indian states of Andhra Pradesh, Goa,Karnataka, Kerala, and Tamil Nadu, and the union territories of Lakshadweep and Pondicherry & Andaman and Nicobar Islands. Natives of these states are referred to as South Indians.

South India is also called Dakshina Nad (Dakshina = South + Nad = land), Dravida Nad (Dravida = Dravidian + Nad = land), or simply Dravida. Culturally and linguistically South India is distinguished as the home of the Dravidians, but not exclusively so; ethnic Dravidians also live in parts of eastern and central India, Sri Lanka, and Southeast Asia, and some non-Dravidian peoples (for example the Konkani people and other Indo-Aryans) also make their home in South India and have adopted the local language.

South Indian Coffee : South Indian Coffee, also known as Madras Filter Coffee is a sweet milky coffee made from dark roasted coffee beans (70%-80%) and chicory (20%-30%), especially popular in the southern states of Karnataka and Tamil Nadu. The most commonly used coffee beans are Peaberry (preferred), Arabica, Malabar and Robusta grown in the hills of Kerala (Malabar), Karnataka (Chikmagalur) and Tamil Nadu (Nilgiris).

South Sikkim : South Sikkim is a district of the Indian state of Sikkim. Its capital is Namchi. South Sikkim lies at an altitude of 400 m to 2000 metres and hence enjoys a temperate climate for most of the year. The people are mainly of Nepali descent. Other ethnic groups include the Lepcha and Bhutia communities. Nepali is the most widely spoken language in the district. It also has one of the lowest populated regions of the state. It is also the most industrialised district in the state, owing to the availability of flattened land. The geology being stable means that the roads are in a good condition as compared to other parts of the state which suffer from landslides. Major urban centres include Teesta Bazaar and Melli. The district is also famous for its Sikkim Tea, which is grown near Namchi.

South Western Ghats Moist Deciduous Forests : The South Western Ghats moist deciduous forests is a tropical moist broadleaf forest ecoregion of southern India. It covers the southern portion of the Western Ghats range and the Nilgiri Hills between 250 and 1000 meters elevation in Kerala, Karnataka and Tamil Nadu states. The ecoregion has an area of 23,800 square kilometers (9,200 square miles). It includes the southern ranges of the Western Ghats, including the Agastyamalai and Anamalai, and the eastward spurs of the Nilgiri Hills and Palni Hills. The forests of Wayanad in northern Kerala mark the transition to the North Western Ghats moist deciduous forests to the north. To the west, the Malabar Coast moist forests ecoregion lies in the coastal strip between the 250 meter contour and the Malabar Coast. To the east, the ecoregion transitions to the South Deccan Plateau dry deciduous forests ecoregion in the drier rain shadow of the Western Ghats. It surrounds the South Western Ghats montane rain forests ecoregion, which lies above 1000 meters elevation.

South Western Ghats Montane Rain Forests : The South Western Ghats montane rain forests are an ecoregion of southern India, covering the southern portion of the Western Ghats range in Kerala and Tamil Nadu, at elevations over 1000 meters. They are cooler and wetter than the lower-elevation South Western Ghats moist deciduous forests, which surround the montane rain forests. The ecoregion is the most species-rich in peninsular India, and is home to numerous endemic species. It covers an area of 22,600 square kilometers. It is estimated that two-thirds of the original forests have been cleared, and only 3,200 square kilometers, or 15% of the intact area, is protected.

Special Protection Group (SPG) : The Special Protection Group (SPG) is the agency responsible for the protection of India's Prime Minister and his/her immediate family members. The force was raised in 1985 in response to the assassination of former Prime Minister Indira Gandhi. Today, the SPG is one of the elite agencies of its kind in Asia. The work of the Special Protection Group was more organised after the assassination of Rajiv Gandhi. After this there were no successful attempts to attack the

Indian Prime Minister and his/her immediate family members.

The Special Protection Group, with about 3000 personnel, is used for the protection of VVIPs such as the Prime Minister. Recruits include the Police and the NSG Commandos and they are trained like the US Secret Service. The Officer cadre is mainly IPS Officers from various state/central cadres. The Special Protection Group provides proximate security to VVIPs and the members of their immediate family. Proximate security includes protection provided from close quarters, journey on foot, road, rail, aircraft, watercraft or any other means of transport, and includes places of functions, engagements, residence, etc. They comprise ring round teams, isolation cordons, the sterile zone, and the rostrum & access control to the person or members of his immediate family. The Special Protection Group, over a period of time, grew both in size as well as in specialisation.

Sri Aurobindo : Sri Aurobindo (August 15, 1872–December 5, 1950) was an Indian nationalist, scholar, poet, Hindu mystic, evolutionary philosopher, yogi and guru. His followers further believe that he was an avatar, an incarnation of the supreme being.

Sri Aurobindo spent his life—through his vast writings and through his own development—working for the freedom of India, the path to the further evolution of life on earth, and to bring down what he called the Supramental Truth Consciousness Force to enable such progress.

Sri Digambar Jain Lal Mandir : Sri Digambar Jain Lal Mandir Is a Jain temple in the Chandni Chowk area of Delhi, India. It is directly across from the Laal Quila. Among other things, it is known for an avian veterinary hospital in a second building behind the main temple. Note that all animal products must be checked at the gate before entry, as they are against Jain precepts.

Sri Krishna Chaitanya Mission : Sri Krishna Chaitanya Mission is a religious organisation in the Gaudiya Vaishnavism tradition founded by Srila Bhakti Vaibhava Puri Maharaj; Maharaj received initiation from Srila Bhaktisiddhanta Saraswati Thakur, so the mission operates in the Saraswat tradition of Bhaktisiddhanta and his Gaudiya Math. Disciples chant the Hare Krishna mana-mantra on prayer beads, wear dhoti or Sari (Sanyasa initiates wear the traditional vesh of their ashram), and preach through traveling, book distribution, singing Kirtan and distribution of prasadam (food offered to Lord Krishna).

The origins of Sri Krishna Chaitanya Mission are found in 1966 with the establishment of Sri Krishna Chaitanya Ashram in Kakinada, Andhra Pradesh, but presumably the organisation was not registered under its current name until 1983. The organisation has eighteen (18) ashrams in India, as well as a worldwide following. Over twenty (20) Sanyasa initiates, as well as Srila BV Puri Maharaj himself, spearhead the preaching campaign to communicate the tenents of Gaudiya Vaishnava Theology.

Sri Padmanabhaswamy Temple : Sri Padmanabhaswamy temple, located inside the East Fort in Thiruvananthapuram, capital of Kerala state, India, is dedicated to Lord Padmanabha, a form of Vishnu. The temple is considered one of the 108 Tirupatis and Vishnu is enshrined here in Anananthasayanam posture, that is, in eternal sleep of yognidra. This is an ancient temple and the city of Thiruvananthapuram derives its name from the name of the presiding deity enshrined in the temple.

Sri Padmanabhaswamy Temple stands at a place, which is considered as one of the seven Parasurama Kshetras, and ancient texts including Puranas, particularly, the Skanda Puranas and Padma Puranas, have extolled the sanctity of this place and the shrine. The tradition states that in this place Lord Vishnu had given darshan to Indian sages like Divakarmuni and Bilvamangalam Swami. An Ezhava couple had also seen the lord in the form of a child and the child had taken morsels of rice from the hands of the couple. In memory of this legend, naivedyam prepared of rice is offered to the deity here in a coconut shell.

Sri Ramana Maharshi : Sri Ramana Maharshi (December 30, 1879 – April 14, 1950) was a great Hindu mystic of the Advaita Vedanta stream and is widely regarded as one of the greatest saints of Hinduism. He lived in the sacred Tiruvannamalai hill near Chennai. The core of his teachings was the practice of atma-vichara (self-enquiry).

Sri Ramcharitmanas : Sri Ramcharitmanas is an epic poem composed by the great 16th-century Indian poet, Goswami Tulsidas (c.1532–1623) (also transliterated as Tulasidasa). As he mentions in Baal Kaand of the composition, he started writing it in Vikram Samvat 1631 (1574 AD) in Avadhpuri, Ayodhya. It was completed in two years and seven months. A large portion of the poem was composed at Varanasi, where the poet spent most of his later life. It is considered one of the greatest works of Hindi literature.

Raamcharitmaanas is a retelling of the events of the Sanskrit epic Ramayana, concerning the amazing exploits of Rama. The great poem is popularly called Tulsi-krita Ramayana, but entitled by its author Raamcharitmaanas, or the Lake of Rama's Deeds. It is as well known among Hindus in northern India as is the Bible among the rural population of England. The composition is in Avadhi, a local dialect of Hindi, spoken in the Gangetic plain of

North India. The language is flowery with free use of metaphors and similes. Many of its verses are popular proverbs in that region; an apt quotation from them by a stranger has the immediate effect of instilling confidence in the listener. As with the King James Bible and Shakespeare, Tulsidas's phrases have passed into common speech, and are used by millions of Hindi speakers (and even speakers of Urdu) without the speakers being conscious of their origin. Not only are his sayings proverbial: his doctrine actually forms the most powerful religious influence in present-day Hinduism; and, though he founded no school and was never known as a guru or master, he is everywhere accepted as both poet and saint, an inspired and authoritative guide in religion and the conduct of life.

Tulsidas professed himself the humble follower of his teacher, Narhari-Das, from whom as a boy in Sukar-khet he first heard the tale of Rama's exploits that would form the subject of the Raamcharitmaanas. (Narhari-Das was the sixth in spiritual descent from Ramananda, the founder of popular Vaishnavism in northern India.) The poem is a revisiting of the great theme of Valmiki (the ancient author of the Ramayana), but is not a mere retelling of the Sanskrit epic. Where Valmiki has condensed the story, Tulsidas has expanded, and, conversely, wherever the elder poet has lingered longest, there his successor has condensed. Raamcharitmaanas consists of seven books, of which the first two, entitled Childhood and Ayodhya, make up more than half the work. (The second book, an expansive recounting of the meeting of Rama with his brother Bharata in the forest, is often the most admired.)

The tale begins at King Dasaratha's court, and tells of the birth and boyhood of Rama and his three brothers, his marriage with Sita, his voluntary exile which is the unfortunate result of Kaikeyi's guile and Dasaratha's rash vow, the dwelling-together of Rama and Sita in the great central Indian forest, her abduction by Ravana, Rama's expedition to Lanka and the overthrow of the ravisher, and life at Ayodhya after the return of the reunited pair. It is written in pure Baiswari or Eastern Hindi, in stanzas called chaupais, broken by dohas or couplets, with an occasional sortha and chhand – the latter a hurrying metre of many rhymes and alliterations.

Sri Sri Ravi Shankar : Sri Sri Ravi Shankar is a spiritual guru and founder of the Art of Living movement to spread the knowledge of breathing, living and spirituality worldwide. Sri Sri Ravi Shankar has given discourses on widely varied spiritual topics, from Krishna to Christ and also conducts Satsangs (Literally, "company of the good people"), where people gather and sing in the praise of divinity. Though born in a Hindu family, he has followers from all religions. His organization is actively involved in many service projects throughout the world.

The Art of Living Foundation, founded by Sri Sri Ravi Shankar, is an international nonprofit educational, charitable, and humanitarian organization active in more than 146 countries around the world. It offeres innovative programs that are aimed to eliminate stress, create a sense of belonging, restore human values, and encourage people from all backgrounds, religions, and cultural traditions to come together in celebration and service. These programmes and service activities have benefitted over 20 million people across the globe.

To live life fully and freely is an art, requiring skill, intuition, creativity, and knowledge. Art of Living, through its many programs, works to bring these values to our society by strengthening the individual. As a Non-Governmental Organization, Art of Living Foundation works in special consultative status with the Economic and Social Council of the United Nations, participating in a variety of committees and activities relating to health, education, sustainable development and conflict resolution.

Sri Sringeri Sharada Peetham : Sri Sringeri Sharada Peetham is one of the important Hindu Advaita mathas. The heads of the matha are known as Sankaracharyas. It is believed to be one of the original mathas started by Sankara. The matha is in the temple town of Sringeri (Shringeri), on the banks of river Tunga, in the Chikmagalur district of the Karnataka state, India. It is 190 kilometres from Mangalore.

The origin of the matha is described in Sankara Vijaya, written by Madhava. According to legends, Sankara and the pair reached Sringeri at an exceptionally hot noon, and as they proceeded to the river Tunga for their ablutions, they saw a frog struggling in the blazing sun to be delivered of its offspring. A cobra, the natural enemy of frog, raised its hood to provide the frog with shelter and protection from the ravages of the tropical sun. Sankara was greatly moved by the sight. If there was paradise on earth, here it was, where the lion and the lamb, the tiger and the cow, the cobra and the frog lived in mutual amity and peace. He turned round when, as she had already stipulated, Bharati, known also as Sarada, decided to stay for good at Sringeri on the banks of the sacred river Tunga.

Vishwarupa, assuming the name of Suresvaracharya, was installed here as the successor of Sankaracharya before the latter resumed his tour to found his three pithas at Puri, Dwaraka and Badrinath. Thus the matha traces its lineage from Suresvaracharya. The Sringeri matha records its history from the 8th century onwards. The recent Sringeri matha sources reported that Sankara was born in the fourteenth year of the reign of Vikramaditya. Some believe him to be the Vikramaditya II of the Western Chalukya Dynasty, which ruled from Badami in Karnataka.

Others believe him to the Vikramaditya of the 1st century BCE. The history of the Sringeri Matha since the period of Sri Bharathi Tirtha (I) and Sri Vidyaranya onwards is well documented. Most of the names from the Sringeri lineage up to Vidyaranya are also found in the Sri Guru Charitra, a 15th-century Marathi work by Gangadhara Saraswathi. The matha continues in existence to this day, and governs many institutions.

Sri Venkateshwara National Park : Sri Venkateshwara National Park extends over two districts of Chittoor and Cuddapah of Andhra Pradesh in an area of 353.62 sq.km. The park established in October 1989, is named after Lord Venkateshwara of Tirupati. It is located in Rajampet of Cuddapah district and Chandragiri and Bailapadu of Chittoor district.

Sri Yukteswar : Sri Yukteswar was born in Serampore, India to Kshetranath Karar and Kadambini. He married and had one daughter. His wife passed away a few years after their marriage, and Sri Yukteswar entered the monastic Swami order some time after that. In 1884, he met his guru, Lahiri Mahasaya, who initiated him into the path of Kriya Yoga. Sri Yukteswar would spend a great deal of time during the next several years in the company of his guru, often visiting Lahiri Mahasaya in Varanasi from his home in Serampore. He converted his family home in Serampore into an ashram, where he had resident students and disciples. Sri Yukteswar had few long-term disciples. However, in 1910, the young Mukunda Lal Ghosh would become Sri Yukteswar's disciple, and spread the teachings of Kriya Yoga throughout the world as Paramahansa Yogananda. Sri Yukteswar was especially skilled in Vedic Astrology, and prescribed various astrological gemstones and bangles to his students. He also studied astronomy and science, as evidenced in the formulation of his Yuga theory in The Holy Science. Sri

Yukteswar passed away at his Puri ashram on March 9, 1936.

Sriharikota : Sriharikota (also Sriharikote) is a barrier island off the coast of Andhra Pradesh in India. It separates the Pulicat Lake from the Bay of Bengal, and is home to the town of Pulicat. It is in Nellore district. The nearest town is Sullurpet, which has the nearest railway station. It houses India's only satellite launch centre in the Satish Dhawan Space Centre used by the Indian Space Research Organisation to launch satellites using multi-stage rockets such as the Polar Satellite Launch Vehicle or the Geosynchronous Satellite Launch Vehicle. Sriharikota is also known as SHAR.

Srikakulam : Srikakulam is a town in Srikakulam District in the north-eastern corner of the state of Andhra Pradesh, India. The town of Srikakulam is the district headquarters and has a population of 109,666 (agglomeration 117,066) (2001 census). It is located on the banks of the River Nagavali at (lat: 18°18' N, lon: 83°54' E).

Srikanthaiah : B M Srikanthaiah or B M Shri (1881-1946) was one of the most influential authors, writers and translators of Kannada literature. Known as the Kannada Kanva for his guardianship of Kannada Literature, he was instrumental in encouraging and promoting Kannada and inspiring writers such as Kuvempu and G. P. Rajarathnam to write in Kannada, at a time when English was becoming the common medium. He was awarded the 'Raja Sevaskta' award by the Maharaja of Mysore and was the president of the Kannada Saithya Sammelana in 1938 at Gulburga.

Srinagar : Srinagar, is the summer capital of the state of Jammu and Kashmir in India, and is situated in the valley of Kashmir. The city lies on both banks of the Jhelum River, a tributary of the Indus River. The city is famous for its lakes and houseboats floating over them. It is also known for traditional Kashmiri handicrafts and dry fruits. Srinagar is 876 km north of Delhi. The headquarters of the Srinagar District are situated in the city.

Sringeri : Sringeri, located in Chikmagalur district in the Indian state of Karnataka is the site of the first matha established by the Adi Sankaracharya, Hindu reformer and exponent of the Advaita Vedanta philosophy, in the 8th century C.E. It is located on the banks of the river Tunga. In a popular legend, Adi Sankaracharya is said to have selected the site when, walking by the Tunga river, he saw a cobra with a raised hood, providing shelter from the hot sun, to a frog about to spawn. Four mathas were eventually established by Sankara, in the north (at Jyotirmath, near Badrinath), south (at Sringeri and according to some disputed accounts, also at Kanchipuram), east (at Puri), and west (at Dwaraka) of India.

The name Sringeri is derived from Rishyashrunga-giri, a nearby hill that is believed to have contained the hermitage of Rishi Vibhandaka and his son Rishyashrunga. Rishyasrhrunga appears in an episode in the Bala-Kanda of the Ramayana where a story, narrated by Vasishta, relates how he brought rains to the drought-stricken kingdom of Romapada.

The most important temple at Sringeri is the Vidyasankara temple built, in commemoration of the pontiff Vidyasankara, around 1357-58 AD. It was built by Vidyaranya, patron-saint of Harihara and Bukka the brothers who founded the Vijayanagara empire. The niches in the temple have a number of sculptures from Hindu, Buddhist and Jain mythologies. Inscriptions in the temple record contributions made by several Vijayanagara emperors, though the temple was probably built on an earlier Hoysala site, and combines the Hoysala and Vijayanagara architectural features. The temple architecture is also an exhibition of astronomoical expertise by our planners. At the start of each solar month in the Indian calendar, the sun rays fall on the pillar designated for that particular month. The location of the pillars also reflect the 12 astrological houses in the Indian astrology.

Srinivasa Ramanujan : Srinivasa Ramanujan was a great Mathematician, who became world famous at the age of twenty six. He was born at Erode in Tamil Nadu on 22 December 1887. Ramanujan could not complete his college education because of illness. He was so interested in mathematics that he learned on his own. He found out new formulas for solving mathematical problems and wrote articles about them. Professor Hardy a scientist in the Cambridge University saw one his article and impressed by his knowledge, took Ramanujan to England.

Ramanujan was considered as the master of theory of numbers. The most outstanding of his contributions was his formula for p (n), the number of 'partitions' of 'n'. It was in 1914, while he was working in Trinity College he developed the 'Number Theory' and for his valuable contribution, was elected fellow of Trinity College on 18th October 1917. He returned to India in 1919 and began Research. He passed away on 26 April 1920. Government of India issued a commemorative stamp in his honour. Indian National Science academy and many other scientific institutions in India are giving various awards in memory of this brilliant mathematician.

Srirangam : Srirangam, also known as Thiruvarangam, is a small island town adjoining Tiruchirapalli in South India. Srirangam is bounded by the Kaveri River on one side, and the Kaveri tributary Kollidam (Coleroon) on the other. Srirangam is home to a significant population of Vaishnavites.

Srirangam is famous for its Sri Ranganathaswamy Temple, a major pilgrimage destination for Hindus (especially Vaishnavites) and one of the largest temple complexes in India. The gopuram of the temple is called the Rajagopuram and is 236 feet (72 m) tall. Myth has it that the coast of Sri Lanka can be seen from the top of the gopuram. The temple is constituted by seven prakaras (elevated enclosures) with gopurams articulating the axial path, the highest at the outermost prakara and the lowest at the innermost.

Srirangapattana : Srirangapattana is a town of great religious, cultural and historic importance located near the city of Mysore in the south Indian state of Karnataka. Although situated a mere 13 km from Mysore city, Srirangapattana lies in the neighbouring district of Mandya. The entire town is enclosed by the river Kaveri to form an island. While the main river flows on the eastern side of the island, the Paschima Vaahini segment of the same river flows to its west. The town is easily accessed by train from Bangalore and Mysore and is also well-connected by road, lying as it does just off the Bangalore-Mysore highway. The highway passes through this town and special care was taken to minimise any impact on the monuments here.

Srisailam : Srisailam is a Jyothirlingam (Hindu shrine to Shiva) located in Kurnool district, Andhra Pradesh, India. It is located about 245 km from Hyderabad and 132 km from Nandyal. Srisailam is situated in the thick and inaccessible forests of the Nallamalai hills, in the northeastern portion of the Nandikotkur Taluk of Kurnool District. It lies on a straight line west of Vijayawada, right as it were in the centre of South India. It is 73 miles north of Nandyal Railway Station. On leaving Nandyal, one has to proceed to Atmakur, which is at a distance of 38 miles by road and from Atmakur to Nagaluti, which is 10 miles off.

There are two routes to reach Srisailam from Nagaluti. One goes via Pedda Cheruvu, and across the hills, and through dense forests by footpath, and the other by road to Dornal, and from Dornal to Srisailam, by the recently opened ghat road. The road from Nagaluti to Pedda Cheruvu is paved with a remarkable series of stone steps, and the forest scenery, and the ravines of the rock are magnificent and hallowed.

Srisailam Project : The Srisailam Project is located in Andhra Pradesh's Rayalaseema Region on the Krishna River. It has a live storage of 250 thousand million cubic feet (TMC). This reservoir was originally designed for hydropower generation only but was later converted to a multi-purpose facility for water supply and irrigation.

St. Angelo Fort : St. Angelo Fort (Kannur Fort) is also known as Kannur Kotta is a fort facing Arabian Sea is situated 3 km from Kannur town of Kerala state, south India. Don Francisco De Almeida of Portuguese constructed this fort in 1505 AD. The Dutch captured the fort from Portuguese in 1663 they sold the fort to the king Ali Raja of Arakkal kingdom. In 1790 the British seized the control over this fort and became one of the important military centres of the British in Malabar. Many people believe that there is a secret tunnel in this fort. This tunnel was built underneath the sea to the Thalassery Fort which is 21 km from Kannur fort. This under passage is said to be used by soldiers to escape. The Moppila Bay Harbor and Arakkal Mosque are near the fort. The fort, is now under the supervision of the Archaeological Survey of India.

St. Joseph High School : St. Joseph High School is a secondary school located at Asad Avenue, Mohammadpur, Dhaka, Bangladesh. Since 1999, the school is recognized by the Board of Secondary and Higher Secondary Education, Dhaka, Bangladesh as St. Joseph Higher Secondary School. It was established as "St. Joseph English Medium School" in 16 Monir Hossain Lane, Narinda in the old section of Dhaka in 1954 by the Congregation of Holy Cross missionaries. The school moved to its present site in 1965. Currently, it is run under the supervision of the Catholic Archdiocese of Dhaka. It is considered one of the top schools of the country, in terms of its success in public examinations.

St. Martin's Island : St. Martin's Island is a small island in the northeast part of the Bay of Bengal, about 9 km south of the tip of the Cox's Bazar-Teknaf peninsula, and forming the southernmost part of Bangladesh. It is about 8 km west of the northwest coast of Myanmar at the mouth of the Naf River. The local name of the island is "Narical Gingira". St. Martin's Island has attracted tourists from home and abroad from the very beginning. Now a days, three shipping liner has regular daily trips to the island. They are Kutubdia, Sea-Truck and Keary-Sindbad. Tourists can book their trip both from the Chittagong city or from the Cox's Bazar city. The surrounding coral reef of the island has an extension named Chera Dwip. It is considered to be a mandatory part of the tour to visit the beautiful Chera Dwip.

Stanley Reservoir : Stanley Reservoir is one of largest fishing reservoirs in South India. Its source of water is the River Cauvery (Kaveri). Its total capacity is more than 90,000,000,000 cubic feet (90 tmc ft). The Stanley Reservoir is one of the largest of its kind in the world. It was completed in 1934. The total length of the dam is 1700 meters. The Mettur Hydro Electrical power project is also quite large. The dam, the park, the major hydroelectric power stations and hills on all sides make Mettur a good tourist attraction.

STAR (Satellite Television for Asian Region) TV : STAR is an Asian TV service owned by the News Corporation. It is based out of Hong Kong but there are also programming offices in India and Australia, as well as in the rest regions in Asia. According to the STAR website, their services has more than 300 million viewers in 53 countries and is watched by approximately 100 million viewers every day. STAR has emerged as India's second-largest media company after "Bennett, Coleman & Co" which publisher of Times-Of-India. STAR's main revenues come from India, with 80% of Indian viewers watching Star Channel.

Star Air : Star Air is a cargo airline based in Karachi, Pakistan. It operates to many cities in Pakistan including Lahore, Islamabad and Peshawar.

Star India Network : Star India Network is India's largest private entertainment company and runs several popular television channels like Star Plus, Star News, Star Movies, Star World, Star One and Channel V. It is partly owned by Rupert Murdoch's News Corp.

Star Monument : Star monument is one of the most breathtaking buildings in Haryana. This building houses the samadhi of Sh Tara Chand fondly called 'Maharaj ji' by his followers. The building is situated in the Radhaswami Satsang Bhawan complex, Dinaud, about 12 km from *Bhiwani, Haryana.*

Star Mosque : Star Mosque is situated in Abdul Khairat Road, Armanitola, in the old part of Dhaka City. The mosque is not dated by any inscription. It is known that one Mirza Golam Pir, whose ancestors had come to Dhaka and settled in Mohalla Ale Abu Sayeed (present-day Armanitola), erected it. Mirza Golam Pir died in 1860, and hence the date of construction of the mosque may conveniently be placed in the first half of the 19th century.

Originally it was an oblong (10.06m × 4.04m) three-domed mosque. There were three mihrabs on the Qibla wall in alignment with the three doorways of the mosque, of which the central one was larger than the side ones. The prayer chamber was roofed with three domes, the central one being taller and larger than the other two. The domes are carried in the interior on squinches. The original mosque building was not as decorated as it is now. The dilapidated plain and naked wall of the western side bears witness to the plainness of the past. The three southern doorways of the mosque are no doubt the old ones.

The mosque, both inside and outside, is decorated with mosaic. Small chips of Chinaware-plate, cup etc and pieces of glass have been used for mosaic. This type of mosaic is called 'Chini Tikri' work. Vase with flowers is an important decorative motif on the spandrel of the arches and elsewhere on the facade. Flower-vases, flower branches, rosset, crescent, star, and Arabic calligraphic writing have been used in the decoration of the mosque. The outer wall between the doors are decorated with the motif of Fujisan (Mount Fuji) on glazed tiles and a crescent-and-star design decorates the upper part of the facade. Hundreds of blue stars have been created on the domes of white marble. All over the mosque the motif of stars dominate the decoration and so the mosque is called the Star Mosque (Tara Masjid).

Star Plus : Star Plus is a Hindi language television channel in India. In its earlier avatar it used to be an English channel, which was later started beaming 24 hour Hindi programming to cater to a wider audience. A new channel called Star World was introduced to take up the space of English Language programming. Star Plus includes many popular Indian dramas such as Kahaani Ghar Ghar Ki and Kyunki Saas Bhi Kabhi Bahu Thi, and the Indian version of Who Wants To Be A Millionaire, known in India as Kaun Banega Crorepati, which is presented by the

Bollywood legend Amitabh Bachchan. STAR PLUS is India's No. 1 cable channel for 5 years running (as of 2005). The channel reaches more than 50 million viewers every week and boasts 45 out of the top 50 shows on Indian cable and satellite television.

State Bank of India (SBI) : State Bank of India (SBI) is the largest bank in India. It is also, measured by the number of branch offices and employees, the largest bank in the world. Established in 1806 as Bank of Bengal, it remains the oldest commercial bank in the Indian Subcontinent and also the most successful one providing various domestic, international and NRI products and services, through its vast network in India and overseas. With an asset base of $126 billion and its reach, it is a regional banking behemoth. The bank was nationalised in 1955 with the Reserve Bank of India having a 60% stake. It has laid emphasis on reducing the huge manpower through Golden handshake schemes and computerizing its operations.

State Emblem of India : The state emblem is an adaptation from the Saranath Lion Capital Of Ashoka. In the Original, there are four lions, standing back to back, mounted on an abacus with a frieze carrying sculptures in high relief of an elephant, a galloping horse, a bull and a lion separated by intervening wheels over a bell shaped lotus. Carved out a single block of polished sandstone, the capital is crowned by the wheel of the law (Dharma Chakra).

In the state emblem, adopted by the government of India on 26 January 1950, only three lions are visible, the fourth being hidden from view. The wheel appears in relief in the center of the abacus with the bull on right and a horse on left and the out lines of other wheels on extreme right and left. The bell shaped lotus has been omitted. The words 'Satyameva Jayate' from Mundaka Upanishad, meaning "Truth Alone Triumphs", are inscribed below the abacus in Devanagari Script.

States Reorganization Acts : Potti Sreeramulu's *fast-unto-death,* and consequent death for the demand of an Andhra State in 1953 sparked a major re-shaping of the Indian Union. Nehru appointed the *States Reorganization Commission,* upon whose recommendations, the States Reorganization Act was passed in 1956. Old states were dissolved and new states created on the lines of shared linguistic and ethnic demographics. The separation of Kerala and the Telugu-speaking regions of Madras State enabled the creation of an exclusively Tamil-speaking state of Tamil Nadu. On May 1, 1960, the states of Maharashtra and Gujarat were created out of the Bombay state.

Stotras : Stotras are Hindu prayers that praise aspects of God, such as Devi, Siva, or Vishnu. Stotras, according to Swami Tapasyananda, are invariably uttered aloud and consist of chanting verses conveying the glory and attributes of God. The three most famous and sacred stotras in Hinduism are Lalitha Sahasranama, Shri Rudram Chamakam, and Vishnu Sahasranama. Other famous Stotras are: Sri Ramraksha Stotra, Sri Maruti Stotra.

Strategic Nuclear Command : The Strategic Nuclear Command, or the Strategic Forces Command, forms part of India's Nuclear Command Authority (NCA; formed on 6 January 2003) responsible for the management of the country's tactical and strategic nuclear weapons. The NCA itself comprises a political council chaired by the prime minister —'the only person entitled to authorise the use of nuclear weapons — served by an executive council chaired by the national security adviser. Their directives are to be operationalised by a new Strategic Forces Command under the control of a Commander-in-Chief of the rank of Air Marshal (or its equivalent) in charge of the management and administration of the tactical and strategic nuclear forces. The NCA may be seen as the first stage in the development of an effective and robust command-and-control (C2) and indications-and-warning (I&W) systems and infrastructure for its strategic nuclear force commensurate with India's strategic requirements.

Sualkuchi : Loated 32km away across the river from Guwahati, Sualkuchi is a famous silk-weaving centre best known for its 'muga' silk which is naturally golden coloured, not dyed. 'Endi' or 'Tassar' and pat silks are also woven here and prices are lower than in Guwahati. There are also brass workers here. There is a regular ferry service across the river daily.

Subash Chandra Bose : Subash Chandra Bose was a great patriot and a determined fighter of national freedom. He was born at Cuttack (Orissa). Unlike other prominent leaders of the Indian freedom struggle, Subash strongly believed that an armed rebellion was necessary to wrest independence from the British. Subash Chandra Bose is popularly known as 'Netaji'.

In 1943, he organized the Indian National Army (I.N.A). He gave to the nation the Salutation and slogan of 'Jai Hind'. The famous words of Subash Chandra Bose are "Give me blood, I will give you freedom". He was posthumously decorated with the title 'Bharat Ratna' in 1992. However, the Supreme Court of India declared on 4th August, 1997 that the press communiqué dated January 23, 1992, used from the Rashtrapati Bhavan to confirm Bharat Ratna "Posthumously" on Netaji should be treated as cancelled as this proposal was dropped by Government in deference to the sentiments expressed by Public and his family members. He is said to have died in an air-crash in 1945.

Subrahmanyan Chandrasekhar : Subrahmanyan Chandrasekhar, a Nobel Laureate in Physics and one of the greatest astrophysicists of modern times was born on October 19, 1910 in Lahore, (now in Pakistan) to parents Chandrasekhara Subrahmanya Ayyaa civil servant and Sita Balakrishnan. Being the nephew of the great, C.V. Raman, a Nobel Prize winner in Physics young Chandrashekhar's interest in the subject came naturally to him.

In 1930, at the age of 19, he completed his degree in Physics from Presidency College, Madras and went to England for postgraduate studies at the Cambridge University. Chandrasekhar was noted for his work in the field of stellar evolution, and in the early 1930s he was the first to theorize that a collapsing massive star would become an object so dense that not even light could escape it; now known as the Black hole. He demonstrated that there is an upper limit (known as 'Chandrasekhar Limit') to the mass of a White dwarf star. His theory challenged the common scientific notion of the 1930s that all stars, after burning up their fuel, became faint, planet-sized remnants known as white dwarfs. But today, the extremely dense neutron stars and black holes implied by Chandrasekhar's early work are a central part of the field of astrophysics. Initially his theory was rejected by peers and professional journals in England. The distinguished astronomer Sir Arthur Eddington publicly ridiculed his suggestion that stars could collapse into such objects(black holes). Disappointed, and reluctant to engage in public debate, Chandrasekhar moved to America and in 1937 joined the faculty as an Assistant Professor of Astrophysics at the University of Chicago and remained there till his death. At Chicago, he immersed himself in a personalized style of research and teaching, tackling first one field of astrophysics and then another in great depth. He wrote more than half a dozen definitive books describing the results of his investigations. More than 100,000 copies of his highly technical books have been sold. He also served as editor of the Astrophysical Journal, the field's leading journal, for nearly 20 years.

Chandrasekhar was a creative, prolific genius whose ability to combine mathematical precision with physical insight changed humanity's view of stellar physics. In addition to his work on star degeneration, he has contributed significantly to many disparate branches of physics, including rotational figures of equilibrium, stellar interiors, radiative transfer of energy through the atmospheres of stars, hydro magnetic stability and many others. He won the Nobel Prize in 1983 and received 20 honorary degrees, was elected to 21 learned societies and received numerous awards in addition to the Nobel Prize, including the Gold Medal of the Royal Astronomical Society of London; the Royal Medal of the Royal Society, London; the National Medal of Science, the Rumford Medal of the American Academy of Arts and Sciences; and the Henry Draper Medal of the National Academy of Sciences. NASA's premier X-ray observatory was named the Chandra X-ray Observatory in his honor. He and his wife, Lalitha became American citizens in 1953. This genius passed away on 21 August 1995 in Chicago, Illinois, USA.

Subramanya Bharathi : Subramanya Bharathi (December 11, 1882 - September 11, 1921) better known as Mahakavi Bharathiar (Maha Kavi meaning Great Poet) in Tamil, is deemed one of the greatest poets of twentieth-century India. A prolific writer, philosopher and a great visionary of immense genius and perspicacity, Bharathiar was also one of the most prominent leaders of the Indian independence movement in South India. Bharathy had an exceptional love and devotion towards his mother tongue Tamil language, which he considered as the sweetest of all the languages known to him. He was fluent in many languages including Bengali, Hindi, Sanskrit, Kutchi, French and English and frequently translated works from other languages into Tamil. He had a voracious appetite for learning ancient and contemporary Tamil literature and had a gifted intellect to derive astonishing truths from ancient poems.

By the early 1900s, Bharathy had become completely involved in the nationalist movement and took active part in the Congress meets through out the country. During this period, Bharathy understood the need to be well-informed of the world outside and took avid interest in the world of journalism and the print media of the West. Bharathy joined as Assistant Editor of the Swadeshamitran, a Tamil daily in 1904. By April 1907, he had started and become the editor of the Tamil weekly India. and the English newspaper Bala Bharatham.

These papers not only served the purpose of enlightening the masses on the affairs of the nation and the world outside, but also as a means of expressing Bharathy's stupendous creativity, which began to peak at this time. Bharathy started to publish his poems regularly in these editions. From complex religious hymns to rousing nationalist anthems, from contemplations on the relationship between God and Man to Songs on the Russian and French revolutions, Bharathy's subjects were truly diverse.

By 1912, Bharathy was already a legend in South India and his political meetings in Pondicherry, where he lived since 1908, were attracting multitudes of young patriots, ready to join the non-violent constitutional agitation against the British rule. This led to a systematic British suppression of what was dubbed as the "militancy". Several arrests and bans on his newspapers followed. The poet's health was badly affected by the imprisonments and by 1920, when a General Amnesty Order finally removed restrictions on his movement, Bharathy was struggling in penury and failing health resulting in his tragic premature death. He died as a result of trampling by an elephant at Parthasarathy temple, Thiruvallikeni on September 11, 1921, not yet forty years of age.

Sudhindranath Dutta : Sudhindranath Dutta was a (1901-1960) post-modern Bengali poet, essayist and journalist, was born on 30 October 1901 at Hatibagan in Kolkata. His father, Hirendranath Dutta, was a philosopher while his second wife, Rajeswari Basudev, was a noted singer. Sudhindranath was among the poets of the 1930's, such as Jibanananda Das and Buddhadev Bose, who broke away from the romantic tradition of Rabindranath Tagore. His poetry was profoundly influenced by the French symbolists such as Mallarme and is marked by a distinct urban outlook and ambience. He died on 25 June 1960 in Kolkata.

Sufi Rock : The term Sufi rock describes the sound of famous Pakistani rock band Junoon. Nadeem F. Paracha claims to have coined the term in 1993 to define Junoon's then pioneering process of fusing conventional rock music with subcontinental Sufi music and imagery. The term became popular in India and Pakistan when it was picked up by MTV-India in the late '90s.

Sufia Kamal : Sufia Kamal (1911-1999) was a poet, writer, organizer, feminist and activist from Bangladesh. She was born to a muslim family in Barisal, Bangladesh. She is one of the most widely recognized cultural personalities in Bangladesh. When she died in 1999, she was buried with full state honors, the first woman in Bangladesh to receive this honor.

Sufiana Music : Sofians musiqui came to Kashmir from Iran in the 15th century. Over the years it has established itself as the classical music form of Kashmir and has incorporated a number of Indian Ragas in its body. Hafiz Nagma in fact, used to be part of sofiana music. The instruments used in this form are Santoor, Sitar, Kashmiri Saz, Wasool or Tabala. In Hafiz Nagma a dancer is a female while her accompanists on various instruments are males. Hafiza moves her feet on musical notes. There are only a few families in Kashmir who are practising this musical form in Kashmir. Whereas the tallest ustad Ghulam Mohd. Qaleenbaft is unable to move out because of health problems, Ustad Ghulam Mohd. Saznawaz and Ustad Abdul Ghani Namathali are imparting training to their family members and are the practising artists.

Sufism : Sufism is a mystic tradition of Islam based on the pursuit of spiritual truth as it is gradually revealed to the heart and mind of the Sufi (one who practices Sufism). It might also be referred to as Islamic mysticism. While other branches of Islam generally focus on exoteric aspects of religion, Sufism is mainly focused on the direct perception of Truth or God through mystic practices based on divine love. Sufism embodies a number of cultures, philosophies, central teachings and bodies of esoteric knowledge. Sufis are active in a diverse range of brotherhoods and sisterhoods, with a wide diversity of thought. Sufi orders ("tariqas") can be Shi'a Islam, Sunni Islam, both or neither.

Suhrawardy Udyan : Suhrawardy Udyan formerly known as Ramna Race Course ground is a national memorial located in Dhaka, Bangladesh. Originally it served as the military club of the British soldiers stationed in Dhaka. It was then called the Ramna Race Course and later Ramna Gymkhana. After the end of colonial rule, the place—sometimes referred to as Dhaka race course—was used for legal horse racing on sundays.

It is the resting place of three great national leaders, Sher-e-Bangla A.K. Fazlul Huq, Khwaja Nazimuddin and Huseyn Shaheed Suhrawardy the place being renamed in honour of the latter. The place is also etched in history as it was here that Sheikh Mujibur Rahman made the first of his stirring speeches in March 7, 1971 months before the outbreak of hostilities between East Pakistan and West Pakistan. The original Flag of Bangladesh was also hoisted here for the second time since it was first unfurled at the University of Dhaka and the first time it was flown at such a large public gathering in Bangladesh. Incidentally it became the setting for the surrender of Pakistan Army under Lt. Gen. A. A. K. Niazi on December 16, 1971 after their defeat in the Bangladesh Liberation War to the allied forces of Mitro Bahini led by Jagjit Singh Aurora. The instrument of surrender was signed at this place and the date is celebrated by Bangladeshis as Victory Day. The place is currently maintained as historic park with an eternal flame setup in 1996 to symbolise freedom.

Sui Northern Gas Pipelines Limited (SNGPL) : Sui Northern Gas Pipelines Limited (SNGPL), is Pakistan's largest integrated gas company serving more than 2 million consumers in North Central Pakistan through an extensive network in Punjab and NWFP. The Company has over 41 years of experience in operation and maintenance of high-pressure gas transmission and distribution systems. It has also expanded its activities to undertake the planning, designing and construction of pipelines, both for itself and other organizations.

Sujoy Kumar Guha : Sujoy Kumar Guha, commonly known as Professor S K Guha or Prof Sujoy K Guha was born in Patna, India in 1939. He did his graduation (B.Tech.) in electrical engineering from IIT Kharagpur. He received his Ph.D. in Medical Physiology from St. Louis, USA. He then founded the Centre for Biomedical Engineering, IIT Delhi and AIIMS and also obtained his MBBS degree from Delhi University. One of the founders of Biomedical engineering in India, Prof. Guha is internationally renowned in the areas of Rehabilitation

Engineering, Bioengineering in Reproductive Medicine and Technology for Rural Health Care. He has received several awards and has more than 100 research papers in cited journals.

His major contributions have been in the indigenously developed non-hormonal polymer based injectable male contraceptive (RISUG) for which the Final Phase-III Clinical trials are underway; Problem-solving at a national level regarding contraceptives in mass usage, especially Copper T; individualized spot air-conditioning system for hospital patients and rehabilitation of the blind, with emphasis on opening automobile repair as an employment avenue.

Sujuni : The first mention of a crafts similar to "Sujuni" comes in the description of bed spreads and wall hanging of uzbeks, they were popular as 'SUJUNI' (from Persion and Tadjik ward for needle). Sujuni is a labour intensive but simple embroidery. Tiny running stitches cover the entire fabric, which is traditionally white or red, with the main outlines of the motive high lighted in a thick chainstitch. Filling stitches inside the motive are done in coloured thread, those outside are done in white or the colour of the base fabrics. The fabric is generally lined with a finer muslin backing before embroidery, giving a quilted effect to the design. Motibs generally cover the gamut of figures, flower and founa, done in naif pictorial style, often illustrating folk look and religious iconography.

Sukhdev : Sukhdev was an Indian revolutionary. He is best known as an accomplice of Bhagat Singh and Shivaram Rajguru in the killing of a British police officer in 1928 in order to take revenge for the death of veteran leader Lala Lajpat Rai due to excessive police beating. All three were convicted of the crime and hanged on March 23, 1931.

Sukhna Lake : The manmade picturesque Sukhna Lake in Chandigarh, India at the foothills of Shivalik hills is an idyllic place for quiet communion with nature, and for offering water sports activities such as boating, yachting, water skiing, etc. The creation of Lake was one of the greatest gift from Le Corbusier and the Chief Engineer P L Varma to the city of Chandigarh. To preserve its tranquility Corbusier insisted that it be forbidden to motor boats and the top of the dam (promenade) prohibited to vehicular traffic. The Lake is fringed by a golf course to the south, and Nek Chand's famous Rock Garden of Chandigarh to its west.

Sukhna is an inseparable part of the city of Chandigarh. Le Corbusier had foreseen that the residents of the city would be drawn it for the 'care of the body and spirit'. The planners of the city will be thrilled to find that this beautiful gift to the city has extended its attraction beyond its boundaries. The city planners were deeply attached to the lake. So much so that Pierre Jeanneret's ashes were immersed in the lake in 1970 as per his wishes by his niece.

Sukkur : Sukkur is the third largest city of Sindh province, situated on the west bank of Indus River in Sukkur District. Sukkur (read as Suck-khar, or sometime Sukhar) is a local variant of Arabic word Saqar which means intense. In the 10th century AD when Arabs invaded Sukkur, they found extreme (hot and cold) climate, and called it saqar. Sukkur is given a title of Darya Dino (means the gift of river), as without the river Indus this would be like Egypt deprived of Nile. Sukkur is the central city of Sindh province in Pakistan.

Sukkur Barrage: The Sukkur barrage is a barrage across the Indus river near the city of Sukkur, Pakistan. It was built from 1923 to 1932. It provides the largest irrigation system in the world, with more than 5 million acres of irrigated land, and has sixty six water doors.

Sulaiman Mountain : Sulaiman Mountain range is located in central Pakistan, extending southward about 280 miles (450 km) from the Gumal Pass to just north of Jacobabad, separating the North-West Frontier Province and Punjab from Balochistan. Its heights gradually decrease toward the south, with summits averaging 6,000–7,000 feet (1,800–2,100 m), the highest being the twin peaks (30 miles [48 km] from the Gumal Pass) called Takht-i Sulaiman, or Solomon's Throne, which legend connects with King Solomon's visit to Pakistan; the higher of the peaks, at 18,481 feet (5,633 m), is the site of a Muslim Ziyarat (shrine) visited annually by many pilgrims. The range's eastern face dips steeply to the Indus River, but on the west the range declines more gradually. Juniper and edible pines abound in the north and olives in the centre, but vegetation is scarce in the south. The Ghat, Zao, Chuhar Khel Dhana, and Sakhi Sarwar are the principal passes in the north. In the south, west of Dera Ghazi Khan, lies the hill station of Fort Munro (6,303 feet).

Sultan Muhammad : Sultan Muhammad (1938 - 1996) popularly known as Sultan Rahi, with his rugged looks, brawny and stocky, with an aggressive style of dialogue delivery was the Pakistani film superstar and the ultimate action hero and firmly established himself as the biggest film personality from Pakistan during the 1980s. He was a Pakistani version of 'Bruce Lee', 'Chuck Norris','Sylvester Stallone', and 'James Bond' all rolled into one with a Punjabi touch.

He was considered a must in any Punjabi movie and played the most number of 'title roles'. Some of his major films include 'Maula Jatt', 'Sher Khan', 'Chan Veryam', 'Kaley Chore', and 'Saakhi Badshah'. A one-man film industry during the 1980s had an extremely successful film career which came to a tragic and premature end with his murder in January 1996.He is in the Guinness Book of

Records for acting in more movies than anyone in the world. He appeared in a little more than 500 movies.

Sultan Quli Qutb Mulk : Sultan Quli Qutb Mulk was the founder of the Qutb Shahi dynasty, which ruled the Sultanate of Golconda in southern India from 1518 to 1687. A Muslim from Turkmenistan, Quli Qutb Mulk migrated to Delhi with some of his relatives and friends in the beginning of the 16th century. Later he migrated south to Deccan and served Bahmani sultan Mohammad Shaw.He conquered Golconda and became the Governor of Telangana in 1518

After the disintegration of the Bahmani Sultanate into the five Deccan sultanates, he declared independence and took title Qutb Shah, and established Qutb Shahi dynasty of Golconda. Quli Qutb Mulk was a contemporary of Krishnadevaraya and Achyutaraya of the Vijayanagara empire. Quli extended his rule by capturing forts at Warnagal, Kondapalli, Eluru, and Rajamundry, while Krishnadevaraya was busy fighting the ruler of Orissa. He defeated Sitapati Raju, the ruler of Khammam, and captured the fort. He forced Orissa's ruler to surrender all the territories between the mouths of Krishna and Godavari rivers. He was able to occupy Eluru, Rajamundry and Machilipatnam extending his rule to coastal Andhra. Quli's campaign against Krishnadevaraya continued until Timmarusu, the Prime Minister of Krishnadevaraya, defeated the Golconda army.

Though, Telugu was not his mother tongue, Quli learned Telugu language. He did not discriminate against Hindus but employed eligible Hindus in his court as governors and officers. He was a patron of the arts, and his dynasty became known for this. Sultan Quli Qutb Mulk died in 1543 when his younger son, Jamsheed Quli Qutb Shah, assassinated him and blinded Kuli's elder son and heir, Kutbuddeen. Jamsheed Quli Qutb Shah then assumed the throne.

Sultanganj : Sultanganj is traditionally associated with the sage Jahnu, whose ashram was a centre of learning and culture. Jahnu Muni's ashram was located on the rock jutting out of the bed of the Ganga River. Now the site has the Shiva temple of Ajgaivinath, also known as Gaibinath Mahadeo. The story is that the river Ganga on her way to the ocean interrupted the Muni in his meditation by the rush of her currents. The sage swallowed the river in a gulp. Bhagiratha intervened and the Muni again let her out by making an incision in his thigh. That is why the river Ganga is also called Jahnavi.

Like many of the ancient temples, the origin of Ajgaivinath temple is also shrouded in mystery. According to one legend, Lord Shiva was given his bow here, known as Ajgav, and so the place came to be known as Ajgaivinath. The ancient name of the place was Jahangira, which was derived from the name of Jahnu Muni. Jahangira is a distorted form of Jahnu giri (the hill of Jahnu) or Jahnu griha (the abode of Jahnu). Jahangira is now a small village forming a part of the town of Sultanganj.

The name Jahangira for the rock had continued till at least1824-25, when Bishop Heber visited the area. In Heber's Journal, Vol. 1, there is a pencil sketch of the temple on the rock tinder the caption of Jahangira. The pencil sketch depicts a mosque by the side of the temple. It is commonly said that Kala Pahar, in the course of his crusade against the Hindu temples, visited the place. He tried his best but failed to demolish Ajgaivinath temple. He could, however, destroy the Parvati temple on the neighboring hill, and built a mosque there. Formerly the hill was much bigger and more spacious. This part of the Ganga has high floods with very strong currents almost every year and the decaying granite rocks of the hill are being slowly worn away.

Sultanganj is a town in Bhagalpur district and has a railway station, of the same name on the loop-line of the Eastern Railway running from Calcutta to Kiul.An excellent all-weather road connecting Bhagalpur with Monghyr and Patna also serves it. It has a cosmopolitan population of about eleven thousand persons. It is a flourishing business place and there are a number of schools and colleges. Sultanganj is a place of hoary antiquity. Traditionally Sultanganj formed a part of the great Anga, State. In the days of the Mahabharata, Karna, the sixth brother of the five Pandavas, ruled in Anga.The capital of Anga was Champa. Champa is the present Champanagar situated three miles to the west of Bhagalpur. King Karna had his castles at Champa (modern Champanagar) and Jahnugiri (modern Sultanganj). At present Champanagar, the- site of Karna's castle, is well known as Karnagarh. Karnagarh is practically a part of Bhagalpur town now.

Some scholars have associated the large plateau of Karnagarh in Bhagalpur, where there are still ramparts of a fort, as one of the famous pre-Buddhist forts. The site had several bastions and ditches. When the British took over, the area wasselected for housing the Hill Rangers, a body of troops raised from among the Santals of Raj-Mahal Hills. For some time this was the headquarters of the wing of an Indian regiment and slowly the bastions have disappeared although the ditches are still there.

The State Constable Training School now mainly occupies the plateau. Karnagarh area of Sultanganj, which had King Karna's castle, is also a large plateau. It is now called Krishnagarh, after the name of a zamindar of the branch of Raj Banaili, by the name of KumarKrishnanand Singh, who built a large residential structure on the site. Sultanganj was also famous during the rule of the Pala and

Sena kings (from 730 A.D. to 1199 A.D.). It is said that Dharmapala, the first king of the Pala dynasty, had laid the foundation of the VikramshilaUniversity at Sultanganj. This claim, however, is now not finding much support and the said famed University is deemed to have been at Patharghatta near Colgong in Bhagalpur district. The relies discovered by excava- tions there, along with other circumstantial evidence, suggest that Patharghatta was probably the real site of Vikramshila University.

Sultanpur : Sultanpur is a district in the state of Uttar Pradesh in northern India. The district is a part of Faizabad Division.It's administrative head is Sultanpur. It has an area of 1713 sq. rn. The surface is generally level, being broken only by ravines in the neighborhood of the rivers. The central portion is highly cultivated, while in the south are widespread arid plains and swampy jhils or marshes. The principal river is the Gumti River, which passes through the centre of the district and affords a valuable highway for commerce. Minor streams are the Kandu, Pili, Tengha and Nandhia, the last two being of onieimiiortanee, as their channels form the outlet for the superfluous water of the jhils, draining into the Sai. There are no forests in the district, only stunted dhdk jungles used for fuel. In the population was 1,083,904, showing an increase of less than 1% over the decade. Sultanpur was a purely agricultural district with a very dense population. The principal crops are rice, pulses, wheat, barley, sugarcane and a little poppy. The main line of the Oudh & Rohilkhand railway from Lucknow to Rae Bareli and Mogul Serai serves the south-western portion.

The only incident worthy of note in the 19th century history of the district since the British annexation of Oudh is the revolt of the native troops stationed at Sultanpur during the Mutiny. The troops rose in rebellion on the 9th of June 1857, and, after murdering two of their officers, sacked the station. Upon the restoration of order, Sultanpur cantonment was strengthened by a detachment of British troops; but in 1861 it was entirely abandoned as a military station.

Sultanpur National Park : Sultanpur National Park and Bird Sanctuary is located in *Gurgaon* district of *Haryana,* about 50 km from Delhi and 15 km from Gurgaon on the Gurgaon—Farukh Nagar Road. This park is best visited in winters when a large number of migratory birds come here. In the old map and district gazetteer of Gurgaon district, this area is shown as marshy land having a 'salt pan' where water accumulates during rains and dries out during summer. A number of organisms like crustaceans, fish and insects thrive during floods which attract a number of birds to this area. It's sanctuary potential was first identified by an enthusiastic bird watcher, *Mr. Peter Jackson.* He convinced Mrs Indira Gandhi, the then Prime Minister of India, of the need for giving protection to this area. Keeping in view it's importance and potential, the area covering 359 acres was declared a Bird Sanctuary in 1971 and was upgraded to the status of National Park in 1991 by *Haryana Government.*

Sumitranandan Pant : Sumitranandan Pant (1900—December 28, 1977) was one of the most famous modern Hindi poets. He is considered one of the major poets of the Chhayavaadi school of Hindi literature. Pant mostly wrote in Sanskritized Hindi. Pant authored twenty eight published works including poetry, verse plays and essays. Pant was born at Kausani village of Almora, in the hills of Kumaon. He later moved to Kalakankar near Allahabad. The mark of the a childhood in the hills can be seen in his works and his poems resound with an echo of the beauty of nature. His mother died when he was very young. He was a shy and girlish child and his classmates often used to tease him calling him 'girl'.

For his graduation, Pant went to Prayag University. On hearing Mahatma Gandhi's call for Satyagraha, he left college. However, he continued his education by reading English, Sanskrit and Bengali literature. After some time, he went to Sri Aurobindo's ashram at Pondicherry. Apart from Chhayavaadipoems, Pant also wrote progressive, philosophical (influenced by Sri Aurobindo), socialist and humanist poems. Pant received Jnanpith Award for collection of his most famous poems, titled Chidambara. He was awarded Nehru Peace Prize by Soviet Union for Lokayatan.

Sun Network : Sun Network is a Rs 600-crore Indian cable television network based in Chennai, Tamil Nadu, India. Established in 1992, it offers a plethora of television channels in 5 languages covering the whole of South India. It was the first fully privately owned Tamil channel in India when it emerged in 1992. Its serials and soaps have generated the maximum TRP rating for viewership all over India, making it the most popular network of channels in India. It is a regional television network in South India and thus most North Indians are unaware of it. Coupled with the DMK-backed Karunanidhi family, it was the largest political-media family in India till the split in November 2005.

All its channels occupy the top spots in their respective languages. Sun TV, in Tamil is the Network's flagship and most popular channel. Being the premier channel, Sun TV is often used to refer to the Sun Network in general. Kalanithi Maran is the Chairman and Managing Director of media giant Sun Network and has been given various awards including the CNBC "Business Excellence Award" in 2005. Sun Network also offers FM Radio Stations and has recently forayed into the print business.

Sun News : The Sun News is a daily newspaper published in Myrtle Beach, South Carolina. It serves the

Grand Strand with a circulation of 45,000 daily, and 55,000 on Sunday. It was founded as a weekly in 1935 by brothers-in-law C. L. Phillips and J. Clarence Macklen, who started a job printing business, and were requested by local merchants to do a local newspaper. It has changed hands numerous times over the years. In 1955 it began publication twice weekly, and with the explosive growth that occurred in the next half century, as the Grand Strand became a major tourist and retirement area, the paper grew into the main daily newspaper.

Sun Temple : About 39 km. From Ranchi on Tata Road near Bundu stands on the desolate bush green the elegant Sun temple fashioned in the form of huge chariot with richly decorated 18 wheels and seven life like horses ready to take of. Built by Sanskrit Vihar headed by Shri Ram Maroo, the managing director of Ranchi Express, the sun temple deserves the title "a poem in stone". The surroundings of the temple, studded with a pond serving as a sacred place for Chhathavratis are actually a natures bounty to the peple of Chotanagpur. A beautiful dharmashala, meant for the pilgrims. The all weather motorable road upto the temple premises is likely to attract tourists who will be captivated to behold the newly built sun temple in the placid and serene surrounding leading to its celestial bueaties.

Sun TV : Sun TV is a regional Tamil language Indian cable television station. It is the premier flagship channel of the Chennai-based Rs 600-crore Sun Network. Sun TV is the most viewed channel in Tamil Nadu. It was the first fully privately owned Tamil channel in India when it emerged in 1992. Its serials and soaps have generated the maximum TRP rating for viewership all over India, making it the most popular channel in India. Coupled with the DMK-backed Karunanidhi family, it was the largest political-media family in India till the split in November

2005. Sun TV has the largest collection of movie titles in its library – about 2,400 films, though according to sources, the real number is pegged at over 6,000 titles. Its service is broadcast through cable or satellite networks throughout India. Sun TV is also available to viewers in the US, Dubai, Europe, Australia, South Africa, Singapore and the Asia Pacific region.

Sunamganj : Sunamganj is a District in (Sylhet division) with an area of 3669.58 sq km, is bounded by Khasia and Jaintia hills (India) on the north, Habiganj and Kishoreganj districts on the south, Sylhet district on the east, Netrokona and greater Mymensingh districts on the west. Annual average temperature: maximum 33.2 C and minimum 13.6 C; annual rainfall 3334mm. There are many haors and beels in Sunamganj. Sunamganj (Town) stands on the bank of the river Surma. It was established in late 18th century. It consists of 9 wards and 44 mahallas. The town has an area of 22.16 sq km. It has a population of 49373; male 52.70%, female 47.30%; density of population is 2228 per sq km. Literacy rate among the town people is 58.8%. The town has five dakbungalows.

Sunamganj mahakuma (sub-division) was upgraded to a district in 1984. This district consists of 10 upazilas, 4 municipalities, 36 wards, 139 mahallas, 82 union parishads, 1711 mouzas and 2813 villages. The upazilas are Bishwamvarpur, Chhatak, Derai, Dharmapasha, Dowarabazar, Jagannathpur, Jamalganj, Tahirpur, Sullah and Sunamganj Sadar. Rebellion of Sukhair in 1922-23 is notable. Many political leaders and activists of Sunamganj were involved in the anti-British movement. The leftist movement spread over the district after the partition of 1947. During the War of Liberation many encounters were held between the freedom fighters and the Pak army; Sunamganj was liberated on 6 December 1971. In 1336 BS a devastating flood occurred as a result of breaking down a damn in Manipur. This flood is popularly known as 'White Water Flood'. A pernicious earthquake on 12 June 1897 caused heavy loss of lives and establishments.

Sundarbans : The Sundarbans delta is the largest mangrove forest in the world. It lies at the mouth of the Ganges and is spread across areas of Bangladesh and West Bengal, India. Interestingly, the Bangladesh and Indian portion of the jungle are listed in the UNESCO world heritage list separately as the Sundarbans and Sundarbans National Park respectively, though they are simply parts of the same forest. The Sundarbans is intersected by a complex network of tidal waterways, mudflats and small islands of salt-tolerant mangrove forests, and presents an excellent example of ongoing ecological processes. The area is known for its wide range of fauna. The most famous among these is the Bengal Tiger, but numerous species of birds, spotted deer, crocodiles and snakes also inhabit it. It is estimated that there are now 400 Bengal tigers and about 30,000 spotted deer in the area.

Most of the plot of prize-winning anthropologist Amitav Ghosh's 2004 novel The Hungry Tide is set in the Sundarbans. The mangrove-dominated Ganges delta – the Sundarbans—is a complex ecosystem comprising one of the three largest single tract mangrove forests of the world. Shared between two neighboring countries, Bangladesh and India, the larger part is situated in the southwest corner of Bangladesh. The western boundary of the Bangladeshi Sundarbans follows the Harinbhanga–Raimangal–Kalindi river system and abuts with the Indian Sundarbans. To the south the forest meets the Bay of Bengal; to the east it is bordered by the Baleswar River and to the north there is a sharp interface with intensively cultivated land. The natural drainage in the upstream areas, other than the main river channels, is everywhere impeded by extensive embankments and polders. The total land area is 4,143 km^2

and the remaining water area of 1,874 km^2 encompasses rivers, small streams and canals. Rivers in the Sundarbans are meeting places of salt water and freshwater. Thus, it is a region of transition between the freshwater of the rivers originating from the Ganges and the saline water of the Bay of Bengal.

In terms of biodiversity, the Sundarbans contrasts the other large mangrove forests for its extraordinarily diverse wildlife and designated as a UNESCO's World Network of International Biosphere Reserves since 2001. The forest also has immense protective and productive functions. Constituting 51% of the total reserved forest estate of Bangladesh it contributes about 41% of total forest revenue and accounts for about 45% of all timber and fuel wood output of the country. A number of industries are based on the raw material obtained from the Sundarbans ecosystem. Various non-timber forest products and plantations help generate considerable employment and income generation opportunities for at least half a million poor coastal population. Besides production functions of the forest, it provides natural protection to life and properties of the coastal population in cyclone prone Bangladesh.

However, despite the fact that the Sundarbans is mostly free of permanent human habitation and retained a forest closure of about 70% according to the Overseas Development Administration (ODA) of the United Kingdom in 1985, forest inventories reveal a decline in standing volume of the two main commercial mangrove species—sundri (*Heritiera fomes*} and gewa (*Excoecaria agallocha*}—by 40% and 45% respectively between 1959 and 1983. Also, despite a total ban on all killing or capture of wildlife other than fish and some invertebrates, there appears to be a pattern of depleted biodiversity or loss of species, and that the "ecological quality of the original mangrove forest is declining".

Sundarbans Freshwater Swamp Forests : The Sundarbans freshwater swamp forests are a tropical moist broadleaf forest ecoregion of India and Bangladesh. The ecoregion covers an area of 14,600 square kilometers (5,600 square miles) of the vast Ganges-Brahmaputra Delta, extending from India's West Bengal state into eastern Bangladesh. The Sundarbans freshwater swamp forests lie between the upland Lower Gangetic plains moist deciduous forests and the brackish-water Sundarbans mangroves bordering the Bay of Bengal.

The fertile soils of the delta have been subject to intensive human use for centuries, and the ecoregion has been mostly converted to intensive agriculture, with few enclaves of forest remaining. The remaining forests, together with the Sundarbans mangroves, are important habitat for the endangered tiger (Panthera tigris).

Sundarbans National Park : Established in 1978 in twenty four Paraganas district in West Bengal, Sunderbans Tiger reserve is spread over an area of 2608 sq. kms. Sixty percent of the demarcated area of the Sunderbans sprawling actually over 9630sq.km, is in Bangladesh. The national park with a core area of 1330sq.km, has been designated as a World Heritage Site in 1985 and is a part of the Project Tiger. The Sunderbans has three wildlife sanctuaries at Sajnekhali, Lothian Island and Haliday Island. Tourism in West Bengal is not flourishing. You will find more and more people heading for destinations outside Bengal. It is not as if they have seen all of Bengal, but it is because other states are selling their destinations better.

Sundargarh : Sundargarh District is situated in the north west part of Orissa, it's headquarter is located in Sundargarh City. The industrial town of Rourkela in this district is a first government sector plant built with foreign (german) collaboration and was the first in India to use LD oxygen technology.

Sundarlal Bahuguna : Sundarlal Bahuguna is a noted environmentalist who has fought for the preservation of the Himalayas. He is also the controversial leader of the Chipko movement.

Sundarnarayan Temple : Sundarnarayan temple stands on the elevated west bank of the Godavari in Maharashtra. There are small carvings of Hanuman, Narayana and Indra on the walls. This Vaishavite temple has three black Vishnu images. The hall is entered through three porches, some damaged, each with balcony seating, lobed arches and slightly bulbous domes. The doorways inside the porches are headed by angled eaves and serpentine pediments.

Sunder Lal Hora : Sunder Lal Hora (1896 - December 8, 1955) was an Indian ichthyologist. Famous for the Satpura Hypothesis, a zoo-geographical hypothesis proposed by him that suggests that the central Indian Satpura Range of hills acted as a bridge providing for the Malayan affinity of many Indian fauna and flora in the peninsula and the Western Ghats of India. A genus of ricefish, Horaichthys ("Hora's Fish"), is named after him.

Sunga Empire : The Sunga empire (or Shunga empire) controlled the eastern part of India from around 185 to 73 BCE. It was established after the fall of the Indian Mauryan empire. The capital of the Sungas was at Pataliputra. The Sunga dynasty was established in 185 BCE, about 50 years after Ashoka's death, when the king Brhadrata, the last of the Mauryan rulers, was brutally murdered by the then commander-in-chief of the Mauryan armed forces, Pusyamitra Sunga, while he was taking the Guard of Honour of his forces. Pusyamitra Sunga then ascended the throne.

Pusyamitra Sunga, a Brahmin, is known for his hostility and persecution towards the Buddhist faith. He is recorded as having "destroyed monasteries and killed

Monks" (Divyavadana, p429-434): 84.000 Buddhist stupas which had been built by the Mauryan king Ashoka were destroyed (R. Thaper), and 100 gold coins were offered for the head of each Buddhist monk. A large number of Buddhist monasteries (viharas) were converted to Hindu temples, in such places as Nalanda, Bodhgaya, Sarnath or Mathura.

From around 180 BCE the Indian territory was invaded as far as Pataliputra by the Greco-Bactrian ruler Demetrius, with the long-term effect of confining the Sungas to the eastern part of India. Demetrius established an Indo-Greek kingdom in the northern and northwestern part of India, which was to last until the end of the 1st century BCE, and under which Buddhism was able to flourish. In particular, one of the successors of Demetrius, the Indo-Greek "Saviour king" Menander (Pali: Milinda) was a strong benefactor of the Buddhist faith at that time. The Indo-Greeks and the Sungas seem to have reconciled and exchanged diplomatic missions around 110 BCE, as indicated by the Heliodorus pillar, which records the dispatch of a Greek ambassador named Heliodorus, from the court of the Indo-Greek king Antialcidas, to the court of the Sunga king Bhagabhadra at the site of Vidisha in central India.

During the historical Sunga period (185 to 73 BCE), Buddhist activity also managed to survive somewhat in central India (Madhya Pradesh) as suggested by some architectural expansions that were done at the stupas of Sanchi and Barhut, originally started under King Ashoka. These stupas, however, are located quite far from the Sunga center of power, and it is questioned whether these works were due to the weakness of the control of the Sungas in these areas, or a late sign of tolerance on their part.

Sunil Bharti Mittal : Sunil Bharti Mittal, founder, Chairman and Managing Director of Bharti Group can be labelled as the most ambitious telecom entrepreneur in India. Sunil a former student of Harvard Business School graduated from Punjab University. The son of a parliamentarian, Sunil did not want to follow his father's footsteps. He had shown an interest in business even from his teenage days. So after graduation, Sunil got together with his friend and formed a small bicycle business with borrowed capital in the1970s. But by 1979, he realized that this business would remain small. So he moved out of Ludhiana, spent a few years in Mumbai and in 1981, was running an import and distribution operation out of New Delhi and Mumbai.

By 1982, Mittal had started a full-fledged business selling portable generators imported from Japan and that gave him the chance to involve himself in activities like marketing and advertising. Things went smoothly until the government banned the import of generators as two Indian companies were awarded licenses to manufacture generators locally.

Sunil Mittal got interested in push button phones while on a trip to Taiwan, and in 1982, introduced the phones to India, replacing the old fashioned, bulky rotary phones that were in use in the country then. Bharti Telecom Limited (BTL) was incorporated and entered into a technical tie up with Siemens AG of Germany for manufacture of electronic push button phones. By the early 1990s, Mittal was making fax machines, cordless phones and other telecom gear.

The turning point came in 1992 when the Indian government was awarding licenses for mobile phone services for the first time. One of the conditions for the Delhi cellular license was that the bidder have some experience as a telecom operator. Mittal clinched a deal with the French telecom group Vivendi. Two years later, Sunil secured rights to serve New Delhi. In 1995, Bharti Cellular Limited (BCL) was formed to offer cellular services under the brand name AirTel. Within a few years Bharti became the first telecom company to cross the 2-million mobile subscriber mark. The company is also instrumental in bringing down the high STD/ISD, cellular rates in the country by rolling the countries first private national as well as international long-distance service under the brand name IndiaOne. In 2001, the company entered into a joint venture with Singapore Telecom International for a $650-million ubmarine cable project, the countries first ever undersea cable link connecting Chennai in India and Singapore.

Always on the move and making an impact and excelling in whatever he did, this clear thinking risk taker has changed the face of the Indian ICT space. For his contributions he has been honoured with several awards. He was chosen as one of the top entrepreneurs in the world for the year 2000 and amongst 'Stars Of Asia', by 'Business Week', he received IT Man of the Year Award 2002 from Dataquest and CEO Of the Year, 2002 Award (World HRD Congress). He is the member of National Council of Confederation of Indian Industry (CII), Federation of Indian Chambers of Commerce & Industry (FICCI), Chairman, Indo-US Joint Business Council, Member, Advisory Committee constituted by Ministry of IT. Mittal has to his credit the breaking up of the 100 year old monopoly of state run companies to operate telecom services in India. Now he heads a successful empire focused on different areas of business through independent Joint Venture companies with a market capitalization of approximately $ 2 billion, employing over 5,000 people and still growing. Bharti Foundation has funded over 50 schools in Madhya Pradesh and also donated Rs 200 million to IIT

Delhi for building a Bharti School of Technology and Management.

In spite of his deep involvement in work, Mittal the man, is calm, seldom ruffled and very down to earth. He says he achieves a sense of detachment and peace with regular practice of yoga. He is thankful for a supportive family including a daughter and twin sons, with whom understandably he doesn't get much time to spend. His brothers Rakesh and Rajan are with him in the business.

Sunil Gangopadhyay : Sunil Gangopadhyay was born on 7 September 1934 at the Faridpur District in what is now Bangladesh. Sunil got his Master's degree in Economics from the Calcutta University in 1954. He is currently associated with the Ananda Bazar group, a major publishing house in Kolkata. Author of well over 200 books, Sunil is a prolific writer who has excelled in different genres but declares poetry to be his "first love". He was the founder editor of Krittibas, a seminal poetry magazine that became a platform for a new generation of poets experimenting with many new forms in poetic themes, rhythms, and words. His Nikhilesh and Neera series of poems (some of which have been translated as For You, Neera and Murmur in the Woods) have been extremely popular.

Sunil Gavaskar : Sunil Manohar Gavaskar (born July 10, 1949 at Bombay, Maharashtra), nicknamed Sunny, was a cricket player during the 1970s and 1980s for Bombay and India. He is considered one of the greatest opening batsmen in the history of the sport. He made a spectacular Test debut in 1971 scoring 774 runs in his first Test series against the West Indies helping India to become one of the few teams to defeat the West Indies at home in the Caribbean. Gavaskar went on to average a mammoth 70.20 runs per innings in the West Indies throughout his career—

a feat no batsman in his era was able to surpass consistently. From then until his retirement in 1987 he was a mainstay of the Indian batting line-up. In 1983 Gavaskar broke one of the oldest and most prestigious records in the game: Donald Bradman's total of 29 Test centuries.

Gavaskar was the holder of the record for the most number of Test centuries (34) until 2005 when his countryman Sachin Tendulkar broke that record. Gavaskar remains the only player to score centuries in each innings, three times. He was also the first batsman to reach 10,000 Test runs and held the record for the most number of runs until it was broken by Allan Border. Along with Hannan Sarkar, Gavaskar holds the dubious distinction of being the only Test cricketer to be dismissed with the first delivery of the Test match on three occasions.

SUPARCO : The Pakistan Space and Upper Atmosphere Research Commission (SUPARCO) is Pakistan's national space agency. It is responsible for the execution of the space science and technology programs in the country, as approved by the Government of Pakistan. SUPARCO is an autonomous R&D organization under the Federal Government. The Commission comprises the Chairman and four Members for Space Technology, Space Research, Space Electronics and Finance, respectively.

Supreme Court of India : The Supreme Court of India is the highest court of the land as established by Part V, Chapter IV of the Constitution of India. Articles 124 to 147 of the Constitution of India lay down the composition and jurisdiction of the Supreme Court of India. Primarily, it is an appellate court which takes up appeals against judgments of the provincial High Courts. But it takes writ petitions in cases of serious human rights violations or if a case involves any serious issue that needs immediate resolution. The Supreme Court of India had its inaugural sitting on January 28, 1950, and since then has delivered more than 24,000 reported judgments.

On January 28, 1950, two days after India became a sovereign democratic republic, the Supreme Court came into being. The inauguration took place in the Chamber of Princes in the Parliament building. The Chamber of Princes had earlier been the seat of the Federal Court of India for 12 years, between 1937 and 1950, and was the seat of the Supreme Court until the Supreme Court acquired its present premises in 1958. After its inauguration on January 28, 1950, the Supreme Court commenced its sittings in the Chamber of Princes in the Parliament House. The Court moved into the present building in 1958. The Supreme Court Bar Association is the bar of the highest court. The current president of the SCBA is Mr. P.H. Parekh.

Supreme Court of Pakistan : The Supreme Court is the apex court in Pakistan's judicial hierarchy, the final arbiter of legal and constitutional disputes. The Court's permanent seat is Islamabad. The Court has a number of de jure powers which are outlined in the Constitution of Pakistan as well as de facto powers which many have considered remarkable given the nation's history of military rule during which part or all of the constitution has been suspended. The Supreme Court has the explicit, de jure power to block the exercise of certain Presidential reserve powers. For example, under Article 58, the President may dismiss the National Assembly (triggering new elections) but the dismissal is subject to Supreme Court approval. The Court also has the power to overturn presidential orders and parliamentary legislation by declaring such orders or laws to be unconstitutional.

Suraiya : Suraiya Jamaal Sheikh (1929—January 31, 2004) was a singer and actress in Indian films, and was popularly known as Suraiya in the film industry.

She became a superstar in the 1940s and 50s during the time when actors sang their own songs.

Suraj Kund : Another place was "Suraj Kund" (the pool of sun). It is about five miles to the South of Multan on the Bahawalpur Road. It was a pond 132 feet in diameter and 10 feet deep when full of water. Sawn Mal the Sikh Diwan surrounded it with an octagonal wall. It was a place of pilgrimage till 1947 and two fairs were held here annually. One on the 7th of the Vanishing moon of Bhadon, and the other on the 7th of the rising moon of Magh, the numbers having references to the seven hours of the Sun's Chariot, according to the Hindu mythology or the seven Rishies.

SurajKund Mela : The very first effort on organizing cultural events on a national level by Haryana Tourism was done with the launching of the annual and now internationally famous Surajkund Crafts Mela, that began in 1981. The Crafts Mela celebrates the finest handlooms and handicrafts traditions of country. It is a fortnight long event that embodies the spirit that runs through the people of India and its rich culture. It is held in the month of February from 1st-15th. The Surajkund Crafts Mela is held just 8 km from south Delhi.

Surat : Surat is a port city in the Indian state of Gujarat and administrative headquarters of the Surat District. It is located at 20.58° N latitute and 72.54° E longitude and as of 2005, Surat and its metropolitan area had a population of approximately 3.6 million. The city is situated on the left bank of the Tapti River, 14 miles from its mouth. A moat indicates the dividing-line between the old city, with its narrow streets and handsome houses, and the newer suburbs, but the city wall has almost disappeared. The city is largely recognized for its textile and diamond businesses.

Surdas : Surdas (1483—1573) was a Hindu poet, sant and musician of India. He is said to have been blind from birth. Surdas' poetry was in the proto-Hindi language of Brij Bhasha. This dialect was considered to be a very plebian language. This was especially pronounced as the literary language of Hinduism was Sanskrit. Surdas' work is one of a number that are credited with raising Brij Bhasha from the status of a vulgate into that of a literary language. Impact on Bhakti movement : The philosophy of Surdas' work is a reflection of the times. He was very much immersed in the Bhakti movement that was sweeping North India. This movement represented a grass roots spiritual empowerment of the masses. For the corresponding spiritual movement of the masses that happened in South India in the first millennium.

Surguja : Surguja is a district in the state of Chattisgarh in India. One of the main towns and the district capital is Ambikapur. Surguja district is located in the northern part of Chhattisgarh State of India. Borders of Uttar Pradesh, Jharkhand, Orissa and Madhya Pradesh States are adjoining to the district. This district has over extension between south-eastern part of Vindhyachal-Baghelkhand region of peninsular India. It lies between 23o 37′ 25″ To 24o 6′ 17″ north latitude and 81o 34′40″ To 84o 4′40″ east longitude . 244.62 km long east to west and 167.37 broad norths to south, this land has as area of about 16359 Sqr Km.

Famous for its enchantingly beautiful natural landscapes and architectural richness, Surguja is one of the most important tourist destinations of Chhattisgarh. The district has some of the most fascinating historic sites, temples, caves and waterfalls of central India. The presence of several ancient temples, stone carvings and archaic remains go on to prove the importance of the city during ancient times.

Surkotda : Around 2300 BC, the Harappans came to Surkotada and build a fortified citadel and residential annexe, made of mud brick, mud lumps and rubble containing houses with bathrooms and drains. They had painted pottery with Indus alphabet painted on the pots, chert blades and copper objects, a typical Harappa seal has also been found. Other interesting finds are clay linga like objects evidently of cult significance. A piece of charred rope adds to the variety of the finds. Bones of the Equus from the earliest levels are the other important discovery in that they show the animal was known to the Harappans. Some important finds are a typical Harappan terracotta seal, a heavy copper chisel, a hoard of copper beads and bangles and terracotta toys, tanks and beads besides animal skeletal remains of the horse, camel, elephant andsheep.

The Harappans buried the bones of their dead in small oval pits and put jars and dishes on a stand probably for keeping food etc. and covered it with a huge slab. This practice is unprecedented in the Harappan burial tradition. The excavations have revealed that the Harappans lived here along with an antecedent culture with all their typical modes of habitation and cultural assemblage and continued even after the mature phase was over. Approachable from Bhuj by road and a regular busservice is available. Nearest Airport Bhuj, Distance from Bhuj to Surkotda 85 Km.

Suryakant Tripathi 'Nirala' : Suryakant Tripathi 'Nirala' (January 22, 1896-October 15, 1961) was one of the most famous figures of the modern Hindi literature. He was a poet, novelist, essayist and story-writer. He also drew many sketches. Nirala's Parimal and Anaamika are considered as the original Chhayavaadi Hindi literature. He was unrecognized during his life. His style of poetry, revolutionary for his time, often was unpublished due to its unconventional nature.

Suryavanshi : Suryavanshi are people belonging to the Suryavansha, or "dynasty of the Sun". According to legend, the Suryavanshis are descended from Surya, the Hindu Sun God. The Suryavanshi lineage is one of the three lineages into which the Kshatriya caste of Hindus is divided, the other two races being the Chandravanshi (descended from Chandra, the Hindu Moon God) and the Agnivanshi, descended from Agni, the Hindu Fire God. All present-day Suryavanshis also claim descent from the Hindu God Rama, who was himself born into a Suryavanshi dynasty

Sushmita Sen : Sushmita Sen, the first Indian to win the Miss Universe pageant held at Manila, Philippines 1994 was born on November 19, 1975 in Hyderabad, Andhra Pradesh. Daughter of an Air Force Commander her family of Bengali origin was posted in Nagpur, then Jorhat, and finally in Delhi. She did her schooling with English Honors predominantly in the Air Force Silver School.

During her school days, she took part in one or two fashion shows. After she finished her plus two she participated in the Femina Miss India contest and from then on there was no looking back. This 172.5cm tall, girl next-door face shot into fame when she became The Femina Miss India in 1994. Her main assets an intelligent mind, poise and linguistic competence finally won her the coveted Miss Universe Crown. Eighteen year old Sushmita Sen the youngest among the 76 contestants charmed a million viewers as well as the judges with her amazing mental acumen.

After she won the crown she got more opportunities for modeling followed by a competitive career in Bollywood. Her first stint in the film world was a south Indian movie, ' Rakshakan' followed by 'Dastak' in Hindi. Some of her other films in Hindi include 'Biwi No.1', 'Sirf

Tum', 'Nayak' and so on. She has proved her mettle in acting especially her dance numbers like 'Shakalaka baby' in Nayak, ' Mehaboob Mere' in Fiza has been much appreciated. Sushmita Sen excels in whatever she does. She has got very rave reviews for convincing portrayal of her character in the film Filhaal. She won the best supporting actress award in the year 2000 for her role in Biwi No 1. Her recent films 'Mein Hoo Naa' in which she got the biggest hit of her career and in 'Vaastu-Shastra' she was appreciated for her role in it. In the personal front, Sushmita likes instrumental music, writes poetry and columns for newspapers and is fond of children. She has adopted a baby girl whom she has named Renee. This ex-Miss Universe remains a much sought after woman today and the common man's ultimate dream and fantasy. This brilliant, down to earth personality has proved that she has much more than a beautiful face.

Sutkagan Dor : The westernmost known site of Indus Valley Civilization was Sutkagan Dor (or Sutkagen Dor). It is located about 480 KM west of Karachi on Makran coast near the Iran border in Baluchistan. The town has typical Harappan city layout, a citadel with an outer city. A defensive wall of 30 feet wide exists. Though inland, may have been near navigable water in ancient times and on a trade route between other centers.

Sutlej : Sutlej is the longest of the five rivers of Punjab that flow through northern India, with its source in Tibet near Mount Kailash to Punjab. It receives the Beas River in the state of Punjab, India and continues into Pakistan to join Chenab river to form Panjnad river which furthur joins Indus river at Mithankot. The Sutlej was known as Shatadru or Sutudri to Indians in Vedic period and Zaradros or Hesidros to the Greeks.

The waters of the river are allocated to India under the Indus Water Treaty between India and Pakistan. At present, most of its water is diverted to irrigation canals and used up in India. The Bhakra-Nangal dam is a huge multipurpose dam on the river. There is substantial evidence to indicate that Sutlej was once an important tributary of the Sarasvati river, instead of the Indus river. Due to some natural tectonic convulsion of earth, Sutlej changed its course to join the Beas river. This resulted in drying of Saraswati, desertification of Cholistan and Sindh, and abandonment of numerous ancient human settlements along the Saraswati river.

Sutlej : The Sutlej (Punjabi: , also known as Satluj, is the longest of the five rivers of Punjab that flows through Northern India, with its source in Tibet near Mount Kailash. It receives the Beas River in the state of Punjab, India and continues into Pakistan to join Chenab river to form Panjnad river which furthur joins Indus river at Mithankot. Sutlej was known as Shatadru or Sutudri to Indians in Vedic period and Zaradros to Greeks.

The waters of the river are allocated to India under the Indus Water Treaty between India and Pakistan. At present, most of its water is diverted to irrigation canals and used up in India. The Bhakra-Nangal dam is a huge multipurpose dam on the river. There is substantial evidence to indicate that Sutlej was once an important tributary of the Sarasvati river, instead of the Indus river. Due to some natural tectonic convulsion of earth, Sutlej changed its course to join the Beas river. This resulted in drying of Saraswati, desertification of Cholistan and Sindh, and abandonment of numerous ancient human settlements along the Saraswati river.

Sutra : Sutra in Sanskrit is derived from the verb siv-, meaning to sew. It literally means a rope or thread that holds things together, and more metaphorically refers to an aphorism (or line, rule, formula), or a collection of such aphorisms in the form of a manual. In Hinduism the 'sutras' form a school of Vedic study, related to and somewhat later than the Upanishads. They served and continue to act as grand treatises on various schools of Hindu Philosophy. They elaborate in succinct verse, sometimes esoteric, Hindu views of metaphysics, cosmogony, the human condition, moksha (liberation), and how to maintain a blissful, dharmic life, in a cosmic spin of karma, reincarnation and desire.

Swabi : Swabi lies between the river Indus and river Kabul, in the north west frontier (NWFP) of Pakistan. Majority of the Yousafzai clan of Pathans have been living here for centuries. The History and culture of the Swabi is very rich. The late historian Roshan Khan Baba from this region wrote a book entitled the "History of Yousafzai tribe". A well known Captain of the Pakistan army Karnal Sher Khan belonged to this region. He was involved in the Kargil War and was killed in action. He was awarded Pakistan's highest Military Honour the Nishan-e-Haider. People in Swabi are well educated.Today many people from this region are found in different parts of the world,but mostly in UK. They have unique characteristics of modern life but within Islam. The People of Swabi are famous for their hospitality and a "romantic" people, they are fair in complexion with rugged expressions as most Mountain People in Pakistan appear.

Swami Chinmayananda : Swami Chinmayananda (May 8, 1916 - Aug 3, 1993) was born Balakrishna Menon (Balan) in Ernakulam, Kerala in a very devout Hindu family. Graduating from Lucknow University, he entered the field of journalism where he felt he could influence political, economic and social reform in India. But his life was changed when he met Swami Sivananda at Rishikesh and became very interested in the Hindu spiritual path.

Balakrishna Menon took sanyas(monkhood) from Swami Sivananda to become Swami Chinmayananda—the one who is saturated in Bliss and Consciousness. Swami Shivananda saw the potential in Swami Chinmayananda and sent him to study under a great Guru in the Himalayas—Swami Tapovan Maharaj under whom he studied for 12 years. At the end of the education he decided to spread his teaching all over the world.

During his forty years of travelling and teaching, Gurudev opened numerous centres and ashrams worldwide, he also built many schools, hospitals, nursing homes and clinics. As well as reinvigorating India's rich cultural heritage, Swami Chinmayananda made Vedanta accessible to everybody regardless of age, nationality, or religious background. On 3 August 1993, in San Diego, USA, Swami Chinmayananda attained Mahasamadhi. His work has created an international organization called the Chinmaya Mission.

S H Vatsyayan : S. H. Vatsyayan (1911–1987), (Sachchidananda Hirananda Vatsyayana), was popularly known by his pen-name Ajneya or Agyeya, was a pioneer of modern trends not only in the realm of poetry, but also fiction, criticism and journalism. He was one of the most prominent exponents of the 'Nayi kavita' (New Poetry) in Hindi, and edited the 'Tar Saptaks'. Amongst the most well-known of his poetry anthologies are 'Aangan ke paar dvaar', 'Chakranta-Shila', 'Kitni naavon mein kitni baar', 'Hari ghaas par kshan-bhar', 'Indradhanu raunde hue ye' etc. 'His major prose works include 'Shekhar: Ek Jeevani'. Agyeya was an extensive traveller, and in course of his travels held visiting positions at various institutions around the world, e.g. UC Berkeley. He received numerous honours such as the Sahitya Akademi Award, Jnanpith Award, Bharatbharati Award and the international Golden Wreath Award for poetry.

Swami Haridas : Swami Haridas has a significant place in Hindustani music. He was considered as a pioneer in creating new methods of music and had a great role in spreading dhrupad. He was deeply learned and widely acquainted with the music of his days. Haridas theology deals with not only the love of Krishna and Radha but also witnessing of love, a state of mind called rasa. The main aspect and theme of all his songs and teachings was the rasa. He gained fame and respect not merely of his musical genius but the literary beauty and simplicity of his dhrupad. His language and music inspired many because of the mystic experience of Bhakti (faith) and he became a leading figure in the Bhakti movement and music.

Swami Sivananda Saraswati : Swami Sivananda Saraswati (Sep 8, 1887—Jul 14, 1963), as he is known under his monastic name, was born Kuppuswamy in Pattamadai, Tamil Nadu, India.

A Hindu by birth, he is a well-known proponent of yoga and vedanta. He is reputed to have written over 300 books, on these and related subjects, during his life. Swami Sivananda organized the All-world Religions Federation in 1945 and established the All-world Sadhus Federation in 1947. He called his yoga the Yoga of Synthesis.

Swami Vivekananda : Swami Vivekananda is considered one of the most famous and influential spiritual leaders of the Vedanta philosophy and is considered by millions of Indians as well as non-indians as a Messenger of God (like Buddha, Jesus etc) . He was the chief disciple of Ramakrishna Paramahamsa and was the founder of Ramakrishna Math and Ramakrishna Mission. He is considered by many as an icon for his fearless courage, his positive exhortations to the youth, his broad outlook to social problems, and countless lectures and discourses on Vedanta philosophy.

Narendranath Dutta was born in Shimla Pally, Kolkata, West Bengal, India on January 12, 1863 as the son of Viswanath Dutta and Bhuvaneswari Devi. Even as he was young, he showed a precocious mind and keen memory. He practiced meditation from a very early age. While at school, he was good at studies, as well as games of various kinds. In 1879, Narendra entered the Presidency College, Calcutta for higher studies. After one year, he joined the Scottish Church College, Calcutta and studied philosophy. During the course, he studied western logic, western philosophy and history of European nations.There started to arise questions about God and the presence of God in young Narendra's mind. This made him associate with the Brahmo Samaj, an important religious movement of the time, led by Keshab Chandra Sen. But the Samaj's congregational prayers and devotional songs could not satisfy Narendra's zeal to realise God. He would ask leaders of Brahma Samaj whether they have seen God. He never got a satisfying answer. It was during this time that Professor Hastie of Scottish Church College told him about Sri Ramakrishna of Dakshineswar.

Narendra met Ramakrishna for the first time in November 1881. Though Narendra could not accept Ramakrishna and his visions, he could not neglect him. He tested Ramakrishna to the maximum, but the master was patient, forgiving, humorous and full of love. In time, Narendra accepted Ramakrishna, and while he accepted, his acceptance was whole-hearted. During the course of five years of his training under Ramakrishna, Narendra was transformed from a restless, puzzled, impatient youth to a mature man who was ready to renounce everything for the sake of God-realization. Soon, Ramakrishna's end came in the form of throat cancer in August 1886. After this Narendra and a core group of Ramakrishna's disciples took vows to become monks and renounce everything, and started living in a supposedly haunted house in Baranagore.

Soon, the young monks of Baranagore wanted to live the life of a wandering monk with rags and a begging bowl and no other possessions. On July 1890, Vivekananda set out for a long journey, without knowing where the journey would take him. The journey that followed took him to the length and breadth of the Indian subcontinent. It is said that he was given the name Vivekananda by Maharaja of Khetri for his discrimination of things, good and bad.

Vivekananda "stole the show" at the 1893 World Parliament of Religions in Chicago, Illinois, where he earned wild applause for beginning his address with the famous words, "Sisters and brothers of America." Within a few years of the Parliament, he had started Vedantic centres in New York City, New York and London, lectured at major universities and generally kindled western interest in Hinduism. After four years of constant touring, lecturing and retreats in the West, he came back to India in the year 1897.Admirers and devotees claim that he was overwhelmed by the reception he received on his return. In India, he delivered a series of lectures, and this set of lectures known as "Lectures from Colombo to Almora" is considered to have uplifted the morale of the then downtrodden Indian society. He founded the Ramakrishna Mission. This institution is now one of the largest monastic orders of Hindu society in India. On July 4, 1902, in the evening he went for meditation in his room facing Ganges and died in Mahasamadhi at the age of 35 at Belur Math near Kolkata.

Swaminarayan Akshardham : Swaminarayan Akshardham is a Hindu temple complex in Delhi, India.

Inaugurated in November 2005 by the President of India, Abdul Kalam, the Prime Minisiter, Manmohan Singh, and the leader of the organisation responsible for the creation of Akshardham, Pramukh Swami Maharaj, this complex has already attracted tens of thousands of visitors from all over the globe.

Swang : The Swang is a folk theatre form peculiar to the Himachal region. The Shivratri celebrations at Mandi, the Dussera festival at Kulu, the Renuka fair at Sirmaur, the Minjar in Chamba, the Jataras at Chattarahandi-Bharmaur and the Holi fairs at Sujanpur, all have Swang shows. These shows are also known as Jhankis or Dole (floats).

Some Swang plays are enacted at festivals. At the Lohadi festival, the village boys act out the Haran Ka Swang and go dancing and singing from door to door. In this a boy is dressed up as a golden deer with a pair of horns upon his head and a deer skin around his shoulders and the rest of the boys stands around him and beat drums and sing. This Swang lasts through the night. In the Kinnaur region Swang shows are organised in which demons are slain ritualistically and prayers invoking the blessing of gods are recited.

Swara : The notes, or swaras, of Indian music are Shadjamam, Rishabham, Gandharam, Madhyamam, Panchamam, Dhaivatam and Nishadam. Collectively these notes are known as the sargam, the Indian solfege. In singing, these become Sa, Ri(Carnatic) or Re(Hindustani), Ga, Ma, Pa, Da(Carnatic) or Dha(Hindustani), and Ni. ("Sargam" stands for "Sa-R(i,e)-Ga-M(a)"). Only these syllables are sung, and further designations are never vocalized. When writing these become, S, R, G, M, P, D, N. A dot above a letter indicates that the note is sung one octave higher, a dot below indicates a note one octave lower.

In certain forms of Indian classical music and quwalli, when a rapid, 16th note sequence of the same note is to be sung, sometimes different sylables are used in a certain sequence to make the whole easier to pronounce. For example instead of "sa-sa-sa-sa-sa-sa-sa-sa" said very quickly, it might be "sa-da-da-li-sa-da-da-li" which lends itself more to a quick and light tongue movement.

Swaraj Party : The Swaraj Party was a political party in India that sought greater self-government and political freedoms for the Indian people from the British Raj. In Hindi and most other languages of India, Swaraj stands for Freedom, Independence and Self-Rule.

The Swaraj Party was formed by Indian politicians and members of the Indian National Congress who had opposed Mahatma Gandhi's suspension of all civil resistance in 1922 in response to the Chauri Chaura tragedy, where policemen were killed by a mob of protestors. Gandhi felt responsible for the killings, reproached himself for not emphasizing non-violence more firmly, and feared that the entire Non-Cooperation Movement would degenerate into an orgy of violence between the British-controlled army and police and mobs of freedom-fighters, alienating and hurting millions of common Indians. He went on a fast-unto-death to convince all Indians to stop civil resistance. The Congress and other nationalist groups disavowed all activities of disobedience.

But many Indians felt that the Non-Cooperation Movement should not have been suspended over an isolated incident of violence, and that its astonishing success was actually close to breaking the back of British rule in India. These people became disillusioned with Gandhi's political judgments and instincts. After his release from prison in 1924, Gandhi sought to bring back the Swarajists to the Congress and re-unite the party. Gandhi's supporters were in a vast majority in the Congress, and the Congress still remained India's largest political party, but Gandhi felt it necessary to heal the divide with the

Swarajists, so as to heal the nation's wounds over the 1922 suspension.

The Swarajists sought more representation in the Congress offices, and an end to the mandatory requirement for Congressmen to spin khadi cloth and do social service as a prerequisite for office. These was opposed by Gandhi's supporters, men like Vallabhbhai Patel, Jawaharlal Nehru and Rajendra Prasad, who became known as the No Changers as opposed to the Swarajist Changers. Gandhi relaxed the rules on spinning and named some Swarajists to important positions in the Congress Party. He also encouraged the Congress to support those Swarajists elected to the councils, so as not to embarass them and leave them rudderless before the British authorities.

When the Simon Commission arrived in India in 1928, millions of Indians were infuriated with the idea of an all-British committee writing proposals for Indian constitutional reforms without any Indian member or consultations with the Indian people. The Congress created a committee to write Indian proposals for constitutional reforms, headed by now Congress President Motilal Nehru. The death of Lala Lajpat Rai, beaten by police in Punjab further infuriated India. People rallied around the Nehru Report and old political divisions and wounds were forgotten, and Vithalbhai Patel and all Swarajist councillors resigned in protest. Between 1929 and 1931, the Indian National Congress would declare the independence of India and launch the Salt Satyagraha. In this tumultuous period, the Swaraj party dissolved into the Congress.

Swarna Bhandar : Two rather strange cave chambers were hollowed out of a single massive rock. One of the chambers is believed to have been the guard room, the rear wall has two straight vertical lines and one horizontal line cut into the rock; this 'doorway' is supposed to lead to king Bimbisara treasury. Inscriptions in the Sankhalipi or shell script, etched into the wall and so far undeciphered, are believed to give the clue to open the doorway. The treasure, according to folklore, is still intact. The second chamber bears a few traces of seated and standing guards etched into the outer wall.

Swat : Swat is a modern district of Pakistan, and historically a Muslim princely state, in the North-West Frontier Province of Pakistan. With high mountains, green meadows, and clear lakes, it is a place of great natural beauty, and a destination for adventure-tourism.

Swat River : Swat River flows from Karakorum Mountains to flows into Kabul River in Swat, Sarhad, Pakistan. Swat river flows through Kalam valley and merges with Kabul River. Swat river irrigates vast area of Swat District. The Swat river has fishing industry. Saidu Group's of teaching hospitalis also located at the banks of Swat river. Malamjaba ski resort is about 10 miles away from the river. Ayub Bridge is one of the attraction for the visitors.The scenery is attracts many tourists from all over Pakistan during the summer. it is said that Alexandar crossed the swat river with part of his army and before turning south subdued the locals at what are now barikoot and odegram. the river swat is a clear water river starting from the Ushu rage of mountains to the spread of the valley of swat.

Swathi Thirunal : Sri Swathi Thirunal Rama Varma (April 16, 1813 - December 25, 1846) was a South Indian king of the state of Travancore, in India. His reign lasted from 1829 to 1846. He was born a king, and was in power even before birth. Therefore, he is called Garbha Sreeman.

Besides being an able ruler, he was a patron of music and a musician by himself. He encouraged both broad systems of Indian music, Hindustani and Carnatic music, though he was essentially a connoisseur of the carnatic music tradition. The king was fluent in Indian languages like Marathi, Telugu, Bengali, Tamil and Oriya to name a few. He even has composed ragas in several ragas. He can be compared to Alexander the Great in some ways. Both died in their early thirties but they are alive even today due to the tremendous influence they had on the generations to come, Alexander in the art of warfare and Swathi Thirunal in the art of composing music, poetry and singing. It is said that he encouraged artists of various genres to come to his place and even if he found the artist not entertaining in his court he would dismiss him richly. He has been called 'King among poets and poet among kings.'

Swedish East India Company : The Swedish East India Company (Swedish: Svenska Ostindiska Companiet or SOIC) was founded in Gothenburg, Sweden in 1731 for the purpose of conducting trade with the far east. The venture was inspired by the success of the British East India Company and grew to become the largest trading company in Sweden during the 18th century, until it folded in 1813.

Swraj Paul : Lord Swraj Paul, the great business magnate was born in 1931 in Jalandhar, Punjab. Having learned business lessons from his father at a young age, he later founded the successful multinational company Caparo, an UK-based steel and engineering group.

Swraj was educated at Punjab University and obtained a master's degree in mechanical engineering from the Massachusetts Institute of Technology (MIT) in the US. In 1953 he returned to India to join the Apeejay Surrendra Group, founded by his father, which he helped build up to a diversified industrial group. Swraj went to England in 1966 hoping to find a cure for his leukemia-stricken two-year-old daughter, Ambika. Shattered by her death, he buried himself in work and there began his spectacular business career in Britain.

In 1968, he started buying and selling steel in a one-man business and acquired a small tube unit, Natural Gas Tubes (NGT), which developed into one of the leading UK producers of welded steel tube and spiral welded pipe. Gradually he bought more units, mainly in the steel products manufacturing industry and founded Caparo Group in 1978. Her Majesty the Queen knighted Swraj Paul in the same year, thereby making him The Lord Paul of Marylebone and a member of the House of Lords.

Lord Paul has been honoured by various international organisations over the years. He has written the biography of Indira Gandhi and was awarded the Padma Bhushan by her in 1983. Among the honours bestowed on him are the Pro-Chancellorship of the Thames University (1998) and its Governorship (1992-97), Chancellorship of Wolverhampton University and the Bharat Gaurav award by the Indian Merchant's Chamber. He is a member of the Foreign and Commonwealth Office's Foreign Policy Centre Advisory Council and MIT's Mechanical Engineering Visiting Committee.

Swraj stepped down from the management of Caparo in 1996, handing over his empire to his three sons. Though he is one of the richest persons in the U.K., in his personal life Lord Paul practices relative simplicity. But he believes in making money so that he can occasionally use it to help the needy or even bail out the London Zoo.

Syama Prasad Mookerjee : Syama Prasad Mookerjee (also spelled as Shyama Prasad Mukherjee) was a nationalist political leader of India, and is considered the Godfather of modern Hindutva and Hindu Nationalism. Mookerjee founded the Bharatiya Jana Sangh, the first Hindu nationalist political party of its kind, and was also the leader of the Hindu Mahasabha and closely associated with the Rashtriya Swayamsevak Sangh.

Syed Ahmad Khan Bahadur : Sir Syed Ahmad Khan Bahadur, born on October 17, 1817 at Delhi, died March 27, 1898 at Aligarh, was a Muslim educator, jurist, and author, founder of the Mohammedan Anglo Oriental College, which later became Aligarh Muslim University, at Aligarh, Uttar Pradesh, India.

He started his career as a clerk with the East India Company in 1838. He qualified three years later as a sub-judge and served in the judicial department. Sir Syed Ahmad was a multitalented man, and his position in the judicial department left him time to be active in many fields. His career as an author (in Urdu) started at the age of 23 with religious tracts. In 1847 he brought out a noteworthy book, Athar Assanadid ("Monuments of the Great"), on the antiquities of Delhi. Even more important was his pamphlet, "The Causes of the Indian Revolt". In this booklet he ably and fearlessly laid bare the weaknesses and errors of the British administration that had led to dissatisfaction and the so-called Sepoy Mutiny of 1857. Widely read by British officials, it had considerable influence on British policy.

The supreme interest of Sir Syed's life was education, in its widest sense. He established schools at Muradabad (1858) and Ghazipur (1863). A more ambitious undertaking was the foundation of the Scientific Society, which published translations of many educational texts and issued a bilingual journal, in Urdu and English. During a visit to England (1869-70) he prepared plans for a great educational institution, a "Muslim Cambridge". On his return he set up a committee for the purpose and also started an influential journal, Tahdhib al-Akhlaq ("Social Reform"), for the "uplift and reform of the Muslim". A Muslim school was established at Aligarh in May 1875, and, after his retirement in 1876, Sir Syed devoted himself to enlarging it into a college. In January 1877 the foundation stone of the college was laid by the Viceroy. This college made rapid progress.

In 1886 Sir Syed organized the All-India Muhammadan Educational Conference, which met annually to promote education and to provide Muslims with a common platform. Sir Syed advised Muslims against joining active politics and to concentrate instead on education. However the attitude of Hindus and the Congress Part compelled Sir Syed to reconsider his ideas, He was pained to see both Congress and Hindus working against the interest of the Muslims. Sir Syed always advocated Hindu Muslim unity and did every effort to bring them closer on one single platform. The membership of British Indian association was kept open for both Hindus and Muslims. In 1886 Sir Syed Founded the British Indian association which worked for the safeguards of the rights of Indian People.

Syed Ameer Ali : Syed Ameer Ali:(1849-1928) was a lawyer, spokesman on Indian Muslim concerns, and writer on Islamic history and society, was born on 6 April 1849 at Cuttack in Orissa. He was the fourth of five sons of Syed Saadat Ali, a descendant of a Shia family from Meshed in Iran. Ameer Ali's great-grandfather had migrated from Iran with the army of Nadir Shah in 1739, serving thereafter at the Mughal and Awadh courts. Soon after his birth his father, who had trained in yunani medicine, and was by inclination scholarly, moved the family first to Calcutta, and then to Chinsura, where they upheld in modest comfort the lifestyle of the ashraf elite. His family's origins were to influence strongly Ameer Ali's sense of his own identity, leading to some criticism of him as alienated from the Bengali environment of his own childhood.

Ameer Ali's greatest contribution was not political, for the confidence-boosting effects of his major publications which eulogised the 'golden ages' of Islam, and stressed the need for Muslims to come to terms with some of the changes caused by colonisation and Westernisation were his major achievements. If he had a lawyer's approach to historical evidence, both in highlighting Islamic achievements and in condemning the shortcomings of other cultures, such buttressing of Muslim self-esteem was certainly a need of the hour. His progressive stance on the status and rights of women in Islam was one of his most notable contributions.

Syed Ansar Ahmed Burney : Born August 14th 1956 in Karachi Pakistan, Syed Ansar Ahmed Burney, son of Syed Mukhtar Ahmed Burney, was the first man to introduce true human rights in Pakistan over 25 years ago. A graduate of Master's and Law from Karachi University and honorary recipient of a PhD. in Philosophy, Ansar Burney, Advocate started his noble mission in 1980 by setting up the "Ansar Burney Welfare Trust", "Prisoners Aid Society" and "Bureau of Missing and Kidnapped Persons" in Karachi Pakistan.

Syed Kamal : Kamal was a popular filmstar of Pakistan in the 1960's and the 1970's.

Kamal, whose film Tauba became a big success has striking resemblance with the Indian superstar Raj Kapoor, and he is not evasive about this issue. He said once, "People used to mistake me for Raj Kapoor while I was in Bombay.

Syed Nazral Islam : Syed Nazral Islam (1925-1975) was a lawyer, politician and the acting President of the Provisional Government of Bangladesh at Mujibnagar. Syed Nazrul Islam was born in 1925 at Jamodal Dampara in Kishoreganj district. He obtained his MA degree in History in 1947 and LLB in 1953 from the Dhaka University. He took active part in politics in his student life, and was the vice president of Salimullah Muslim Hall Student Union (1946-47) and secretary of Muslim Student League. Syed Nazral Islam was the captain of the Dhaka University cricket and hockey team and secretary of games and sports of Dhaka University Central Students Union (DUCSU).

Syed Nazrul Islam successfully competed in the Pakistan Central Superior Service in 1949 and joined as an officer in the Department of Taxation. He resigned from government service in 1951 to join Anandamohan College (Mymensingh) as Professor of History. Subsequently he joined the Mymensingh district bar. He took active part in the Language Movement as a member of the all party Action Committee. After the assassination of Bangabandhu Sheikh Mujibur Rahman by a group of army personnel on 15 August 1975 martial law was promulgated and Khondakar Mostaq Ahmad was made President of the country. Khondakar Mostaq managed to get some of his old collegues into his cabinet. But the top four leaders of Awami League Syed Nazrul Islam, Tajuddin Ahmed, M Mansur Ali and Ahm Qamaruzzaman having expressed their reluctance in joining the cabinet were arrested on 23 August and kept confined in the Dhaka central jail. Syed Nazrul Islam along with three others were ruthlessly killed inside the jail on 3 November 1975. He lies buried at Banani graveyard.

Syed Noor : Syed Noor is Pakistani film director based in Lahore. He has to his credits some of Lollywood's biggest hits like Choorian, Jeeva and Deewane Tere Pyar Ke.

Syed Rasel : Syed Rasel (born July 3, 1984 in Jessore) is a Bangladeshi cricketer. He is a left-handed batsman and a left-handed medium-fast bowler who came up through the ranks of the under-19s, to the Bangladesh A team, to the full Bangladesh team, while playing for Khulna Division.

Syed Sultan Ali : Syed Sultan Ali (1876-1966) was a lawyer, politician, legislator and a social worker. Born in the village of Ranbijaypur in Bagerhat district, Syed Sultan Ali, son of a local pleader Syed Emdad Ali, graduated from Ripon College, Calcutta. He joined legal profession as a pleader in 1905. He was a member of Bengal Legislative Council from 1924 to 1926. Politically he was a Khilafatist and a Congress nationalist initially and subsequently an activist of the Muslim League. He was a founding member of P C College, Bagerhat. In recognition of his contributions as a social worker, Ali was awarded the title of Khan Sahib in 1939 and Khan Bahadur in 1946.

Syed Waliullah : Syed Waliullah (1922-1971) was a Bangladeshi novelist, short-story writer and playwright. He is most well known in Bangla literature for his first novel, Lalsalu (translated as "Tree Without Roots", though it literally means "Red cloth").

Sylhet : Sylhet is a major city in north-eastern Bangladesh. It is the capital of Sylhet Division and Sylhet District. The city has approximately 290,000 residents. Sylhet is an ancient settlement. Historians believe that Sylhet or, as it was known in ancient times, Sreehatta (enriched marketplace), was an expanded commercial center from the ancient period, which explains its original namesake. During this time, Sreehatta was probably inhabited by Indo-Aryan Hindu Bengalis, though genetically much of the population would also have been of Munda, Assamese and Dravidian ancestry.

In the ancient and early medieval period, Sylhet was ruled primarily by local chieftains. There is evidence to suggest that the Maharaja Sri Chandra, of northern Bengal, conquered Bengal in the 10th century, although this is a much disputed topic amongst Bangladeshi historians and archaeologists. This was a period of relative prosperity and there is little evidence to suggest this was marred by wars or feuds. Sylhet was certainly known by the rest of India, and is even referred to in the ancient Hindu sacred Tantric text, the Shakti Sangama Tantra, as 'Silhatta'. The last chieftain to reign Sylhet was Gaur Gobinda.

The 14th century marked the beginning of Islamic influence in Sylhet. In the early 14th Century, a Turkish Muslim saint arrived in Sylhet from Yemen, Hazrat Shah Jalal, and his companions (reported to be about 360) triumphed over Sylhet and began to spread Islam. Although Shah Jalal was a native of Konya in Turkey, it didn't take much time for him to become a very respected figure in Sylhet. He died in Sylhet a few years later; his tomb is a revered shrine in Bangladesh. Saints such as Shah Jalal and Shah Paran were responsible for the conversion of most of the populace from Hinduism to Islam. Shortly thereafter, Sylhet became a centre of Islam in Bengal. During this era of Muslim rule, Sylhet was often known as 'Jalalabad' in official documents and historical accounts, such as that of Ibn Battuta.

Much later, the British East India Company began to be interested in Sylhet as early as 1765, as an area of strategic importance in the war against Burma. Sylhet gradually was absorbed into British control and administration and was governed as a part of Bengal. After the British administrative reorganization of India, Sylhet was incorporated into Assam. It remained a part of Assam for the rest of the era of British rule. In 1947, Sylhet became a part of East Pakistan. Important historical places include the Stone Monument of Jaintapur, Mound of Gharduara, Gaiyabi Mosque, tombs of Hazrat Shah Jalal and Shah Paran, Abu Torab Mosque, Nawabi Masque,

Mughal Mosque at Akhalia, Dhaka Dakshmin Temple and the Thin Mandir (trio temple).

Sylhet Division : Sylhet division is the Northeastern division (Bibhag) of Bangladesh, named after its main city, Sylhet. It is bounded by Meghalaya State of India on the north, Tripura State on the south, Assam State of India on the east and Dhaka and Chittagong divisions on the west. The Sylhet division is subdivided into 4 districts (Zila): Habiganj, Moulvibazar, Sunamganj and Sylhet. Further, the Sylhet division contains 35 sub-districts (Upazila/Thana), 323 unions, 10185 villages and 14 municipalities.

Sylhet Osmani Medical College : Sylhet Osmani Medical College is a state funded medical college in Bangladesh. It is located in the north-eastern city of Sylhet in Sylhet District. The college is named after General Muhammad Ataul Gani Osmani, a native of Sylhet, and the commander-in-chief of Bangladesh Army during Bangladesh Liberation War of 1971. The college provides 5 year MBBS degrees, and admits approximately 150 students each year. The college is affiliated to Shahjalal University of Science and Technology under School of Medical Sciences.

Sylheti : Sylheti (native name Silôti; Bengali name Sileti) is the language of Sylhet proper, the North Eastern region of Bangladesh and southern districts of Assam around Silchar. It is also spoken by a significant population in the other north-eastern states of India. It is similar enough to Bengali (Bangla) and is considered to be a dialect of that language, but at times it is probably better seen as a separate language. Given that Sylhet was part of the ancient kingdom of Kamarupa, the language has many common features with Assamese, including the existence of a larger set of fricatives than other East Indic languages. According to Grierson (Language Survey of

India, Vol II, Pt 1, p224), "The inflections also differ from those of regular Bengali, and in one or two instances assimilate to those of Assamese". Indeed it was formerly written in its own script, Sylheti Nagari, similar in style to Kaithi but with differences. Now it is almost invariably written in Bengali script.

Syndicate Bank : Syndicate Bank, established in 1925 in Udupi (Karnataka state, India) by Upendra Ananth Pai, Vaman Kudva and Dr, T. M. A. Pai, is one of the oldest and major commercial bank of India. At the time of its establishment, the bank was known as Canara Industrial and Banking Syndicate Limited. The bank, along with 13 other major commercial banks of India, was nationalized on 19th July, 1969, by the Government of India.